BROOKEBOROUGH
The making of a Prime Minister

To Deirdre and Allen

BROOKEBOROUGH
The making of a
Prime Minister

BRIAN BARTON

THE INSTITUTE OF IRISH STUDIES

THE QUEEN'S UNIVERSITY OF BELFAST

Published 1988
The Institute of Irish Studies,
The Queen's University of Belfast,
Belfast

ISBN 0 85389 316 0

Printed by W. & G. Baird Ltd., Antrim.

Acknowledgments

I wish to thank the staffs of the following institutions for their assistance: the Public Record Office of Northern Ireland, in particular, Trevor Parkhill and Bryan Follis; the Public Record Office, London; the House of Lords Record Office, London; the Imperial War Museum, London; the British Library (Reference Division), Newspaper Library, London; the Liddell-Hart Centre for Military Archives, London; the Army Record Centre, Hayes, Middlesex; the Tom-Harrisson Mass Observation Archive, Brighton, especially Ms Dorothy Sheridan; the State Paper Office of Ireland; the University College, Dublin, Archives Department; the National Library of Ireland; the Main Library, Queen's University, Belfast; the Central Library, Belfast; and the Linen Hall Library, Belfast, particularly John Killen.

I must also express my gratitude to the Deputy Keeper of the Records, Public Record Office of Northern Ireland, for granting permission to quote from material deposited at P.R.O.N.I. I am very deeply indebted to Rosemary, Viscountess Brookeborough, for giving me permission to quote from the Brooke Papers, to Brian Dingwell for giving me access to the Spender Papers and to Lady Harkness for permitting me to consult the Harkness Papers. I wish to thank the Clerk of the Records, House of Lords Record Office, and the Trustees of the Beaverbrook Foundation for permission to reproduce material from the Wakehurst Papers, the Lloyd George Papers and the Beaverbrook Papers. The Mass-Observation material is reproduced by permission of the Trustees of the Mass-Observation Archive, University of Sussex. The Trustees of the Liddell Hart Centre for Military Archives allowed me to include extracts from the Alanbrooke Papers and the Trustees of the Imperial War Museum permitted references to the diaries of Field Marshall Sir Henry Wilson. I am grateful to the committee of Fermanagh Unionist Association for permission to quote from the Association's letter-books and also to Miss Sandra Granlees formerly of the University of Ulster, for allowing me to refer to her thesis which is listed in the bibliography.

Amongst my other creditors are people whose encouragement, advice and criticism have been crucial to my embarking on this research and who have helped to ensure its completion. Professor L. Warren, of the History Department, Queen's first instilled in me an interest in research whilst I was an undergraduate student there. I must thank my supervisor for the PhD thesis on which this book is based, Professor D. W. Harkness, also of Queen's, for his guidance and kindness. I benefited from the helpful comments of Dr A. T. Q. Stewart, my internal examiner, and Dr M. T. Foy.

I also wish to express my gratitude to the Institute of Irish Studies, Queen's

University, my publishers, and, in particular, to Dr B. M. Walker who with patience and competence has guided this work into print.

In addition, I must record my deep sense of debt to John Warden Brooke, the Second Viscount Brookeborough. He not only provided me with enthusiastic support but also made his father's private papers available to me – a crucial source both for this volume and for the second part of his biography, now in preparation.

Last, but by no means least, I would like to thank Miss Anne Cunningham, who undertook the task of typing the original thesis and this book, for her promptitude and efficiency.

Contents

Introduction

In 1913, at the age of twenty-five, Sir Basil Brooke inherited the family's estates at Colebrooke in County Fermanagh, under the terms of his father's will. They had been in Brooke ownership since the Cromwellian plantation and, despite prolonged absences from them particularly in his earlier years, they became 'the great love' of his life.[1] They might well in different circumstances have provided him with all the challenge and stimulation that he needed for complete earthly contentment. But this was not to be.

During the 1880s, the decade of Sir Basil's birth, a threat to the survival of the Anglo-Irish gentry and to the Union itself emerged. It was only comparable in its gravity to the crises which had erupted almost three hundred years earlier in the course of which his ancestors had first set foot in Ireland. The threat must have seemed all-embracing. On the one hand the downward trend of prices and rents began to erode the economic position of the old Anglican aristocracy. On the other hand, its political power was jeopardised by the land agitation which infused a new element of class feeling into the traditionally hereditary pattern of national politics.

Meanwhile imperial legislation trebled the size of the Irish electorate and in the process transformed the existing marginal catholic majority on the electoral rolls into a massive numerical superiority, so providing the home rule movement with its largest and most effective majority to date. In the 1885 and 1886 general elections Parnellite candidates decisively transformed Ireland's electoral topography which remained unchanged for a generation. In Fermanagh, on both occasions, home rulers swept to victory in the county's two newly-created constituencies. This and the shock news of Gladstone's conversion instilled within the local landowning élite deep feelings of desperation, impotence and foreboding.[2]

Under the sustained pressure of recurrent home rule crises, however, Fermanagh's small, amateur, conservative clique of the 1880s gradually evolved, by 1914, into a cohesive, mass, unionist movement. At the same time, as part of this process, the political power and social leadership of the Anglo-Irish gentry was perpetuated, counteracting the effect of their declining economic position and the rising sentiments of democracy and class awareness within the county. They continued to be looked upon as the natural leaders of those who favoured the union, their military traditions and training having additional relevance in the turbulent political atmosphere immediately before the world war.[3]

Sir Basil Brooke grew to maturity in the context of these tumultuous years. His first portentous steps in public life were taken in direct response to the challenge of the third home rule bill as it affected his beloved, native county and as a conscious perpetuation of the traditions of his family and of his class. In 1912, whilst on leave from the 10th Hussars, he helped organise and train local companies of the Ulster Volunteer Force. Soon after the war, with the political future still uncertain, he once more applied his military experience in forming 'Fermanagh Vigilance', an embryo of the 'B' specials. Months later he played a leading role in the formation of the special constabulary. As a result of these activities he rose to a position of prominence not only within Fermanagh but throughout the province as a whole and in so doing laid firm foundations for his later career in politics. His subsequent political rise in the recently established Northern Ireland parliament was, by contemporary standards, meteoric. He moved from the back-benches to junior minister inside four years and, ten years later, in 1943, reached the premiership in highly controversial circumstances. In the fullness of time he became the province's longest serving prime minister and, in all, held government office for an unbroken period of thirty years, a record unequalled by anyone either at Westminster or at Stormont. In 1952 he was raised to the peerage as Viscount Brookeborough of Colebrooke.

Brooke has not been well served by posterity. His importance in the history of the Northern Ireland state arguably ranks along with that of Carson or Craig. Yet no commemorative monument has ever been erected in his honour, the only exception being a modest plaque recessed into the wall of the small Anglican church on his estate. No study of his long life in politics has been written or attempted,[4] and nothing exists beyond compilations of newspaper interviews conducted at Colebrooke in his declining years and his own brief unpublished autobiography. Historians have preferred to focus their attentions on the inception of the state and on the present 'troubles', neglecting the period of his premiership altogether or dismissing it as a time of 'change without change'.[5] The purpose of this narrative is to trace and to analyse the source and early development of his remarkable, improbable and hitherto neglected career.

CHAPTER I

The Brookes of Colebrooke

In some perplexity an eighteenth-century Fermanagh historian, John Dolan, after observing the Brooke family coat of arms in the banqueting hall at Donegal Castle, confessed that he 'could not directly explain' its origins.[1] It does, nevertheless, provide some clue as to the antecedents of the first Basil Brooke, the soldier-adventurer who came to Ireland in the late sixteenth century. It suggests that his family was descended from 'the ancient Cheshire family of Brooke', the Brookes of Leighton, whose arms are almost identical. This was possibly through Rafe Brooke of Nantwich, governor of Calais, and second son of Thomas Brooke of Leighton.[2]

Brooke came as a captain in the English army bringing reinforcements to Ireland, and later commanded a cavalry regiment under Sir Henry Docwra in the conquest of Ulster. He distinguished himself as a servitor during the Tyrone wars and was one of those selected by the king for a proportion of the plantation. He was knighted in 1619, styled Magherabeg and Brooke Manor, became a governor of Donegal, and later, was a member of the commission ordered by Charles I to enquire into how thoroughly the undertakers had fulfilled the conditions of their grants.[3]

Thus the Brookes first entered Ireland under English arms and initially held their property in Donegal and not Fermanagh. The former was never really colonised. Due in part to its wildness and inaccessibility colonists proved reluctant to attempt settlement. In addition, Sir Arthur Chichester described its native population as 'a people inclined to blood and trouble'. In 1619, Pynnar recorded of estate after estate that nothing was built and that there were no British tenants.[4] One historian has thus described it as 'the danger spot of the whole plantation'. He continues 'it was the pluck, skill and tact of hard-bitten, experienced soldiers, such as Sir Henry Folliott and Sir Basil Brooke that held Donegal quiet and so gave protection to the infant colony'.[5] Certainly the latter appears to have been an energetic, determined and resourceful planter, eager to establish himself permanently in his adopted home.

Sir Basil's grant of 1,000 acres was in a rugged precinct set aside for servitors and natives, and was 'to be held forever . . . as of the castle of Dublin, in common socage and subject to the conditions of the plantation of Ulster'.[6] The land was of poor quality, the barony in which the land was located being described in the book of survey and distribution fifty years later as 'mountainous, boggy, rocky and with many . . . ways hardly passable'.[7] By 1622,

1

however, Brooke was reported as having repaired a round bawn of lime and stone, 13 feet high, 7 feet thick and 220 feet in compass within which a house was standing which had been occupied by an English settler in 1619.[8]

He also acquired other property. One of the written complaints of the earl of Tyrconnell was that the lord deputy had appointed Captain Brooke to live in his castle, and 'constrained the earl to accept such rents as he had given order of to the said captain to pay and to pass a lease thereof and four acres of the best lands thereunto annexed, for one and twenty years unto the said captain'.[9] By 1611, with the help of a royal grant Brooke had repaired the castle, voluntarily built a bawn to enclose it, and a strong house of lime and stone adjacent to it.[10] This relatively secure and less isolated dwelling he occupied with his English wife. Thirty-five British men were said to be present in Donegal town in 1622, their houses constructed 'after the manner of the Pale'. That same year a commission suggested that if Brooke had 'the inheritance of the castle, he would make it a strong and defensible place for his majesty's service as he affirmeth'.[11] He was in fact appointed constable of the castle and given the ownership of it and the town of Donegal, both of which were inherited, with his other property, in 1633 by his only son Henry, who was then married and of full age.[12]

The latter fulfilled the confidence which the commissioners had earlier expressed in his father. During the rising of 1641, he was successful in 'preserving from plunder' the town and castle and the surrounding district. He afterwards fought on the parliamentary side in the civil war, serving as a captain of foot. In consequence, he acquired a substantial area of land, worth more than £900 yearly, mostly by grant 'for his said personal services and for arrears thereof services', and one-third of it by purchase, selling in the process some of his Donegal property.[13] These new estates lay in the adjacent counties of Monaghan and Fermanagh, and had become available through the forfeitures of property by two leading local native landholders. In Monaghan, Henry gained possession of some of the lands of Hugh MacMahon in the barony of Cremorne.[14] In Fermanagh he acquired most of the confiscated estates, including the old ancestral home at Largie, of Lord Maguire, who had been hanged at Tyburn and whose family had ruled the county for most of three centuries from their base at Lisnaskea. The latter's property, which had until then survived 'as a little bit of Gaelic Ireland left untouched', now became the basis of the future Colebrooke estate. Despite this slightly belated entry of the Brookes into Fermanagh as major landowners, only two of its leading early twentieth-century estate-holders could claim earlier links with the county. Of the names of the original British undertakers, only one survived, the Archdales, and the Coles represented the only servitor to survive. Moreover, when Sir William Cole was assigned the town of Enniskillen, together with covenants for 'building and inhabiting' it, he was to do so 'according to a plan set down by the lord deputy for Sir Ralph Bingley and Captain Basil Brooke'.[15]

Henry, who became high sheriff, governor and member of parliament for Donegal, was knighted in 1664, and died seven years later. He was succeeded by Basil Brooke, eldest son of his marriage to his first wife, Elizabeth Wynter. Soon afterwards a legal dispute arose between Basil and Thomas Brooke, eldest son of Anne St George, whom Henry had married in 1652. The former, who was chancellor of Oxford University, claimed all of his father's property, both the 'ancient inheritance' in Donegal and also the land in Fermanagh and Monaghan, mainly under the entailment clauses contained in a deed of enfeoffment drawn up by his grandfather in 1630. In 1680, he accordingly initiated proceedings in the chancery court. During the following year, in an exchequer bill, Thomas claimed that it had been agreed by a settlement, in 1652, just before Henry's marriage to Anne, that he 'would settle on his children by her all his new estate'. Eventually, the issue was resolved, and articles of agreement were drawn up under which Basil swore to 'acquit and release all his right, title and interest' in Henry's estates in County Fermanagh, and that 'his heirs and assignees . . . . [would] . . . never pretend, sue for, or molest the said Thomas Brooke, his heirs or assignees or any of the issue of the said Anne'. A financial settlement was also entered into, whereby the value of the disputed land in Monaghan was shared.[16]

The Donegal estates of the senior branch of the family passed by direct descent through three generations to Henry Vaughan Brooke, member of parliament for the county in the late eighteenth century. His seat was a 'distinction', one contemporary wrote, that he owed 'to the general opinion of his integrity and honour entertained by his . . . spirited and independent . . . constituents, . . . for the powerful interests in the county were combined against him'.[17] In 1807, he died intestate, leaving his paternal property to a nephew, Thomas Grove, 'on condition that he took the name and arms of Brooke'. However, their identification with the original plantation grant was only briefly prolonged, as on the death of the latter's wife in 1863, the estates passed to her nephew James Wood, who was not bound by the earlier conditions of inheritance.[18]

The 'issue of . . . Anne', the younger branch of the family have survived on their Fermanagh property through ten succeeding generations. Thomas, married Catherine, daughter of Sir John Cole, of Newlands, County Dublin, and from this marriage came the name Colebrooke, given later both to the estate and to the house.[19] Prior to the Williamite wars, then a soldier in the army, Thomas was dismissed by Tyrconnell, later reinstated by William III, and his name together with about 120 other Fermanagh landholders, as well as that of his half-brother Basil, appears on bills of attainder passed by the parliament of James II. In the more settled times that followed the family made useful marriages and consolidated their position to the 1770s. Colebrooke was then regarded as a good estate and the Brookes as having with the Archdales, the 'principal interest'[20] in Fermanagh.

In 1761, however, Thomas's grandson, Sir Arthur, a spendthrift, unconscious of the value of money and a gambler on a large scale, wasted his patrimony. Though he had inherited through his grandmother's brother, Lord Ranelagh, large and valuable property in the city of Dublin, Tipperary, Clare and Wiltshire, at his death in 1785 nothing was left but Colebrooke denuded of trees and heavily encumbered. Nonetheless, the latter remained in the words of an informed contemporary, in 1783, 'a good estate but involved', and in the years preceding the act of union the family continued to be regarded as having one of the chief interests in the political life of the county.[21] Sir Arthur's immediate successors, his brother Francis, and his eldest son, Sir Henry, first baronet of the 1822 creation, diligently set to work to restore the fortunes of the estate, living frugally, and investing rents in land drainage and replanting. At the time of the 1876 return of owners of land in Ireland, its size was recorded as almost 28,000 acres, the third largest in the county, only slightly smaller than Crom or Florencecourt.[22]

Gradually also the quality of its soil was improved. The barony of Maghera-steffany was described in a book of distribution and survey at the time of the original grant as 'part mountain and part lowland, the mountain is for the most part pastureable, and the lowland is intermingled with many bogs, loughs and heathy grounds'.[23] Though the house and property were described as 'well improved and elegant' by a contemporary traveller in the 1730s, a professional survey by Starratt, commissioned at this time, indicates that the overall quality of the land had changed little from the earlier assessment. However, two generations later, Sir Henry could write that Starratt was 'not entirely to be relied upon . . . the several distinctions are very faulty, there being more bog set down than there is on each farm, and the same of mountain and moor. Most of what is called moor . . . is now brought in and is good land'.[24]

Sir Henry himself spent £10,000 on rebuilding Colebrooke on the site of the original house,[25] and the ordnance survey memoirs suggest that he was one of the most enterprising landlords in the county. They commented that 'by his attention to the habits and comforts of the tenantry, [he] . . . went far towards giving his dependants an opportunity of raising their general standards. The effect is evident in the very respectable appearance of the present occupiers of the district'.[26] This evaluation is confirmed by an improbable source, the *Impartial Reporter*. Though bitterly anti-landlord, it described Colebrooke, in 1874, as 'one of the most prosperous and cultivated . . .[estates] . . . in the Kingdom', and stated a decade later that

for as long as we can remember the Brooke tenantry have been regarded as the most comfortable in Fermanagh. . . . When, in 1841, Arthur Brooke . . . brought his bride back . . . [there] . . ., it was noted that the cavalcade of horsemen which welcomed him was such that no other estate in the county could turn out.[27]

Clearly, over the years the Brookes came to identify closely with the county and country of their adoption, its prosperity and stability they helped promote, its idiosyncrasies they enjoyed, its humour and sentiment they increasingly shared. They cherished its natural beauty, knew well its history, lived and worked by and large comfortably with its people. Yet they, like others of their class, perceived Ireland ultimately in a British context, a fact reflected in the collective contribution of the Anglo-Irish gentry, particularly those of the Ulster plantation, to the history of the British Army. The roll-call of their field-marshals and generals 'echoes down the last two centuries like the music of some noble ceremonial march',[28] whilst often related to them, but far outnumbering them, are others, the regimental officers that they provided through generation after generation. A recent authority writes:

second to none were the Brookes of Colebrooke. They had come to Ireland with swords in their hands unashamedly. They tenaciously defended the British crown and the protestant succession, with which their own fortunes as a family had been intertwined. Not only loyalty, but leadership in the community and zest for military service came as naturally as breathing. They had the stimulus which comes from challenge and from more than a touch of insecurity.[29]

Over the past three hundred years, the Brookes have established a remarkably consistent record of military service. In that period, through each successive generation, they have served with every leading regiment and in every major British theatre of war in Europe, the empire and elsewhere. It is the most outstanding feature of the family's long recorded history. The army was the almost inevitable career of their younger sons and the sons of younger sons, few entering either the church or the professions. Unless when war came to Ireland, such service was less common for the eldest son, and in any case disrupted at some stage by the inevitable burdens of inheritance. Their function was rather to use their influence to launch younger relatives in military careers, and meanwhile preserve eternal vigilance and preparedness at home 'encouraging the loyal, and never taking their eyes off the doubtful'.[30] In Ireland, ancient bitterness survived, 'danger and instability were never far below the surface of elegance, amusement and affection . . . such an atmosphere breeds fighting men'.[31]

The Brookes acquired their estates in the seventeenth century, at the expense of three of the province's leading native families and mainly as a reward for military service. In the Williamite wars Thomas Brooke served in the regiment raised by his brother-in-law, Lord Drogheda, Basil helped to defend Donegal against Sarsfield's army, and his brother was staff officer to the duke of Schomberg, whilst three of their relatives, a colonel, a lieutenant and a pikeman, helped to defend Derry during the siege.[32]

In the Napoleonic wars, Sir Henry Brooke had three brothers holding high military rank. For one of them, Arthur, whose 'fame was not surpassed in the family until Alanbrooke',[33] the highlight of his twenty years of active service in Flanders, Italy, Egypt and elsewhere was when he succeeded General Ross of Bladensburg in command of the expedition which burnt the Capitol, Washington, in the war of 1812. In his diary he recorded the firing, amongst other structures, of the House of Representatives, the Senate House, 'supposed to be one of the finest buildings in the world', and the presidential home, where he had found 'everything ready for dinner'. He concluded, 'I think that this was one of the finest, and at the same time, most awful sights I ever witnessed'.[34] Of his two brothers, Richard served, like his father, in the 18th Light Dragoons, and Colonel Francis commanded the 4th Foot. The latter was wounded in the battle of New Orleans and retired four years later after almost thirty years service.[35]

Sir Henry's second son, Arthur, served in the Royal Navy and succeeded as the second baronet of Colebrooke. Typical of the family were the five sons of his younger brother, George, three of whom joined the army and two the Royal Navy. Characteristic also, were the family of Sir Arthur Brooke's second son, Sir Henry Brooke of the 92nd Highlanders. Two of his sons died in their father's regiment in the great war, one winning the Victoria Cross, another was wounded in operations with the Indian army, and a fourth, the youngest, was killed in 1917, whilst serving in the Royal Navy.[36]

Indisputably, the greatest soldier to emerge from the family's records was Alan Brooke, one of four soldier sons of Sir Victor Brooke, and recently described as 'the best chief of imperial general staff ever produced by the army and . . . produced at the vital hour. Britain was fortunate indeed'.[37] Churchill recalled how at the outset of their wartime partnership he had 'a personal link' with Brooke 'through his two gallant brothers, the friends of my early military life'. Of one, Victor, he wrote that he had 'perished gloriously of sheer exhaustion', whilst acting as liaison officer with the French cavalry corps in the retreat from Mons in 1914. Sir Winston was with the second, Ronald, in South Africa and states that he 'served with distinction in all campaigns that occurred', having earlier 'shone at the staff college amongst his contemporaries'.[38]

At the Delhi Durbar in 1911, four Brookes were in the king's escort. A total of twenty-six Brookes of Colebrooke served in the Great War and twenty-seven in the war of 1939–1945, and in those wars or from wounds received in them, twelve died. Of the four who died in the second world war, two, Julian and Henry, were the sons of Sir Basil Brooke. When thirty years earlier, Sir Basil himself began to consider his own immediate career, family tradition spoke overwhelmingly in favour of the army. There were, however, exceptions to fire his imagination. Sir Basil Vernon Brooke, a nephew of Sir Victor, served with the Grand Fleet through world war I, commanded the royal yacht 'Alexandria', and retired with the rank of rear-admiral.[39]

The Brookes of Colebrooke, as with most of the Anglo-Irish gentry, made little contribution to the intellect and to the imagination of the province, though this is less true of collateral branches, notably the Brookes of Dromovana.[40] They did, however, exercise and preserve an important governing role, particularly at county level, acting as governors, sheriffs, lieutenants, deputy-lieutenants and magistrates, as well as sitting on various county committees and councils, and as members of parliament. Partly in recognition of such services, two members of the family were knighted, and two separate baronetcies created.[41]

If the political tradition of the Brookes over the centuries is less sustained, less illustrious and altogether less impressive than the military, it is nonetheless an important aspect of the family's history and of its significance. From the late seventeenth century, they held one of the leading political interests in Fermanagh, and particularly in the years prior to the act of union they competed with success for the county's two seats in parliament. The continuity of their parliamentary representation, nonetheless, compares unfavourably with such families as the Archdales, who successfully contested the county without disruption from 1731–1885, and the Coles and the Crichtons who controlled the boroughs of Enniskillen and of Lifford respectively and who normally provided the county's second member.[42]

The most consistent period of Brooke parliamentary representation occurred in the years up to 1785. For a short time in the 1690s, Thomas Brooke was M.P. for Antrim borough. His son, Henry, after sitting briefly for Dundalk, represented County Fermanagh between 1727–1761 and was thus the first of his family to do so.[43] He was succeeded in the seat by his son, Arthur, who defended it successfully to 1783. He became a baronet in 1764, a title which lapsed at his death, and was made a privy councillor by Lord Townshend.[44] In later years he sought a peerage, without success.[45] Both the Crichtons and the Coles were ennobled in the 1760s, of Abraham Crichton it being noted that he had thoroughly supported the government, and had entered into a stipulation to return one member at the general election who would do likewise.[46] On the basis of either criterion, Sir Arthur's claims were somewhat defective. In 1775 he was described as 'against government in his heart, . . . [though] . . .

generally esteemed . . . . in private life, . . . in public, very insincere, ungrateful to the crown and never to be depended on'.[47]

Meanwhile, Sir Arthur's political influence appears also to have declined, almost certainly reflecting the corrosive effects of his life-long extravagance. Thus his urgent requests for a peerage in the early 1780s were prompted, a contemporary observed, by his being afraid of losing the county.[48] If this was the case, such fears were realised. In the 1783 election when he and Colonel Mervyn Archdale were opposed by Viscount Cole, eldest son of the first earl of Enniskillen, Archdale and Cole were returned.[49] However, Sir Arthur did succeed in retaining a seat in parliament. Sir John Parnell, who married his daughter Letitia, who was thus the great grandmother of Charles Stewart Parnell, brought him in for Maryborough, County Leix, which he represented until his death in 1785.[50] Nonetheless, the pattern of Brooke representation for Fermanagh was broken. Sir Arthur's successor, his brother Major Francis, failed to regain the seat in 1790.[51]

Between 1783–1929, the only member of the family to represent the county in parliament was Sir Arthur Brindsley Brooke, grandson of Sir Arthur. In April 1840, he replaced Viscount Cole who succeeded to his father's peerage, so leaving one of the county's two seats vacant, and was returned unopposed until his death in December 1854. He was a voluble and not ineffective parliamentarian and a deeply committed conservative, who spoke with all 'the opposition in [his] . . . power' against the Maynooth College grant in 1845, and protested the following year against corn law repeal. He was nicknamed 'good Sir Arthur' by his tenants for his generosity during the famine having become chairman of the board of guardians in 1840.[52]

He was also closely identified with the revival of the Orange Order in Fermanagh. Following a government order in February 1836, the county grand lodge had formally disbanded in April, Sir Arthur seconding the motion of dissolution. However, by the 1840s, what were regarded as 'concessions to the popish party', including the emancipation act and the reform act, also the strength of the repeal movement and Ribbonism, as well as the government's refusal 'to arm the loyal people of this part of the country' led to local pressure to reorganise the movement. Initially it was led mainly by local clerics. Though threatened with the withdrawal of electoral support for their candidacy in future elections, some of the local aristocracy were reluctant to commit themselves openly at first. In September 1845, the News Letter, however, described Sir Arthur as 'one of the champions of the cause' and reported his agreement at a conference held in Enniskillen to a series of resolutions which it referred to as 'a plan for future protestant organisations'. The resolutions expressed support for the regeneration of the order, unflinching commitment to 'the legislative union' and to 'the blessings of civil and religious liberty'. Brooke himself introduced a motion which reflected the extent of his own commitment: 'we look with the greatest confidence to obtaining the co-operation of all classes from the highest to the lowest in the carrying out of these principles'.[53]

The Brookes did not remain for long at the centre of political affairs in Fermanagh. When Sir Arthur Brooke died in 1854, his eldest son Victor was then aged eleven and attending school in Cheshire.[54] The seat reverted to the Cole family for the next generation. In February 1853, Victor had written home

to his father promising 'to do . . . [his] . . . best to get on', and after referring to
two of his father's recent speeches, he added 'we are glad to see you stick up for
the protestants and for Ireland, I will stick up for them for as long as I live'.[55]
Though the letter, carefully preserved amongst his father's press cuttings,
provides an insight into the political attitudes of the family, the intentions
expressed were to remain largely unfulfilled. Soon after leaving Harrow,
Victor began to travel, first in Scandinavia, and later in the Far East. When his
coming of age was celebrated at Colebrooke in 1864, he was hunting in India.
He was a keen and versatile sportsman for whom the exhilaration of shooting
and hunting, particularly for big game, proved irresistible. The German tutor
of his children described him as 'a Siegfried figure of perfect proportions . . .
noble winning features, blue eyes, blond beard'.[56] He had also a consuming
interest in natural history and zoology, fostered through contact with William
Fowler in the 1870s, and wrote prolifically in the recognised journals. His
grandson, Sir Basil Brooke commented with some recrimination, 'he lacked
that love of Colebrooke which I had developed as a small boy', tending to
regard it 'as a shooting lodge to be visited occasionally'.[57] Its rooms, filled with
trophies of the hunt, and the well-stocked deerpark testify eloquently to the
owner's priorities.

His itinerant instincts were confirmed when he married Alice Bellingham in
1864. After a few years living at Colebrooke she developed symptoms of
delicacy, thus they spent a growing proportion of their time abroad and
eventually bought a villa in the south of France at Pau.[58] It was an international
town and winter resort with varied leisure and sporting activities; 'as expensive
as the Riviera', he wrote, 'but to my mind infinitely preferable. . . . The climate
suits my wife as well as Italy'.[59] During his long absences the estate was looked
after at first by his uncle, and later his brother. Nonetheless, an academic who
accompanied him on one of his occasional return visits was 'struck' by the
extent to which the tenants regarded Sir Victor as 'the providence who would
put everything right', a role which the latter accepted 'as a matter of course'.[60]
He did, however, fight a series of court cases in an unsuccessful attempt to
prove that 'Ulster custom' did not apply to his property.[61]

After considering his effectiveness as a public speaker, fine intellect, powers
of 'personal attraction, . . . undoubted influence over men of all classes' and
confident manner, his biographer expressed regret 'that he never turned his
attention to public life. . . . The way was open . . . [and he had] the aptitude
and capacity for [it], . . . but when it was most feasible he was deeply occupied
with his natural history studies'.[62] The *Fermanagh Times* likewise commented
'there only wanted desire on his part to lead him to a prominent part in public
and political life'.[63] This verdict was confirmed by Basil G. Brooke, one of the
Brookes of Somerton, a collateral branch of the family, who alleged that he
overheard a conversation between his father and Sir Edward Carson. In the
course of it, he claims that the Ulster leader spoke of the 'Parnellite days, when
we suffered for lack of leadership', and concluded, 'in my opinion there was
one man who could have made the difference, Sir Victor Brooke'.[64]

Throughout his life, his political opinions, though infrequently expounded in
public were, like his father's, fervently conservative. In the 1860s, it was said
that he had supplied all the tenants that he considered to be 'sound, with very
superior rifles'[65] in response to the growing levels of Fenian activity. In the

1880s he was one of the largest subscribers in the division to the South Fermanagh Registration Association.[66] He spoke with conviction and considerable force against church disestablishment, and against home rule at meetings of the Irish Loyalist and Patriotic Union, and the landlords' convention in Dublin. He also addressed, occasionally, gatherings of the Orange Order. He became a member, somewhat belatedly, in 1872, when his absences from Colebrooke were already becoming more frequent and prolonged.[67]

In a speech in 1875, he justified the existence of the order in terms reminiscent of his childhood letter to his father, stating, 'there is but one institution in this country which has for its specific object the defence of protestants and protestantism and that is the Orange Institution'. After quoting extensively from Gladstone's writings, he concluded that 'the Roman church . . . aimed at universal supremacy in things temporal and spiritual', and that this was the main justification for the existence of their organisation. He ended, as was his habit, with an appeal to the Orangemen that they might show 'peace and charity' to all.[68] His children's tutor recalled a similar meeting held the following year, and stated that Sir Victor, in contrast to the other platform speakers, 'refrained from all fanaticism and was restricted to a clear matter-of-fact presentation of the serious religious and political issues of the day'.[69]

In 1891 he died of pneumonia at Pau, never having fully recovered from a hunting accident sustained four years before. Characteristically, in his last years he had continued to travel, to Egypt in 1888, and finally to the United States, seeking to invest in the latter some of the proceeds of recent land sales.[70] In the long term, these sales which, by 1914, had reduced the estate to 1,300 acres were bound to erode the family's local influence. More immediately, Sir Victor's absenteeism from the 1870s, as well as the electoral reforms of 1884 which placed Colebrooke in the constituency of South Fermanagh, a division which was for unionists unwinnable, necessarily curtailed the political role of the Brookes during these vital decades.

Nonetheless, that role was by no means insignificant. In 1885, when leading local families appear to have been reluctant to contest South Fermanagh and face certain defeat, Frank Brooke informed the party secretary that he was 'anxious that some one should be started' and expressed a willingness to do so himself, if his expenses were paid.[71] He was a land agent who lived in Ashbrooke, and a cousin of Sir Victor's, whose father had looked after the estate during the latter's minority. His candidacy was subsequently approved by Lord Erne and at a public meeting held soon afterwards. The *Impartial Reporter* commented, acidly but no doubt accurately, that if there had been 'any chance of winning, Archdale and Cole would have been in the front'. The paper was, however, enthusiastic about Brooke, describing him as 'typical of the advance of young Conservatives to suit the altered condition of the times'.[72] He stood on a relatively advanced programme which included tenant purchase and local government reform. Above all he stood for the union, stating that 'I am as all my family have been, a Conservative'.[73]

After predictable defeat, he commented that though he 'had many friends amongst the Roman catholics . . . he could fairly presume that every catholic voted for Mr Campbell',[74] his opponent. The description 'land agent' on his nomination papers, some observers suggested, was unlikely to have appealed to tenant farmers.[75] Immediately after the election, he worked to reorganise the party in the constituency, becoming the first chairman of South Fermanagh Registration Committee. He also joined the Orange Order. At an Orange soirée, at Colebrooke, in January 1886, he declared 'we will meet every rebel demand, first with every legal and constitutional means to uphold the integrity of the empire. Second, should this course fail and the people of England refuse to hear our cry, then we men of Ulster will meet our enemies with rifles in our hands'. These, and other speeches in which he expressed similar sentiments were raised in the House of Commons, but appeals that he be struck off the commission of the peace were rejected by the lord chancellor.[76]

Soon after the defeat of the first home rule bill, he was defeated for a second time, in July 1886, on the same register. Three months later he left Fermanagh to serve as land agent to Lord Fitzwilliam in Wicklow and Kildare, though remaining for some time a substantial subscriber to party funds in his old division.[77] On 30 July 1920, by then an Irish privy councillor and an official at Dublin Castle, he was shot dead whilst working in his office. One colleague, Mark Sturgis, described the incident as a 'dirty, cold-blooded, senseless murder', which he believed helped undermine plans, then being considered, for 'a quick and generous settlement based on dominion home rule'.[78] Certainly it led to other officials taking up residence in the Castle for their own safety, and to appeals by Warren Fisher that they be sent back to their departments in London, as he claimed that the incident marked the end of civil administration in Ireland.[79]

In April 1887, Sir Victor Brooke began handing over responsibility for running Colebrooke to his eldest son, Douglas, who was then aged twenty-one. He wrote 'I know you will show yourself equal to the call upon you, . . . remember this is the crisis of your life, . . . it will mean constant study of the work for at least two years, . . . on your shoulders will rest the tremendous responsibility'. It was a responsibility Douglas seems willingly to have accepted, and one for which he was by no means unprepared. After attendance at Marlborough College, considered by Sir Victor to be 'the best school in England',[80] he had gone to Sandhurst, and had then for a time ranched at Calgary in Alberta, Canada. In 1887, he took up residence at Colebrooke, with his wife, Gertrude Isabella Batson, whom he had married in the summer of that year.[81] Thereafter, they lived together on the estate virtually all year around. Within twelve months, Basil, the first of their five children was born into the somewhat austere, disciplined family atmosphere favoured by their father.[82] Sir Douglas enjoyed shooting, fishing and natural history, but indulged these interests mainly within the confines of his property. He had a genuine interest in farming, and worked to build up the stock on the home farm which had been so neglected by Sir Victor.

He perpetuated the family's tradition of public service, particularly at a local level. He served on the Fermanagh Farming Society, and the Agricultural Committee, and was a member of the Royal Dublin Society. He was a justice of the peace, a deputy-lieutenant and a sheriff for the county, and represented Maguiresbridge district on the county council, for a time acting as its vice-chairman. With justification, the Fermanagh Times commented that 'in the neighbourhood of Colebrooke . . . no local movement of any significance, no public work of any kind was undertaken without first obtaining . . . [his] . . . advice and consent'. As a further indication of this, he was also a strong supporter of the Church of Ireland, active in the temperance movement and a vice-chairman of the Clogher Valley railway company.[83]

In addition, he was a member of the Orange Order but not, as he was once described, its 'constant supporter and advocate'. Despite the widespread presumption that he would join when he first took up permanent residence at Colebrooke, he did not do so until 1892, five years after his arrival, and one year after his father's death. In the course of his first public speech as one of the initiated, ignoring the causes for his earlier hesitancy, he justified membership on the grounds that the order helped 'uphold law and order, and civil and religious liberty'.[84] Privately, he wrote before Sir Victor's death, that they both felt it 'unwise to throw cold water on the Orange . . . in these times. Whatever their faults may be, they are staunch to protestant interests . . . and on the whole have behaved most creditably during the land agitation'.[85] He became one of the leading figures in the order, acting as district master for Brooke-borough district, regularly attending meetings of Fermanagh grand lodge, sitting on county deputations and serving as an Orange delegate to the Ulster Unionist Council.[86]

Sir Douglas was also active politically. In 1893 he made known his intention of standing as a parliamentary candidate for South Fermanagh.[87] He did so not in the expectation of victory, but partly, as the *Fermanagh Times* states, 'out of a sense of duty'. He himself commented publicly that 'it was a most unwelcome burden, . . . I do not want to get into parliament, but', he added, 'I want to see the best possible fight made'. Earlier he had referred to 'the disgrace of letting a nationalist in unopposed'.[88] This, however, understated his real determination to stand in the election as Unionist candidate. From early 1894, as Sir Douglas was aware, W. C. Trimble had been 'feeling the pulse of the electors',[89] and for a time their rival candidacy threatened the unity of the party in the consti-tuency. Trimble told Hugh de Fellenberg Montgomery that he had 'no doubt . . . what a public meeting would decide' in respect of their competing claims. Further, he was confident that he could attract the support, not only of unionist farmers, but also of protestant home rulers and the Parnellites, so reducing the nationalist majority to 'vanishing point'. By contrast, he predicted that if Sir Douglas stood, despite his greater 'influence . . . with the Orange body', he would lose by up to 1,200 votes due to unionist tenant abstentionism.[90]

Though in March 1895, Sir Douglas offered 'to stand down if the farmers . . . [wanted] . . . somone else', providing his replacement opposed home rule, Trimble had some ten months before been 'induced to retire'.[91] His candidacy had consistently been opposed by influential local party members, the Irish Unionist Alliance, and even 'liberal' Unionist landlords, like Montgomery.[92] Apart from other considerations, his political conversion was for many too recent, and his optimism concerning possible victory unfounded. In order to counteract suggestions that he was the nominee of the landlords, Sir Douglas's election agent, Charles Dudgeon, had stressed throughout the 'necessity' of his candidate being 'selected at a thoroughly representative meeting . . . [of] delegates duly chosen by the electors . . . in the several polling districts'.[93] In May 1894, such an assembly resolved the issue, in favour of Brooke, after 'heated discussion'.[94]

Dudgeon also encouraged Sir Douglas to 'meet electors' wants on local matters', by taking, if possible, a 'strong position' on land purchase, supporting local government reform, state purchase of the railways, a housing scheme, and even some measure of self-government for Ireland. Sir Douglas incorporated a number of these ideas into his election address, including, though not as a priority, a scheme of compulsory purchase, if it was 'fair and equitable'.[95] He also drew attention to his record of permanent residence in Ireland, and the generous terms on which the farms on his own estate were being sold off. However, as he declared on one occasion, the essence of his policy could be distilled into three words 'no home rule'. He was, he said, its 'bitter and determined opponent'; he stood, 'not as a politician, but as a loyalist'. Unionist tenants who attended land agitation meetings, he castigated as the 'dupes and laughing stocks of the rebels', deluded into imagining that the home rule danger was past. The land issue was, he suggested, 'a red herring'.[96]

Sir Douglas's defeat was inevitable, given the size of the nationalist majority, despite Dudgeon's enthusiastic claims of success in 'knocking off . . . the rebels'[97] from the electoral register at the revision sessions. Also Jeremiah Jordon was an exceptional opponent and the local Unionist organisation defective. The defeat was, nonetheless, not on the scale that Trimble had predicted; Sir Douglas's own figures corroborated from other sources suggest that approximately 300 unionists failed to vote.[98] However, it was clear, as the county inspector stated at the outset, that the party had 'not the remotest chance' of victory.[99] Shortly before the succeeding election in 1900, Sir Douglas indicated that it was his intention not to stand; no one else came forward and the seat was uncontested.[100] Throughout these years he continued to serve as chairman of the South Fermanagh Registration Association, and was one of the leading subscribers to party funds in the division.

Two weeks before the 1895 election, Jeremiah Jordon wrote to Sir Douglas to 'assure . . . [him] . . . that if South Fermanagh should be lost . . . there . . . [was] . . . no one in the county or Ireland I should rather see Conservative member for it than you', and that he considered his candidacy as a 'guarantee' of a 'fair and gentlemanly' contest.[101] In similar tones the *Fermanagh Herald* referred to him as a 'strong conservative, but one of those men who whilst holding their own views allowed other men to do the same'.[102] Nonetheless, such fulsome statements cannot obscure the fact that he remained throughout his life an implacable opponent of home rule. In 1906, at Maguiresbridge, he made the most controversial speech of his career, and one which precipitated questions at Westminster. In it he referred to the existence of an armoury at Colebrooke, the contents of which would be distributed if required, in order to resist home rule.[103] He died in November 1907 and was buried at his own request with Orange honours. Earlier that month, the county grand lodge had passed a resolution, in silence, the brethren standing, which expressed regret at the illness of one 'who has taken such a leading part in our society'.[104]

Thus, the Brookes were, in many regards, a typical Anglo-Irish family. They first came to Ireland in the 1590s, their precise antecedents somewhat obscure. They directly benefited from the land forfeitures of three leading native Irish families and throughout the next three hundred years demonstrated, as at the outset, both a determination and a capacity to survive. Their estate was a source of profit, power and pleasure. Their record was one of competent, even enlightened, land-holding, combined with an exceptional military tradition, and a consistent pattern of public service. They provided leadership in the community, instinctively, as arising naturally from their social class, and also from a genuine and profound sense of duty. In the late nineteenth century, amidst the increasingly persistent pressures from nationalism, democracy, and growing class consciousness, and the corrosive influence of land reform, they successfully preserved their governing role.

Their political attitudes, in these years, have been uniformly conservative and unionist. Unlike a minority of neighbouring gentry, their family has never produced any dissident liberals or home rulers. The *Fermanagh Times* wrote with considerable justification, in 1907, that 'their name is synonymous with the principles of loyalty and protestantism'.[105] Though they did not think of themselves as other than Irish, to the Brookes 'standing up for Ireland' meant standing up for the protestants of Ireland. Loyalty to the crown, and to the preservation of the protestant succession in Britain, they regarded primarily as a means of preserving the protestant position in Ireland. Though personal friendships with catholics might be enjoyed, the ancient fear and distrust of their collective threat have constantly been both endemic and intuitive. It is not without significance that the townlands in the neighbourhood of Colebrooke have survived into the twentieth century as a predominantly protestant and unionist enclave in an otherwise catholic and nationalist-controlled constituency.[106] Thus, in 1895, Jeremiah Jordon enquired of Sir Douglas Brooke: 'If I thought it advisable to hold a meeting at Brookeborough, would I be permitted to do so without molestation?'[107]

Through each recent generation, the Brookes have been clearly identified with the Orange Order. Their participation has generally been at a local level and almost hereditary in character. Their membership has sprung, in part, from class interests, consciousness of the value of the society as a means of social control, particularly in containing the land agitation. But their involvement has mainly sprung from conviction, the considered judgement held with growing force that such a large, sectionally exclusive, and socially heterogeneous institution was an essential bulwark in the defence of protestant interests.

Overall, from the mid-nineteenth century, their political leadership was moderate and widely respected within the county, and on occasion, beyond. Nonetheless, during these years, they have emerged as consistent and irreconcilable opponents of home rule. They have articulated a defiant and aggressive unionism, with an explicit threat of non-constitutional action, if it should prove necessary. They have done so not to divert attention away from the class issues and conflicts of Fermanagh; such views they expressed with equal force before the land question had emerged, and after it had been resolved. Thus, when the third home rule crisis arose, the rhetoric of violent resistance expressed by Sir Douglas Brooke was unhesitatingly laid aside in favour of action, by his successor, his eldest son, Basil, on whom the 'tremendous responsibility' of Colebrooke was about to fall.

These consistent responses on the part of the Brookes were indulged in during a period when sympathy for them was by no means unanimous amongst the gentry of Fermanagh. Indeed large sections of the county's landowning aristocracy responded to the threat from the home rule movement with a remarkable degree of hesitancy and inertia even on a constitutional level. Total Parnellite victory in the elections of the mid-1880s reflected in no small measure the apathy and dilatoriness of local conservatives in devising adequate party structures in response to changing circumstances.[108] During the spring of 1893, when Gladstone introduced his second measure granting Ireland self-government, once again the level of agitation in the county was minimal when compared with other parts of the province.[109] Though the volume of protest increased later in the year much of it was orchestrated by the improving Unionist party organisation in Belfast rather than the product of local initiative.[110]

Similarly, throughout the early stages of the third home rule crisis Fermanagh's Unionist leaders responded with by now customary lethargy.[111] Police and press reports confirm that it was not until the latter part of 1913 that the pace and militancy of the county's organised resistance quickened and subsequently did not falter until after the outbreak of world war. It was only in this period that the leading landed families abandoned their caution and contributed to the marked increase in Unionist Club and Orange Order activity and the acceleration in recruitment for the Ulster Volunteer Force.[112]

In the course of this latter crisis the differing nature and levels of reaction within Fermanagh's landed class are clearer. The most aggressive leadership came, then, not from the county's nobility, the Ernes and the Enniskillens, but from sections of what might be described as the upper squirearchy, the Archdales, the Irvines, the Porter-Porters and, of course, the Brookes. Such families, for example, openly and actively encouraged the formation of the U.V.F. in Fermanagh from its inception in December 1912. This may reflect merely accidental factors such as age and personality, or it may indicate that the two noble families felt a greater initial unwillingness to accept the risks and possible costs of acting illegally or of fostering violent responses amongst the populace. It may even suggest that the latter felt, or could afford to feel, a less complete commitment to the preservation of Fermanagh within the union. It is true that eventually, during late 1913, both noble families, were at last drawn into and accepted their familiar predominant positions within the protest movement. It was, however, for the last time. In the post-war years, when the crisis, still unresolved, re-emerged, the landed families which provided leadership were again drawn from the upper squirearchy. The role of individuals like Sir Basil Brooke and his older neighbour, E.M. Archdale, was enhanced by the non-participation of their noble neighbours. In Sir Basil much of the tradition of the Anglo-Irish gentry and many of the attitudes and unspoken assumptions of his own family were preserved and cherished into the third quarter of the twentieth century.

CHAPTER II

Basil Brooke – Childhood, Soldiering in Peace, First World War

On 9 June 1888, Basil Stanlake Brooke was born at Colebrooke, a large, 52-roomed house built half a century before to the designs of a Dublin architect, William Farrell. Though 'never enough in itself, it was', he wrote,

the great love of my life, leaving personal attachments out of it . . . Whatever I have encountered, whether of sorrow, or joy, satisfaction or frustration, always my instinct has been to take it to that peaceful place . . . I know how fortunate I was always to have it in the background, a retreat, a place of resuscitation.[1]

It was the place of his birth, and eighty five years later, in deference to his expressed wishes, his ashes were scattered over the demesne.

In the 1880s, the house was the hub of a 30,000-acre estate, owned and lived in by the Brooke family for most of 250 years. It was located in Fermanagh, to Sir Basil, 'the loveliest of Irish counties'. Many years later, he recalled with obvious relish his early childhood there when he 'had everything a country-loving boy could wish'.[2] He quickly acquired a profound love and considerable knowledge of nature and of all country pursuits. He fished, rode and trapped, until the age of eight, untroubled by schooling or tutor. In these early years, skills, habits and affections were formed which endured throughout his long life. Fishing he regarded as 'the most pleasurable pastime in the world'.[3] A diary entry for 1 May 1943, reads 'Governor invites me to form cabinet . . . caught 1 pound 6 ounce trout in the Narrows'. The action was as he himself stated 'typical'.[4]

His sister, Sheelagh, recollected his childhood, his 'keen interest in the various kinds of deer in the park and . . . in the Australian ostriches' and his 'being friendly with everyone on the estate'.[5] He was the oldest of five children and, perhaps partly because his younger brother was physically frail, some of his closest childhood companions were drawn from families on the estate. Amongst them was Arthur Duncan, later his head game-keeper and forester and, in the summer of 1965, one of the four personal friends invited by the then Lord Brookeborough to the garter ceremony at Buckingham Palace. More like a brother to him was his uncle Alan Brooke who was just four and a half years his senior. After the death of his father, Sir Victor Brooke in 1891, Alan stated my brother [Arthur Douglas, Basil's father] became virtually a second father to me, I practically dropped into his family. Even after joining the army, I continued to treat Colebrooke as my home and was always received there as one of the family, . . . it was he who grounded me in shooting, fishing and the love of natural history.[6]

His sister, many years later, recalled the 'important relationship'[7] that grew up between them. It was not, however, a relationship between equals. 'It is to be uncle Alan', the latter had at the age of eight, told Basil, and he maintained order firmly.[8] He exercised his periodic responsibilities as chaperone to his young nephew on their journeys from school in France to Ireland, with 'scrupulousness and exact discipline, threatening dire punishment should Basil fail to observe his instructions'.[9] The warmth of their childhood friendship never faded. In unpublished memoirs written near the end of his life Alan recalled April 1925, when his wife died in a motoring accident:

I took many months to recover . . . I owe an immeasurable debt of gratitude to Basil and his wife for all their sympathy in that period and the years that followed. It was thanks to them that I recovered the desire to live and renewal of interest in life.[10]

Douglas Brooke was to his much younger brother, Alan, a 'mentor, . . . the kindest of instructors'.[11] However, Basil's recollections of his father are somewhat less flattering. He describes him as a 'truly Victorian parent, . . . stern disciplinarian, one of . . . the Jehovah-type'.[12] Orders had to be obeyed by his sons and all the household. The farmyard was a prohibited area in case the facts of life were learned at too early an age. The disciplinarian atmosphere was heightened when his grandfather, Sir Victor Brooke, was present. Sir Basil could recall the latter's stern admonition, 'no Brooke ever cries'.[13] He formed the distinct impression at an early age that those who died were either killed in battle or in an accident. On hearing that some friend of the family had died, he vividly remembered asking, with lively interest, 'Who shot him?'[14] Though he regarded his strict upbringing as possibly of some value in later life, it was resented at the time, and a model which he strove to avoid in bringing up his own children. Life was made more 'tolerable' for him by his mother, born Gertrude Isabella Batson, the youngest child of Stanlake Ricketts Batson, whose family had owned a manor in Cambridgeshire from the eighteenth century. She was, he writes, 'kind and gentle, and shared my love for the hills and streams'.[15] He bore for her a deep affection until suddenly and permanently this cooled whilst he was on military leave during the summer of 1912.

In 1896 came the inevitable but nonetheless 'painful wrench',[16] when, at the age of eight, Brooke was sent to boarding school at Pau in the south-west corner of France, at the foot of the Pyrenees, following in his Uncle Alan's footsteps. For the next 25 years, Colebrooke was only glimpsed occasionally during fleeting school holidays and army leaves. From the late 1860s Brooke's grand-parents had lived with increasing permanence at Pau, a fashionable resort, with its exclusive but growing British colony and in 1879, they had bought the 'Villa Jouvence'. Basil's education began nearby at Saint George's school. On his arrival, he could neither read or write. It was a small, private institution, but not expensive, run by a Bavarian doctor, according to his own ideas. The pupils, mostly English, with some Americans and French, selected their own subjects and were taught in the language of their choice. The

Americans, Sir Victor noted 'when educated there could speak French as fluently and purely as their own lingo'.[17]

Because of delicate health, Alan received all his education at Pau until the age of sixteen and though he regarded the school as 'excellent' and 'meticulous', non-attendance at an English public school was the cause of an 'acute inferiority complex'[18] at the time he entered Sandhurst. For most of Basil's five years at Saint George's they were constant companions, only returning to Colebrooke during summer vacations. The outward journey took four to five days. They started out from Colebrooke station on the picturesque but rarely profitable narrow gauge Clogher Valley railway to meet the main Belfast-Dublin line. There, they changed trains for Greenore, a small port in County Louth, went by boat to Holyhead and train to Liverpool, where they caught a small steamer for Bordeaux and finally the train to Pau. Occasionally, during holiday periods, they travelled together in the south of France, to Biarritz, then a small fishing village and on at least one occasion to Lourdes, where Basil recorded only being 'impressed by the size of a procession of pilgrims'.[19]

In 1901, at the age of thirteen, he proceeded to Winchester, having struggled through the entrance examinations. It was then under the headmastership of Dr Burge, a future bishop of Oxford, his reputation being a factor in his father's choice. Academically Basil's school career was undistinguished. He was in 'D' house, under an ageing housemaster, and rose no higher than the second division (of three) of middle part V, never reaching senior part or sixth book to which the Wykehamist élite aspired. Promotion at the school was strictly on academic merit, the qualities encouraged being those of critical analysis, and the control of one's emotions, rather than creativity. In Pau, he had been taught in French and German, and his lack of any grounding in the classics was a disadvantage at England's oldest public school where the classical education was the high ideal.[20] He was active in few societies, and despite his later choice of career, his name does not appear in the records of the debating society. However, in sport he was more active, playing cricket and football (under Winchester rules, which precluded passing and dribbling) and fishing the Itchen, upon which the school had three miles of the water. In shooting he excelled and was a member of the college VIII from 1903 to 1905. He was reckoned to be the best shot in the school, became captain of the team, and under his leadership, Winchester enjoyed one of its rare successes in winning the Ashburton Shield at Bisley in 1904. But clearly his contentment there was in no small measure due to its greater proximity to Colebrooke, which was, he wrote 'always tugging at my heart'.[21] Opportunities to return home were more frequent. Nonetheless, the experience helped to develop his social poise and confidence and widen his range of social contacts, both of inestimable value in later life.

During his schooling, he later observed, 'no great thought had been put into the idea of a career'. However, his development continued to mirror precisely the well-worn paths and traditions of his class, the Anglo-Irish gentry; public school in England followed by a period of service in the armed forces of the crown, which for the oldest son would inevitably be interrupted when he, in turn, assumed the responsibilities of his inheritance. Soldiering, he regarded as the 'most obvious'[22] service for him to enter, given the family tradition, and the immediate example of his three uncles Ronald, Victor and most recently Alan.

Though he considered the navy and always preserved a passionate interest in it, which was reflected in his choice of reading, this option was finally rejected. After a brief spell at a 'cramming' establishment (Bosworth and Stern) he went up for the entrance examination to the Royal Military Academy, and passed, to his own self-confessed relief and his father's unconcealed surprise.[23]

Sandhurst was a highly competitive establishment, strenuous both physically and intellectually. Subjects studied included history, geography, European languages, military administration, topography, tactics and of particular future significance for Brooke, Hindustani. India's defence in the aftermath of the Boer war and before the crisis in Europe was regarded as the primary task of the British army. He did well at riding and musketry, was captain of the Sandhurst VIII and was described in his last report as being of 'excellent' character.[24]

On 26 September 1908, at the age of twenty, Basil was commissioned into the 7th Royal Fusiliers, City of London regiment, as a second lieutenant.[25] Three months later, on Christmas eve, he joined his fellow officers at Secunderabad in central India, travelling via Port Said. He served in India for the next four years. Throughout he kept in close contact with home, writing regularly and asking for local newspapers to be sent out. Typically, his first letter contained the request 'oil my rods and reels and put them away carefully'. His early correspondence, mostly with his mother, was descriptive, uncomplaining and affectionate, containing such phrases as: 'the climate is grand . . . I like everybody'.[26] Certainly, the life was not uncomfortable. He lived in his own bungalow, soon built up a personal menagerie of ponies, mules and dogs and there was no shortage of domestic servants to make meals or carry rods. 'Thank goodness' he wrote, 'in this place one sacks one's butler and about 20 turn up to take his place'.[27] He learnt to play polo, for, he observed, 'there is nothing to do unless you do play polo'. He shot and hunted almost daily – pigsticking from the start, hunting jackal with dogs, shooting snipe or teal, or deer and bison, and sought every opportunity for tracking down the occasional panther. Away from India's mountains and jungles, he fished, a typical early entry in his diary running: 'saw some grand fish rising but cannot find what they like'.[28]

Contacts with the local population came mainly through sport, whether negotiating with villagers to borrow their dogs, playing polo or occasionally roulette with the Indian social élite. Specifically military activity was confined to infrequent manoeuvres or ceremonial occasions. Infrequently, letters home did hint at the danger of 'trouble with the natives', especially if the monsoon was late, or referred to 'the very seditious state of the country'.[29] In general, such references tend to be somewhat condescending and unflattering in tone. In spite of his affection for Indian companions in sport, or high regard for the quality of his servants, in his general attitudes he was a young man of his time. Nor does his correspondence convey any sense of the empire undergoing a process of change or ultimately of disintegration.

From mid-1910, there was growing indications that he was becoming less content for reasons that went deeper than the 'awfully trying' summer heat or occasional 'merry troubles'.[30] There was the discomfort of marching with the infantry under the Indian sun, as a junior officer in the rear. Though such experiences were infrequent they helped confirm his desire to join the cavalry and experience, like his uncles Victor and Alan, 'the glamour of being an

Hussar'.[31] He wrote to his mother 'the whole time one feels that one does not really belong to the regiment . . . I expect I would have had a very much better time if I had been in a good cavalry regiment'; and again, 'I should get home for a year every two years, . . . the only way to soldier out here'. After the failure of attempts to get him into the 11th Hussars, made on his behalf by his uncle and guardian, Ronald, his frustration heightened almost to breaking point. As he informed his mother, 'If I cannot get a cavalry regiment, I think I will chuck it'.[32]

His discontent sprang also from homesickness and a deep desire to return to Colebrooke. He wrote often of his longing to see it and of his desire 'to get it on its legs'.[33] His father had died on 27 November 1907, during his final year at Sandhurst. Basil, as eldest son, inherited the baronetcy but, under the terms of Sir Douglas's will, the property was held in trust for him by two guardians until his attaining the age of twenty five years.[34] His letters home convey a deep concern for his mother, expressing a keen interest in her gardening, fund-raising and birthdays and commending her 'bravery' in bringing up her young family alone on the estate. He promised 'I shall not try to come out here again' and stated that he wished to do what she liked, which would be discussed and decided upon when he next returned to Fermanagh.[35] The gathering political tensions in Ireland may have added to his worries, though his letters betray little evidence that this was the case.

In January 1911, after having served with the infantry at Secunderabad and Jupplepore, his hopes were realised.[36] He transferred to the 10th Hussars, joining them in North India at Rawalpindi, where they were completing their final two years of service in India. He served with them until his retirement in 1919. As a result of the transfer, his unbroken service in India continued without the opportunity to return home until mid-1912. It did, however, enable him to attend the Durbar at Delhi, an unforgettable spectacle, apotheosis of British India, and the undoubted highlight of his peacetime soldiering. He took part in the great review, with 50,000 troops on parade. The 10th Hussars, watched by his sister, Sylvia, formed part of the royal escort on Durbar day, accompanying the king from his camp for the three miles to the Durbar enclosure and back.[37] Alan, also in the escort, wrote that it left 'a deep groove in my memory of the grandeur of British rule in India at its best'.[38]

For Basil, the final term of service in the sub-continent was altogether more contented. Being a hussar was, he recalled, a 'glorious life for a young man, full of adventure and sport'.[39] Like many members of his generation, he would later regard these years as amongst the happiest and most carefree of his life. India was a country in which 'every variety of experience, travel and sport was to be obtained and cheaply'.[40] This was the India of 'Kim', and of Kipling, and of the British Raj before 1914. The training had changed little since before the Crimea, though it may have been under closer scrutiny after the sobering experiences of the Boer war and as the shadows in Europe grew longer. In any case, it did not seriously interfere with the 'adventure and sport'. With obvious pride Sir Basil recounted to his mother the successes of the regimental polo team, winning the subaltern's cup and the inter-regimental contest for the 6th successive year. 'It was' he assured her, 'an absolute record'. Sport was considered an excellent formative of character. To ride well was a prerequisite of efficiency in an officer and sport promoted competent riding, as well as speed of reaction, judgement and physical fitness. Though the basic elements of life and of field sports were still inexpensive, officers were paid little and army income had to be supplemented therefore from private means. Brooke regarded his £400 annual allowance from his guardian as an 'absolute minimum, . . . if one plays polo, it is practically impossible to stay out of debt'.[41]

To his own immense relief, in February 1912, leave for eight months was sanctioned to begin on 1 July of that year. Thus, he could return home to Fermanagh and to Colebrooke for the first time after almost four years of unbroken absence. The prospect, he told his mother, left him 'most fearfully excited'.[42] In late July, he arrived home to the exuberant scenes of welcome which generally accompanied the return to Fermanagh of her aristocratic sons. There were popular demonstrations at Brookeborough and at Colebrooke, church bells rang, a flute band played and there was a display of fireworks provided by Lady Brooke.[43]

The eight months of leave that followed were notable for Sir Basil in a number of respects. It marks the beginning of a souring in his relationship with his mother, who had been from childhood almost his inspiration and certainly his confidante. Subsequently, the flow of letters home to her diminished to a trickle, became cold and formal, and were clearly written, as he himself phrased it, 'from a sense of duty'. The cause of this domestic crisis is unclear, but almost certainly the crucial factor was Lady Brooke's increasing alcoholic addiction. Recently widowed, living on a large and remote estate, with a son, Victor, incurably ill, in an atmosphere of mounting political tension, it was, perhaps, a not altogether surprising development. However, Basil, though sympathetic to her position, was alienated by her response. He clearly felt hurt, disappointed and embittered. He grew increasingly alienated from and indifferent towards her, informing his sister some years later 'I have finished with her unless she makes some kind of improvement'.[44] Eventually, with much recrimination on both sides, she left Colebrooke in late 1915, to live out her final days at Laputa House in Ballyshannon. Soon afterwards, Brooke's sister, Sheelagh, recently married, moved into his vacated home. She and especially Sylvia, now became the focal point of his affections and the pivot of his future plans.

There was a further significant development; just before leaving for India, in 1908, at a meeting of Hanover L.O.L. 1639, the Orange lodge which served the estate and in which Brooke had succeeded his father as worshipful master, the hope was expressed that he would be 'long spared to support the old cause'.[45] This leave, four years later, provided him with his first opportunity to do so, and he did zealously identify with the anti-home rule movement. On 18 September 1912, he was one of the glittering platform party during Carson's visit to Enniskillen, and ten days later he signed the covenant, appropriately at Colebrooke.[46] Moreover, at a time when many of the other county families were distancing themselves from the emerging military response the Brookes, and Sir Basil in particular, were deeply implicated. Many years later, the latter recalled training members of the Ulster Volunteer Force during their Wednesday drill nights in a barn on the estate.[47] Certainly he was a member of the small county sub-committee appointed, in mid-December 1912, by Orange Order delegates to inaugurate and organise the force in the county, and later he was appointed to a further committee, responsible for its military training.[48]

Colebrooke itself was throughout this period one of the most active unionist centres in Fermanagh. It had its own half-company of the U.V.F. which appears to have been a highly efficient one.[49] The Enniskillen Horse held parades there.[50] Its armoury became during these years the biggest in the county. Police statistics, based on the information of a private informer, suggest that it held one-quarter of all the arms in Unionist hands and it was earmarked as one of the area's main distribution centres for the guns 'run' through Larne.[51]

Long before the 'Clydevalley' delivered its cargo, however, Brooke had rejoined his regiment. Nonetheless, he had indicated by his actions during these months that he readily and fully identified with the aggressive and defiant attitudes which had characterised the recent history of his family's political involvement. After hearing one of his speeches, in January 1913, a local Orange leader commented on 'the genuineness of the principle and the earnestness of . . . [his] unionism. [He] shows no hesitation to tread in his father's footsteps. He is proud to do so'. There is further evidence to this effect. In February, just before leaving to resume his duties with the Hussars, now in South Africa, Brooke told the local brethren of 'the great importance of Ulstermen and Orangemen, standing united together . . . . to defeat home rule'. He concluded with a promise that 'if they stood by him, he would stand by them'. He fulfilled this pledge. One year later, on 26 March 1914, against the background of the Curragh mutiny, the *Fermanagh Times* carried a small report which, though veiled in anonymity, is nonetheless unmistakable. It ran 'Mr Falls [commander of the 3rd battalion of the U.V.F.] received a cablegram from an officer on active service in South Africa, asking if he should return to help the loyalists in Ulster'.[52] Certainly, Brooke did offer to resign his commission and go back to Fermanagh. He had inherited Colebrooke outright in June the previous year and he wished, he stated later, to be at hand if needed to help the unionist cause.[53] But for injury, he might well have returned as he considered that his 'loyalties were to . . . [his] . . . home and to . . . [his] . . . people'.[54]

In the Transvaal Sir Basil had his first taste of military action. In mid-1913, a strike had broken out amongst the Rand miners, and the troops, vastly outnumbered, were used to maintain order in a tense and potentially explosive situation. He wrote to his sister:

we have been having a rotten time . . . I shall be very glad when we are out of it and away . . . Martial law will be declared as soon as the first bomb is thrown . . . the worst part of the whole thing is having to wait to be shot at.[55]

In later years he expressed deep appreciation for the tactics adopted by Botha and Smuts, describing their response as 'calm and decisive'. He remembered vividly how 'all officers were called into the Rand club for a briefing . . . we were told there was to be no reading of the riot act or allowing matters to become really bad before dealing with them'. The troops were given

an indemnification in writing for the consequences of any necessary order, . . . later, . . . I was to remember the lessons this affair taught me . . . the importance of giving full support to the forces of authority in times of stress.[56]

The implications of this 'lesson' lay in the future. For the present, the crisis subsided and more leisurely training and activity followed. His first serious injury occurred early the following year, and resulted from a motor cycle accident which shattered his jaw in twelve pieces and caused wounds which later turned septic. The incident caused him great suffering, and but for his youth and fitness, it could well have proved fatal. When the war in Europe began, his jaw was still painful and tender, and he still required a device to soften his food.[57] However, the army medical board declared that he was fit for service. His uncle, Ronald, had been surprised by the speed of Sir Basil's recovery and that he was so 'very little disfigured'.[58]

Churchill described the former as 'a rising star in the British Army . . . [until] stricken down by arthritis'. In September 1914, he was training troops at Aldershot, and found them as 'keen as mustard . . . so that they can go and fight the Germans'.[59] It was an emotion Basil shared. He had recently been promoted to full lieutenant (19 September 1914) and disliked greatly the posting forced upon him through injury.[60] In late October, at Tedworth barracks, waiting to cross to France he complained, 'I am fed up, no one has left for a fortnight . . . I can't stick this drill instruction job. I do hate hanging about'. During the following week, he himself crossed the Channel. His final instructions to his agent were: 'See to it that any . . . who enlist shall have their place kept open for them when they return . . . Let them know this'.[61]

When Brooke arrived in France, on 4 November, the tide of the great German advance had already ebbed, to be followed by the battle of the Aisne and the 'race to the sea'.[62] This led to the indecisive encounter known as first Ypres and the extension of the deadlock at appalling cost. The 10th Hussars formed part of the 6th Brigade of the 3rd Cavalry Division which was commanded by Major General Julian Byng. Initially they were deployed as reinforcements covering the retreat of the rear and flank of the allied army.[63] At first Ypres, where it has been said the old British Army died, they fought from holes and trenches to hold an enemy which still had overwhelming superiority of numbers. During the week after Brooke's arrival, the regimental diary records their being 'under heavy attack from the Germans . . . [who got] . . . up to a few yards from the trenches, however, the squadron with a severe fire mowed them down'. These first few months left a deep and lasting impression on Sir Basil, in his own phrase: 'it burned into my memory'. At the time, he described how 'in one week, we were in the trenches for 2 goes of 48 hours, and when out were on mobile reserve, . . . [we] saddled up . . . and turned out five times'.[64] Long afterwards he recalled an incident during November, his closest 'experience of the slaughter', in which he fired 'round after round, for four hours, at the Prussian Guard advancing across no man's land'.[65]

Temporary relief came, on 20 November, when the regiment moved into billets and enjoyed its 'first rest since operations began'. However, they were shortly afterwards despatched back to Ypres to take over a section of the French line. They were so close to the German lines that it was possible for a German to throw a match box into their trenches with the message, 'we are an Alsace Regiment, don't shoot us and we won't shoot you, vive la France, but Germany comes first'.[66]

From the spring of 1915, Brooke's letters home indicate a predictable and deepening depression, though there were lighter moments. He was able to return to Colebrooke briefly in March, and for a short time Edward, later duke of Windsor, was attached to the squadron of which he was troop leader.[67] Still, his health was poor, he had suffered from mild gas poisoning and was struck by shrapnel on at least two occasions, once on his jaw, aggravating old wounds, and contributing to digestion problems. For a time, it seemed possible that he might be invalided out.[68] The fighting itself he found 'very uninteresting, . . . one fails to see how we will ever be used for proper cavalry work'. For a time he tried to join the flying corps, but was unsuccessful. He was philosophical: 'the colonel can't spare officers who know cavalry work, . . . I am very disappointed . . .[but] . . . I can see his point of view'. He suffered inevitable weariness, as the conflict settled into an apparently unending war of attrition, and with the death and mutilation of comrades. Of one letter written at this time, he commented later, 'I very nearly didn't send it, . . . it seemed so hopeless'.[69]

His spirits were raised, at least temporarily, when in mid-April General Byng unexpectedly asked him to act as his A.D.C. the appointment to date from 7 May 1915. For Brooke, it was the fulfilment of an ambition. He wrote next day to his sister, 'on the staff at last'.[70] Days later, however, he sought permission from the general to be allowed to return to his regiment. At the time the 10th Hussars were suffering possibly the highest casualty rate in their history, between 7–13 May forty per cent were killed or wounded, and Sir Basil considered that he ought to be serving alongside his comrades. Byng firmly refused the request and the two served together for the remainder of the war.[71] The general was personally fond of Brooke, and recognised his suitability for promotion based on his seven years of active service, proven courage, and the fact that, in addition, he could speak French fluently. For his part Brooke had, like his uncle Alan, a deep admiration for his superior. Byng's reputation was one of seeking always to alleviate the disabilities of the rank and file and thus, after the armistice, he was detailed with Haig to deal with the demobilisation problems at Boulogne. He was a man of great sincerity and simple habits who shunned controversy. At his own request his funeral was private and without military ceremonial and his private papers were burnt. They became close friends. Byng became the godfather of Brooke's first son, who was called Julian after him.[72] To Basil, the appointment brought both pride and pleasure. The work he now reported to be 'interesting', he enjoyed higher standards of comfort, and the dangers 'were not as considerable as of old',[73] though Byng's exacting sense of duty ensured that they entered the shell zone almost every day.

The period immediately following was uneventful. 'Things very dull', he reported, 'absolutely no news of any description'. Then as is typical in war, at a few hours notice, Byng was transferred to the mid-eastern expeditionary force to take over command of IX Corps.[74] Lady Byng recorded in her autobiography:

when I received his telegram giving me the bitter news, I felt as if his death warrant had been signed, . . . no place was more hopeless strategically, . . . my only consolation was . . . that he had with him two of his A.D.C.s who would do their best for him, one was Sir Basil Brooke, the other Lord Tichfield.[75]

Their efforts on Byng's behalf were not always favourably received. Shortly after their arrival at Suvla, the two successfully scrounged glass windows and furniture from the Royal Navy for Byng's quarters, only to receive a severe reprimand: 'When I want to live in greater comfort than the rest I will let you know'.[76] Conditions compared unfavourably with those they had left in France, particularly the climatic extremes, flies, living in dug-outs cut into the hills, constant shelling, and for Brooke, amongst many other discomforts, recurrent dysentery, 'a damnable complaint'. One of the few compensations was close cooperation wtih the navy. He wrote with obvious relish of going on reconnaissance in a destroyer, and of the 'perfectly magnificent' submarine bombardment of railway lines and columns of troops.[77]

Byng quickly came to the conclusion, like Sir Charles Munroe, that there was no alternative to evacuation. Brooke, at the time in letters home and in his memoirs, expressed deep admiration for the speed and efficiency with which this was conducted. He told his sister that 'the Turk never fired a gun until the next morning . . . that we had completely evacuated, I am sure never entered his mind until well on in the day'.[78] One month later, he added: 'There was not a single thing left at Suvla, . . . even at the very end Byng . . . and I loaded up an old Ford with rifles and wheels we had found'.[79] Others shared his enthusiastic assessment. A German account concluded that the evacuation would stand before the eyes of all strategists of defeat as a hitherto unattained masterpiece.[80] Brooke's expectations, however, that the 'old general will get great praise' were not fulfilled. Early in 1916, he wrote, 'There has not been much mention of his name, as he does not advertise. I think the people that matter realise what he has done, but it makes one all the more determined to get out of the army as soon as one can'.[81]

But for the intervention of the war Sir Basil's military career would by this time almost certainly have been over and he would have been back in his beloved Fermanagh estate. Increasingly his thoughts were drawn back to Colebrooke, no doubt partly from necessity as high taxation was eating into the depleted income from his neglected property, but it was also from homesickness and war-weariness. These feelings were reinforced when his sister Sheelagh moved into the house with her husband in November 1915. Some weeks earlier he wrote to Sylvia, 'the thoughts of the time we will have at Colebrooke when it is all over are the only thing that keep me alive'. Later, he returned to this theme 'I sometimes get Colebrooke so bad that I have to go away by myself and walk hard. I always spend half an hour before getting up in thinking about the place. I often wish the government would order me back saying I would be more use to them at home'.[82]

His letters home contain few references to his own direct experiences of the carnage of war and still less to the political situation in Ireland. Comments relating to the enemy are similarly infrequent and are rarely tainted by that very understandable hatred which loss and misery, exacerbated by propaganda, were so freely to generate. Prolonged exposure to the horrors of the Western Front did however have a profound impact. This was well illustrated on the one occasion, in early 1916, where he did address himself to 'the domestic troubles in Ireland'. His attitude then would no doubt have been widely supported by many other Ulstermen directly involved in the war. He wrote

I think one's views become modified to a great extent when one has been at this game for a bit. In a few words I . . . [have come] . . . to the conclusion that of the two evils civil war or home rule, the former is the worse for Ireland. People at home who have not seen war will shout for it but I am sure if some of us who do know its horrors can take a firm stand, we could make them see it.

At the time of writing Brooke was in Egypt, which he found 'a pleasant rest, . . . there is as much chance of a brick landing on me here as there is at Colebrooke'.[83] He had gone with Byng who, after the Suvla evacuation, was transferred for a brief period to command a section of the Suez Canal defences. However, in early February, the general took over the 17th Army Corps, at Vimy, and Brooke again went with him back to the Western Front, but only for a matter of weeks. On 22 February he left France and returned to Fermanagh. His enforced leave was due to deteriorating health and weariness induced by his recent experiences in the Dardanelles and the almost daily routine of 'going up the line' with Byng. The latter wrote to Brooke's sister: 'I had to pack him off . . . as he was getting a nasty, irritating inflammation behind the eye'. He added later, 'I think his nerves got a bit of a shake at Gallipoli, . . . he is fussing about his being away and thinks I will get someone else in his place, which I certainly shall *not* do, as I am far too fond of him'. Aware of Sir Basil's eagerness to return, he stressed, 'keep him at home until he is really well'.[84]

Thus, Brooke spent the spring and early summer of 1916 recuperating at Colebrooke. In early March a concert was organised to welcome him home. During it he repeated at least some of the sentiments which he had expressed earlier to his sister privately. He is reported as having said that it would be 'a good thing to lay aside their own little petty troubles and think of the great troubles of the empire'.[85] Such emotions were rapidly overtaken by the traumatic events in Dublin during the weeks which followed. Brooke first heard of the rising when a note, indicating in broad outline something of what had happened, was passed to him during Easter service at the small Anglican church on his estate. Many years later he recorded his personal feelings of bitterness as a long serving soldier at this 'stab in the back' for the British war effort on the western front, and his sense of shame that it should have been perpetrated by Irishmen.[86] In July 1916 he himself returned to the battle-zone.

Meanwhile, Sir Basil had been mentioned in dispatches by General Munroe during the Gallipoli campaign and before returning to France was decorated with the Military Cross at Buckingham Palace, on the king's birthday, 24 June 1916, in 'recognition of his gallantry and devotion to duty in the field'. Three weeks later he rejoined Byng's staff and served with him in some of the major theatres of war until the armistice. Byng had just taken over the command of the Canadian Corps.[87] He led them at the Somme, and in early 1917, in the attack on Vimy Ridge. Alan Brooke was directly involved in both engagements. At the Somme, his 18th Division gave the Canadians support, he organised the 'creeping barrage', and was awarded the Distinguished Service Order. On 8 September 1916, he wrote of 'everything broken and smashed . . . absolute desolation and destruction . . . everything seems broken except the morale of the men'.[88] By the time of Vimy Ridge he was on the staff of the Canadian corps, and again coordinated the artillery barrage prior to the assault.

In June 1917, Byng was given his last and most demanding wartime posting, the command of the Third Army, and Brooke, now a captain, accompanied him.[89] The Third Army was subsequently involved in three major engagements, the Cambrai offensive, the defensive struggle in the spring of 1918, holding the German attack at Arras, and the final advance in the autumn of that year, prior to the armistice. The Canadian troops were moved to Passchendaele, in Alan Brooke's words 'to flounder in a sea of mud with no hope of ultimate success'. He felt it 'incomprehensible that they were not sent to the Cambrai attack which was short of reserves'. In the latter Byng sought, controversially, the elusive strategic break-through. As with Gallipoli, Basil regretted that his commander failed to receive 'the credit he deserved' for the tactics adopted.[90] On 26 March 1918, he attended, as a member of Byng's staff, the Doullens conference at which Foch became commander-in-chief of the Allied forces in France. Later during the spring offensive, he acted as interpreter at a meeting between Foch and Byng at Albert. His reconnaissance work in the Villers-Brittonneux area at this time was recognised when he received the Croix-de-Guerre the following October.[91]

In the autumn of 1918 the tide finally turned and British troops at last had the unprecedented sense of German resistance steadily weakening. The Third Army won eighteen decisive battles and drove the enemy back over sixty miles between 21 August and armistice day. Brooke wrote to his sister 'these are very thrilling days . . . the Bosch is broken and will go when we want him to go. I expect things ought to have developed in a month and then I can get home'. He concluded, in typical fashion, 'let me know any farm news'.[92]

Many years later Brooke could recall armistice day with total clarity, travelling in a cattle wagon, near Valenciennes, on his way to Mons, which had just been captured by the Third Canadian division. For him, as for so many others, the war ended within a few miles of where it had begun. In his final letter home on 15 November, he expressed his immense sense of relief: 'I am just beginning to realise that the whole thing is over, I said realise but I don't, . . . I am so b. . . .y happy, I don't know what to do'.[93]

In Fermanagh, claims were made that Enniskillen was the first town in the United Kingdom to hear of the armistice. The military barracks picked up a faint message at 6.30 am and conveyed the news to the town by launching a series of rockets. Soon church bells joined in, as crowds gathered for the November hiring fair. Brooke arrived home three weeks later, and was once again greeted by the kind of reception reserved for the sons of county families returning from the war. Fog signals placed on the line exploded as his train entered Maguiresbridge station. A large crowd had assembled and formed a procession behind his car, torchbearers laid the way and local bands played 'lively airs'. At a more formal occasion, later, he was officially welcomed back by the tenants of the estate, his taking up permanent residence at Colebrooke was celebrated and the hope expressed that he would now 'live the life of a country gentleman . . . amongst them'.[94]

His military career ended officially on 9 March 1919. On that date he retired with a gratuity from the 10th Hussars and was appointed to the regiment's reserve of officers.[95] Thus his partnership, though not his friendship, with Sir Julian Byng, future governor general of Canada and metropolitan police commissioner, ended. On the same day, the 3rd Cavalry Division broke up and his old regiment subsequently took up duty in one of the zones of occupation on the Rhine.[96]

The post-war plans graphically described in his wartime correspondence contain no hint of one further significant development in early 1919. In mid-April he became engaged to Cynthia Mary Surgison of Cuckfield Park, Sussex. They had met in the final weeks of the war, their families being already linked through the marriage of Miss Surgison's sister to Brooke's cousin.[97] Just one newspaper struck a discordant note, describing Sir Basil's father as 'a rabid Orangeman who publicly declared a few years ago that he had an armoury at his mansion and would serve out rifles to Orangemen should occasion arise'.[98]

In the Sussex press Miss Surgison was described as 'charming . . . and intensely interested in the romantic history of Cuckfield Park and Surgison traditions'.[99] However, she rapidly came to identify fully with her adopted home. Not long after her arrival, Mrs Archdale, wife of the county's imperial member of parliament, spoke of 'how proud [she was] . . . to see Lady Brooke, an English woman like herself, taking her part as an Ulster woman'.[100] Initially the marriage appeared to confirm Brooke's current domestic preoccupations, but ultimately his wife was to play a crucial role in forwarding his broader political career. In the years that followed, for half a century, she was to provide him with that domestic warmth and stability at Colebrooke for which he had yearned in wartime and which he was ever relieved to return to. She filled a void in Brooke's life, real even if not consciously appreciated, and there especially after the cooling of his feelings towards his mother. It was a relationship tested and strengthened through bereavement and illness. Lady Brooke's social competence, unquestioning devotion, her resilience and determination sharpened his ambition and contributed to its fulfilment. Many of his political ideas originated in conversation with his wife and his debt to her he frequently and willingly avowed in public.

They were married on 3 June 1919 at St George's Chapel, Hanover Square. The guest list was drawn mainly from the landed aristocracy and a number of military figures, including Byng, 'very soldierly . . . despite his well cut grey overcoat and bowler',[101] and the marquis of Tichfield who had been, like Brooke, one of the general's A.D.C.s. The redoubtable E. M. Archdale was the only politician present. Three days later, on 6 June, they returned to Fermanagh and were welcomed by over 400 residents and tenants of the old Colebrooke estate. After receiving gifts, and compliments regarding his 'distinguished' military record, 'kindly disposition and unaffected manner', Brooke indicated his pleasure at being home, stated that he had thought about Colebrooke a great deal and that now they had 'come back . . . prepared to do all they could to help the neighbourhood'.[102]

No one could doubt his genuine delight at returning to Fermanagh. Twenty-five years of absence had served to strengthen his love for and commitment to the family estates. As he wrote many years later, 'when the war ended I had no ideas in my head but to go back to Colebrooke of which I had seen so little, my heart was set on farming'. This he now began to do 'with great happiness'.[103] In part it was a gentlemanly necessity. The 1,300 acre estate had inevitably suffered from the neglect caused by his unexpectedly prolonged military career, farm profits were low and the long-term trend of food prices was downwards. He did, however, also have a real and abiding interest in agriculture. In 1916, he had written to his sister 'I think if I get through this war, I shall settle down to drain-cleaner in chief'. Throughout the war he had bombarded his agent with queries relating to prices, techniques of production, staff numbers, the leasing of shooting rights and balance-sheets. With regard to the latter he wrote 'my questions are not in the nature of criticisms . . . simply I am not used to these accounts and I want to get to grips with them'. He had prepared and developed detailed plans and stratagems for the future 'working on the principle of each year doing a little to get the place right'. In France he was constantly on the lookout for new farming practices that might be successfully applied on his own estates. He was confident with regard to their ultimate profitability so long as 'a business-like approach was adopted', and they concentrated on livestock 'the only way to make the farm really pay . . . As long as we go slow, we shall soon be working the whole land'.[104]

On taking up residence he set in motion a process of gradual reclamation, unblocking drains, pushing back the rushes that had encroached on once productive land, replenishing the livestock herds, planting trees and increasing the numbers of deer in the depleted woodlands.[105] Each year the house itself was gradually restored and renovated. In 1923 electric lights were installed. The walls were repainted in parts for the first time in fifty years. Lady Brooke helped restore the gardens, where some of the flowers she noted, dated to the 1850s. She wrote: 'it is the most complete wilderness, disease in almost all the roots'. Leisure interests were not neglected, 10,000 trout were put down in one of the streams, banks cleared for fishing, and shooting butts set in position. Both shared a passion for shooting and fishing. Soon after her arrival Lady Brooke recorded, with obvious pleasure, learning to make flies and catching her first salmon.[106]

Though he attended meetings of and subscribed to the Fermanagh Unionist Association, the chief way in which Brooke initially sought to 'help the neighbourhood' was to help the farmer. He was active in the Ulster Farmers' Union. It was at such an assemblage that his wife made her 'first public appearance'. He regarded it as an indispensable pressure group, stating, in July 1919, at Brookeborough that its 'object was to see that every farmer's interest was looked after . . . there was no use their writing to parliament if they had a grievance'.[107] He was instrumental also in setting up a highly successful Farmers' Cooperative Store 'despite a good deal of opposition from local shop-keepers'.[108] He was also a member of Fermanagh Farming Society and a county representative to the Irish landowners' convention in Dublin in July 1919.[109]

Thus for the first eighteen months after his return from France, events followed fairly closely the course that Brooke had hoped they would. The time had been spent happily, restoring his estates, responding to the needs of the local community, and living the life of a country gentleman. Throughout this period, it can have been no disappointment to him that his most militaristic activity had been to preside over the first meeting of the British Comrades of the Great War, at Enniskillen courthouse.[110] However in mid-1920, his career took a new, entirely unpredicted, but portentous turn. Many years later, he wrote, 'I had thought that my soldiering days were over but they were not. For in the next few years I was to become a soldier of a very different sort . . . but I had the added stimulant of defending my own birthplace'.[111] In June 1920, Lady Brooke recorded simply in her diary, 'BSB started the vigilantes, an arrangement for mutual protection against Sinn Fein, in which two men from each town land do sentry duty one night per week, BSB did likewise'.[112]

CHAPTER III

The Formation of the
Special Constabulary 1919–23

In compelling prose Churchill caricatured the impact of war on the west of the province: 'As the deluge subsides and the waters fall we see the dreary steeples of Fermanagh and Tyrone emerging once again. The integrity of their quarrel is one of the few institutions that has been left unaltered in the cataclysm which has swept the world'.[1] Certainly, after his return to Colebrooke in November, 1918, Brooke can have found little that was new or unfamiliar in his immediate political environment from five years before. Wartime police reports continued repeatedly to stress that, despite their apparent quiescence, unionist opposition to home rule was unabated, and the U.V.F. was ready to resume activity should the occasion arise.[2] One important change, had, however, occurred. Editions of the local newspapers which bore news of Sir Basil's return referred also to the recent 'historic poll', and to the victory of Sinn Fein, a striking indication of how crucial the period of war had been in the development of Irish and of Fermanagh nationalism.[3] The R.I.C. regarded this new movement as 'thoroughly anti-British and disloyal in character'.[4]

Sinn Fein first achieved significant support in the county during the aftermath of the Easter rising. As elsewhere, the execution of its leaders served to polarise opinion. Police reports stated that it aroused party feeling 'not as regards the rebellion itself or its repression but . . . the military measures after the surrender'.[5] The *Fermanagh Times* observed, in mid-May: 'we are no longer under any delusions as to the revolt . . . it has elicited the sympathy of 90 per cent of the nationalists of the country' and it expressed fears two weeks later, of government panic and of Fermanagh 'thrown to the wolves'.[6]

The impact of the rising on nationalist opinion was reinforced by the deepening conviction that the old constitutional movement had failed, and by gathering fears of conscription. The decisive impetus, however, to the growth of a more extreme nationalism within the county, came from local catholic clergy. The county inspector's reports in the autumn of 1917 and spring of 1918, described Sinn Fein as spreading 'under the fostering care of the majority of catholic priests' and claimed that, 'where priests stand in this direction, clubs are formed'. Its other local leaders were dismissed as 'hardly men at all in the ordinary sense of the word'. According to these confidential assessments, the moderating influence of Cardinal Logue was counteracted by the activities of the local bishop, who gave both clergy and national school-teachers every

29

licence and encouragement, while local priests, many of them born in Monaghan, were held to have organised and led nationalist opposition to exclusion.[7] The latter helped ensure that most of the county's delegates to the Nationalist party's convention, held in June 1916, voted against partition and some led A.O.H. branches in secession as a protest against the majority decision there. The county inspector felt that they influenced the opinion of many 'who would have acquiesced in exclusion', though, he added, 'there . . . [was] . . . a strong supposition' that this would be 'temporary and not under an Orange administration'. Later, the local priesthood exhorted the faithful to 'go to the sacraments as, . . . in the event of conscription, . . . numbers will be killed'.[8]

By mid-1918 Sinn Fein strength in Fermanagh was estimated at 2,200, but its influence was thought to be greater than its numerical support, with nationalist magistrates allegedly afraid to discharge their duties fairly, Nationalist party members inhibited in expressing opposition to it by the priests and the local nationalist press said to be 'tainted' by the movement. In 1919, however, its support stabilised and even declined. Poor attendance at its meetings, lack of funds, and the steady flow of recruits from the region into the R.I.C. suggest that the organisation was losing momentum and influence. The extent of party toleration was illustrated when unionists and nationalists celebrated the armistice and later the peace settlement together in Enniskillen, a phenomenon almost unique in Ireland.[9]

Sinn Fein appeal was diminished when conscription ceased to be a threat, and it suffered also from governmental proclamation and suppression. In Fermanagh its gathering campaign of violence alienated moderate opinion, many of its supporters locally apparently being of a 'mild type, . . . really constitutionalists'. In addition, the strength of the Orange Order and A.O.H. were thought to have inhibited its activities because if the latter 'perpetrated outrages . . . [its members] . . . would be attacked or at least given away'. The county inspector believed that without the support of the priests, it would have collapsed altogether in most areas. The influence of the church had been graphically illustrated earlier during the 1918 election. That Sinn Fein should have contested South Fermanagh was Cardinal Logue's decision whilst the movement's choice of candidate in the northern division was effectively determined by local clergy. Police estimates suggested that the Irish party was stronger throughout the county, but its supporters followed clerical direction, and voted Sinn Fein, to keep the Unionist candidates out.[10]

Nonetheless, before the end of 1919, Sinn Fein activity was causing police concern, particularly in those areas bordering counties Leitrim, Cavan and Monaghan, where it had taken firm root. Local leadership and tradition helped to determine the geography of its support within the county. Greatest unease was felt by the R.I.C. in relation to the area around Brookeborough. At Lisnaskea, Newtownbutler and Maguiresbridge, Sinn Fein appears to have had strong support. Nationalists were said to be bitterly hostile towards the police there, relations strained by arrests and the baton-charging of meetings.[11]

From late 1919 community tensions in Fermanagh steadily deepened and there are indications of Sinn Fein strength beginning to increase once more. The movement was helped by the disintegration of the Irish Nationalist Party and the sharpening of the partition issue. This imminent prospect once more increased the symbolic significance of the local government elections in 1920. The revision sessions were very keenly contested by all parties, as with proportional representation no one could easily predict the outcome. Local priests tried desperately to arrange an electoral pact, with agreed Nationalist and Sinn Fein candidates.[12] Voting was on strictly religious and sectarian grounds. Unionist efforts to achieve control of Enniskillen urban council and the county council were predictably frustrated and party supporters made bitter allegations of intimidation and personation against their opponents.

Their apprehension was heightened by the extent of Sinn Fein success in the rest of Ireland, with its obvious threat to their own exposed county, their suspicion of governmental weakness, and the growing confidence of Fermanagh nationalists that they would soon be in an Irish republic. The former fully shared the fears of the county inspector that Fermanagh was being 'infected by the general spread of lawlessness in the country'. Sinn Fein was, he reported, 'working secretly, with a fairly large following', holding courts, organising collections, and carrying out raids for arms. Though violence within the county was still rare, he expressed concern, in February, that the 'concentration of police on the defence of personnel and barracks' was increasing the opportunities for outrage. Later he referred to the possiblity that 'the U.V.F. . . . [was] . . . being reorganised but the police . . . [had] . . . no confirmation of this'.[13]

The original stimulus for Brooke to initiate a vigilante force, however, did not arise directly from conditions in Fermanagh itself. The idea germinated during his wife's confinement at 40 Upper Fitzwilliam Street, Dublin, from March to late May 1920. Though their first son, Julian, was born on Sunday evening, April 18, their visit was unexpectedly prolonged owing to the critical illness of Lady Brooke, giving her husband time to observe and absorb the mood of the capital. He recorded later his sense of shock 'at the anarchy that had taken over the city' and the suffering of people not sympathetic to the rebel regime.[14] The murder, some weeks later, of Frank Brooke, in his office at Dublin Castle, must have served to reinforce this impression. At the time, Sir Basil was particularly horrified by the success of a hunger strike amongst prisoners at Mountjoy, which he felt had coerced Hamar Greenwood into authorising their premature release. The latter believed that their 'martyrdom [would do] . . . the government more harm than their freedom'.[15] Brooke resolved that 'whatever the cost' such a state of lawlessness should not be permitted to spread to Ulster.[16] His concern was shared by others. The government's apparent capitulation was condemned in both Fermanagh's unionist newspapers, and in mid-May Frederick Crawford advised Carson on what ought to be done. He suggested mobilising the U.V.F. again, and obtaining official recognition for it, otherwise, he claimed, 'we will have the protestants breaking out here and killing a lot of Sinn Fein leaders'.[17]

On his return, in June 1920, Brooke proceeded to organise his illegal vigilante force. He began with the formation of a nucleus of fourteen on the demesne at Colebrooke. They were armed, using the U.V.F. guns 'run in' by Crawford at Larne. They had never been surrendered but carefully concealed, he claimed later, for just such an eventuality.[18] To act aggressively in defence of their property and of the union was a deep and enduring Brooke family tradition, and one which Sir Basil had already, during his leave in 1912–13, shown himself to be an heir to. In addition the estate was located in a particularly tense and vulnerable area, an exposed and insecure unionist enclave. Police reports suggest that it was the most actively Sinn Fein portion of the county. It was also adjacent to the border with Cavan, Monaghan, and Tyrone, from which the county inspector believed 'their orders came'.[19]

In a letter to General Macready, in July 1920, Brooke summarised his motives for forming the force and requested that it be recognised by the government. He wrote:

I am out solely to do what is possible to maintain order . . . If the government will help [the people] . . . they will do all they can to help the government, but if they are left without any means of protection owing to lack of police, long distances to the nearest military barracks, and the possession of arms denied them, then they have only two alternatives. The hotheads will take matters into their own hands and threaten retaliation should any of their own side be injured, and so commit acts which will inevitably lead to rioting, or else those who wish for a quiet life, and failing to find protection from any other quarter, will inevitably become adherents of Sinn Fein . . . I am not speaking about what I think but what I know to be the feeling amongst the people. They are very nervous and do not know what will happen from day to day. If the government will not help . . . I am afraid that a very serious situation may develop . . . I have tried to explain the matter as I know it to be.[20]

In letters to both Macready and later Sir Ernest Clark he suggested that 'the threat of raids . . . was . . . increasing',[21] and that his 'patrols' reported considerable traffic on the roads. There were 'no police to stop them', however, and his men had 'no power to stop them'.[22]

Many of these fears and expectations were being echoed at the same time in local police reports to Dublin Castle. As early as February, these expressed concern at the rising tide of Sinn Fein outrages within the county, and the view that, particularly in areas where barracks had been vacated, the level of police protection was inadequate. For instance, at Lisbellaw it was reported in June that 'police and military patrols went there at uncertain hours but . . . this method of dealing with a party of Irish Volunteers [was] . . . almost useless as . . . [they] . . . are no doubt watched and can easily be prevented from arriving in time'. The growing danger that unionist hotheads might, in Brooke's phrase, 'take matters into their own hands' was obvious. The county inspector predicted after two raids on Lisbellaw, in late May and early June, that 'a very serious encounter may be expected involving considerable loss of life and very bitter party feeling if a further attack is made by Irish Volunteers', and implied the need for some form of protective organisation. In neighbouring counties, R.I.C. reports described moderate nationalists being driven into the arms of Sinn Fein through inadequate protection. The June report for Tyrone referred to 'constitutional nationalists [who had] . . . become more extreme . . . throwing their lot in with Sinn Fein as they see the activities of this party unchecked'.[23] In Donegal, it was reported that 'people who would be moderate are afraid to go against the movement, . . . [and that] . . . quiet law-abiding people live in constant dread . . . Sinn Fein entirely dominate the community'.[24]

The nature of the organisation with which Brooke hoped to nullify these dangers was, at least initially, simple. It was comprised, as Lady Brooke stated, of 'two men from each townland [doing] . . . sentry duty, one night per week'.[25] Sir Basil sought to reassure Macready that its sole purpose was to assist in maintaining law and order and that 'all creeds and shades of political thought would be enrolled if they so desired'.[26] He had little success in the latter objective, though this does seem to have been his main reason for adopting the name 'Fermanagh Vigilance'. He explained this to Sir Ernest Clark, then assistant under-secretary and based in Belfast, stating that 'while using the material of the U.V.F., I did not call it by the old name. "Vigilance" force seemed to meet the situation'. He went on to list his reasons:

1. U.V.F. implied political aims, in my opinion, the situation was too serious for that
2. Being more or less political, the government could not possibly take sides
3. I wished to enrol law-abiding Roman catholics, who could not do so under the old name . . . Originally, there were three working for us, two have since dropped out, one an ex-police sergeant, remains.

His conclusion was that 'in theory it was right but in practice owing to distrust it failed'.[27]

From the beginning he was convinced that this force needed arms, an important factor in requesting government recognition. It had, he estimated, about 40 per cent of what was required. Clearly this was likely to be the major stumbling block at the Castle. Accordingly, he stated his case forcefully to Macready:

I fully appreciate the difficulty of supplying us with arms, yet I for one would hesitate before I asked men to go on patrol who by so doing would attract attention to themselves, if they had no means of protection. I am convinced that if the law-abiding citizens were made to take an oath, that these arms would not be used for any other purpose from that for which they were given.

He expressed the hope that the government would 'help these people, by at any rate allowing them to obtain firearms for their protection'.[28]

Brooke's action in forming a local protection force was certainly not unique in mid-1920. It was paralleled by similar groups formed by northern unionists elsewhere, as the need was widely and independently felt. The inspector general had consistently warned Dublin Castle of the probable re-emergence of the Ulster Volunteer Force after the War. Subsequent to the Easter rising it was described as still a potentially effective organisation. From early 1918, the force was closely scrutinised. It was predicted, in May, that its estimated 50,000 members would become active again during the following six months. In fact, it remained quiescent, and three months later many of its arms were voluntarily handed in to military custody. In July 1919, Carson threatened to revive it if Ulster's rights and liberties were interfered with and the Ulster Unionist Council four weeks later, decided to resuscitate the Unionist Clubs in preparation for the mobilisation of resistance to any measure of self-government.[29] But soon afterwards the introduction of the Government of Ireland bill proved reassuring, and no further action was taken.

However, from early the following year, the rising levels of Sinn Fein violence, unionist doubts regarding both the commitment of the R.I.C. and the dependability of the military, their suspicions that the Castle lacked the political will to impose order and growing party feeling, all contributed to the deepening conviction that some form of protective force was necessary.[30] On 25 June 1920 therefore, the U.U.C. standing committee decided to revive the U.V.F. and Wilfrid Spender was asked to command the force. He himself regarded it as 'the best and safest way' to avoid 'serious trouble'.[31] From police reports, it can be seen to have been active in all six north-eastern counties, except Down, by August. It was referred to first in Belfast and Fermanagh, and subsequently Tyrone, followed by Armagh, Antrim and Londonderry.[32] It is not clear whether these references would have included local civilian forces like Brooke's 'vigilance'. Soon after his arrival in mid-September 1920, Sir Ernest Clark listed seven bodies similar to the latter. In each case the initiative and leadership usually came from ex-military officers, though occasionally it was provided by clerics or committees whose membership is not specified. They were predominantly involved in patrol work and surveillance and, in some instances he noted that they offered intelligence to the R.I.C.[33]

Thus Brooke's force was not unique within the province in this period, nor was the idea of forming such a force original within Fermanagh itself. During the war, the Easter rising had prompted local U.V.F. leaders to offer, 'in view of the situation, to hold the available members of their organisation (around 2,300) at the disposal of the authorities'.[34] In response to the political initiatives which followed the rising, the *Fermanagh Times* asked: 'What is being done for our protection? . . . It would be wise if every county did something on the common behalf, but an exceptional position renders it imperative that Fermanagh should certainly lose no time in doing so'.[35] However, there is no evidence of anything being done. Similarly, in May 1920, the month before Brooke began to form his protection force, the *Impartial Reporter* encouraged citizens to form an organisation for their own mutual defence, as they could no longer rely on the government to fulfill this function.[36]

Newspaper reports suggest that Lisbellaw unionists had already done so. When the home of an ex-army sergeant was attacked on May 22, local volunteers were summoned by church bells and mill-sirens, up to 300 arriving in thirty minutes. It was stated that civilian patrols of U.V.F. men had been functioning in the village 'for the last few weeks', since the R.I.C. vacated the local barracks.[37] It was an exposed unionist area, near the Monaghan-Cavan border, like Brookeborough. There is evidence that Fermanagh's first Orange lodge was formed at Lisbellaw.[38] Local newspapers also suggest that the first Orange hall in the county was built there and that its first Unionist club met there in May 1911.[39] At a meeting in December 1920, to launch the special constabulary, one speaker acknowledged the seminal role that Lisbellaw had performed in initiating the new force, stating that it had given the 'lead . . . The whole thought of this organisation sprang from what they had done in that small village . . . They, in Fermanagh, were therefore the first to start the organisation'.[40]

Though Brooke is frequently regarded as a founder of the special constabulary, clearly he did not pioneer either the idea or the practice of such a force within the county or the province. Nonetheless he did encourage the spread of 'vigilance' units at a very early stage and was identified closely with this movement at a time when, in Fermanagh, respectable opinion still held aloof from, or opposed, it. Moreover, his claim to be 'one of the originators'[41] of the specials is justified in other ways. Thus, for example, he used all of his influence to get government recognition for the force through written and direct personal appeals to the Castle and later to Sir Ernest Clark. In June, he argued his case in the presence of General Macready, Sir John Anderson, and General Brind.

In early July, in response to a letter from the former containing the government's proposals for unarmed protection committees, he replied repeating his arguments and concluding, 'I am not signing my name . . . and not posting the letter locally but I am sure you know who the writer is'.[42] He also contacted Clark, in September, and provided him with a draft scheme for the new force. This may, in fact, have been his most significant single contribution to its formation.[43]

Many individuals could legitimately claim to have exercised a formative influence over the emergence of the special constabulary. Clark later wrote of them, with evident pride, as 'the success of one's own children . . . after all, I was primarily responsible for the early stages'.[44] Their organisation was a major part of his official responsibilities, together with any other 'matters arising out of the political situation'.[45] In drawing up the scheme, however, he sought instruction and advice not only from his superiors in Dublin Castle but from a considerable number of people of various religious and political opinions in the north.[46] Amongst the political, military and police leaders consulted were General Hackett-Pain, Colonel Wickham, Craig, Spender, and Brooke. S. G. Tallents later wrote of the specials as being Craig's 'invention'.[47] Clark himself stated that the Unionist Association got the force 'practically on their own conditions'.[48] In late August 1920, Spender gave a detailed list of suggestions to Craig. His wife later noted that her husband was 'fairly satisfied, 6½ of the 8 proposals he put forward . . . have been accepted', adding characteristically, 'the scheme is almost entirely his'.[49] Spender himself makes less sweeping claims. Some years after, he recalled that he and Brooke had put forward their suggestions after consultation with some military figures in England. This recollection is substantiated by Clark's correspondence at the time.[50]

Brooke's recommendations appear to have followed on closely from his immediate experience and practice in Fermanagh. In June 1920, he initially organised a nucleus of fourteen men at Colebrooke, two acting as sentries one night per week. In the following months he encouraged the spread of this organisation through neighbouring townlands with members regularly drilling and manning patrols, seeking to eliminate gaps in 'the screen of defence'.[51] Meanwhile its structure became more complex and sophisticated. The scheme which he submitted to Clark was, the assistant under-secretary stated, 'in regard to a force which already exists in Fermanagh under the name of Fermanagh Vigilance, and is to all intents and purposes a special constabulary'.[52] It bears a striking similarity to the scheme ultimately adopted for the 'B' Specials.

In his submission, Sir Basil suggested that the county be put under one leader elected by district leaders who were in turn to be elected by townland leaders. The county leader was to collect information and distribute it, and coordinate the work of the district leaders who would act as his committee. District leaders were to command districts of a size that they could conveniently supervise, and decide with townland leaders how much patrolling and what level of defence was necessary. Under each townland leader, there were to be fourteen men which would enable two men to do duty each night of the week. In his letter to Clark, he listed his reasons for this structure:

The county leader was not in a position to take an active part in the defence as he could not know the requirements of the various districts

The district leader on the other hand by his local knowledge could decide on what action was to be taken. In some cases this only amounted to the collection of information but in others a complete defence scheme was worked out

There was little correspondence as little had to be referred to the county leaders – any there was being passed by hand

The townland leaders having a thorough knowledge of their neighbours were in a good position to select the right man for their patrols and could further keep a watch on those whose actions were suspicious

Owing to the necessity of secrecy during the preliminary stages, meetings could not be held, but the townland leaders on their own could get in touch with men whom they knew were in favour of the movement but also as yet were unorganised and so increase the organisation without attracting undue attention

Members of the patrol would not be on duty far from their homes, a point which I found much appreciated.[53]

In conversation with Clark, Brooke also suggested that men who gave one night's service per week should be paid, and that arms might in certain circumstances be distributed.

The assistant under-secretary was impressed by Brooke, and by Fermanagh Vigilance, praising in particular its 'excellent intelligence and outpost system'. Brooke's submission was perfectly timed as the special constabulary scheme was just being formulated. Clark sent a copy of it to Sir John Anderson and, in an accompanying note, described it as

the most valuable information I have received, . . . [Brooke] realised before he formed his force that it must be a supervisional force and could not act as a volunteer force, although its nucleus of organisation and membership may have derived from the old U.V.F.[54]

It, at least, served to confirm Clark's own views as to how the special constabulary should function. In a personal file, he described it as 'identical' to his own scheme.[55] He pointed this out to Anderson also, writing 'it will be noticed that the general organisation is in the main essentials of organisation and subordination of officers much on the lines of the scheme I have put forward'. He proceeded to use Brooke's opinion in support of his arguments:

I put to Sir Basil the main points of the organisation of the proposed special constabulary, and he said that so far as a man could be sure of anything, he was quite sure that the force proposed . . . could be formed and would be effective . . . [and] . . . there would be no difficulty in getting the proper link with the regular police force.[56]

Brooke gave no indication in his written submission as to how this might be achieved. In mid-1922, some of the deputations to Tallents regarded the inadequate coordination with and supervision of the specials by the R.I.C. to be the most critical defect in the operation of the whole scheme.[57]

At Dublin Castle, Anderson and Macready, in particular, were extremely reluctant to recognise and arm civilian vigilance forces like Brooke's. In early July, the general sent Sir Basil the details of a system of protection committees, which the administration there had adopted after 'careful consideration . . . [of] . . . suggestions from various quarters' and for which 'excellent results' were claimed in Londonderry.[58] He hoped that these bodies might act 'as a grain of mustard seed in a holy war'.[59] The committees were to be as 'fully representative as possible and . . . bear no political label'. Their function was one of 'advising and cooperating with the local police and military authorities in the execution of measures for the prevention of crime'. Members were to 'meet at frequent intervals . . . be freely consulted by the responsible police authorities' . . . and, it was suggested, 'in their individual capacity they may often be able to do much by personal influence to avert the beginnings of disorder'. In conjunction with these committees, responsible citizens, similarly representative, could be organised to undertake 'under the control of the police and in a purely civilian capacity patrol work and keeping the authorities in touch'. The note concluded: 'distinctive armlets and police whistles could be supplied if desired. The issue of arms is not contemplated'.[60] Copies of these instructions were also sent to county inspectors as well as to Clark and Brooke.

Sir Basil later described the scheme as 'idiotic', and 'derided in Ulster'.[61] Certainly, it had no success whatever in Fermanagh and, at best, a transient significance elsewhere even in Londonderry where the committees had emerged spontaneously in late May. The Fermanagh county police report for July 1920 commented:

It has been quite impossible to get nationalists and unionists to join in forming unarmed protection committees. Nationalists will not take any action to assist the government and unionists will not form any such committees unless they are officially recognised as part of the forces of the crown and are promised the arms necessary to defend themselves.[62]

Anderson and Macready, however, continued to oppose 'the raising of Carson's army from the grave'. The former warned Bonar Law, in early September, 'you cannot in the midst of a faction fight recognise one of the contending parties'; this view was not shared by Lord French, the lord lieutenant.[63]

The impact of such a course of action on the north was, in the last analysis, however, just one consideration and not the most important one, for Lloyd George. The case for letting Ulster unionists protect themselves became increasingly attractive, in the autumn of 1920 with the steadily deteriorating military situation in the rest of Ireland, the R.I.C. evidently exhausted, and worsening labour problems in England. In late July, the prime minister decided that the proposal 'should be examined'.[64] Meanwhile these same factors made unionist demands for such a force all the more strident. Craig's doom-laden predictions of civil war as loyalists lost faith in the government's determination or ability to protect them, were fully supported by Clark, the self-styled 'John the Baptist', preparing the way, from mid-September, for the Northern Ireland government.[65] Later that month, he was urging that 'the psychological moment' had arrived, 'men have been approached', further delay would create a deep and dangerous 'sense of anti-climax', and damage the potential effectiveness of the new constabulary.[66] He was nonetheless acutely conscious of the risks involved. He later described to the Castle 'the state of distrust and fear' in the province, and expressed the 'frank opinion' that 'however the fact is obscured sectarian differences are at the root of all political and administrative differences here'.[67]

The decision to set up the force was taken, in principle, on 8 September 1920. During the weeks that followed the details of the scheme were discussed and decided on, and eventually made public in late October. For the prime minister the main consideration was that it would enable troops and police to be deployed elsewhere in Ireland.[68] Bonar Law was struck by Craig's warning of 'something like a genuine massacre' in the event of 'the Orangemen getting completely out of hand'. He wrote, on September 2, to Lloyd George: 'we cannot afford to have everyone in Ireland against us, and I think now the time has come when we ought to make special arrangements to let the loyalists in Ulster be in a position to preserve order there'.[69]

The scheme was first introduced into the Tyrone and Belfast areas where it was felt to be most urgently required and then gradually elsewhere. This staggered intake eased the problems of training those who enrolled. On 11 November 1920, public notices appeared appealing for applicants in Down, Armagh and Fermanagh, thus, Clark stated, 'completing the southern border of the divisional area'.[70] The establishment for the latter was 230 'A' and 2,500 'B' specials. The level of violence had actually remained comparatively low within the county during preceding months; a fact which W. C. Trimble attributed to the volunteers. Thus, of thirty-three police barracks destroyed in the six counties up to 10 November just three were in Fermanagh. Nonetheless, there had been attacks on other government property and the level of outrages had increased markedly from mid-1920.[71] Brooke did not expect much Sinn Fein activity inside the county but anticipated incursions from neighbouring counties.[72]

From the mid-summer, however, the county inspector had viewed the future with deepening gloom. After failure of Macready's protection committees he predicted that unionists in response to 'any aggressive move . . . made by the Sinn Feiners, . . . will obtain arms secretly and they will take independent action, . . . nationalists will then take sides with Sinn Fein'. In October, he mentioned that there had been threats of reprisals and counter-reprisals after an attack on Tempo R.I.C. barracks.[73] Similar reports had appeared in the local press during the previous month, a loyalist volunteer threatening in the event of further Sinn Fein activity, that it would not be 'an eye for an eye and a tooth for a tooth, but two eyes and two teeth'. It was hoped that the government decision to create a new force would relieve some of these tensions and dangers. Certainly, most unionists welcomed the scheme. It would, E. M. Archdale felt, help contain Sinn Fein who would otherwise attempt 'to stir up trouble to get Fermanagh into Southern Ireland'.[74] The *Fermanagh Herald* in contrast ominously predicted that the new constabulary would be 'nothing more or less than the dregs of the Orange lodges, equipped to overawe . . . catholics, . . . they are the very classes that an upright government would try to keep powerless'.[75]

Somewhat surprisingly, Brooke was not initially selected as county commandant for Fermanagh. On November 15, Spender received a coded telegram from the 'leaders of the county', indicating that they wished Viscount Cole to be offered the appointment. Spender, when informing Clark, stated 'I do not know very much about [Cole] . . . but I am very sorry that Sir Basil . . . has not been selected'. He concluded by emphasising that the latter 'was most anxious not to compete with Viscount Cole if he seemed agreeable to take up the duties', and that Brooke would 'no doubt . . . give all the help' that he could. It was left to Colonel Wickham, the divisional police commissioner, to decide whether or not to act on the county's suggestion. Meanwhile, the assistant under-secretary thought that Brooke might accept the adjutancy.[76]

The nomination of Cole may well indicate nothing more than the continuing strength of local deference towards the county's leading family. However, it may be that Brooke's aggressive role in the preceding months and his close association with an illegal civilian volunteer force made him somewhat suspect in the eyes of respectable county opinion. The *Fermanagh Times* had shown noticeably less enthusiasm for such activities than the *Impartial Reporter*. Also in early November, Clark wrote to Collum, Fermanagh's lord lieutenant, apparently in reply to criticisms by the latter of Brooke's activities. He stated 'I understand that [Brooke] . . . was taking part in an organisation which is at the moment doing somewhat of the work that is before the special constabulary', but the letter continued reassuringly, 'he is not acting to bring into force the proclamation except to get the necessary information laid'.[77]

It seems extremely unlikely that Cole would ever have been prepared to take on the onerous duties of county commandant. The office was the linchpin of the county organisation, from the outset a paid and virtually full-time position with extensive organisational and disciplinary functions. It was, Clark stated, 'a necessity . . . to the scheme for each county' and 'in every case . . . [Wickham sought] . . . a man of fair rank in the army'.[78] After consultations with both Cole and Brooke, the latter was finally selected and the appointment was subsequently approved by Dublin Castle. The former does not appear to have been active at any stage in raising the new force. Six months later, when Craig asked him to allow his name to go forward for the Senate, and suggested that sacrifices were necessary, and that this was the unanimous desire of the cabinet, his request was rejected. The viscount stated in reply 'the circumstances under which I live make my acceptance impossible'.[79]

Sir Basil's appointment took effect from 18 November 1920. In the weeks and months that followed the campaign was launched to raise the county's establishment. Clark assiduously ensured that Brooke, like the other commandants, complied with the cumbersome but necessary legal preliminaries, under the 1832 special constables act. The former was concerned that 'each process [should be] . . . watertight against future criticism'.[80] Thus a 'credible witness' had to state on oath before two magistrates his opinion that the ordinary police force was 'not sufficient for the preservation of the public peace', so empowering the latter to authorise the enrolment of special constables.[81]

The prospects for enrolment in Fermanagh were uncertain. Clark, who regarded the scheme as a test of the capacity for good government, thought the response in Belfast to the call for 'B' specials most unsatisfactory, and anticipated a similar reaction in contiguous counties. He felt, nonetheless, under no obligation to act as a recruiting agent. Likewise it was soon clear that nationalists, with few exceptions, were not joining the force.[82] On the other hand, Sir Ernest was confident that recruitment targets would be reached in Tyrone and that 'if the machinery works in the first county, [he had] . . . no doubt as to its doing so in others . . . in outlying counties we will cover our estimate'. From his contacts with Fermanagh he was far from being impressed by the quality of the county inspector, whom he described as not having 'a particularly good head-piece'. However, he felt that the county was more advanced than Down or Armagh, with plenty of good material for the force.

He informed Anderson that there were 'already 1,500 men with their names down waiting for the official machinery to work'. Collum had told the assistant under-secretary that 'both sides [were] . . . likely to join . . . to stop the spread of lawlessness'.[83]

Sir Basil himself, whilst throwing himself energetically into the campaign, predicted accurately that recruitment would 'go on all right . . . but be a little slow'.[84] Stephen Tallents' terse assessment of the former's motivation and attitudes, though written almost two years later still seems broadly accurate in relation to 1920. 'Brooke', he wrote, 'has taken his position as commandant of the constabulary from a sense of duty, regards the whole business as a military job. No special party colour'.[85] He undoubtedly, had accepted the appointment from a strong sense of duty, combined with deep conviction, and showed throughout a greater willingness to serve than ambition. His public statements at the time, however, indicate a certain ambiguity in his approach. In December 1920, he stated, in phrases similar to those in his letter to Macready, that 'the movement is not political or religious, but only aimed at terrorism . . . it is for the sake of safeguarding the public'.[86] Nonetheless, his appeal for support was clearly political. He wrote: 'you have now the great test of your loyalty, before you, . . . I am convinced that the loyalty and devotion to empire and country . . . will only shine the brighter when you are called upon to fight the agents of murder, anarchy and terrorism, . . . by answering the call of the empire, you are helping your country and defending yourself'. Likewise, though he admonished those who enlisted to be 'tolerant in your actions, for there are many of other persuasions who, while disapproving of these deeds of violence, are yet unable to take an active part in suppressing them',[87] at the first major recruitment meeting, he spoke with less restraint. He stated that 'if anyone can join and does not join, that man will not be considered a well-disposed citizen'.[88]

Despite much exhortation, recruitment remained gradual, but steady. Initially, there were fears that the 'A' Special establishment had overestimated the capacity of the county.[89] Also, unlike Tyrone, where 'B' Specials had enrolled quickly and unevenly with groups or batches enlisting at one time, in Fermanagh the pace was consistent but slow.[90] A number of local Unionist leaders chided the apathy of the shopkeepers and employers in Enniskillen, and of the farmers amongst whom the response appears to have been particularly poor. Sir Charles Falls stated that it was not fair that it should be left to the 'clerks and servant boys to come out and defend those who had a stake in the country'.[91] Clark suggested to Brooke 'just one thought' that might help 'B' enlistment: 'a man who is not a special constable will obviously have no right to be in possession of firearms'. This point was made forcefully by the latter in subsequent speeches.[92] Despite the apathy of some and the genuine doubts of others as to the need for the new force, by mid-March 1921, Fermanagh was the only area in the six counties apart from Tyrone to reach its establishment quota for both 'A' and 'B' classes. This was due in no small degree to the energy and efficiency of Brooke. In April, Clark wrote to him to express his 'very many congratulations . . . on the achievements of your specials, . . . it must have been wonderfully well organised and was most highly successful'.[93]

Clark's note was not, however, written solely to offer congratulations but also to advise Brooke to impress on . . . [the special constabulary] . . . that they are acting in the best interests of Ulster and the empire if they hold themselves properly in hand and always remember that they are there to keep order and finally to make this province a fit place for peaceful citizens to live in.[94]

These observations were justified by the fact that levels of tension and violence within the county had risen markedly during the first half of 1921, with the obvious risk of escalating reprisals and counter-reprisals and of indiscipline within the new force. This deterioration in community relations was due in part to the imminence of partition, though the county inspector felt that all business people were apprehensive at the prospect, fearing the disruption of commercial activity. He also noted, surprisingly, that there was very little interest being shown locally in the elections for Northern Ireland's first parliament during the weeks before polling day. He regarded the boycott of Belfast goods, initiated by Sinn Fein during the summer of 1920, as the chief cause of growing political and religious feeling. This appears to have been the case particularly in the Lisnaskea area, remaining parts of the county, including Enniskillen, being described, in March 1921, as normal.[95] These impressions were confirmed by a unionist deputation to Colonel Wickham from this district, also in March, which projected the boycott as the culmination of a campaign against them which had included raids on their houses, threatening letters and damage to property.[96]

The locality had a tradition of sectional conflict, was the strongest centre of Sinn Fein support in the county, and was near the borders of Monaghan, Cavan and Tyrone where this movement's orders were thought to originate. Indeed, Clark regarded Monaghan as the key 'to a good deal of the trouble' not only in East Fermanagh but also along its borders with other northern counties.[97] The county inspector in Monaghan was also concerned about, but powerless to prevent, the activities of I.R.A. flying columns based in the mountainous areas adjacent to Fermanagh. These clearly operated with considerable success, so that by June 1921, the average number of outrages per month in the latter had reached double the county's already high January figure. Much of this campaign was directed against the specials. The deputation to Wickham stated that 'in our opinion class "B" men . . . in that part of Fermanagh are exposed to the very gravest of risks by reason of their isolation and their total inability to defend themselves against a concentrated attack'. They feared that unless the authorities took immediate action, there would be reprisals and a general increase in the level of lawlessness, as the attacks aroused the 'greatest resentment and anger'.

The deputation had not overstated the gravity of the situation. In February, the county inspector reported that the *Impartial Reporter* had begun to advocate reprisals during that month and added ominously that lists had been prepared of every Sinn Fein leader in every district. Next month, he stated that a number of Sinn Fein houses in Rosslea had been burnt down by 'the U.V.F.', in reprisal for the shooting of a special. This led, in consequence, to the murder of two 'B' special sergeants and the destruction of the houses and property of almost 20 loyalists nearly all connected with the special constabulary along the Monaghan border, hence the timing of Clark's admonition to Brooke in April.

During the course of the same month both police numbers and activity were increased, particularly in the Rosslea area with the stated objective of protecting unionists from possible raids from the County Monaghan side.[98] A guard of six R.I.C. men was placed at Colebrooke, though to Lady Brooke their acquisition was of dubious value. 'No one has much opinion of them', she commented.[99] Meanwhile the county's 'B' Special establishment was increased to 3,000, a measure Clark had enthusiastically supported.[100] The *Impartial Reporter* had earlier expressed the hope that the attempt 'to cow men from joining . . . [would] . . . rouse loyalists to a sense of their duty'.[101] The number actually sworn-in increased substantially, rising by 600 to 2,620 between 9 April – 9 July, 1921, and government arms and ammunition were served out to a large number of them. Brooke's greatest admiration was reserved for those who enlisted from the remote areas along the future Free State border, almost one-third of the total as he enthusiastically informed the Boundary Commission several years later.[102]

However, despite this increased security provision, throughout the spring the number of outrages continued to increase, and as before the Lisnaskea district was the area worst affected. In June, the county inspector reported that 'Sinn Fein intimidation . . . [had] . . . increased especially against the 'B' specials', and inevitably the problem of holding these 'properly in hand' became acute.[103] The most serious incident occurred on May 29, when a patrol was ambushed and two of its members killed, at Mullaghfad, on the fringes of Brooke's own estate. The action was carried out by an I.R.A. flying column based on the Monaghan border. Brooke immediately called a meeting of leading local figures to 'discuss the very high feeling running through the county'. He informed Craig, candidly, that if there was a

further repetition of these outrages . . . nothing can stop reprisals on a large scale . . . I have managed to hold the men so far but I do not believe that anything will stop them if their blood is really up.

The county inspector was equally sanguine about the future: 'the unionist population become daily more incensed against Sinn Fein' he wrote, 'I fear something untoward will occur should they continue'.[104]

Police reports suggest that these gloomy predictions were not fulfilled. In late May, some cottages belonging to alleged Sinn Feiners were burnt in retribution, and there followed a succession of petty reprisals and counter-reprisals which, in June, boosted the number of outrages to their highest monthly total since the war. The 11 July Anglo-Irish truce was the crucial factor in reversing these alarming trends, as at least temporarily the consistently escalating pattern of violence was arrested and community tension relieved. Initially, it was reported to have been welcomed throughout the county and its terms respected. For the rest of the month no outrages of a political nature occurred, and no political activity was observed by the police.[105]

Almost imperceptibly and certainly unconsciously, during the twelve dramatic months after his return from Dublin in May 1920, Brooke had risen to a position of prominence within the county. In June 1921, the *Fermanagh Times* referred to his 'universal popularity',[106] and undoubtedly he had already become a trusted and admired local unionist leader. His willingness to accept the key appointment of county commandant and his energy and efficiency in first mobilising and later restraining the special constabulary had also favourably impressed key government figures such as Wickham, the divisional commissioner, and Spender, fellow Wykehamist and 'B' Special and now a somewhat reluctant cabinet secretary. By mid-1921, Brooke could legitimately boast that Fermanagh had a higher proportion of 'its unionist population enrolled in the 'B' Special constabulary than any other county in Northern Ireland'.[107] Sir Ernest Clark expressed appreciation not only of his administrative ability, but his character, describing him to Sir John Anderson as 'an eminently level-headed, active and moderate man, who . . . [had] . . . seen service in the war'.[108]

Craig acknowledged Brooke's services by awarding him a C.B.E. on the occasion of the king's visit for the opening of the Northern Ireland parliament. The investiture at the Ulster Hall was a somewhat unconventional occasion. After George V's historic speech which was cheered for two minutes and delivered, according to Lady Spender, without a trace of German accent, the cheering continued at varying levels according to the popularity of the recipients of decorations. At the sight of Frederick Crawford, his coat concealing his revolver, Lady Carson cried out 'so that the king might hear, 'Here is the gun-runner!' Brooke was himself well received, wearing his uniform as county commandant of Fermanagh special constabulary.[109]

Meanwhile, Sir Basil's services had received a further and more problematical acknowledgement. In early April, Craig visited Fermanagh amidst 'lorries of police, armed to the teeth'.[110] It was probably his first visit to the county since his by-election defeat almost twenty years before. At the time he was organising and nominating his ministerial and parliamentary team, and in the course of his visit almost certainly asked Archdale to act as minister of agriculture. During lunch at 'Riversdale' he asked Brooke to allow his name to go forward for the Senate and so take his first step into politics.[111]

Sir Basil's was one of twenty-four names which had been drawn up after consultation with the recently nominated Unionist candidates for the Northern Ireland parliamentary elections. Craig expected his party to secure fifteen Senate seats. The additional nine names were included, Sir James explained, as 'a precautionary measure, . . . [in case] . . . the Sinn Feiners and nationalists refuse to function and in consequence forfeit their right to elect their quota'.[112] Representation was to be on a broadly territorial basis and to include, in effect, the province's social élite. The completed list was sub-divided into fifteen first and nine second choice candidates. Fermanagh's representatives on the former were John Porter-Porter and Lord Cole, with Brooke's the only name from the county on the latter. In late May, when it became clear that these additional seats would fall to the Unionist party, his name was amongst those confirmed at a second conference of the now newly-elected M.P.s. He gladly accepted, advising the prime minister, who himself personally seconded his nomination: 'use my name in any way you think best, . . . if there is any other way in which I can assist you and the country I hope you will tell me'.[113]

Sir Basil's election, however, precipitated a sequel which appears to have been entirely unforeseen. On June 15, the lords commissioners informed Brooke that he must resign his position as county commandant, an office of profit under the crown, before taking the oath as senator. Otherwise they stated that he would infringe section 18 (2) of the government of Ireland act. He immediately informed Craig and Clark, stressing that he would be 'very unwilling to let down the county'.[114] He then sought Wickham's approval for his continuing in an honorary capacity, but made it clear that this was only until the matter could 'be arranged'. He felt unable to continue indefinitely the work which was taking up all of his time unless he could have 'some assurance' from the government that his case would 'be adjusted'.[115]

The divisional commissioner shared Clark's view that Sir Basil's resignation would be 'a serious loss to the special constabulary', but could only suggest that if all else failed, he should resign from the Senate. There proved to be no ready solution to Brooke's difficulty, as amending legislation would have been required. This, the assistant under-secretary commented 'would not be easy without involving very wide issues . . .[adding] . . . The question as to the course of action meantime must be left to his own decision'.[116] In fact, Brooke decided to remain as county commandant in an unpaid, honorary capacity. Resignation amid the tensions of late June cannot have been given much serious consideration. However after the July truce, community bitterness relaxed and the burdens of office lightened. No further enrolments of specials took place whilst it was in operation, and all 'B' specials sworn for duty were suspended and remained so until February 1922.[117]

In mid-July the general mood in the county was reported to be one of desire and hope for a final settlement. However, the truce was the prelude to a period of prolonged political uncertainty and sectarian tension which cast a dark and permanent shadow over the subsequent history of Fermanagh. This was caused initially by a growing awareness that its terms were being breached. Though for the first few weeks it was apparently well observed, police reports for August and September contain a lengthening catalogue of I.R.A. activity, including recruitment meetings, drilling, attendance at training camps, the operation of illegal courts, attempts at enforcing the Belfast boycott, kidnapping, intimidation and attacks on R.I.C. barracks.[118]

The county inspector described these activities, in September, as 'a source of grave anxiety to loyalist inhabitants'. In the local unionist press, after the expectations raised in the recent elections, the truce was soon condemned as a farce and the attitude expressed was one of shock, disillusion and betrayal. It was alleged that police and troops had stood inertly by whilst Fermanagh became 'a veritable hotbed of sedition, conspiracy and intimidation'.[119] It was claimed that through their inaction they had permitted Sinn Fein to prepare 'for a final swoop on Ulster'[120] and to train men 'how to shoot protestants . . . especially when they . . . [could get] . . . them in twos and threes, unarmed, after the truce'.[121] The enforced inactivity of the 'B' specials was lamented and resented and once more there were calls for people 'to take active steps for their own safety'.[122] In October, presumably as a protest at, or due to the frustration caused by, their prolonged inactivity resignation levels from the force were high, and its membership fell by over 10 per cent.[123]

At the same time the course of the Anglo-Irish negotiations was watched by unionists with acute uneasiness. As early as August the county inspector reported that the political future was being looked upon with anxiety.[124] Apprehension that they would be 'sacrificed' increased as gradually the British and Irish press focused more attention on the case of Fermanagh and Tyrone. In mid-October, Lloyd George himself felt this issue was 'going to wreck a settlement', but eventually saw 'one possible way out', a boundary commission.[125] This proved to be an extremely effective ploy in the context of the negotiations. However, it left the issue, in Churchill's words, 'unclear . . . it was inevitable that it should be left in a certain vagueness'.[126] As a result it also inevitably exacerbated the political divisions in Northern Ireland.

Meanwhile, unionist anxiety was further heightened by the attitudes and activities of Fermanagh nationalists. The latter became excessively optimistic, refusing to consider the possibility of partition as a permanent reality. They sent delegations to de Valera to stiffen his resolve with regard to the London talks. The county council, of which they had control, resolved that 'the authority [of the Northern Ireland parliament] . . . could only be exercised by force and coercion' and subsequently pledged support to Dail Eireann. Even the majority who welcomed the treaty as a respite from violence were utterly convinced that clause 12, which made provision for the creation of a boundary commission, would ultimately ensure the essential unity of Ireland.[127] Given this context, when power was finally transferred to the Northern government after being delayed by the negotiations, it was welcomed by unionists who wished to see order at last being firmly restored, recalcitrant local governments being superseded, and effective repression of the boycotting campaign. As for the boundary, there was an increased determination 'not to yield up any portion of the county . . . to any rebel government established in Ireland'.[128]

Thus the truce and treaty prolonged political uncertainty in the county and in the province, increased levels of intransigence and aggravated existing sectarian tensions. The Boundary Commission, which had made the Anglo-Irish agreement possible, was described by Craig as 'the predominant threat confronting the loyalists of Ulster'.[129] It induced in border areas something approaching panic amongst protestants. It gave the nationalist population, the militant section of which was now better organized for violence, every reason to expect that the state would not survive. It justified the connivance of southern politicians, who had believed that the commission would be a gateway to unity not a modification of partition, with those who wished to achieve Irish unity through force. This was particularly the case after the conflicting interpretations regarding its function became clear during the Collins-Craig talks in early 1922. Overall, the freedom of manoeuvre for the new and inexperienced northern government was gravely compromised. It was indicative of Unionist distrust of the imperial authorities that soon after power had been transferred, Craig's policy priority was to become independent of British military support.[130]

In December 1921, Lady Brooke recorded in her diary that the boundary question was a 'cause of great dissatisfaction', but added with rather naive optimism that 'trouble [was] . . . now expected gradually to subside, as there . . . [was] . . . no reason for further aggression on the part of Sinn Fein', and that her husband was 'trying to give up command of the specials'.[131] In fact, during the months that followed, Fermanagh drifted from comparative peace to the brink of civil war. In late 1921, political feeling was already running high. The position deteriorated further due to uncertainty about the political future, the inadequacy of police provision, the impact of disorder in neighbouring counties, especially Donegal, and what Tallents described as 'the organised conspiracy of murder and violence against the northern government'[132] directed towards creating an independent Irish republic. This campaign sought to illustrate that large areas of the northern territory were disaffected and that the northern government was incapable of maintaining law and order. There were also hopes of precipitating a confrontation with British troops and thus drawing republican forces and provisional government troops together against the common enemy, so averting civil war. Fermanagh was inevitably in the front-line of the conflict.[133] In the course of succeeding events, Brooke was drawn back into full-time police service and subsequently his commitment to and identification with the special constabulary became complete.

In early February 1922, Sir Basil was holidaying with his wife in London, when news arrived that over forty Unionists had been kidnapped along the Fermanagh–Tyrone border. Over half of those taken were special constables, mainly from Newtownbutler. Approximately fifteen men in cars carrying high explosives were later arrested by police. All were from Leitrim and Longford, though their raid had been assisted by local people acting as guides.[134] Immediately, Brooke called to see Craig, who was in London for the Lords' debate on the boundary question and was asked to resume his position as full-time paid county commandant. He then hurried back to Fermanagh to urge restraint on angry loyalists in border areas.[135] He also resigned from his seat in the Senate. His senatorial career had not been a distinguished one: he had spoken just once and then it was to complain about the inadequate briefing of members on what business was due for debate. Nonetheless, there may have been a tacit understanding reached during his meeting with the prime minister to the effect that once the county had stabilised he would once again pick up the threads of his political career.[136]

The kidnappings were almost certainly not, as Craig claimed, part of a deliberate and organised attack on Ulster. A more probably motive was the seizure of hostages in a bid to force the Belfast government to reprieve three I.R.A. members who were being held at Londonderry under sentence of death. This was Arthur Griffith's view.[137] Certainly a number of pro-Collins I.R.A. leaders from Monaghan who had been arrested in Tyrone some weeks before had been carrying papers which suggested that their objective was the release of these prisoners. Alfred Cope, assistant under-secretary for Ireland and clerk of the Irish privy council, stated that subsequently Collins had been having difficulty 'holding in . . . sections of the I.R.A. who were out for hostages'.[138]

In the aftermath of this event tension in Fermanagh rose to dangerously high levels. Newspapers reported that Cahir Healy had been informed that he would be held personally responsible for the return of Ivan Carson, an ex-high sheriff abducted from Enniskillen.[139] Immediately after arriving home, Brooke was met by a deputation of 'B' Special constables, who threatened 'bloody murder' if their colleagues were not quickly released. He warned that such a course might well result in the death of those held, and no retaliatory action appears to have been taken.[140] The local unionist press made strident calls for a restoration of the pre-truce security arrangements. Craig himself attributed the incident to Britain's lack of courage and the demobilisation of the special constabulary.[141] By late March both the unionist hostages and the Monaghan I.R.A. men had been released.

But, meanwhile, the measures taken to strengthen the forces of law and order precipitated an incident which ironically further exacerbated sectional feeling. The 'B' specials were mobilised for the first time since the truce, and additional troops were moved into the county, implementing a decision made before the kidnappings.[142] More portentously, 'A' force reinforcements were despatched by train from Newtownards depot to Enniskillen in order to bring their numbers in the county up to fixed strength. This involved changing trains across the border at Clones. When travelling on the same route with her husband twelve months before, Lady Craig had described it as 'a very Sinn Fein spot . . . if ferocious looks could kill, we would have dropped dead on the platform'.[143] On 11 February 1922, minutes after their arrival at this station, the 'A' specials became involved in a gun battle with the I.R.A. and as a result four of their number died, nine were wounded, and five others were captured. The I.R.A. commandant was also killed. The precise circumstances of the conflict are unclear. The southern authorities appear to have received no preliminary warning that the 'A' force would be passing through. The violence began when its members were asked to surrender.[144]

The effect was immediate. When the bullet-ridden, blood-stained train reached Lisbellaw, its appearance so incensed loyalists that those regarded as Sinn Feiners were driven out of the village. Before the boundary commissioners Brooke condemned the incident as a 'murderous attack . . . no offence whatever had been committed by the special constabulary'.[145] The *Impartial Reporter* wrote of the 'hatred and venom' showered on the specials because they bore the Ulster uniform, and suggested that reprisals were the 'only effective check'. The *Fermanagh Times* stated that this, with other outrages, had brought 'civil war . . . within measureable distance'.[146]

On 12 February, Brooke travelled to Belfast to consult the prime minister and Spender, deeply concerned at the grave situation along the border and anxious about his ability to prevent retaliatory outrages. One week later, amidst tight security, Craig came to Fermanagh, in his wife's words, 'to back up the specials'.[147] With Wickham he reviewed the 'A' and 'B' forces, stopped at Newtownbutler, the most sensitive area, and spoke to men who had been wounded as well as those kidnapped on 7 February and since released. Throughout he appealed for 'strict discipline and restraint'.[148] Partly in response to strong pressure from a parliamentary ginger-group, which included Cooper and Coote, border security was strengthened. The county's 'B' Special establishment was increased, and in the weeks following, the numbers actually on patrol reached their peak. The *Fermanagh Times* claimed that enrolment was spontaneous because the absolute necessity for the force had been demonstrated.[149] Undoubtedly the psychological commitment of the unionist community to the force was now almost total, though the press continued to deride the inadequate enlistment of professional and business people, particularly in Enniskillen. Meanwhile by early March all but seven roads leading across the border had been trenched, those left open were heavily guarded and a motor curfew had been imposed. Border liaison committees were also formed, probably on Collins' suggestion.[150] However, given the tension, distrust and deep sense of outstanding grievances, these had little chance of success and proved ineffectual. The special constables taken at Clones were still being held and as Cope remarked despondently: 'even if the orders . . . [had been] . . . given [for their release] . . . it . . . [was] . . . unlikely they would be obeyed'. He added, 'No expedient for restoring peace . . . has much chance of succeeding'.[151]

Rumours of I.R.A. men massing on the border and fears of further violence and kidnappings were widespread. Thus soon after returning from London, Brooke had himself taken the precaution of sending his son, Julian, to stay with relatives in England.[152] For a time, he appears to have been successful in preventing serious reprisals. However when in late March, two special constables were murdered in Ballinamallard on the Tyrone border, three men were shot almost simultaneously in obvious retaliation. The *Impartial Reporter* described the incident under the heading 'An eye for an eye', and reported the widespread 'pilgrimage to the hills' as men fled from their homes fearing further murder. It was claimed that in the area around the villages of Trillick and Dromore families cowered by their firesides through the night, and if footsteps were heard hurried into the fields. The *Fermanagh Times* urged restraint, warning its readership, in an editorial, on the dangers of a 'murder competition'.[153]

These incidents, particularly the kidnappings and the violence at Clones, had much more than local significance. Throughout the province they helped fuel unionist resentment against Britain and sharpened hostility and suspicion towards the south. This was reflected in Craig's press statement on February 8 which emphatically declared 'What Ulster has she holds, . . . I absolutely decline to enter into further conferences on the subject'. It was a stance widely applauded in Fermanagh.[154] Sir James's policy priorities, which he defined later as preserving 'Ulster's safety' and 'keeping the people's confidence', led him to set in motion far-reaching security measures. Apart from further increases in the special constabulary, these included the introduction of a special powers bill and the appointment of a military adviser.[155] Nonetheless, he never lost sight of his final dependence on Britain. Thus, he advised his cabinet, on 14 February, that in no circumstances could Ulster survive in any campaign of atrocity with the South. Partly for this reason he was also anxious to prevent reprisals, willing to hold a 'Clones enquiry' and most controversially prepared to meet Collins in late March and agree the terms of a pact with him. With regard to the latter, James Cooper commented 'the people in my constituency are very suspicious of the tone of these terms'.[156] Sir Henry Wilson also recorded his shock at the extent of Collins' interference with internal arrangements in Ulster.[157]

British ministers were likewise deeply concerned about these recurring border incidents which threatened to undermine the treaty and lead to civil war. However, they still hoped that a little imperial aid, discreet pressure, and a measure of goodwill might yet be sufficient to establish both Irish governments. It is, perhaps, significant that it was on 9 February that the British chancellor agreed to pay £1,500,000 to cover the cost of the special constabulary until September 1922.[158] Overall, British support was effective and unobtrusive, but not something that Craig felt he could rely on.[159] Lloyd George bluntly told Sir James that there would be no peace in Ireland as long as he was there. The British government was throughout concerned that it might depart too far from 'the spirit of . . . [its] . . . bargain with the south', and so undermine Collins' resolve and ability to implement the treaty.[160] Also it was aware of the risk that its direct involvement might lead to a military confrontation with the I.R.A. and possibly unleash another Anglo-Irish war.

This latter consideration had important repercussions for Fermanagh and for

Brooke as its county commandant. It determined that the defence of the border should remain primarily a special constabulary rather than British military responsibility. Sir Basil had himself originally envisaged the former as primarily a force having police functions rather than acting as a first line of defence. Its imposed dual function was a grave responsibility and caused him deep concern. Amidst the bitterness generated by recent events the essential police virtues of non-aggression, courtesy, and absolute impartiality were, in themselves, difficult, perhaps impossible, to sustain. This additional close contact with the I.R.A. on the long and often wild mountainous terrain of the border, which in many areas was virtually indefensible, was always likely to lead to violent confrontation.

In the months following, some of these difficulties were graphically illustrated as trouble shifted with dramatic suddenness westwards from Monaghan to those portions of the county contiguous with Cavan, Leitrim and later Donegal. In mid-April, an 'A' special patrol was ambushed in a remote area near Garrison by seventy-five men who had crossed from Leitrim. Unionist opinion was outraged by the report that one constable had, in Brooke's words, been 'taken into hostile territory . . . the body then being mutilated beyond all recognition',[161] though this claim was disputed, at the time, by a local priest. Subsequently in this inflamed atmosphere, newspapers described with some alarm how, at Belcoo, a nearby village bisected by the border, armed sentries from the Free State and specials on the northern side were marching constantly up and down within yards of one another. In an attempt to reduce the dangers of a collision on 11 April Brooke crossed over to Blacklion for a conference with the commandant of the Free State troops.[162] As a result, it was amicably arranged that both sides withdraw their forces to a distance of 400 yards from the frontier.

However, the most serious border incident, both for Fermanagh and the state, and one which proved to be beyond the capacity of Brooke and the county's special constabulary, occurred the following month, when Irregulars occupied Belleek and Pettigo and the countryside between these two villages. The area lay inside Northern Ireland, but was cut off from the rest of the county by lower Lough Erne. All access roads passed through Free State territory. If these were closed, the only means of approach was by water. Progressively, R.I.C. and British military provision in this vulnerable salient had been reduced. From mid-1920 to early 1922, five barracks in the immediate neighbourhood were either captured or evacuated, and though Belleek's eighteenth-century fort was occupied by British troops in February 1922, they vacated it after just four weeks.[163] Thus from late April, the *Fermanagh Times* felt justified in running a series of emotive articles relating to the area alleging 'betrayal' and 'Free State rule in Fermanagh'. In late May, protestant families resident there applied for protection.[164]

The crisis erupted when a body of Irregulars invaded and occupied the segment, on 27 May, and arrested a number of local unionists. Their intrusion was unchallenged by Free State forces, any response apparently being impeded by internal divisions over the treaty.[165] The cause of the attack is unclear. It may have been related to the launching of a new police force in the province on 1 June. Possibly, it represented a despairing final attempt at provoking a confrontation with British troops in the hope of avoiding civil war in the south.

Macready attributed it in part to the arrival of a new Irregular commandant into the area three weeks earlier who, with his 'undisciplined hooligans, . . . [had] . . . terrorised the neighbourhood'. He also regarded it as an aggressive riposte to Craig's recent introduction of internment, and almost certainly a number of those involved had crossed the border in order to escape its imposition. Unionist claims of 'invasion' he dismissed as symptomatic of 'a strong attack of nerves'.[166]

At Colebrooke, Lady Brooke recorded in her diary that these events represented 'a really serious crisis for the border counties, . . . [with] . . . Sinn Fein pressure . . . [being] . . . felt all along the border, . . . the firing . . . almost continuous, . . . [and the] . . . atmosphere very tense and more alarming than hitherto'. Many years later, her husband could vividly remember summoning the specials by the ringing of church bells during service on the last Sunday in May; an action which recalled the summoning of the Enniskilleners to meet the forces of King James.[167] A composite force of sixty-four 'A' and 'B' men was quickly organised. It crossed into the salient by water, and occupied Magherameena Castle, but next day was forced to evacuate its exposed base, when police reinforcements failed to get through.[168] In consequence, Craig, having consulted the local police and military authorities, pressed Churchill for 'immediate action', otherwise, he claimed, more land would be seized and 'people . . . [would] . . . take things into their own hands'.[169] He confided to his cabinet that he was not hopeful of a positive British response. However, after the colonial secretary had discussed the situation with the provisional government, on 3–4 June the orders were sent out, and Pettigo was recaptured. The ninety or so Irregulars in occupation were totally unprepared for an assault by British troops using modern artillery. To the reverberations of sniper fire, General Wyatt, the officer commanding, entered the village accompanied by Sir Basil and his wife.[170]

Lloyd George received the report of these events in a mood of profound gloom. He feared that his government was being manoeuvered into war by border incidents caused mainly by de Valera and Sir Henry Wilson, and was convinced that 'conflict [with the south] must be avoided except on the issue of the constitution itself'. He was no doubt influenced by Collins' complaints after the Pettigo action at Britain's 'unwarrantable interference', and by his calls for an inquiry in order to prevent a 'very serious situation' from developing in Fermanagh.[171] However, this response was not shared by all of his colleagues. Though the prime minister might question both Churchill's loyalty and his sanity, the latter was determined, to the point of resignation and even at the expense of the treaty itself, to reject any inquiry whatsoever, and to expel the Irregulars from the rest of the salient. Sir Winston was convinced that this would 'show the Free State government that H.M.G. . . . [was] . . . ready to act'. He added later that 'we could not have met the H of C . . . with the admission that we did not know what was going on in a British village and did not dare to find out'. Accordingly, he pursued a policy described by Keith Middlemas as the 'epitome of . . . thorough'.[172] After some slight delay during which Collins was forewarned, on 8 June, British troops took Belleek. Brooke witnessed the twenty shells and 400 rounds which were fired and which proved sufficient to drive out the 500–600 Irregulars. The action was almost without casualties, so enabling a relieved Lloyd George to celebrate with champagne 'the great bloodless battle of Belleek, . . . a famous victory'.[173]

Whatever the motives for the Irregulars' offensive, it happened, as Collins realised, very conveniently for the Northern government. Though Churchill's response to the incursion was symptomatic of a growing sympathy for Craig, especially amongst Conservative M.P.s, there had also been genuine concern felt in Britain at the security measures being taken in the province. In late May, Sir James was summoned to attend the British cabinet to discuss the imposition of martial law on Belfast, and the holding of a full-scale judicial enquiry into the activities of his government.[174] Both intentions were overwhelmed by events. The only outcome was a brief investigation by Stephen Tallents, in June–July 1922, and he advised against any further enquiry which he considered would only revive 'propaganda about matters . . . best forgotten', and encourage non-recognition of the northern administration.[175]

As for Fermanagh, after the Belleek-Pettigo salient had been cleared, Lady Brooke recorded that 'the pressure was eased', and this view was shared by the local unionist press.[176] The deepening divisions in the south undoubtedly had a devastating impact on the campaign of violence against the north. Macready noted, that during the weeks that followed, Free State and Irregular forces were withdrawing all along the border. He also believed that the recent decisive military action had markedly reduced the likelihood of future incursions across the frontier. Subsequently, plans for creating a neutral zone, occupied by British troops, were devised for the southern portion of the county, with Brooke's enthusiastic support.[177]

A further factor in reducing the level of Sinn Fein violence was the effectiveness of the security measures taken by the Northern Ireland government. Thus by mid-1922, there was an establishment of 3,500 'A' and 'B' Specials in Fermanagh, a curfew was still in operation and most border roads remained blocked. Cabinet consideration was given to the complete closure of the border but this was found to lie beyond its devolved powers.[178] More controversially, Brooke, as county commandant, was actively involved in the arrest of a number of leading local republicans. In mid-April, the government had lists prepared of those suspected of 'evil design' throughout the province and, on 20 May, in response to the Collins–de Valera electoral pact, ordered that those named should be interned at once. In Fermanagh, over fifty were apprehended, Lady Brooke recording with evident pleasure that only two had escaped.[179] Amongst those arrested was Cahir Healy whom unionists regarded as 'the brains of Sinn Fein locally'. His case aroused controversy, particularly after he had become a Westminister M.P. in November 1922. The suggestion has been made that the motivation behind his arrest was to impede the compilation of a strong anti-partitionist case for the county. Several years later, the Boundary Commission questioned Brooke closely on the whole question of actions taken by specials which betrayed political bias. At the time, Healy himself wrote: 'all my life, I have been a man of peace . . . the whole object of this illegal arrest . . . was to paralyse public opinion along the boundary'.[180]

Healy's internment was not, however, without a measure of justification. He had played a key role in the county council debates on whether to recognise the northern government, and supported a motion pledging allegiance to Dáil Eireann. Earlier he had introduced a resolution stating that the authority of the

Belfast parliament could 'only be exercised by force and coercion'.[181] During the week prior to his arrest he had told Collins' north-eastern advisory committee that a 'good' obstruction policy, 'would have to embrace every branch of activity . . . in every way to do all they could against the northern government. It would be hard to say where passive resistance would end and other activities begin'. He himself went on to support a 'destructive policy . . . the destruction of roads, bridges and all other ways in which we can make the government impossible in the six county area'.[182]

The arrest of Healy and other Fermanagh nationalists may well have stifled the flow of anti-partition propaganda relating to the county. Certainly the attention of northern nationalists, as well as southern leaders, in this period, was much more firmly centred on Tyrone. However, there are alternative explanations. Thus Sean Milroy explained to Collins, in August 1922 that

County Tyrone is in the opinion of those who are conversant with the six counties the key . . . If we retain Tyrone, we automatically retain Fermanagh as there is no territorial connection with Fermanagh and the other four counties save through Tyrone.[183]

Healy was held for almost two years before being belatedly released on conditions which initially banned him from the west of the county. Long before this, however, the levels of violence and of tension in Fermanagh had begun to subside. As a result, from mid-1922, Brooke's duties as county commandant diminished, allowing more time for farming and leisure, both neglected since the spring. By October, the maximum number of 'B' specials on daily patrol had fallen to 30 from a June peak of 360.[184] The pressure on the force eased. In April 1925, Sir Basil could recall no attacks or injuries to any member of the special constabulary since the expulsion of the Irregulars from Belleek. Meanwhile, earlier security precautions had gradually been relaxed. During the late summer of 1923, Brooke's headquarters provided the county council with a list of thirteen bridges on border roads that it was felt could safely be repaired.[185] Brooke himself represented the Northern Ireland government, with Wickham, Tallents and the county inspector, in negotiations which led to the British military evacuation of Belleek fort in 1924.[186] Pettigo had been evacuated the previous year, and the number of troops based at Enniskillen had been reduced to pre-war levels.[187]

For a time it seemed possible that Brooke's post of county commandant might itself become redundant. On 27 July 1922, the cabinet decided that all special constabulary expenditure should stop from 1 April 1923, provided the situation merited the disbandment of the force. Though reductions subsequently occurred, numbers actually fell little below peak figures. In April 1925, Brooke informed the Boundary Commission that there were still 2,700 'B' and over 500 'A' specials serving in the county.[188] Craig justified their retention ostensibly on the grounds of political circumstances – the persistence of the boundary issue, the fear of disturbances in border areas and concern at the prospect of a republican government in Dublin. Certainly, in Fermanagh, though levels of violence declined very sharply, genuine uneasiness undoubtedly still persisted in many areas, confirmed and strengthened by occasional raids from the Free State.

An unsuccessful petition to Craig from the Garrison area seeking increased protection, in November 1923, reflected these worries. It stated that 'a big rush of Sinn Feiners might come over the border at any time . . . this border is a dangerous one. It was always said that it was the neck of the six counties . . . One night would wipe all the loyalists here clean out'. Wickham agreed that they were 'badly placed and exceedingly vulnerable'. An address, similar in tone, was delivered to Lord Derby during his visit in April 1923 on behalf of the citizens of Enniskillen.[189] In the course of that year Craig visited the county on three occasions giving reassurance on the boundary question and attempting to dispel feelings of insecurity. At Colebrooke, he stated that the specials would not be disbanded 'until all danger be past'. It was a sentiment with which Brooke wholeheartedly agreed.[190]

However, other factors, apart from the needs of border security and internal order, or presumptions as to their efficiency and cheapness, account for Craig's retention of such large constabulary forces. Their strength helped to obviate Northern Ireland's high unemployment levels, a circumstance which added to the already immense political difficulties involved in reducing their numbers. It was also likely to prove difficult to recover their arms. In Fermanagh, this had been the greatest problem in the creation of a neutral zone in the Belleek–Pettigo area after the Irregulars had been expelled.[191] In the last analysis, however, the willingness of the British government to pay for their maintenance was crucial. The final impossibility of convincing Westminster that such expenditure was still justified, precipitated reductions in their numbers at the end of 1925. The 'B' specials, always regarded, in Wickham's phrase, as 'the best value for money' remained.[192] The 'A' force which Clark from the outset had regarded as being overpaid, was disbanded.[193]

The decision provoked a protest movement, in mid-December 1925, against the government's demobilisation terms. Its chief centres were Londonderry and Prince's Dock, Belfast, but ripples reached Fermanagh when a platoon of 'A' Specials at county headquarters, Enniskillen, arrested their officers and closed the station. As elsewhere, resistance crumbled when confronted by a tactful but obdurate government, and generally unsympathetic public. A report prepared for the Home Office suggests that its roots in the county were shallow. It states that all local action collapsed after 'the return of two delegates despatched . . . to a conference at Londonderry, in a state of blind intoxication . . . and unable to confirm to their colleagues whether they had reached the conference at all'.[194]

Throughout Brooke worked to resolve the dispute and undermine the protest. 'A' force members of mobile platoons came directly under his command; the remainder, about 25 per cent of fixed strength, served as reinforcements to barracks under the authority of police officers. He toured all the platoons and reported that nine were 'steady and loyal', adding typically of those disaffected at headquarters, 'this is remarkable . . . as the men on the border had done all the work, have suffered the hardship, had long anxious patrols'.[195] The split command structure may partly account for Brooke's rather ambivalent attitude towards the 'A' specials, despite their very considerable casualty figures in Fermanagh. He himself stated that, 'in ways . . . [they were] . . . more trouble than they were worth. Many of them were ex-soldiers . . . delighted to have lucrative short-service appointments, . . . a wild crowd'.[196] It is possibly also significant that so many came from outside the county, as it was government policy that recruits should serve away from their own home regions. In 1925, more than 90 per cent were from other parts of Northern Ireland, particularly the Belfast area, where the force had from the beginning been oversubscribed.[197]

In stark contrast Brooke expressed, throughout his long life, warm affection and almost uncritical enthusiasm for the 'B' force. In May 1929, when resigning his post as county commandant, he spoke of the honour it had been to lead 'the loyal men of . . . [his] . . . native county' and offered to resume his duties should danger again threaten. Forty years later, in response to the Hunt report, he stated: 'I am proud still to be an honorary commandant. They [the 'B' specials], are always close to my heart'.[198] He frequently spoke with evident pride of being a founder, or the founder, of the force and though he regarded its formation as 'a calculated risk', it was one which he felt had been totally vindicated. He stated that 'the reassuring effect of having a properly organised and strictly disciplined force on the roads . . . every night gave the people confidence, and stabilised what had been growing into a very dangerous situation'.[199] He deeply admired those who, he believed, had with dedication and for very little reward, voluntarily come forward to defend the union and protect their community. He always did eulogise the farmer with an almost Jeffersonian zeal, but none more so than those who joined the specials, especially in border areas, despite the obvious dangers of their isolation, beyond the protection of any barracks. He criticised those Englishmen who inclined 'to judge the whole of Ulster by the hooligans in Belfast'. As he told a journalist from the *Morning Post*, 'you will see when you come, all we want is to be left alone and not threatened'.[200]

When, in 1925, he came to write his submission to the Boundary Commission, he appealed only briefly to demographic, historical, cultural or economic factors and rested his case predominantly on the sacrifices of the special constabulary. He depicted loyal inhabitants left unprotected, responding magnificently to the challenge of protecting themselves. He listed the casualties of the force, the dead and their dependants, the wounded and the kidnapped. All this, he claimed, had been borne to frustrate those 'intent on arson and murder'. He concluded:

it would be most unjust now to hand over any portion of Fermanagh to the Free State, where it would entail . . . the handing over of a single inhabitant who has carried out his duties to his county and to the empire.[201]

Brooke's favourable assessment was far from being unanimously endorsed by others. The *Fermanagh Herald* from the outset contained a constant stream of allegations, particularly against the 'B' specials, claiming indiscipline, sectarian bias, gratuitous harassment and violence. Dáil Eireann also published a list of outrages which were reported to have been committed by the force in Fermanagh. One local historian concluded that 'the effect of their activities was to subdue and terrorise the nationalist people'.[202]

Further evidence to this effect comes from other less predictable sources. The boundary commissioners closely questioned Brooke and others about political abuses, including voting malpractice and attempts to disrupt the Nationalist registration machinery, said to have been committed by the special constabulary.[203] Police reports confirm that the latter certainly did not prevent loyalist reprisals, and the possibility that these might be perpetrated by those under his own command was one of Brooke's most haunting fears. However, some of the most trenchant criticisms of the force came from within Unionist ranks. In mid-1922 Stephen Tallents recorded that during his inquiries, prominent figures within the party had told him privately that its partisan activities were sowing feuds in the countryside which would not be eradicated for generations.[204]

Amongst these was General A. St Q. Ricardo who, in June 1922, provided him with a well-informed critical analysis of the role of the special constabulary based on his experiences in County Tyrone. With regard to the 'B' force he drew particular attention to the difficulties of adequately training part-time men, and the problems of discipline where those enlisted were virtually unpaid, and the officers were neighbours and personal friends of lower ranks. He doubted that they could ever be disarmed. He claimed, from personal knowledge, that they had acted in a violent and sectarian manner, committing reprisals, drawing up death-lists, and acting almost without supervision by, or coordination with, the regular police. Overall he considered that their performance compared very unfavourably with the pre-war U.V.F. He concluded with a prediction that civil war was inevitable unless a state of martial law was declared, the special constabulary was brought under the complete control of the R.U.C. and British troops took over border defence.[205]

Brooke was certainly concerned about some of these issues. The problem of enforcing discipline prompted him strenuously to advise Clark in December 1920, that payment for head constables should be introduced into the 'B' force. He regarded them as 'the pivot of the whole county organisation', and suggested that their being unpaid left 'the commander without any hold upon them, . . . [and] . . . owing to the work being voluntary it would be extremely difficult to get rid of an inefficient man or to enforce satisfactory work'. This suggestion, which he regarded as 'almost essential', was rejected.[206]

Nevertheless, the evidence would suggest that Sir Basil did have considerable success in maintaining discipline within the 'B' force, despite the death of 16 of its members.[207] Though county inspector reports in the period up to the truce refer to political feeling running high, and lists of nationalists being prepared, they indicate also that unionist reprisals for Sinn Fein violence did not go beyond damage to property, and none of these actions was attributed overtly to the special constabulary. Home office figures for the weeks between 24 March and 17 June 1922, the period when tension in the county was at its peak, suggest that five deaths occurred, and that all of those whose religion was known were protestant.[208] Surprisingly, a report prepared for the southern government, in July 1923, commented on the 'commendable restraint' that had been shown by the Fermanagh specials, stating that over the preceding months they had remained 'quiet and unoffensive'. Another related that in the area around Derrylin, such was the sensitivity and impartiality displayed by the district inspector that local nationalists were said to 'prefer six-county rule' and that those directly across the border were considering voting themselves into the north.[209]

In addition, it was much easier to identify flaws in the existing scheme than to suggest realistic alternative solutions. General Ricardo himself, though critical of the special constabulary, thought that it had, nonetheless, 'done magnificent work under immense difficulties' and that prior to the formation of the R.U.C.

at least, its creation as in independent force 'may have been a necessity'.[210] He stressed that imperial troops had taken 'no hand in subduing the present rebellion against the northern government'. A British cabinet committee report some weeks earlier concluded, in similar vein, that 'in the absence of any . . . effective measures on the part of the British government to keep the border intact . . . the Northern Ireland government was entitled to . . . provide that protection against invasion which citizens of the U.K. have a right to claim'.[211] Unionist confidence in the dependability of British troops had been undermined particularly during and after the truce. Hence Craig had considered imperial support to be unlikely during the June crisis of 1922, and had been striving for some months before it to achieve independence for Ulster in security matters. Sir Henry Wilson, in April, advised him to 'prepare for the worst: a republic in the south and Lloyd George's withdrawal of troops from Northern Ireland'.[212]

At the same time the mounting levels of violence were also clearly beyond the resources of the local R.I.C., a fact of which the small beleagured force in Fermanagh was increasingly aware from the summer of 1920.[213] At an early stage it lost the confidence of local unionists, at least until the redistribution of its personnel in mid-May 1922. It is significant that already in 1920 the force did not patrol the county's main Orange demonstration, on 12 July, at Maguiresbridge. This distrust no doubt partly stemmed from its predominantly catholic membership. Also the troubles in the south led to a number, of what Tallents described as the 'less efficient and trustworthy members' of the R.I.C. being drafted into the then comparative quiet of the six counties.[214] Ricardo describes it as increasingly demoralised, permeated with Sinn Fein sympathies, and 'latterly . . . a force awaiting disbandment, . . . [which] . . . had no heart in . . . [its] . . . work, and had therefore to be ignored to some extent'. The *Impartial Reporter* made strong allegations, almost certainly justified, that 'treachery [had been] . . . the cause of the surrender'[215] of a number of its barracks in the county during 1922.

There was thus a strong case both for forming and maintaining a special constabulary in this period to fill the security vacuum. The circumstances of its birth determined its main characteristics. From the beginning there were strong unionist pressures on Clark to ensure that it should 'act with and not be subordinate to the R.I.C.'; he himself described this as the 'rock upon which the whole scheme may split'. Ambiguity in their relationship arose in part from the fact that the legislation under which the force was launched, in Sir Ernest's words, 'never contemplated the present developments'.[216] Though Brooke sought to reassure the latter with regard to police relations with the new constabulary, his own scheme was ambiguous as to how this might best be achieved.

It was probably inevitably that the new force would in the course of the next two years become increasingly independent of the small, demoralised and increasingly suspect regular police establishment. The devolution of power to the county commandants was also actively encouraged by the government's zealous military adviser, Major General Arthur Solly Flood. He did so in the face of warnings from General Cameron, G.O.C., that this was a fundamental error which would increase the risk of reprisals and escalate tension.[217] However, Sir Henry Wilson supported Solly Flood's policy, despite his impression that the commandants, were 'only a fairly good team'.[218] The central role of the specials was perpetuated by the fact that the R.U.C. was inaugurated, on 1 June 1922, at just one-third of its fixed strength, and practically unsupported by any system of criminal intelligence.[219]

Finally, given the context of sectional tension it was, from the outset, unlikely that the new force would enlist many nationalist recruits, though this appears to have been a cause of genuine disappointment to Clark.[220] Those from the minority who joined obviously exposed themselves to the danger of I.R.A. retribution and to ostracism within their own community and also, by implication, they would not only be accepting partition but actively helping to enforce it. Dr Gillespie stressed at Collins' north-eastern advisory committee in mid-1922 that 'nothing will give the northern parliament greater recognition than a thing like this'. There was general agreement that it would compromise the nationalist position before the Boundary Commission and that, particularly in Tyrone and Fermanagh, it 'would not be useful'.[221] The lack of a more positive response relieved unionist fears of infiltration by those seeking to perpetuate disorder. In 1925, Brooke informed the commissioners that in Fermanagh his assistant adjutant was Catholic, and between one-eighth and one-quarter of the 'A' force and 'quite a number' of the 'C' specials. However, he also said of the latter that as it was composed of 'older men, willing to serve in case of trouble . . . you might say that every unionist in the county is a 'C' man' and he conceded that the 'B' force was without exception protestant.[222]

No doubt partly because of its sectional composition, the special constabulary had, by mid-1922, won throughout the province the enduring affection and almost unanimous support of the protestant population. Though specific instances of indiscipline in the force might be mildly censured, the Unionist press and political leaders in Fermanagh frequently expressed immense pride in its achievements. Profound gratitude was felt towards those who, at all hours of the night and in all sorts of weather, had acted to resist the 'wholesale pillage' which it was assumed would otherwise have engulfed them.[223] Events in Donegal confirmed this conviction as well as stiffening determination within the county to fight rather than be transferred into Southern Ireland; a response which was shared by General Ricardo.[224]

These sentiments of appreciation and trust were felt in equal measure for Brooke himself. The *Fermanagh Times* attributed their comparative immunity from serious outbreaks of violence to his 'exceeding tact and ability', and wrote glowingly of the universal confidence and respect that surrounded his leadership.[225] W.C. Trimble forcefully expressed a viewpoint shared by many, that 'when the county was once in a critical position and others shrunk from it, he responded to the appeal, and came forward as county commandant . . . and saved them from peril and raids'.[226] Sir Basil had, during these difficult years, acted decisively and courageously motivated, not by ambition, but by a genuine sense of duty. He showed himself as willing to serve, in the tradition of his forebears and of his own upbringing and training, in defence of order and of property and, from a broader perspective, in defence of the union and of the empire. Within Fermanagh, he embodied and perpetuated the role and the attitudes of the Anglo-Irish gentry, when the members of many other county families, the erstwhile leaders of local unionism, had ceased to provide their accustomed leadership. Their retreat enhanced his role and significance.

At the outset, in July 1920, when urging Macready to organise and arm a civilian force, he had written 'I am not a politician in any sense of the word' but, he added, 'I know what is being thought by the people here'.[227] Some might regard the latter phrase as the *leitmotif* of his later career in politics, one for which his present activities helped lay firm foundations. Certainly, during these years from the comparative obscurity caused by his own prolonged absence and the somewhat circumscribed role played by his family through successive recent Ulster crises, Brooke rose to a position of prominence not only in the county, but in the province. He had favourably impressed Clark, Spender and Wickham. When Tallents drew up coded descriptions of six Northern Ireland political leaders, in mid-1922, Brooke was the only non-cabinet member included on the list. The reference was brief but unmistakable, beginning, 'served with Byng in France, . . . young'.[228] His services to the state were recognised in his receipt of the C.B.E. and appointments first to the Senate and later as honorary A.D.C. to the governor.

Also for the first time, Sir Basil came into frequent contact with Craig. The latter was totally committed to the specials; causing Tallents to complain that he would 'hear nothing to [their] . . . detriment'.[229] Sir James was clearly impressed and surprised by the success of Fermanagh's county commandant in a difficult and demanding post. This, he expressed when, in January 1924, he came to Colebrooke to meet the county's police officers. For Lady Craig the visit was not an undiluted pleasure. She described luncheon being served 'in a large room that had not been used for some time . . . the damp and cold was something I shall remember . . . the water was running down the walls'. In typical fashion she added that 'James made a fine speech'.[230] In it he paid glowing tribute to Brooke, stating that 'he had neither spared his time nor his pocket in doing everything that lay in his power . . . to make Fermanagh peaceful, happy and contented. Sir Basil', he continued, 'was one of the finest leaders in Ulster today'. After referring to his 'genial personality' and 'extra-ordinary activity' he reflected on 'the wonderful way in which he had borne the duties that had fallen on his shoulders'. All in all the prime minister concluded Brooke's performance had 'been an eye-opener'.[231]

CHAPTER IV

Brooke's Political Career to 1933

Gradually from the winter of 1922–3, the military phase of Brooke's career receded at least for the next fifteen years. His duties in the special constabulary steadily lightened, though occasional border incidents continued to occur, and the spectre of the Boundary Commission helped to keep local fears and rumours alive and deepen those psychological scars which permanently influenced the county's political structures. The duration of his military activities which had begun in 1908 in the arid heat of India, was as unexpected as their ultimate setting, the villages and countryside of Fermanagh, and the unsought prominence both within his native county and the province that resulted. After this experience, and given his class and family background, a career in politics was always likely to follow. Its features would inevitably be influenced by the traumatic context in which he had first reached political consciousness.

During the 1920s Brooke's life came to approximate most closely to that role which he had so eagerly anticipated during the war years, that of landowner and 'drain-cleaner in-chief'.[1] From late 1922 to 1929 his pursuits were more Fermanagh-centred than at any other time between early childhood and retirement from the Northern Ireland premiership in 1963. Indeed he later claimed with little exaggeration that throughout this period, he had not once visited Belfast.[2]

Throughout 'the troubles', as he himself wrote, 'Life went on normally . . . [I was] . . . fully engaged in farming my estate, watching my family grow'.[3] The estate consisted of about 1500 acres, half of it wood, and small portions continued to be sold off under 1920s' land legislation. Farming was his greatest recreation as well as being an economic necessity, and his success is reflected in the frequency with which he won prizes for livestock in the county's agricultural shows.[4] Nonetheless, despite his enthusiasm and competence it provided only a frugal income, in part the legacy of his grandfather's and his own absenteeism. His son recalled that in his childhood,

Fun was plentiful, money was not. We were very short. My father when he came to Colebrooke had £1,000 a year from investments and the rest came from the farm . . . We wanted all sorts of things we could not get . . . the stress was on self-sufficiency.[5]

At Eton, he had suffered from feelings of embarrassment at his relative lack of money. A leading Ministry of Agriculture official recorded his impressions of Colebrooke from the early 1930s as being 'comfortable but with many rooms

59

unused, meals spartan, and run by Lady Brooke with a butler and a couple of maids'.[6]

Family life brought both pain and pleasure. Within a few years of his return from France, death had struck three generations of Brookes. Sir Basil's grandmother died at Pau, his mother at Laputa House, Ballyshannon, and most tragically, in May 1921, his sister Sylvia, for whom he had so much affection, died at a private nursing home in Dublin, fifteen months after her marriage to Charles Mulholland. At her funeral fifty special constables provided a guard of honour and Lord French, General Macready and E. M. Archdale were amongst those who sent wreaths.[7] Meanwhile, Brooke's own family grew to include three sons. After Basil Julian's birth in Dublin, by general agreement the closest in personality to his father, John Warden*, now his sole surviving son and heir, was born in November 1922 at home, and Henry Alan almost one year later, on the same day, his mother noted, as the electric light installation at Colebrooke was completed.[8] They were brought up in a consciously more relaxed atmosphere than that which had pervaded Brooke's own late Victorian childhood. Everyday discipline, particularly from the late 20s when their father entered parliament, was provided by Lady Brooke, Sir Basil dealing with matters out of the ordinary, occasionally losing his temper, but his son recalls, 'that was the end of it, he did not hold grudges'.[9]

Apart from farming Brooke indulged in his enduring love of country pursuits, educating his children as his forebears had done through nine generations in the seasonal rhythms of nature on the estate, and with his wife, inducing in his sons a passion for shooting and fishing. The records of his shooting, often the first activity before going to his constabulary office in Enniskillen, or a weekend relaxation shared within his social circle, are more meticulously recorded than any other aspect of his life.[10] Fly-fishing was a more solitary pastime, though again frequently pursued in the company of his family on local Ulster rivers, the Colebrooke or the Mourne, almost two miles of which he eventually leased, on Scottish estates, or during summer vacations with Lady Brooke spent on Norwegian fjords where the success of their holiday was measured by the weight of the catch. On at least one occasion pleasure almost gave way to tragedy. Whilst fishing on the river Erne, in the summer of 1924, their boat was swept out of control but luckily entrapped itself on rocks, some yards short of the thirty feet deep Falls of Asseroe.[11] Recreation and travel were frequently combined. Both interests had been strengthened by his years at school abroad and later in the army but they never became for him the obsession they had been for his grandfather. Most notable during these years was his visit with Lady Brooke, to see General Byng prior to the latter relinquishing the governorship of Canada in 1926.[12] Generally travel, like social entertainment, was rarely indulged in for its own pleasure alone, but rather had some clear purpose in view.

Though Brooke many years later wrote of the 1920s 'Even if I have been interested, I would not have had much spare time for politics,' and had declared in 1920 that he was not a politician, he was ineluctably drawn in during this decade.[13] From the outset, he was active at a local level. He regarded those members of the gentry who remained resident in the country as the 'natural leaders' of the community, as their established wealth permitted objective judgement, and he himself consistently throughout his career acted from that

*John Warden Brooke died 5 March 1987.

profound sense of duty characteristic of his class and of his own family.[14] John Brooke, reflecting on his parents' influence commented that they inculcated in their children not only an 'appreciation of moral values, and of patriotism, and loyalty to the empire . . . but above all [of] . . . service. They imbued you with a sense of guilt if you were not doing something for other people'.[15]

His father, by the late 1920s, had a wide range of responsibilities and commitments far beyond his positions as county commandant and, from 1924 aide de camp to the governor of Northern Ireland. Inevitably many of these reflected his keen agricultural interests. He encouraged improvements in local farming not only by example on his estate, but through his presidency of the Ballylurgan co-operative which he had himself helped to establish in order to meet the needs of neighbouring farmers, and through his active involvement in the Ulster Farmers' Union. He was instrumental in setting up local branches of the latter, and they discussed under his chairmanship a wide range of practical issues from the abolition of luck pennies to the analysis of price trends. In 1929, after serving for several years on the movement's executive he became its vice-president, and later president. In addition, he was a member of the agricultural committee of the county, and of the Royal Ulster Agricultural Society.[16]

He also served on the board of the Clogher Valley railway company, was a county grand juror, and on a more overtly political level both Brooke and his wife were, throughout the 1920s, active members of Fermanagh Unionist Association. Their membership might be regarded as virtually inevitable as, during this period, the association confronted the gravest challenge in its history. In 1920, William Eames, county secretary, stressed to Archdale 'there was never a time when it was more necessary to keep the association alive, every point must be strained to keep Fermanagh in the north'.[17] However, his task of responding to the political crisis as well as coping with the expanding electorate was made no easier by the historic organisational lethargy of local unionism. At the time of his letter to Archdale, the county had only 150 regular subscribers out of 13,000 registered party voters, and had accumulated debts of over £500. At least the widened franchise simplified revision work, to such an extent that the association's solicitors concluded, in 1925, that their function had become superfluous.[18]

Brooke was a member of a twelve-man county executive committee, amongst the largest contributors of party funds, and one of the four trustees in whose name the Unionist headquarters in Enniskillen was held.[19] It was Lady Brooke, however, who took the more active part in the day to day running of the association. With the reform of the franchise it was vital, as Eames recognised to organise the female vote and re-cast the party organisation so as to give women representation on county committees. In these uniquely favourable circumstances, Lady Brooke's role was formidable. From the moment of her arrival at Colebrooke she identified herself totally with the unionist cause. She worked enthusiastically as chair-person of ladies' registration committees, and impatient with any hint of slackness, constantly chided the association secretary if voting lists were not sent out with sufficient promptitude or inadequate notice was given of party meetings. After her thirtieth birthday, in May 1927, she politely demanded that her name be entered on the electoral roll.[20] Brooke was justifiably proud of his wife's achievements and claimed, in

1931, that she had been responsible for establishing fourteen women's unionist branches in the county.[21] She had meanwhile become a member of the Ulster Women's Unionist Council. She was successful not only in forming branches, and raising money, but in overcoming initial local hostility to such involvement by an 'outsider'.

By the late 1920s, the morale of the association was high. The electoral divisions had been redrawn, proportional representation was banished, it was firmly in credit, and Wilson Hungerford could congratulate Eames on the 'wonderful state of organisation' in the county, which he regretted was rare elsewhere.[22] If, as one leading local unionist suggested, this healthy state was 'owing to the exertions of the Fermanagh Women's Association', then Lady Brooke could legitimately claim a considerable share of the credit. Through these activities she contributed positively to her husband's emerging political career. She not only provided him with a valuable entrée into women's unionist circles in both county and province but more fundamentally, her political commitment encouraged his involvement in politics. Thus in August 1925, Eames enquired whether Sir Basil would be 'willing to act as chairman of all the [registration] committees in the area on which Lady Brooke is chairman of the ladies' committees'. From the outset their political involvement was on a shared team-like basis. Thus, earlier that year she helped organise, at Colebrooke, the first of what proved to be annual gatherings of active unionist workers in the Lisnaskea area. They were held in order to raise funds, for mutual edification, and by way of recognition of past services by party workers. With typical thoroughness she first sought Eames' advice on who should be invited.[23] Sir Douglas Harkness recalled his impressions of her from the early 1930s:

She was . . . a good and economical manager, . . . most capable, . . . and possessed of a very sharp intelligence and shrewd head. Rightly or wrongly the impression in the Ministry of Agriculture was that she was the dominant partner in the marriage, although there was never any question that she attempted to intervene in ministerial affairs. But where Brooke's personal interests were concerned, she was a wise judge and adviser.[24]

Also John Brooke, after identifying her qualities of kindness, determination, and competence, stated that 'she was a very much better judge of character' than his father and the main source of ideas within the partnership.[25] Her determination to defend her husband's interests was illustrated when, after their trip to the Ottawa conference in 1932, Brooke was billed mistakenly for the hire of a typewriter used by the entire Ulster delegation. She sent a caustic reply to the Ministry of Finance promising that she would 'fight them to the death'.[26] Ultimately her services not only to Ulster unionism but to bodies ranging from the Women's Royal Air Corps to the Save the Children Fund were recognised when she became a dame of the British empire and was awarded an honorary doctorate at Queen's University.[27]

The first major step in Brooke's political career came in 1924, when he became a Unionist county councillor. The local government elections of that year were the first since partition and with justification were described in the *Irish News* at the time as 'a farce'.[28] Nationalist candidates refused to contest a single seat in Fermanagh and Tyrone. Political alienation and misjudgement with regard to the forthcoming Boundary Commission played a part in their calculations, but above all their non-participation indicated a determination not to legitimise procedures, implemented prior to the election, which the party regarded as gerrymandering.

In November 1921 the Northern Ireland government inherited the whole pre-partition local government structure, including franchise, voting system, and council membership. Of those bodies under nationalist control none proved to be more intransigent or uncooperative than Fermanagh county council. It persisted in its refusal to recognise the partition parliament in Belfast and continued to pledge 'allegiance to Dáil Eireann'. These provocative attitudes contributed to local unionist alarm particularly as the boundary remained uncertain, and also because of the growing patronage and power of local government, and the conviction, based on rates payments and property ownership, that Fermanagh was 'a protestant county notwithstanding the population'. The government shared this concern. In late December Fermanagh county council was the first of twelve recalcitrant councils to be dissolved, their duties taken over by appointed commissioners.[29]

Such a solution could only be temporary. On 12 May 1922, the Northern Ireland cabinet decided to abolish proportional representation in local government and to assume powers to redraw the electoral divisions, before the elections due in 1923. The decision was prompted by the non-cooperative attitude of nationalist councils, mounting disorder within Northern Ireland, and numerous representations from Unionist associations.[30] The legality, propriety and timing of the bill aroused great controversy. Collins formally protested against this ploy 'to paint the counties of Fermanagh and Tyrone with a deep Orange tint'.[31] The British government, obviously embarrassed, withheld the royal assent for two months. It finally relented when it became clear that the reform lay within the powers delegated to the Northern Ireland government, that Craig's cabinet would resign unless the assent was given, and that meanwhile Collins had begun to implement the treaty in the south.[32]

Fermanagh unionists viewed abolition with mixed feelings. Eames, the county's Unionist secretary, had welcomed P.R. when it was first introduced in 1919. He informed Archdale 'we certainly cannot do worse than we are now', and expressed the hope that the Local Government Board might be pressed to revise the electoral boundaries 'to our advantage'.[33] The board did indeed subsequently make changes which reduced the number of Nationalist controlled councils. Meanwhile James Cooper who later described himself as busy 'manufacturing votes' throughout 1921, was increasingly confident that the party would regain control of the county at the next election under the P.R. system. However, once the latter was abolished, such hopes were dashed and he urged the adoption of new boundaries rather than revert to those that had existed before the introduction of proportional representation. He wrote 'if we are to go back to the old system . . . We are swamped . . . it would knock the heart out of the people altogether'.[34] From December 1921 at least, rumours were current that border unionists were preparing new divisions. Certainly, by the following spring, substantially in advance of the Northern Ireland cabinet decision to abolish P.R., such schemes were well in hand. In April 1922, Parke, secretary to Tyrone Unionist Association, wrote to his Fermanagh counterpart

I suppose you are engaged in preparing a scheme to make Fermanagh boundaries safe
. . . [I am] gerrymandering at night . . . it is the hardest job I ever undertook . . . we
have a big nationalist majority against us.[35]

Eames found it no easier, observing privately that 'No one [would] ever realise
the amount of work that . . . [he] . . . had perfecting the . . . schemes'.[36]

From the autumn pressure was exerted on the Northern Ireland government
to accept these schemes and to proceed with the elections when they fell due in
1923. Hugh de Fellenberg Montgomery advised Craig that 'to put them off
would be discouraging . . . the other side are given a whole year to find out
what we are doing and make preparations to oppose it'.[37] In the event the rural
district and county council elections were postponed, and the government held
public enquiries prior to the introduction of the new boundaries where it was
felt that circumstances required them. As elsewhere, Fermanagh nationalists
refused to participate. To do so would, they felt, merely 'give public approval
to a cut and dried scheme which the unionists had in readiness'.[38] The scheme
which was finally adopted virtually guaranteed unionist control of all Fermanagh's councils. Cahir Healy predicted that if there had been no local government reform nationalist candidates would have had a majority of two on the
county council, but that the new scheme would result in them having five fewer
seats than the opposition.[39] Hence their party boycott, and the electoral 'farce'
resulted whereby, in 1924, the government's commissioner was replaced by a
body for which no votes had been cast. It was described by the *Impartial
Reporter* as 'the most influential that ever sat in the council chamber', composed 'of the leading gentlemen of the county, all large rate-payers and men of
standing'.[40] Brooke was one of those alluded to.

Sir Basil had not been immediately involved in these preliminary proceedings but he was a direct beneficiary. He was selected for the newly-created local
government division of Brookeborough, which James Cooper, the co-opted
chairman of the new council and mastermind of the new boundaries, estimated
had a unionist majority of fifty.[41] Brooke's selection was hardly surprising,
given his family's traditions and his own sense of duty and local pre-eminence.
In addition, the division was, as he informed the boundary commissioners the
following year, 'practically altogether a portion of my estate . . . an area which
I have known all my life'.[42] This he proceeded to demonstrate by describing in
detail for their benefit its political topography. Some localities were, he stated,
'equally divided', or 'half and half', and parts were 'the other way', but it was,
he assured them, overall, predominantly Unionist, adding with some humour
'unless they had changed their minds'. That majority, he stated, had been
reinforced since 1920 by an influx into the division of some fifty protestant
families from neighbouring southern counties, out of a possible total of one
thousand who entered Fermanagh during this period.[43] Whatever the figures
the division provided him with a safe seat, and the first important step on his
political career.

Brooke was an active council member. At an early stage he was voted onto
committees dealing with agriculture, education, and later the management of
the Clogher Valley railway.[44] He spoke and introduced resolutions frequently.
As was predictable, farming interests were not neglected. Thus, in 1927, one of
his resolutions urged on the government 'the dire necessity that at present
exists for the restoration of the full grant in relief of rates'. As a member of the

Pirrie committee, he had supported a similar recommendation four years earlier. His attention also focussed on other issues. In 1924 he strongly opposed too-great economy in local government as a serious threat to efficiency. On his initiative, in 1925, it was decided that persons canvassing for positions within the appointment of the council would be disqualified. In addition, he put forward practical suggestions as to how cross-border trade might be stimulated.[45]

Amidst the mundane and ephemeral content of much council business, one issue transcended all others, the Irish Boundary Commission. Local unionist opinion had unanimously opposed the loss of any portion of the county from the moment the commission was first mooted, though before the 'troubles' views had been more diverse. Stephen Tallents noted, in July 1922, that even amongst border moderates, opinion on the issue had, by then, hardened appreciably.[46] In a letter to Spender, in 1924, James Cooper stated the case simply: 'we want to remain in Fermanagh exactly as we are'.[47] This intransigence was passionately shared and expressed by Craig and helps to account for the depth of his popularity in border districts. Thus Spender could reply reassuringly that the premier 'would never accept . . . any lake division' of the county. Such a scheme had apparently been favoured by Sir Henry Wilson as 'the real strategic frontier from the military point of view'.[48]

Undoubtedly Brooke's most important contribution to the council's deliberations in these years lay in helping it to define and articulate its response to the commission. Local unionist opinion was split on whether to boycott the latter or alternatively to recognise it and try to influence its findings. In late 1924, F. B. Bourdillon, secretary to the commissioners, requested that the council prepare a case and submit evidence to help with their enquiry. It responded in a resolution proposed by Brooke, which was favourable to the request but contained a condition that the commissioners should first give an 'assurance . . . that their duties are confined to a mere rectification of anomalies on both sides of the existing borders'.[49] The commission's reply was equivocal, stating that it did 'not propose at the present stage to make a pronouncement on the questions raised by this resolution'. But it suggested that the councillors 'supplement' their letter 'by putting forward considerations in support of the interpretation of the article' (article 12) which it implied, and that the commissioners 'would be glad to hear representatives appointed' for this purpose.[50]

In the council debate which followed, Brooke continued to support a positive response. He argued pragmatically that the commissioner's report would in any case be ratified by the British government, and that if unionists failed to present a case to it, public opinion in Britain could legitimately charge that they had been given ample opportunity to do so but had refused to grasp it. He proposed a reply, unanimously adopted, which expressed regret that the commission had refused to define its interpretation of article 12, sought to justify its own interpretation of that clause, and concluded by stating that the council would 'present a statement of fact to the Boundary Commission and . . . support this with evidence'. Brooke was one of the fourteen councillors entrusted with this task, though as he himself willingly acknowledged, James Cooper played the key role in preparing the council's case. His arguments were subsequently dismissed by Healy, as based on 'land, bullocks, and poor rates . . . not the will of human beings'.[51] However, geographical and other points were raised to justify boundary extension and stress laid on the recent protestant influx from the south, in negating nationalist census statistics.

Brooke himself submitted both written and verbal evidence in support of this view. He urged that any boundary change should increase the land area of the county, using arguments relating to economic and cultural factors, but resting mainly on the loyalty and sacrifices of the special constabulary since their formation.[52] The Free State government was however convinced that this force had been used in more clandestine ways by the northern authorities to influence the work of the commissioners. In mid-1923 it received reports of provocative action by specials along the south Fermanagh border. Their officials concluded that the object of these activities was to produce a war atmosphere, and ultimately to create a position of actual warfare, that they were being attacked from the south, and so prejudice the commissioner's findings in their favour. Whether such incidents occurred and, if so, the extent of Brooke's involvement is unclear but the southern leaders regarded this information as of sufficient gravity to merit the transfer of seasoned and reliable troops to this section of their frontier.[53]

The final dramatic outcome of the Boundary Commission was greeted with unionist euphoria and nationalist gloom. Craig confessed to his wife that 'in his wildest dreams he had never expected to keep Ulster intact'. In contrast the *Fermanagh Herald* bore the headlines 'Border nationalists deserted', and Healy spoke of 'betrayal'.[54] Churchill told a meeting between government ministers and commissioners that in the history of the Anglo-Irish negotiations since 1910,

this very question of Fermanagh and Tyrone had been found to be the most insoluble.

He concluded:

now suddenly the two parties had settled the matter out of court, over the whole area of the empire it will be felt that something has happened which has brought peace.[55]

In Fermanagh, the county council once more adopted a resolution, proposed by Brooke, which expressed similar optimism,

We believe that the solving of that problem [the boundary question] . . . will remove many difficulties which have hitherto prevented men of different shades of opinion from working together for the common good of the county.[56]

The significance of Brooke's contribution to the council's affairs was acknowledged in 1928. In the June of that year, James Cooper resigned as chairman, and warmly supported Sir Basil as his successor. The latter was elected unopposed, and remained so until forced to relinquish the position owing to the pressure of his ministerial responsibilities.[57]

Reflecting back on his own experience, Brooke once expressed the view that local government was 'a natural training ground for parlimentary career'.[58] However, though he did not enter parliament until 1929, his name was being suggested as a prospective Unionist candidate from much earlier. There were press reports in early 1921, that he had been approached and had agreed to stand as a representative of the farming and labouring interests.[59] His name, however, is not mentioned at the subsequent delegates' meetings. Later that year E. M. Archdale publicly indicated his intention to stand down before the next election, and suggested that Sir Basil would be a worthy successor. In fact, mainly due to pressure from Craig he continued to serve as minister of agriculture until 1933, and sat in parliament until 1938.[60]

Again Brooke informed the Boundary Commission that prior to the 1925 election, a number of Roman catholic friends and large farmers had urged him to stand as an agricultural representative. He had rejected their request stating that he would 'always be a unionist, . . . was not anxious to stand', and that he considered that they were being 'perfectly well represented'. However, he clearly did not rule out such a possibility at a future date, stating that 'when the time came [he] . . . would see about it'.[61] The retirement of James Cooper provided him with his opportunity. Cooper was the central figure in Fermanagh unionism in the 1920s. He was a local solicitor, ex-member of the U.V.F., B Special, and member of parliament from 1921. He had been mainly responsible for redrawing the county's local government boundaries in 1923, and in preparing the unionist case for the Boundary Commission. In 1926, he indicated his intention of retiring from public life after he had fulfilled one final objective, which he openly stated:

the parliamentary divisions are the only thing left which require attention in this constituency, . . . I intend before I retire to see that made right if I can.[62]

When proportional representation was abolished for local government elections, there was a widespread assumption that it would soon be removed in parliamentary elections also. In early 1923, Wilson Hungerford had warned the already overworked Eames that the onerous task of creating new single-member seats 'will have to be faced before very long'.[63] When, at this time, W. T. Miller, M.P. for the Fermanagh–Tyrone constituency, informed Spender that he strongly opposed the change, Herbert Dixon tersely expressed the government view, 'there is no room in Ulster for diversities of opinion and the people have got to learn that sooner or later'.[64] The cabinet considered introducing legislation in 1924, but on Craig's recommendation agreed to defer doing so until after the Boundary Commission had reported.[65] When this obstacle was removed the reform proceeded. Thus in the winter of 1928–29, Miller (whose opinions had changed in the interim), and Cooper worked to produce schemes for their respective counties. Hungerford confidently reassured Craig: 'I think we will have no difficulty in having something we can stand over. It will be a very big job . . . Miller is quite alright and I think we will be able to fix Cooper'.[66] Amidst nationalist protests of political treachery details of Fermanagh's three new single-member seats were disclosed in the March of 1929.[67]

Having fulfilled his political objectives and partly as a result of business pressures Cooper duly retired from public life. During this period Brooke spoke of him frequently, with uncritical praise and affection, referring to his tact, sense of humour, political skills, and personal qualities. Evaluating his contribution to local party fortunes, Sir Basil declared that he was 'the man who had done more for the unionist cause in Fermanagh than he or anyone else could do, . . . [who] knew the county and the needs of the county', and who had left 'no political storm on the horizon'.[68] For his part, Cooper played a vital role in the formative stages of Brooke's own career. He had already provided him with a safe county council seat and supported his succession as county council chairman in 1928. Now before his retirement he privately urged Brooke to 'take over' the newly created parliamentary division of Lisnaskea, with its substantial in-built unionist majority, stressing to him 'after all you live right in the middle of the constituency'.[69] Also, from early 1927, he publicly supported Brooke's candidacy and in glowing tributes testified to his suitability.

He did however, mildly rebuke Sir Basil on one point, his comparative lack of involvement in the Orange Order, and recalled, by contrast, his childhood pleasures at seeing his father, Sir Douglas, faithfully lead the Brookeborough Orangemen into Enniskillen. Certainly Brooke had attended and spoken very rarely at Orange meetings, and had even earlier on this same occasion, criticised the Order, when referring to those people who wore sashes on the 12th 'and that was as far as they got'.[70] In response to Cooper's public criticism, Sir Basil justified his minor role, by stating that his status as county commandant had not permitted him to take a more prominent part,[71] and proceeded lavishly to praise the institution.

With such support Brooke was well placed to win the nomination for Lisnaskea division, but he was in any case a formidable candidate. Cooper in promoting his attributes had stressed his record of loyal service as county commandant and county councillor, his deep interest in farming issues, and his family tradition, stating that the Brookes had come to Colebrooke, 'when the rebels were burning the protestants out, . . . and from then they had been in every scrap in Ireland'. The *Impartial Reporter* referred to his 'one great asset, . . . the Brookes were the best of landlords and in consequence the tenants were instinctively attracted to them'.[72] His opponent for the nomination, Sir Charles Falls, was an ageing solicitor, who had served local unionism from the 1890s and had represented the county at Westminster from 1925. He accepted defeat with grace, and paid special tribute to Brooke's personal qualities, his youth – though he was already over forty years of age – energy, charm, generosity, keen intellect, and fluent speaking ability. At his own request he was the first to sign Brooke's nomination papers.[73]

Brooke's speeches at the time of his acceptance were a familiar blend of modesty and colloquial humour, commenting that 'if he did not please them he would do his best to please them'. In his speeches, he stressed two key commitments; not to forget the farmers as he was one himself, and total loyalty to Craig.[74] In the election twenty-two seats were uncontested, and sixteen of these were retained by Unionists. Despite rumours of an independent farmers' candidate standing, Sir Basil was amongst those returned unopposed, as he was on all but one occasion until his retirement in 1967. Once more the residual influence and appeal of the Anglo-Irish gentry was demonstrated as Fermanagh was represented by the heads of the two families, the Archdales and the Brookes, for the first time in almost one hundred years.[75]

On the brink of a new career, Brooke later recalled his own diverse emotions. He felt some 'reluctance', as a parliamentary career would take him away from family and home, and concern that if he refused to go forward he would in some way be letting people down. He concluded that 'after some soul-searching I agreed'.[76] There is no doubt that the sense of obligation, and of service, were important factors in influencing his decision. This is confirmed by contemporary accounts. The *Impartial Reporter* stated clearly that Brooke was not a candidate because he put himself forward, but because he was 'invited to become one' by the Unionist Association.[77] But such an interpretation is perhaps misleading in laying such stress on Sir Basil's own passivity, at this turning-point in his life. As a witness before the Boundary Commission he had made it clear that he was not adverse to the idea of becoming an M.P. Also, from that time, both he and Lady Brooke had been active in both mobilising and encouraging party workers within the Lisnaskea district. This had been one of the main objectives of the annual rallies of up to 100 leading local unionists held at Colebrooke from the mid-twenties. In 1926, Brooke himself suggested that one of their functions was 'to build up party organisation in preparation for the new constituencies'.[78] On the same occasion, Cooper indicated the probability that in the near future Fermanagh would be divided into three single member seats. It may not have been Brooke's unblinking ambition to become an M.P. but it seems likely that he foresaw the possibility of a seat becoming available, and if he did not reach out and grab this opportunity, he certainly appears to have consciously taken steps to enhance his claims to it, and soon showed a strong commitment to this new development in his career.

In the short-term at least, Brooke's life-style was modified rather than fundamentally altered by his entry into parliament. Regular travel to Belfast became a familiar routine for the next four decades, though before the second world war not a single weekend was spent in the city. He had rarely visited it before 1929, and had in the early 1920s somewhat disparagingly referred to the 'hooligans' there with the implied contrast to his own more peaceful county. Visits to the Free State also ceased. Almost certainly he did not travel south between entering parliament and his retirement from the premiership. His son suggests that Sir Basil was unwilling to ask the southern authorities for the protection he would have required had he crossed the border.[79]

In the meantime he had a town-house built in Massey Avenue, adjacent to Stormont, in 1934. Such a substantial financial outlay was a clear demonstration of his commitment to a future political career. In addition, it clearly helped to lessen the disruption of his family life, and time spent travelling, and was done partly in response to his own growing ministerial responsibilities.[80] Perhaps the most obvious change for Brooke was the unaccustomed frequency with which he now began to speak on public platforms in Fermanagh and elsewhere. Thus when speaking at the various localities within the county he frequently prefaced his remarks by making nostalgic references to his last public appearance there, almost invariably in the early twenties, when appealing for volunteers to join the special constabulary. Further eulogistic comments as to the historically vital role of the force served to enhance his own credibility, and helped him establish a rapport with his audience. The latter was an important element. Such occasions were for years to come amongst his most potent means of taking the pulse of unionist attitudes and feelings.

Unionist party meetings provided the usual context for speeches as well as those gatherings of the Orange Order which he had previously been charged with neglecting. He had clearly not forgotten Cooper's earlier criticism. Thus, on one occasion, at Enniskillen whilst addressing a demonstration in 1930, he informed his audience that he had travelled the five-day journey from Norway in order to have the honour of leading his father's old district to the field and to welcome the prime minister, who shared the platform. However the delivery of such speeches to the brethren remained for the moment the extent of Brooke's increased involvement in the order. Though he consistently lavished it with praise, referring to it as the main prop against Bolshevism, the saving of Ulster, or praising its tolerance, and appealing for new membership, at this stage he did not himself take a leading part in the organisation.[81] He remained as he had been, the humble district master of Brookeborough district. He was later to become deputy grand master of Ireland. His political rise was to a considerable extent mirrored by his rise within the institution.

Prior to 1933–4 the content of his speeches was uncontroversial. They were characteristically well prepared, informal in tone, educational in content, direct in delivery, and conformed to a predictable pattern. In sincere and unpretentious phrases he sought to convince his audience that they should be unionist not from habit or family tradition alone, but from conviction. Drawing on the essentials of his own political faith he suggested that unionism was based partly on sentiment, 'ties and feelings' which were rooted in their common descent from British stock and their shared language and culture.[82] He suggested that because of this unionists felt an instinctive pride in the empire, which he claimed was the greatest power for peace and justice in the world, and identified with the national anthem and union jack. He also stressed that 'Ulster's welfare lay in her association with Great Britain'. Consideration of the material advantages of the union invariably led to a comparison between Northern Ireland and the Free State with regard to such aspects as social welfare provision, agricultural conditions and educational facilities. This might be followed by an appeal for party unity and organisational vigilance with independent unionists projected as a nationalist fifth column whose true objective was the dissolution of the union.[83] In the recent election, Brooke appears to have been genuinely perturbed by faults in the local electoral machinery, particularly lapses in registration, and the need to improve the means of getting 'out-voters' to the county's polling booths.[84]

The discussion of government policy was another recurring theme. In early speeches he often criticised the Labour administration, which he claimed had no coherent policy to counteract unemployment and had failed to introduce protection, a measure which he justified himself, partly on strategic grounds.[85] He took pride in the claim that 'In our towns are many industrial workers who to their credit instead of being mostly socialist as in England are as strong unionists as you or I'.[86] He consistently defended the policies of the Northern Ireland government, stressing its lack of culpability for deepening depression, the merits of its legislation, its even-handed treatment of the minority, and throughout emphasised his own personal loyalty to Craig.[87] Aware of the proclivities of his Fermanagh audience and following his own interests he spoke in particular detail on agricultural policy. In the early 1930s this was arousing much criticism in Fermanagh, sufficient to cause concern with regard to Unionist party unity. In the county council, resolutions were introduced calling for the abolition of the department. Beyond the chamber, experienced politicians like Devlin and Healy skilfully exploited the symptoms of unease, attacked Brooke's 'alluring promises', and jibed at what they alleged was his suddenly discovered concern for the small farmer. In December 1930, the *Fermanagh Times* wrote of their 'insidious . . . attempt to split unionist ranks'.[88] Against such skilled opponents Brooke moved with circumspection adapting an approach which he himself would have described in a favourite hunting phrase: 'never shoot until you see the whites of their eyes'.[89]

Thus, for example when in late 1930, the two Nationalist leaders organised a campaign culminating in a rally at Enniskillen to press for the introduction into Northern Ireland of an equivalent to the British agricultural credit act, Brooke was evasive initially, and excused his non-attendance on grounds of previous commitments. He meanwhile had been contacting the Ministries of Agriculture and Finance and received in return detailed written replies from Gordon and Pollock dealing with the issue, and armed with their cogent explanations spoke authoritatively at his next Orange Order engagement in Fermanagh in defence of the status quo. Healy himself described his speech as 'lengthy and able', and it was fervently praised in the local unionist press, for its alleged success in refuting nationalist criticism.[90] On a number of occasions, on major policy areas, Brooke sought illumination and advice from government ministers and officials, which he then used to defend policy more effectively.[91]

Brooke's regular speech-making in the country was not mirrored in the House of Commons. His parliamentary debut was singularly unimpressive. During his first three sessions he spoke just once and then, characteristically, he intervened briefly in defence of a controversial resolution by the prime minister which stated that the house should not be recalled for three weeks.[92] He failed to make a recognisable maiden speech and in fact never was a backbencher. In the early afternoon of 29 May 1929, he was sworn in as a member of parliament, and several hours later that same day moved the adjournment.[93] He was already junior whip, and assistant parliamentary secretary to the Ministry of Finance, a department in which he had very little interest. On his own admission this rapid elevation caused him 'one of the most embarrassing moments' of his life. Shortly after entering parliament and whilst still unfamiliar with commons' procedure, the opposition forced a division. Herbert Dixon, the chief whip, had meanwhile left for the Balmoral show leaving Brooke in charge. The latter, in panic and feeling 'most uncomfortable' had to consult the front bench in order to establish what his duties were.[94]

His initial parliamentary reticence may indicate an elementary caution on Sir Basil's part whilst he gradually accustomed himself to his new environment. Alternatively he may have felt the restraints of convention as whips do not usually take part in debates. It was in any case a temporary phase. From late 1932 onwards, his verbal contributions in the commons were increasingly frequent and assured if somewhat innocuous. Despite his links with the Ministry of Finance he spoke almost exclusively on agricultural issues, such as land drainage, marketing and abbatoir inspection, or matters relating specifically to Fermanagh.[95] Nonetheless, in a clash with Joseph Devlin in early 1932, he did illustrate that he could be an extremely effective parliamentary performer.

The immediate background to their confrontation lay in a threat by the British government in the spring of that year, to impose a 10 per cent duty on maize, under the terms of the import duties act. At this time approximately £2.5 million worth of the crop was imported into Northern Ireland yearly, representing one-third of total United Kingdom consumption.[96] It provided indispensable fodder supplies for local, small livestock farmers, and as a result, poultry, pig and cattle production faced possible ruin if the tariff was introduced. In response, the Northern Ireland government spear-headed a campaign to have maize placed on the 'free-list'. Brooke himself, played a central role which earned a public statement of gratitude from Craig. In mid-February he led a deputation of local farmers, millers and merchants to lobby Sir John Gilmore, minister of agriculture and fisheries, and was later personally involved in Pollock's negotiations with the Treasury.[97]

Subsequently in a public speech at Lisnaskea Brooke criticised both Devlin and Healy for their lack of interest in the campaign. He alleged that when asked to assist 'Mr Devlin paid no attention', and Mr Healy went 'to the Free State . . . [to] . . . talk for Fianna Fail'.[98] Two days later Devlin responded to this provocation, by defending his role in the house during the debate on account. He stated that he had not been invited to serve on the London delegation, claimed that the U.F.U. had written to thank him for his speeches at Westminster on the farmers' behalf, and flatly accused Brooke of having 'uttered a statement that was not only untrue but, to the honourable and gallant gentleman, was well known to be untrue'. Brooke sat in silence throughout, despite Devlin's challenge that 'if he had decency, [he] . . . would rise up . . . and apologise for the statement he made'.[99]

Exactly one week passed, before Sir Basil rose to make a personal statement to the house. He chose his words carefully. It was the first prepared and substantial speech of his parliamentary career. He defended his lack of response at the time by arguing that Devlin's onslaught had been procedurally out of order, and it was also, he claimed, so vague that he had needed to check Hansard 'to get the general drift of the attack'. A further critical factor was mentioned in earlier drafts of his speech, but expunged from the final text. It was that Devlin had given him only five minutes warning that his name would be mentioned, and that 'The absence of this usual courtesy placed . . . [him] . . . at a disadvantage at the time'. Certainly, Brooke used the intervening period extremely profitably. Having checked the Westminster debates, he now accused Devlin of not having spoken in any of the relevant debates there, and of voting only once. He followed this up by quoting from a letter in which the secretary of the U.F.U. stated emphatically that he was 'not aware of any steps taken by Messrs Devlin or Healy to influence the minister of agriculture or the members of the imperial parliament'.[100]

Devlin who had apparently been expecting Brooke to withdraw his original statement was taken totally by surprise. He attacked the latitude given to Brooke by the speaker, he protested that Sir Basil had been 'inspired by sinister influences beside him', and that 'an ordinary member . . . with ordinary intelligence would have risen when the incident occurred'. But in the end, he conceded that it was a 'well prepared brief, . . . he has really, I believe, made the best speech of his life in defence of his statement'. Finally he withdrew his original accusation with its 'implication on the honourable and gallant gentleman's honour'.[101]

Significantly, in the course of their confrontation Devlin described Brooke as one of the members of the cabinet council if not a member of the cabinet. The comment was premature rather than inaccurate as Sir Basil was already beginning to emerge as a probable successor to E.M. Archdale at the Ministry of Agriculture. By the standards of the house the rapidity of his political rise was exceptional, and occasioned some acrid observations from other members.

When the appointment was made Thomas Henderson bluntly asserted that he had 'got the job because he needed it'. Whilst a Nationalist M.P. proferred the opinion that it was a reward for speeches he made at this time which contained 'attacks on catholics'.[102] No single factor accounts for his success, but it was certainly not entirely surprising. Cahir Healy calculated that sixteen out of thirty-seven Unionist M.P.s in the late twenties had cabinet posts or were parliamentary secretaries. Northern Ireland was therefore he suggested a 'bureaucracy rather than democracy'.[103] At the same time, the lack of talent within the ranks of the party was a potent justification for the continuity of interwar cabinet membership.

Also despite Brooke's relative youth, few if any members had the range of experience or qualifications which he offered. He had the confidence and authority derived from his aristocratic background, public school education, and distinguished military service. To this he had added an impressive record of varied activity after his return from France. He had shown initiative, courage, and competence during the formation of the special constabulary. He had proven an effective county councillor, an enthusiastic member of the county Unionist Association and had risen to prominence within the Ulster Farmers' Union. If his interventions in the house had been rare they had also shown political skill. Contemporary assessments of Brooke also laid particular emphasis on those personal qualities which in the long term helped him to acquire such an enduring hold on Unionist affections. His lack of pomposity, simple habits and tastes, and modest, friendly manner erased social barriers.[104] His innate charm and wit, and skill as a raconteur contributed to his growing personal popularity.

In addition, Sir Basil had extremely useful contacts through family and friends, a fact which facilitated his entrée into the highest conclaves of the Unionist party, and later enabled him to treat British ministers and officials on equal terms. His connections at the highest social level were underlined when the duke of Gloucester honeymooned at Colebrooke in the early thirties.[105] Sir Wilfrid Spender records, later in the decade, the suggestion being mooted that Sir Basil's personal contacts in the services might be used to bring arms contracts to the province, normal government channels having apparently failed.[106] Within Northern Ireland, members of the family also held positions of influence. His cousin, Lieutenant General Brooke, was a leading political journalist with the *News Letter*.[107] His brother-in-law, Henry Mulholland, a close personal friend of James Craig, succeeded Hugh O'Neill as speaker of the new house, in May 1929. Brooke in turn succeeded Mulholland as assistant parliamentary secretary to the Ministry of Finance.[108]

Even before becoming an M.P., Brooke was well acquainted with key figures within the Unionist party leadership. In January 1929 Herbert Dixon, the chief whip, was his guest at Colebrooke for the annual Unionist gathering and spoke in glowing terms of his host and of the Brooke family. Crucially, Sir Basil had also enjoyed for some years a warm personal friendship with Craig which deepened over the next decade. He himself commented

It was a source of the greatest satisfaction to me that he and I had a very good relationship. Craig was a founding father of Ulster and a great man whom I admired immensely. Even before I entered parliament I had a close association with him . . . he was very interested in the work I was doing with the special constabulary, . . . kept in close touch at all times, and provided some impeccable advice, and actual assistance on many occasions.[109]

Brooke offered Craig his unwavering loyalty, an attitude sometimes tested but never shaken. It was a constant theme of his own and of Lady Brooke's public speeches through the 1920s and 30s. In 1933, reflecting back on his first four years in parliament, he took pride in having honoured his two deepest commitments to the Fermanagh electorate through his unstinting loyalty to the prime minister, and his efforts on behalf of the farmers.[110] Such sentiments did not pass unnoticed. One of Brooke's early speeches, in which he had stated 'I am an absolute supporter of Lord Craigavon', had the peculiar distinction of being extensively quoted by Lady Craig in her diary, including the audience's enthusiastic response.[111]

Brooke's high opinion of the prime minister, was reciprocated. Craig had not forgotten Sir Basil's 'eye-opening' performance as county commandant. He had a strong affection for Fermanagh and he deeply revered the force, having according to his wife 'always said that as long as he was P.M. there would be . . . "B" specials'.[112] In 1930, he unveiled a tablet at Enniskillen Courthouse in memory of those members who had lost their lives in the recent disturbances. The parade of constables he told Dawson Bates 'gladdened' his heart. In the course of his speech he paid special tribute to Brooke, whose company he had requested throughout the tour, stating, 'When the province was in danger no one could have acted more honourably or more to the satisfaction of his fellow citizens than his old friend and their neighbour'. On other occasions, he spoke of his qualities as a politician, 'one of the best M.P.s at Stormont'; there was 'no man . . . more energetic in looking after the interests of the people'.[113]

Given his knowledge of and interest in agriculture, Brooke must have appeared as an eminently suitable successor to Archdale. His selection conformed to the general pattern of Craig's past appointments which were based on ability, past services to unionism, and considerations of social and geographical balance. It may also be that there was a tacit understanding between the two men regarding Brooke's political future dating back to the spring of 1922, when Sir Basil's senatorial career was prematurely terminated in order that he could assume full-time constabulary duties. His son believes on the basis of conversations later with his father, that it was agreed at this time that Sir Basil would re-enter politics when the province had stabilised, with a possible implication even then that a cabinet post would be available. On similar evidence, he suggests that his father was conscious after he entered parliament, that Craig was grooming him for promotion, possibly even for the succession to the premiership. Whether or not such claims are justified, certainly Brooke was being 'groomed' for the Ministry of Agriculture from an early stage, and there is no doubt that his relationship with Craig became very close in the course of this decade, closer than that of other more senior colleagues.[114]

Both Brooke's willingness to serve and the competence which had characterised his actions in the early twenties were equally in evidence as gradually these ministerial responsibilities were devolved to him during 1932–3, and must have helped to seal his position on the front bench. He showed these qualities during the maize duty negotiations, and more demonstrably in the grander setting of the imperial conference at Ottawa. In April 1932, the Northern Ireland cabinet decided to press for the inclusion of representatives from the province on the British delegation. At an early stage in the negotiations the Ministry of Agriculture and Fisheries accepted that Craig should appoint two members to the Newton committee, which was to be composed of non-official agricultural interests, and was charged with the duty of submitting advice to its chairman, in London, as part of the preparations for the conference. Craig, apparently under the misapprehension that its members would be attending Ottawa, appointed Scott Robertson and Brooke.[115] When the position was clarified the former withdrew and Sir Basil became the province's sole representative. The choice was totally vindicated, as the friendships which he formed there proved valuable when the conference proper began. After his return from Canada, Scott Robertson informed Pollock that they had enabled Brooke and himself 'to secure an exceedingly close and effective contact with official and unofficial views, and to influence both in a manner which would not otherwise have been possible'.[116]

In late May, Craig asked Brooke to serve on the official Northern Ireland delegation to Ottawa, as an adviser on matters relating to agriculture, concluding, 'I sincerely trust you will make it convenient'. Brooke's reply was typical, stating 'needless to say . . . [I am] . . . only too glad and honoured to act in any way you may suggest. I very much appreciate the fact that you have selected me'.[117] The delegation was led by Pollock, Minister of Finance and veteran of the Irish convention, and included three civil servants and two other advisers with responsibility for linen and tariffs. Each travelled at Northern Ireland expense. Their precise status was somewhat anomalous as they were neither recognised as an independent delegation in their own right, nor as fully accredited members of the British team. Pollock was attached as an adviser to Walter Runciman's staff, and the civil servants were to be allowed any necessary contact with British official advisers before and during the conference. Thus any influence which they might collectively exercise would depend largely on informal contacts and the goodwill of British ministers and officials.[118]

The trip began inauspiciously. Brooke, with his wife and colleagues, travelled to Canada on the same ship as the Free State delegation. During the latter stages of the journey, the air was filled with patriotic songs, a tricolour flew from the mast-head, and they were finally greeted at Montreal by such a noisy demonstration staged by Irish emigrants that they thought it advisable to slip away unobtrusively.[119] More ominously when the conference eventually began, they found the British delegation aloof, and formed the opinion that the Canadian authorities had been instructed to show every consideration to the southern representatives, with the object of 'softening their attitude by unlimited kindness'.[120]

During the weeks that followed the Ulster delegation experienced perhaps more success than they had anticipated. Pollock was permitted to attend meetings of British ministers, and Scott Robertson sat on a number of high-powered agricultural committees, but, overall, it was hardly enough to justify the claim made by one of the civil servants present that 'Northern Ireland is having its fair share of a place in the sun'.[121] Lewis Gray, the group's adviser on linen, wrote to Craig 'The actual work of the conference has been confined to the delegates . . . [to the] cabinet ministers and officials'. He himself had 'not been allowed to take any part in the proceedings' . . . and would 'have very little to say to [his] . . . constituents in the trade' on his return. Likewise, Senator McCorkell found that there were not many 'demands on his time'.[122] Brooke experienced similar frustration. He later told the house that, 'as an adviser . . . [he was] . . . not in a position to influence the Ottawa conference' adding 'That was not my fault'.[123] During its proceedings he felt very seriously handicapped by the fact that his opposite numbers from the dominions were kept far better informed by their ministers than he was, and he also found British industrial representatives quite unsympathetic to agricultural interests.

Despite this colleagues certainly valued Sir Basil's own personal contribution in Ottawa. In one of his early reports, Pollock stated that Brooke had 'rendered invaluable service on agricultural questions, . . . I cannot think that we could have made a better selection to watch our interests'. He later reiterated these sentiments in parliament. Scott Robertson, an official not given to passing effusive compliments, was impressed by the informal social contacts which Brooke and Senator McCorkill established which he felt 'helped particularly with the United Kingdom representatives who, at first, were apt to fight shy'.[124] In this regard, Brooke was also to the forefront in setting up a small private bar in one of the bedrooms which was used to entertain dominion ministers, secretaries and officials. Robertson regarded this as 'of exceptional value'. He claimed that in its relaxed atmosphere the Northern Ireland representatives were able to explain the province's relationship to Great Britain, and to counteract Free State 'propaganda', so that 'in spite of our unofficial standing the Ulster delegation acquired a dominating position in the sympathy and regard of dominion delegates'. He concluded 'it will . . . be of permanent value'. He described both the Brookes and the McCorkells as 'a tremendous acquisition', their work was 'truly magnificent . . . so fundamental that I do feel that it should be put on record'.[125]

When it was over the delegates found it difficult to assess how productive attendance at the conference had been. The precise impact of the agreements was not easy to predict, and in any case they had gone as much for political as economic reasons. Scott Robertson felt that they had been more successful than he had expected.[126] Brooke, some months after his return, sought clarification from the Ministry of Agriculture regarding the real value of the conference, but expressed the opinion at the time that participation had been worthwhile. He told Craig that the delegation had successfully 'kept the position of Northern Ireland before them', and he valued particularly a commitment by Baldwin that 'no permanent arrangement with the south in respect of tariffs would be made without bringing our government into conference'.[127] However when he was faced with criticisms of the delegation in the house regarding its expense, lack of status and final irrelevance in the face of deepening agricultural depression, he found it difficult to defend. He suggested that some food prices had benefited from conference decisions, and pleaded for more time before passing judgement, but conceded that industry had inevitably got 'the lion's share of the Ottawa benefits'.[128]

Nevertheless, Sir Basil clearly enjoyed the conference, and personally benefited from it. He especially revelled in the relaxed social occasions, where as he told Craig he had the pleasure of 'meeting many old friends from the Canadian Corps days and making many new ones'. He described with some amusement how, owing to his contacts with the authorities, he was able to 'roar through the city in a police car with greater ease' than Baldwin or Chamberlain. He even found time for six days fishing with his wife in New Brunswick after the official proceedings had ended.[129] Overall, attendance heightened his sense of pride in empire, a theme given greater prominence in speeches after his return.[130] Speaking retrospectively he also felt that involvement had helped him in his future career. It 'proved a good training ground in a more rarified atmosphere of politics than I previously experienced, . . . [and] . . . I made many friends in high places which were to prove useful to me and to Ulster in the years to come'.[131] He might have added that it also strengthened his claims to become the next minister of agriculture. Certainly the process of delegating departmental responsibilities to him continued uninterrupted though not without some friction.

In November 1932, Healy jibed at the 'duet' of Brooke and Archdale, the latter had just described Sir Basil as 'the shining light of Ottawa'.[132] However, their relationship was not entirely harmonious. Sir Douglas Harkness recalls how Sir Edward became 'more reluctant to retire as the heir apparent become more apparent'. This was illustrated in the spring of 1933, when the agricultural marketing bill, the Department's most important inter-war piece of legislation, came before the House. Craig informed ministry officials in the gallery that he would arrange for Brooke to reply, and requested that they brief him on any points that arose in the debate. Harkness writes

Whether he had told Archdale of what he had done I do not know but after . . . [Sir Basil] . . . had spoken and replied . . . as we thought, Archdale rose to his feet and replied again, . . . including a reply to Brooke. So long as Archdale was minister he would exercise his full authority as minister and suffer no interloper.[133]

After many months of press speculation, the official announcement of Sir Edward's retirement came in November 1933.[134] He was in his eightieth year, and had almost completed a remarkable career. He had seen service with the Royal Navy at Gallipoli during the great Eastern crisis, and forty years later witnessed personally the Easter rising in Dublin. His first 'retirement' in 1903, had been followed by the humiliating loss of his seat by James Craig, now his prime minister. He had represented Fermanagh in both Northern Ireland and British parliaments. He had also chaired the standing committee of the U.U.C. after its formation in 1904, been a privy councillor from 1921, and a baronet from 1928, and meantime been made imperial grand master of the Orange Order. To Harkness who regarded him with 'unstinted affection and regard', he exemplified the first generation of Northern Ireland's politicians, men,

who by virtue of their position, intellect and character led the state, . . . natural leaders, . . . unambitious, . . . not party politicians in the ordinary sense.

their only concern to ensure 'that the new form of government worked'.[135]

When parliament opened in mid-December 1933, the local press reflected on the lack of change. The one exception was Brooke's anticipated move to the government benches, the displaced Archdale actually retaining a front bench position, but now below the gang-way.[136] Sir Basil recalled the occasion shortly before Christmas when Craig summoned him to his office and asked him to become minister of agriculture. Despite his growing experience and confidence, it was a daunting proposition. The rural economy was undergoing what the prime minister himself described as 'one of the greatest revolutions in the history of our country'. One newspaper described the position as the 'most difficult in the cabinet'.[137] Brooke remembers having felt 'troubled by such a degree of responsibility'. He continued

I shall not easily forget what Craig said to me that day, for I think his words are a key to the man.

He said

these schemes will be very tricky indeed and you will have to be very careful . . . you could bring the government down, . . . I could carry this one through myself but I want you to do it. You may be sure that I will be fully behind you in whatever you do and you can count on me for every support.

It was Brooke concludes 'a wonderful education for a young man'.[138] The news of his acceptance was reported in the press on 7 December.[139]

Craig's fears regarding the agricultural marketing schemes were genuine, but no more so than his promises to give Brooke his full support, a commitment which was soon to be tested. The latter had already emerged as a figure of controversy. At the time of his appointment, the *News Letter* observed that Sir Basil was best known in Fermanagh for his work on the county council and on county committees, but elsewhere for his speeches.[140] To mid-1933, these had continued to be predominantly educational and moderate, with occasional florid phrases decrying Irish unity, or attacking the Church of Rome. Since Ottawa, they had been mainly concerned with the merits of conference agreements and the predictable defence of agricultural policy.[141] Thereafter for a period of almost twelve months, they became controversial and emotive. This new phase began on 12 July 1933, in a speech made at Newtownbutler. Sandwiched between an appeal for Orange Order moderation and a discussion on agricultural imports, Brooke remarked that

a great number of protestants . . . employed Roman catholics . . . He felt that he could speak freely on this subject as he had not a Roman catholic about his own place . . . He would point out that the Roman catholics were endeavouring to get in everywhere and were out with all their force and might to destroy the power and constitution of Ulster. There was a definite plot to overpower the vote of unionists in the north. He would appeal to loyalists, therefore, wherever possible, to employ protestant lads and lassies (cheers) . . . Roman catholics . . . had got too many appointments for men who were really out to cut their throats if opportunity arose.

In conclusion he appealed for unity in the face of nationalist attempts to foment division.[142] One month later, at Londonderry (on 12 August), he stated that despite the controversy over his earlier remarks, he would not withdraw a single word. He proceeded to repeat much of what he had said earlier, adding that if nationalist infiltration into Northern Ireland from the south 'were allowed to continue unchecked . . . it . . . would result in their becoming in a few years so numerous that they would be able to vote Ulster into the Free State'. Once more he advised loyalists if possible to employ protestant boys and girls, and gave dire warnings that if protestants 'were put in the power of the Free State . . . not only would they be condemned to death, but might be . . . drawn and quartered'. He then appealed for unionist unity, referring to

Fermanagh as 'the gate of Ulster'. On this occasion, he stressed in conclusion that he was not speaking from the religious point of view but because of his conviction that 'the vast majority of Roman catholics in Ireland were disloyal'.[143]

Speaking in Enniskillen again in October, he returned to these themes, and affirmed that his comments were 'not a political stunt as some say, . . . he believed from the bottom of his heart all he said'. He then sought to justify his remarks by claiming that the number of protestants employed by Roman catholics in the town, could be counted on one's fingers. Such statements continued into the new year, and after his promotion to the front bench. Thus, on 19 March 1934, again in Londonderry he stated categorically that he had 'not lost a night's sleep' over any of his earlier speeches. He had spoken 'after careful consideration . . . I recommend people not to employ catholics . . . their religion is so politically minded, . . . [they are] . . . out to destroy us as a body'.[144]

From the outset this series of speeches by Brooke aroused controversy. Within the county, the *Fermanagh Times* consistently endorsed them. It described his first such statement as 'a clear outline of Unionist policy and . . . very welcome . . . exposure of nationalist tactics'.[145] In contrast, it prompted the Reverend W. J. Mitchell, a Church of Ireland rector from County Cavan, publicly to protest that 'many Free State protestants were repelled by . . . [Brooke's] . . . excited tone', and to draw attention to the fact that the local protestant population was dependent upon Roman catholic employees.[146] Captain T. T. Verschoyle, a large protestant landowner from Fermanagh, in August 1933, condemned one of Brooke's later speeches as 'inconsistent with the right of civil and religious liberty', and making no pretence 'to reconcile . . . protestantism and christianity'. He concluded, 'He who sows the wind will reap the whirlwind, . . . it remains to be seen whether the Colebrooke Hitler will receive a well-merited rebuke from a responsible member of the government'.[147]

No such rebuke was forthcoming. In parliament however, Healy and other Nationalist leaders sought to force the prime minister to define the government's position with regard to the growing controversy. In so doing they helped focus the attention of the province on these speeches. Much of the initial criticism had come from a number of local unionists from the west of the province. After Verschoyle's attack, the *Irish News* gave greatly increased coverage to Brooke's comments, thereafter referring to him as 'Captain Boycott Brooke' and challenging him to reply to the attack. But it also with justification, drew attention to under-reporting of his remarks by the Belfast unionist press, stating that the latter 'pass his utterances by without the comment we should like to see'.[148]

Healy first raised the question in the Commons, slightly ambiguously, in mid-October 1933, when he alleged that 'regrettable utterances . . . outside this house around about 12 July' had embittered feelings and so helped cause sectarian murders in Belfast, during the following months.[149] On 20 March 1934, the day following Sir Basil's controversial remarks in Londonderry, he directly challenged Craig. After referring to Brooke's speeches as 'one of the most disgraceful episodes in the history of this institution', he asked whether the latter was 'speaking on his own account . . . or whether he represented the

considered policy of the government'.[150] Other opposition members suggested
that the speeches violated the constitution, and one admonished the front
bench with the remark, 'if you want peace in this community you will have to
stop the spirit of hatred and bitterness and rancour for the purpose of leading
the mob'.[151]

Brooke spoke little beyond reiterating earlier claims that 100 per cent of
Roman catholics were nationalist, and that the Nationalist party was out to
destroy Ulster. He repeated the claim that he was 'not questioning any person's
method of worshipping his God'.[152] Craig's intervention in the debate served to
heighten the controversy. He stated that Brooke 'spoke as a member of his
majesty's government'. He continued

He spoke entirely on his own when he made the speech, . . . but there is not one of my
colleagues who does not entirely agree with him, and I would not ask him to withdraw
one word . . . I do not think that a single word said . . . [by Brooke] . . . could cause any
offence to those who are loyal to the constitution of Northern Ireland.

Using imagery drawn from Fermanagh's past, he concluded by warning of the
dangers of the south 'sending swallows across the border'.[153] The *Fermanagh
Times* commented 'The whole country will rejoice at the strong and frank
attitude taken up by the prime minister . . . and not one of his colleagues did
not agree'.[154]

On 24 April, the issue was once more forced upon the attention of parliament. Healy moved a motion stating that

in the opinion of the house the campaign against the employment of catholics promulgated by the minister of agriculture, and expressly sanctioned by the prime minister, is a
grave violation of the rights and liberties of the minority.

He bitterly attacked Brooke, referring to him as 'the Lisnaskea Cromwell
whose speeches were not merely anti-catholic but anti-christian, . . . stirring up
sectarian and political bias, . . . in common with others I did not reckon on the
degree of anti-catholic hate that seems to well up in him periodically like a
spring'. He warned the front bench that in its treatment of the minority it was
'moulding a policy that may soon drive the nationalists out of this house
altogether'.[155] Colleagues joined in condemning the alleged government campaign for a boycott of catholics.

Craig countered by introducing a motion of his own which stated that the

employment of disloyalists entering Northern Ireland is prejudicial not only to the
interests of law and order and the safety of the state, but also to the prior claims of loyal
Ulster-born citizens seeking employment.[156]

The cross-border infiltration that this implied was strongly denied by Nationalist members in the heated debate which followed. They also attacked the use
of the term 'disloyalist', as Brooke's original statements were not made against
'disloyalists' but against 'catholic Irishmen bred and born in the six counties'.[157]

Brooke rose near the end of the debate. During the previous few days,
leading Fermanagh unionists had provided him with material that he might use.
Eames, secretary of the county association, had checked through his recent
speeches as reported in the *Fermanagh Times*, and citing times and places
reassured him that 'it was to political creed that you referred, not religion'. He
also enclosed details of the number of protestants employed by Roman

catholics in Enniskillen. Ritchie, editor of the *Fermanagh Times*, provided him with a resumé of Healy's allegedly inconsistent political career.[158] Brooke now wove these points into his comments. He stated that he had 'never approached the problem from a religious point of view'. He claimed that catholic employers in Enniskillen had given employment to just three protestant workers. He surveyed critically Healy's record of public service. His conclusion, however, appears to derive from no other source than his own innermost convictions at the time. He said

There is . . . a catholic political party which ranges from what I might call benevolent nationalism, to what I might call the extreme of the extreme, . . . but the one plank in its platform is the destruction of Ulster, as a unit and as a constitution . . . That is the policy and it simply varies in method . . . Anyone who is out to break up . . . [the] . . . constitution . . . established by Great Britain is to my mind disloyal . . . I shall . . . use all my energies and whatever powers I possess to defeat the aims of those who are out to destroy the constitution of Ulster, be they protestants or Roman catholics.[159]

At 6.30 p.m. the debate was adjourned without a division.

This series of speeches made by Brooke echoed through the rest of his long career. He himself acknowledged that nothing else that he ever said or wrote imprinted itself so indelibly in the popular memory. No single factor would appear to acount for their timing or their content. It may well be that he failed to anticipate the degree of criticism and controversy that his original comments in July 1933, would arouse. The sentiments that he expressed could almost be regarded as part of the traditional rhetoric of such unionist gatherings in Fermanagh. An anthology could be produced of similar comments made particularly in the early 1930s by local party leaders and politicians including his parliamentary colleague E. M. Archdale. In 1934, Eames, the association secretary, stated, 'Protestant employers should employ those of their own faith only, catholic workers were not there as workers but as spies'.[160] At the time, Brooke's July speech was given modest though entirely favourable coverage in the *Fermanagh Times*, being superseded in both its editorial and its reports of the Orange demonstrations, by Archdale's slightly more restrained utterances at Irvinestown.[161] Having raised these issues, Sir Basil's subsequent statements became to an extent self-perpetuating, and made in reply to criticisms of the original remarks. Thus, his August speech was essentially a reply to the Reverend W. J. Mitchell. In Enniskillen, in October, he responded to the criticisms of Cahir Healy and Captain Verschoyle. Most of his later comments were made in response to Nationalist M.P.s during commons debates in the spring of 1934. However these debates were themselves provoked mainly by Brooke's earlier speeches, particularly his Londonderry speech in late March. After the heated exchanges on Healy's motion, the series ended.

Throughout, the essential content of Brooke's controversial remarks changed little. He simply reiterated his claim that most Roman catholics were disloyal; the precise percentage might vary but that their constant objective was to destroy the state by one means or another, and that they ought not therefore to be given employment by protestants. He attempted to justify his initial remarks rather than amend them, apart from professing more prominently later that his concern was with the political objectives of the minority, and not their religious doctrines or practices.

Allegations were made at the time that the speeches were made to win favour with Craig and to procure promotion. One M.P. stated bluntly,

Why he got the job was because he did so well at these public meetings, and in these attacks he made on Roman catholics. That is why the cabinet made him minister of agriculture . . . I could quite understand . . . [him] . . . making these speeches when he was in the running.[162]

Healy also suggested that Brooke 'was not slow to take the hint . . . The more intolerant the policy the better apparently it would please the prime minister'.[163] Such views would appear to be superficial. Both the content and frequency of the speeches would suggest that they sprang more from his political convictions at this time rather than political calculation. In any case, it seems virtually certain that, long before July 1933, Brooke had established his claim to be the next minister of agriculture, and that the appointment awaited only Archdale's resignation. This had probably been the situation at least from the end of the Ottawa conference, possibly much earlier, and it is confirmed by the continuing delegation of departmental responsibilities to him. When Dr James S. Gordon was retiring in mid-1933, Spender even suggested that Sir Edward's successor might be consulted regarding his replacement as permanent secretary, though Craig thought this course of action 'inopportune'.[164] Also from the moment that his controversial speeches began he was being referred to in the nationalist press, as Archdale's very probable successor.[165]

In addition, however much Sir James and his cabinet may have felt anxiety with regard to disloyalist infiltration, it is not clear that Brooke's speeches would have met with the former's approval. Whilst the prime minister proved willing to support Sir Basil in the house, he did nonetheless, make it clear in the March debate that the latter was speaking 'entirely on his own when he made the speech'. Though he also stated that his colleagues would 'entirely agree'[166] with what Brooke had said, no-one else from the front bench spoke on Sir Basil's behalf either during the interchanges that followed or on 24 April. Craig's motion on the latter occasion noticeably avoided using the phrase 'Roman catholic', a phrase repeatedly used by Brooke, but substituted the term 'disloyalist'. This prompted one Nationalist member to state, 'What it means is that the government, having regard to the terms of the 1920 act, are afraid to stand over the declarations of the minister of agriculture . . . They are afraid to use the word catholic'.[167] Brooke many years later expressed regret that he had not used the term 'disloyalist' himself.[168] The *Irish News* commented particularly after the April debate on the conciliatory nature of Craig's performance, that he had not tried to justify the catholic boycott, and had 'emphasised more than once his desire to deal justly by all'. This is borne out further by a speech made in Belfast by Sir James, on 27 April, which referred to the extent that his opponents had 'played the game', both in the house and beyond it, over the preceding twelve or thirteen years.[169]

Craig may have also been apprehensive about the timing of Brooke's speeches. From mid-1932, the cabinet had been increasingly concerned at the threat to law and order posed by the increasing levels of tension within the province. The eucharistic conference was reported to have caused 'excitement amounting almost to frenzy . . . along the border'. The election of a Fianna Fail government aggravated the situation. Victory celebrations sparked off riots in

Enniskillen,[170] whilst one of Healy's correspondents reflected on 'De Valera's mad policy' which 'estranged' the north: 'what is a border today will be a frontier tomorrow'.[171] In addition, Dawson Bates predicted in June 1932 that deepening depression would cause 'a large body of the population [to be] . . . driven to desperation by poverty and hunger, 'and that rural distress would far exceed the capacity of the boards of guardians to provide relief'.[172] In response to these pressures the cabinet immediately agreed to introduce emergency security measures, which included the calling out of the 'B' specials. In these volatile circumstances Craig warned his colleagues that they should 'avoid provocative actions', and gave an undertaking that he would 'see the press to calm their comments'.[173] This may help account for the initial under-reporting of Brooke's speeches in the Belfast unionist press.

Nothing that happened subsequently could have justified any change of mind on Sir James's part, regarding the need for those in positions of influence to exercise caution. In the twelve months after his appeal, the government's security measures were tightened rather than relaxed.[174] It is interesting also to note the *Irish News* comment on the 12 July speeches of 1933, that 'almost as if by general consent, the customary attacks on popery were shorn of their usual venomous character'.[175] Whatever the reason for this, the prime minister's admonitions [in cabinet] would appear to have been justified. After the serious riots in Belfast, in 1935, the city coroner commented that those involved were influenced almost entirely by the public speeches of men in high and responsible positions.[176]

The context of rural distress was almost certainly an important factor in determining the timing of Brooke's speeches. Even in 1929, the economist, Maynard Keynes, had described the low level of income and living standards of Northern Ireland's small farmers as 'almost unbelievable'.[177] Subsequently prices had fallen and the depression intensified. The Ottawa agreements totally failed to provide significant relief, despite Brooke's hopes and promises. He himself conceded, amidst a chorus of Commons' criticism, that the conference had failed to bring the 'millenium, . . . such a colossal slump . . . [was] . . . not anticipated', and he reflected on the 'considerable blame . . . [which had] . . . fallen upon . . . [his own] . . . shoulders'.[178]

In January 1933, the U.F.U. executive committee stated that the agricultural industry was on the point of collapse. In Fermanagh, as elsewhere, petitions, deputations and mass meetings were organised to urge upon the government the need to reduce rents and rates and, above all, abolish land annuities.[179] Craig had, some months earlier, forseen the probable emergence of the latter demand. He had written to Pollock, then still in Ottawa:

What perturbs me more than anything else at the moment is the ruthless campaign proceeding in the Free State by De Valera and his cabinet, which may resolve itself into purchasing the support of the farming community by cancelling the payment of annuities, in which case I dread the effect on our people who in such an event would be spurred on by the nationalists to obtain similar forgiveness.[180]

His fears proved well-founded. The Fianna Fail government did indeed repudiate the land annuity payments, and certainly in Fermanagh Nationalist leaders took a leading role in the agitation to achieve abolition in the north. Repeatedly during the spring of 1933, the *Fermanagh Times* drew attention to what they termed 'the insidious methods' used by their opponents of 'dividing and splitting up' unionists, through 'the guise of land annuity meetings and Farmers Union meetings'. It reported that 'well meaning unionists . . . [were being] . . . completely hood-winked'.[181] These meetings were strongly critical of the Unionist leadership and of Brooke himself. Though the Northern Ireland government might give grants, provide cheap loans or reduce rates, its slender financial means and powers precluded any possibility of abolishing annuity payments. Brooke defended this policy describing even a moratorium as one of the very greatest evils, and appealing to Orangemen not to join the agitation.[182]

These class strains paralleled those of the late-nineteenth century and similarly threatened unionist unity. The *News Letter* expressed the view that no department of the government had been singled out for more unfair criticism than the Ministry of Agriculture.[183] In the house, Beattie gave dire warnings that a new party would emerge due to 'the apathy of the old party to the agricultural interests of this country'. In Fermanagh, the reality of these political dangers was underlined when, in June 1933, the party lost the hitherto safe local government division of Lisnaskea, a village once described by Brooke as the 'capital town' of his constituency.[184] Such propitious circumstances the county's nationalists had traditionally exploited by supporting independent parliamentary candidates. At this time, there was speculation that a farmer's representative might be selected to stand for one of the Unionist-held Fermanagh seats in the forthcoming Stormont election. A relatively small defection by the party's supporters would have been sufficient to precipitate defeat.

This was the immediate context for Brooke's first controversial speech in July 1933. His advice not to employ Roman catholics was immediately prefaced by comments on the 'slackening of discipline' at Lisnaskea and nationalist success in fomenting internal unionist dissension. His extreme comments might be regarded in part as a means of reassuring his audience regarding his own loyalty against the background of so much government criticism, and also as an attempt to counteract the divisive class pressures which were straining unionist unity, by reminding audiences of the insidious external threat. The *Fermanagh Times* lauded his exposure of nationalist tactics. During the run-up to the election, Sir Basil proceeded to make a number of further bitter attacks on independents, describing them as 'a trap for fools', 'semi-protestants and semi-loyalists', and offering on one occasion a slogan 'no truck with traitors and stand united'.[185] In the end he was himself returned unopposed, along with all other members of the cabinet which he now joined.[186]

Brooke's speeches also constantly reiterated warnings of a definite plot to overturn the unionist majority in the north, and vote the six counties into the Free State. He spoke of Roman catholics 'getting in everywhere', of their 'infiltration', and 'peaceful penetration', all of which he used to justify his advice to employ 'protestant lads and lasses'.[187] In Fermanagh, unionist concern over such issues became acute from the moment when the catholic community in the county was able to translate its numerical superiority into political power. Though after partition electoral boundaries had been devised to counteract the party's numerical weakness, such arrangements could easily be upset. This is reflected, at least partly, in the lack of local government housing built in the county by Unionist councils, once described by Healy as a 'liquidating policy'.[188] Craig touched a sensitive chord in the county, when he referred during the Common's debate to the 'swallows', as a reminder of how easily an apparently safe majority might be overturned by infiltration.[189] Such fears were no doubt heightened in the context of rural depression. At such times employment issues were more divisive, and more farms were likely to change hands. During previous distress Falls had written to Craig, describing how the best class of farmers were selling out and 'the less desirable . . . financed from some unknown source . . . [were] . . . buying farms offered for sale'. On 12 July 1933, E. M. Archdale had declared himself to be a 'bigot' on the issue of catholics buying protestant property.[190]

Brooke justified the conclusions expressed in his speeches at this time partly by focusing attention on the actions of local nationalists in supporting independents and their alleged job discrimination against protestants, and also by citing the aggressive statements of their leadership north and south. In October 1933, he claimed that Cahir Healy had publicly boasted that he 'could convert the unionist majority in Fermanagh into a nationalist majority' and that this had directly prompted him to make his speeches in July and August. Later he attacked Healy's schemes of 'peaceful penetration'.[191] Though Brooke's speeches throughout these years were frequently prompted by the comments of political opponents it is not improbable that this explanation was more of an attempted counter-attack in response to Healy's earlier slightly veiled accusation that Sir Basil's speeches had helped cause murder in Belfast. The former denied ever having used the phrase but accepted that he would 'do . . . [his] . . . best to bring Ulster into a United Ireland, by the power of the vote or by peaceful penetration, . . . I see no objection to it'.[192] The evidence would suggest that Brooke's statements were, as he said, considered statements, rooted in personal conviction rather than spontaneous responses to external provocation. This is suggested by the notes for his October speech, which read 'Religion is for clergy, politics is for your member. Warning when I started the specials, warn you now, no political stunt, for you to decide and act'.[193]

There is other evidence to this effect. Brooke's views may have been influenced by earlier correspondence contained in his private papers, dated 21 October 1932, and 6 June 1933, which detailed the demographic trends for the main religious denominations in Ireland from 1871 to the 1926 census.[194] This indicated that uniquely amongst the six counties the catholic proportion of the population in Fermanagh had increased, though very marginally. Southern infiltration could be used to provide at least a partial explanation. Ritchie reassured Brooke, in April 1934, that Healy's 'anger' at the exposure of his schemes was for 'obvious' reasons:

It is computed that in the parliamentary constituency of Fermanagh and Tyrone, there are 12–15,000 farm labourers and others imported . . . from the Free State . . ., engaged . . . by protestant employers, . . . [without them] . . . there would be a large unionist majority . . . it is a curious and anomalous position.[195]

Such claims had long been made by local party members and were used to justify the viewpoint that, despite their minority position, Fermanagh really was a unionist county.

Local concern with the whole issue of catholic employment was also indicated by a circular from this period, dated 10 August 1932, and distributed by the Fermanagh intelligence branch of the Ulster special constabulary. It referred to a great danger that was threatening Ulster due to 'peaceful penetration' schemes. As evidence it quoted from a document said to have been taken from the pocket of a drunken man at Ardress. This was alleged to have been circularised by the Irish Foresters and stated that it was the duty of all members not to employ protestants. It stressed the value of catholics gaining employment in such sectors as labour exchanges, post offices, and railways, 'which would put us in a position to shake . . . protestantism to the foundations'. The constabulary officials advised readers

should you represent unionist interests in any district or county council or in any other public capacity, . . . [we] . . . would impress upon you the vital necessity of seeing that unionists of sound standing are established in all places. It is only by playing the rebels at their own game that we can hope to succeed.[196]

Whether Brooke was influenced by such a circular is impossible to establish, but he almost certainly read it, as it is preserved amongst his private papers, and from his public statements he would clearly have shared the sentiments it expressed. In making his controversial speeches, he himself felt that he was 'only performing his duty'.[197]

Unionist concern over the issues raised in Brooke's speeches was manifestly not unique either to Fermanagh or Sir Basil himself and never had been. Sir Ernest Clark, assistant under-secretary in Northern Ireland and the state's self-professed 'John the Baptist', realised within days of his arrival in Belfast that, when employing local people, he must 'take protestants' as to do otherwise 'would be fatal to any chance of success'.[198] An important reason given for holding a census in 1926 was to identify the general trend of catholic population.[199] However, fears regarding both catholic employment and total numbers appear to have been especially strong in the early 30s. This is reflected in the tone of many public speeches made by leading unionists at this time and not just those of Brooke. Particularly in these years, Sir Wilfrid Spender received many queries regarding religious proportions in the civil service and in schools.[200] In May 1932, the issue of 'infiltration' from the south was reviewed at a meeting of the Ulster Unionist parliamentary party, and in April 1934, it was considered by the cabinet.[201] Ministers subsequently agreed to raise the residence qualification for unemployment assistance claimants, and discussed the creation of a register for all who entered the province, as well as whether Northern Ireland government voters should be made to affirm loyalty to the king.[202]

During the commons debates, in early 1934, News Letter editorials, even if belatedly, supported Brooke's statements. The paper said of him in December 1933, 'he has already shown that he has the courage of his convictions'.[203] Thus, however uneasy some may have felt about the timing and bluntness of Brooke's speeches, clearly his worries were widely shared at the highest level. The impact of depression, the eucharistic conference, the elections north and south, and the statements and policy of De Valera all contributed to this alarmist atmosphere. In fact, though the number of Roman catholics in Northern Ireland rose by almost 8,000 between the 1926 and 1937 censuses, their proportion of the total population remained stable, and in Fermanagh, it actually fell.[204]

During the commons debates in April 1934, Brooke gave one additional explanation for his contentious remarks. He stated 'I was informed . . . that a scheme was afoot whereby my oldest son was to be kidnapped . . . Therefore, I took every precaution . . . and got rid of every man in my place who I thought might betray me'.[205] Later, this threat was used to explain and justify not only his statement that he had 'not a Roman catholic about his own place', but also to project his advice about employing protestants as a spontaneous outburst made under this intense strain.[206]

Such an explanation is inadequate. The kidnap threat to Julian was made in 1922, whilst his controversial statements began eleven years later, in a series delivered and defended over a ten-month period. Nonetheless, responding to criticism after his retirement, he reflected back on these years and passed a remark which merits consideration. He said 'What they forget is that I lived through one of the most terrible times in this county. Therefore, I am not as ecumenical as the others'.[207] It is impossible to doubt the formative significance of the war period and of the early 1920s, in the development of Brooke's political perception. In 1929, he admitted to a Lisnaskea audience that until the war, he was 'not interested in politics' but that 'since then his ideas had changed. Politics was a necessity of life'.[208] This process of change began in 1916. In the spring of that year he had written from the western front to say that home rule would be preferable to civil war. Some weeks later, whilst he was at home on leave at Colebrooke, the Easter rising occurred. He described his reaction:

I regarded it as treachery. I felt it personally, to the extent that I had been fighting since 1914 . . . This was a stab in the back not only for England but for me personally . . . I refused to describe myself as an Irishman thereafter.[209]

Bitterness and disillusion soon deepened after his permanent return to Ireland, caused no doubt in part by his direct experiences in the special constabulary, but also by the unwillingness of Irish nationalists to accept the government of Ireland act and the treaty as a final solution. The real scars from these years were not physical, not a single shot was fired at him as county commandant, but psychological. When he addressed his first 12 July Orange demonstration in 1921, days after the truce, his speech was moderate, constructive and optimistic. He stated that the special constabulary was

not formed to coerce anyone but simply to defend us from those who have called us the enemies of Ireland because our ideals happen to differ from theirs. All we want is to be left alone.

Further Sinn Fein violence, he suggested would 'drive the wedge in further between north and south'.

He challenged the south to operate the 1920 act and

show that they can govern justly . . . and not consider us in the north their enemies because we differ from them. They must prove to us beyond any measure of doubt that they are willing to work with us for the good of Ireland and not endeavour to coerce us. They must face the fact that it will take time to heal the wounds.

In conclusion, he expressed his hope for 'an honourable settlement' and that 'within the next few days the healing process will begin whereby all Irishmen can unite for the good of their country'.[210] Several weeks later he strongly defended the appointment of catholic officials at the Ministry of Agriculture, stating,

> it did not matter what his religion was so long as he was a good man and knew his job, . . . how could they expect fair treatment not only in Ulster but in other parts of the country if they tried to block the appointments that Mr Archdale had made.[211]

In late 1921, he was hopeful that he might soon be able to resign from his post as county commandant, as it was his expectation that the 'troubles'[212] were over.

However, the treaty negotiations were not the prelude to peace but to a crescendo of violence which served to imprint feelings of fear, hatred, and distrust throughout the north. During these months, Stephen Tallents noted in border areas, even amongst moderate unionists, a willingness to fight rather than be transferred to the south.[213] When in July 1922, Brooke addressed his second orange demonstration, this time as a full-time constabulary officer, his mood had changed. Referring to his optimistic statements twelve months before, he said, 'these hopes were shattered'. He reviewed the record of 'dastardly crimes' by Sinn Fein, and spoke of the 'bitterness and hatred turned against Ulster'. He declared defiantly that 'they were not going to be coerced . . . Sinn Fein instead of bringing Ulster closer to Ireland was dividing them further and further apart'.[214]

The peaceful resolution of the boundary question in 1925 appears to have restored for a time Brooke's hopes for the future. The resolution which he then introduced into the county council suggested that the agreement had removed many of the difficulties which had hitherto 'prevented men of different shades of opinion from working together for the common good of the county'.[215] Clearly by 1933–4, his earlier mood of despondency had returned and was no doubt reinforced by the recent formation of a Fianna Fail government in the Free State. A sense of disillusionment reverberates through his most controversial speeches in this period. 'Loyalists', he suggested, 'were too often on the defensive and could legitimately feel bitter at constant nationalist efforts to get them into the south'.[216] In the house he accused the opposition of having 'taken no active part in the corporate life of this country, . . . surely we unionists . . . who believe in the constitution of Ulster naturally feel sore and pained'. He told Healy that 'If the honourable gentleman's people . . . would do their share . . . it might be a different question'. When he was criticised on the grounds that his remarks were 'making catholics bitter', his reply was that he did not believe that 'if loyalists remained silent, large numbers of . . . [them] . . . would become loyal citizens', and that he wished he could believe it. In essence, he regarded the minority as being irrevocably committed to the ending of the partition: 'There is a catholic political party which ranges from . . . benevolent nationalism to the extreme of the extreme . . . but the one plank in their platform is the destruction of Ulster'.[217]

Nationalist unwillingness to accept the legitimacy of the Northern Ireland state appears to have been particularly resilient within his own county. One member of that party, the Reverend J. McShane, described a visit by an *Irish News* reporter, in the mid-30s, to the west of the province, and how the latter had expressed great surprise that the partition issue was as much alive in Fermanagh today as if it had happened only a few weeks ago. This attitude he regarded as a thing to be deplored.

The priest did not agree, stating that he 'dreaded the development of a certain mentality prepared to acquiesce in the status quo', because if such emerged, 'the permanence of partition would be assured, . . . time is definitely not on our side'.[218]

From the spring of 1934 Brooke's speeches reverted to their earlier predominantly educational content, explaining and defending government policy, calling for party unity and organisational vigilance and occasionally, in temperate terms, referring to the threat from the south. Nonetheless he had by then acquired a reputation. When in early 1934, a cottage within the grounds of Stormont was allocated to a catholic ex-serviceman said to have been personally known to the prince of wales, Joseph Davison, who had in August 1933 advised protestants only to employ protestants, and who was grand master of the Orange Order in Belfast, wrote to Brooke, a junior minister and mere district master, to protest that the institution could not stand over the decision.[219] As far as his political opponents are concerned, the *Fermanagh Times* was probably correct when it described him as 'the best hated member of the Ulster government by the patriots of the Free State, and the nationalists of Northern Ireland'.[220]

Popular recollection of his contentious remarks lingered on through the years, partly because he had repeated them so often in these months, and partly because of Healy's skill in raising them in parliament and so forcing a response from the government. In addition, their propaganda value to his critics was increased as his political career blossomed. Within days of his reaching the premiership his controversial speeches were once more raised during debate in the House of Commons. They were as he himself appreciated 'the only lasting memory' from this period.[221] His son continued to reflect on how 'extraordinary' it was that because of these remarks 'anti-unionists should have . . . condemned him' thereafter.[222] Certainly the collective memory has been selective, his moderate statements were ignored or soon forgotten. It would however, be unfair to presume that his political assumptions remain unaltered. Many years later, and in his own words 'older and wiser',[223] he expressed regret that these controversial comments had been made. Such rhetoric was a response to a particular situation and it should not be deduced that the distrust of the minority that he then expressed proved as enduring as its place in popular recollection.

CHAPTER V

Peacetime Minister of Agriculture
(1933–39)

(1) The Marketing Legislation

No government post could have better suited Brooke's temperament, experience or interests than his appointment as minister of agriculture, the first of two junior cabinet positions which he held before becoming premier. Farming was for him an enduring passion. Even when serving on the western front it was a frequently recurring topic in letters home to his family. One of his strongest commitments on becoming an M.P. had been to defend the farmer's interest. Such a commitment acquired greater urgency in the context of deepening rural depression caused by factors apparently remote from his Fermanagh audience, such as competitive currency devaluation in Europe, industrial recession and glutted world food markets. He enjoyed his new position, he wrote later, 'far more than if I had been minister of finance', and indeed when being considered for the latter in 1941, he indicated a clear lack of interest.[1] At agriculture there was less administrative routine and some opportunity, however circumscribed, for a creative and positive response to the immense problems of rural Ulster. To the end of his tenure he genuinely relished the immediate contact with the countryside which the position permitted.

Brooke was firmly convinced of the significance of his department, due to 'the importance of agriculture in the economic life'[2] of the province, and of the merits of its policies. Certainly agriculture remained the backbone of the Northern Ireland economy. It was its largest and most extensive single industry, whether judged by size of labour force, volume and value of output and exports, scope and diversity of operations or its overall influence on the province's social and political life. Also, the establishment of a responsible regional government department certainly did provide the opportunity to develop a distinct policy geared to Northern Ireland's particular needs.

Local farming was small scale on under-mechanised mixed farms of one-third the average size in Great Britain. It was characterised by an acute scarcity of capital, inadequate investment, backward production, low living standards, and an obsolete system of marketing; all of which were compounded by high transport costs to mainland markets. In the 1920s the average number of workers per 100 acres was twice that found in England and Wales, and after

91

making allowance for production costs, the average return to a small farmer was at best a labourer's wage. These circumstances were aggravated by the effects of war which induced complacency amongst local producers. During hostilities they received high prices almost regardless of quality, freshness and presentation. After its conclusion the old primary production system of Ulster could not cope with the new competing imports of fresh, well-packaged and expertly-marketed produce which began to appear on the British market. With so many unorganised though politically influential independent owner-occupiers, some cooperation, or bulk method of marketing, based on the standardisation of high quality produce had become essential. Reports in the 1920s and early 30s confirmed that the initiative would necessarily have to come from the government.[3]

There were, however, immense difficulties in devising a successful regional policy. There was the context of pre-Keynesian ideology which favoured a reliance on free-market forces, and in any case the effectiveness of increased government spending would have been restricted by Northern Ireland's high propensity to import. The province was not a separate economy, but 'an undifferentiated part of a single economic system embracing the whole United Kingdom'.[4] Its government had restricted powers and such slender financial means that it had very little revenue for positive economic action. The negative aspect of devolution was the danger of remoteness from the centre of power and influence and certainly until the late 1930s Northern Ireland was treated less generously by the imperial government than other depressed areas.[5] Nonetheless during the previous decade the local administration had been more interventionist than Westminster, energetically building up a marketing structure aimed at enhancing the quality, reputation and price of Northern Ireland's agricultural exports. However, any radical initiative had necessarily to await changes in imperial fiscal and trading policy, some of which Brooke had suggested in his earlier criticisms of the Labour government.

Brooke was fortunate in that his appointment as minister was closely preceded by Britain's abandonment of free-trade and laissez-faire, some relaxation in public spending, and the beginnings of economic recovery. As a consequence of this new departure, agriculture was assisted by a variety of measures, including tariffs, import quotas, subsidies and consumer levies. A central feature was the marketing legislation of 1931 and 1933 which provided for compulsory co-operation, organised collective bargaining and control of home production within a government-provided framework and behind protective tariffs. This change of course provided the stimulus and sometimes the necessity for introducing similar measures into Northern Ireland. Their purpose was to integrate the province into British schemes, modify Westminster measures to suit local conditions, and generally provide farmers with the same assistance as in Great Britain. In 1939, Brooke thus defined

the keystone of . . . [his] . . . policy . . . [as] . . . to secure for [Northern Ireland] producers . . . a degree of assistance strictly similar to that which is extended by the Imperial government to producers in Britain.[6]

Such a marketing programme was well under way by the time he became minister. He himself frequently acknowledged that it was his predecessor, Sir Edward Archdale, who 'laid the foundations on which . . . [he had] . . . been able to build'.[7] The *News Letter*'s annual farming review pinpointed the year 1933 as 'the most important experienced by the agricultural interest since the war', as during it the agricultural marketing act (Northern Ireland) had been passed, marketing schemes for pigs and bacon initiated, and the preparation of others for milk and potatoes begun.[8]

From the outset departmental officials played a decisive role in devising these measures. Uniquely in Northern Ireland, responsibility for their preparation was vested exclusively in the local ministry, a feature justified by their complexity, the need for extensive knowledge of the economic position and prospects of the industry, and because they inevitably required close cooperation with the boards in Britain. Here again Brooke was fortunate. He inherited an experienced, talented and enthusiastic department, which he himself claimed was 'not to be beaten in any country of the world'.[9] His officials eagerly anticipated their increased control and direction of the province's food production. Thus Harkness wrote to Brooke, just after the Ottawa conference: 'You cannot change in a day from a *laissez-faire* policy of free imports . . . but when this new policy is in operation it cannot fail to be of immense benefit'.[10]

Thus at the beginning of his ministerial career, Brooke was associated with a novel and imaginative programme which had originated with changes in imperial policy just as he was for a second time identified with the similarly progressive social welfare legislation of the third labour government shortly after becoming premier. Both generated friction within the province, and before the war the success of the former was far from universally accepted. Nonetheless, though its implementation aroused entirely predictable difficulties, in the longer term, it played a significant role in laying the basis of Brooke's reputation as a competent and effective minister.

Northern Ireland farmers were by tradition self-reliant, suspicious of government and extremely conservative. Brooke wrote later that 'they resented that the quality of their produce was controlled by a . . . department . . . [and] . . . felt that they had lost their independence'.[11] Though the local ministry recognised the need to involve them in the decision-making process it frequently proved more resolute than other departments in persisting with its policies. Also within the Unionist party there were from the outset ominous indications of disquiet. The *News Letter* described Dr Addison's bill in 1931, as 'quite useless', and Sir Robert Lynn claimed that the marketing legislation had been 'fought from the first line to the last' by the Unionist party at Westminster. In the interwar period backbench M.P.s at Stormont divided against the government more often on farming issues than on any other.[12] Their misgivings were heightened by awareness that some of the innovative measures being adapted were unsuited to the province, having been devised in response to the different structure and needs of British agriculture.

At cabinet level, there was also obvious concern. During discussion on the agricultural marketing bill, Andrews expressed the fear that 'if we control farmer's actions more than a measureable degree . . . we [would be] . . . running the risk of becoming liable for the financial position of many of them'. He also stated characteristically, 'we are really introducing this bill, following the British measure . . . [and] . . . as far as reasonably possible we should follow the conditions and practices set out in the British bill'.[13] Craig seems to have been genuinely convinced that the marketing legislation would benefit the farmer, that they would eventually come to recognise this and thus that his government should be prepared to accept responsibility for its introduction.[14] However, he was described as feeling 'a great deal of anxiety' about the schemes and had indicated this to Brooke in the clearest possible terms when asking him to become minister. Sir James' fear was that 'unless the very best men were nominated [to the boards] . . . there might be a breakdown which would cast very grave reflections on the Ministry of Agriculture and also upon the government'. Thus he was determined that Dr J.S. Gordon should, after retiring as permanent secretary, in mid-1933, become chairman of the new marketing boards, as 'anyone else . . . might easily produce a fiasco; . . . in our small province, boards should have in large measure identical personnel'. Both Pollock and Spender were equally concerned at the political risk which the schemes involved, but far from convinced that they would result in the economic benefits anticipated by their prime minister.[15]

In December 1933, when considering Brooke's suitability for his new appointment, the *Northern Whig* mirrored this context of anxiety. It expressed the hope that Sir Basil would assert his 'independence' and would 'not allow himself to be dominated by the official mind'. It recommended 'practical experience rather than bureaucratic theory . . . in the framing of policy' and as evidence of the need for caution suggested that the department's first scheme, for the marketing of pigs and bacon, was already 'near breakdown' and would require his urgent attention.[16] In fact the relationship that developed between Brooke and his officials, particularly his permanent secretary, was to become a cause of increasing comment and criticism both in parliament and within the party by the late 1930s and the flow of departmental legislation continued so that from 1924 to 1939 a total of twenty-one statutes was passed concerning the marketing of the province's agricultural produce.

The pig and bacon scheme certainly did require Brooke's urgent and indeed frequent attention. It was the first, arguably the most successful as well as the most controversial of all his ministry's initiatives in the 1930s. In due course the problems that it generated led to severe parliamentary criticism of Sir Basil and his officials and ultimately precipitated a vote of censure in the government itself. In 1933 however, few doubted the need to reorganise this sector of the agricultural industry. Though pig production was well suited to the province's small farm, under-capitalised structure, in the late 1920s Northern Ireland had a substantially lower pig density than England and Wales, and almost 40 per cent of pigs cured locally were imported from Eire. Their commercial exploitation was delayed mainly because their prices were not only depressed, but volatile and extremely variable at a local level owing to an unregulated and chaotic marketing system.

The imperial scheme introduced import controls, and created pig and bacon marketing boards to organise the production of a domestic quota, to determine pig and bacon prices and to encourage import substitution. Though welcomed in the province, it was not applied there because of the different characteristics of the local industry, a fact fully recognised in the simultaneous scheme devised by the Northern Ireland ministry. Under the latter two similar boards were created to organise and develop the province's share of the now partially-protected British market. Their function was to fix prices through mutual negotiation aiming to distribute profits fairly between producers and curers, eradicate price fluctuation and provide the farmer with the security for progressive, efficient and expanded production. The ministry also sought to improve quality through a grading system and to diversify output. The British market for Northern Ireland's traditional product, roll bacon, was depressed. The department therefore encouraged the adoption of the Wiltshire cure, demand for which was growing on the buoyant south England market, in part because competing imports were regulated. This involved a change in pig breed, a process which was encouraged by board propaganda, price incentives and the licensing of suitable curing factories. With regard to the latter an important objective was to have every pig possible cured in Northern Ireland, so creating employment and enhancing producer profit, whilst encouraging product diversification.[17]

Though no board showed greater initiative and enterprise than the Pig Marketing Board, the scheme proved difficult to operate as to a unique degree its stability was determined by factors beyond local control, including the strength of the British market, the level of competing imports, and the price of feedstuffs. As experience was gained, its features were steadily restructured, and generally as a result, ministry control was increased. The attempt to fix prices was perhaps its most intractable difficulty. During its first months public confidence was shaken by an unexpected glut on the home market which prompted early predictions that the whole scheme was in imminent danger of collapse. This was because the imperial Fox-Lane reorganisation commission initially permitted too high import levels, having underestimated British ham and bacon output. Producers anticipating improved prices had held back supplies until the scheme began. Curers, therefore, unsure what they could dispose of, in some cases refused to purchase pigs. Thus the Northern Ireland government acted to guarantee them against any loss entailed in adhering to the guaranteed price, by means of a loan.[18]

Soon afterwards, further difficulties were caused by abnormal trading conditions on mainland markets in early 1934. Due mainly to import restrictions British curers had insufficient pigs, live pig prices therefore increased and their export from Northern Ireland rose as a consequence. This threatened supplies for local curers who also suffered from a surge in local dead pig prices. After promptings from the boards the ministry reacted by introducing regulations to control live pig exports. Also the Pig Marketing Board which was throughout obliged to purchase any live pigs offered to it for sale took over the live trade on behalf of the producer. This enabled it to reduce market fluctuation, and, as it proceeded to set up marketing depots all over the province, it helped to break the stranglehold of isolation that had encouraged the dead marketing of pigs particularly in remote areas.[19]

Other fundamental problems remained. In particular, the joint negotiations between the pig and bacon marketing boards over price-fixing generated constant friction. This forced the ministry to introduce remedial legislation in 1934. As a result the P.M.B. duly expired, its powers to regulate bacon production were transferred to the department, and a Pig Industry Council was established. The latter was a mixed board, with equal curer and producer representation, as well as two appointed officials. It had powers to fix prices and to advise the ministry on the granting of new curing licences. Both of these functions were fraught with very great difficulty.[20]

Nonetheless, despite persistent and severe crises the scheme had considerable success. It proved to be flexible and sensitive to the province's needs and it provided ample opportunity for local participation almost throughout. Producers and curers benefited from stable even rising prices and assured markets. Pig supplies became more regular, quality improved, and total numbers more than trebled. By the late 1930s the region accounted for one-quarter of all United Kingdom production and had the highest pig density of any area in the British Isles. The scale of Northern Ireland output rose from £1,140,000 to £4,423,000, from 1931–32 to 1937–8 representing by the latter date 27 per cent of the total value of farm production, and by then the most valuable branch of the local agricultural industry. In addition the Wiltshire cure was firmly established, and this with the introduction of grading made an important contribution to the future prosperity of this sector, whilst in the short term enabling producers to take greater advantage of the British market. Overall, it was the numerous small family-worked farms to the east of the province, which were ideally suited to pig production, who benefited most from the scheme.[21]

Meanwhile other projected marketing schemes had proceeded. In his report after the imperial conference at Ottawa in 1932, Scott Robertson noted with some disappointment that the dominions had 'been conceded continued free entry'[22] into the United Kingdom market for cheese, butter and other milk products for at least three years. In 1933 the British government introduced milk marketing legislation, its first such scheme, subsidising the manufacturing sector against such competing imports. This led to widespread demands for similar assistance in Northern Ireland. The local dairying industry, which was regarded by Brooke and his officials as the most important branch of agriculture in the province, was by the early 1930s approaching crisis. About 70 per cent of producer milk output went to co-operative creameries and post-war manufactured milk prices were acutely depressed. This was partly due to competing imports, but in addition the creameries themselves urgently required rationalisation. They suffered from excessive competition and from seasonal milk supplies as a result of which they operated in winter at only one-half to one-quarter capacity, so inflating their production costs. In mid-1933, butter prices were 20 per cent below pre-war levels, farmers were reported to be receiving as little as 2½d per gallon for manufacturing milk, and fears were being expressed that the whole creamery movement would collapse. Such a prospect also threatened greatly to reduce the numbers of calves, store cattle, pigs and poultry in the province.[23]

In mid-May 1934, the Treasury agreed to amend current Westminster legislation so enabling £200,000 to be used to subsidise the price that Northern Ireland creameries paid producers for their milk. Such financial aid was a vital precondition of the subsequent legislation devised by the local ministry. This was once more delicately attuned to the province's needs. In England and Wales where only 30 per cent of milk production was used for manufacturing purposes, boards pooled milk receipts, and paid a level price to all farmers, so giving an enhanced price to manufactured milk producers at the expense of those who produced liquid milk. Though the Northern Ireland ministry regarded it as essential that farmers should receive a remunerative price for milk sent to creameries, it felt that the mainland's approach would have been impracticable and unfair if applied locally.[24] This was mainly because Ulster's liquid trade was too small to support milk manufacture to the same extent as in Great Britain. The department not only attempted to help all milk producers, but also to ensure that consumers were provided with a better and safer milk supply.[25]

Brooke described the resulting measure, the milk and milk products bill, as 'the most important piece of legislation . . . ever attempted by my ministry'. Under its terms, a milk fund was created. This, with the agreed Treasury grant, was used to pay a remunerative price to creamery suppliers of milk in a carefully modulated system aimed at raising the volume, improving the quality, and increasing the regularity of milk supplies. Subsequently subsidies were increased in response to changes in British rates, rising feeding stuff costs and variations in the supply of milk to creameries.[26] The act also established a Joint Milk Council which determined wholesale and retail prices for the liquid trade, and supervised milk contracts. In addition, the ministry sought to improve milk quality through milk grading, differential bonuses and levies, the examination of animals and their housing, and milk sampling and testing. It also encouraged a more diversified output of milk products in favour of those with higher prices, whose imports were controlled.

Once more the Northern Ireland scheme was well suited to local conditions. It catered for the needs not just of producers but of consumers and of the broader community, and was concerned with quality and consumption levels as well as with volume. Its regulations were tight, the marketing system efficient and its methods of price support unique and apparently not ineffective. From 1935 to 1938 the volume of manufacturing milk produced in Northern Ireland increased from 15.7 million gallons to 19.03 million gallons,[27] and by 1936 Brooke could justifiably boast to the house that the Ulster consumer had 'by far the cheapest milk supply in the United Kingdom'.[28] In addition it was of better quality. Overall the Northern Ireland scheme was more far-reaching than the British counterpart and was widely recognised as being a superior measure.

Both Brooke and his officials however, regarded the egg marketing scheme as the most challenging of all those initiated by the ministry during these years. Sir Douglas Harkness described it as 'the most exacting' because unlike those for pigs and milk it was devised in a 'completely uncharted' field. Brooke himself claimed that it was 'an innovation without parallel in Great Britain',[29] which was emulated elsewhere, and which underlined the advantages of devolved government. In Northern Ireland, eggs and poultry were second only to store cattle in importance within the agricultural industry. Egg production was characterised by non-specialist, backward producers, with marginal supplies, selling in small, dispersed markets and suffering severely from more efficient foreign competition on the British market.

The government's reforms were throughout broadly consultative, and evolutionary; its legislation building on the experience, structure and regulations of the previous decade. In 1936, when introducing the marketing of eggs bill, a comprehensive amending measure, Brooke stated: 'the ministry feel and I am convinced as their political head that if we do not take this opportunity but stand still . . . the whole of this trade will disappear'.[30] In the background the price of Northern Ireland eggs had just been reduced by the London trade. The new act enabled the ministry, with the advice of an eggs marketing committee to determine the price each week at which eggs might be purchased by licensed wholesalers. Eggs were to be bought on a quality basis, and it was hoped through the operation of a contract system to eliminate price fluctuations, and with it to end that endemic hoarding by dealers in anticipation of a rising market which had previously damaged the reputation of local output.[31]

Many years later Sir Douglas Harkness wrote, 'past experience of fluctuating egg supplies and prices suggested that an attempt to introduce fixed prices for eggs was almost certainly doomed to failure', but he concluded the scheme was 'a complete success'.[32] By 1937, Northern Ireland eggs exported to Britain were second in price only to those sold under the select English mark. The scheme also contributed to a rise in the province's poultry numbers, and though the latter remained unregulated, an improvement in stock was encouraged by the department through the operation of accredited farms, poultry stations, laying tests and blood sampling. In September 1938, when Brooke was illustrating to the cabinet the importance of the agricultural sector, he stated that if present egg output could be doubled 'it would be worth to the province the equivalent of the shipbuilding industry'.[33]

Tillage provided less opportunity for departmental innovation and it remained relatively unprofitable throughout the inter-war period. Its contraction from the late nineteenth century had been temporarily reversed in wartime, but by 1923 acreage had receded to pre-war levels, and by 1930 had retreated virtually to its limits. Farm size, climate and relative price trends favoured grassland and livestock production, and the province failed to benefit from early imperial measures which aimed to stimulate sugar beet and wheat output. With regard to Northern Ireland's traditional tillage crops, oats production declined after the war due to declining demand, cheap competing fodder imports and the absence of any government guaranteed price. From 1937, acreage revived a little benefiting from a subsidy scheme for oats and barley introduced at Westminster. Flax was left unregulated throughout despite local pressures for a flax board, guaranteed prices, grading and inspection. A modest state grant and the creation of a flax committee failed to compensate for consistently low prices, and production fell to the late 1930s.

Potatoes were the only major Northern Ireland field crop. They were well suited to the local climate and generally more profitable than flax. Legislation in the early 1920s sought to reduce disease levels and, in 1928, the state began to regulate the size and quality sold and introduced grading and the licensing of exporters. These measures had considerable success. When Britain initiated a marketing scheme in 1933, this existing machinery was expanded and modified. In 1935, the Northern Ireland Potato Marketing Association was established. Its function was to collaborate with its English equivalent, and it was also concerned with improving the quality and regulating the quantity and price of potatoes exported. Though the province's total production fell in the interwar years, suffering like oats from cheap imports of feedstuff, these and other measures adopted by the ministry probably prevented worse decline, contributed to an improvement in quality and to the buoyancy of seed potato exports to the mid-1930s.[34]

Meanwhile, Brooke and his officials persevered with the fruit marketing scheme launched in 1931, which sought, mainly through grading, improved packaging and a licensing system, to improve the quality and increase the quantity of apple exports. From its inception the fruit act provoked fierce opposition in County Armagh, and growers and traders there continued to attribute their difficulties to state regulation and interference. Thus, in 1934, the Ulster Fruit-Growers' Defence Association called for the abolition of Stormont, and three years later, amid claims that inclement weather had destroyed one-quarter of the apple crop, producers once more agitated for the freedom to market all that they produced. Nevertheless, the evidence of improved quality as reflected in rising export levels, helped to justify Brooke's verdict, given at Stormont in 1937, that 'the much maligned fruit act has as it was intended borne fruit in abundance'.[35]

In the same setting two years later Sir Basil recited with evident satisfaction the substantial and still growing list of measures taken by the government to assist agriculture. He mentioned the marketing schemes and import controls, the great variety of direct subsidies, the derating of agricultural land, the grants available for the improvement of holdings, the ministry's provision of fertilisers at cheap rates and made reference to an agricultural wages board which would soon be operational.[36] During the early and mid-30s this emerging programme illicited a broadly favourable response throughout the province. A post-war government enquiry explained that:

In contrast to the position they had suffered for so long of being largely at the mercy of the merchant in agricultural produce, farmers welcomed wholeheartedly measures which appeared to give them the opportunity of controlling through an elected marketing board all the produce available for sale and for determining the price at which it should be sold . . . Previously the dice were loaded . . . heavily . . . against the producer.[37]

This perhaps dangerously high level of rural expectation and enthusiasm was reflected in the 23 per cent increase in Ulster's pig population during the twelve months before this inaugural scheme was launched, and the fact that 80 per cent of those eligible participated in the first P.M.B. elections in 1934.[38] Particularly after its experience with the fruit act the government regarded it as essential that agricultural interests should be widely consulted regarding new measures in order to sustain producer confidence. In cabinet, Craig himself suggested that before proceeding with the agricultural marketing bill arrangements should be made for favourable resolutions to be passed by the U.F.U. and other representative bodies.[39]

In parliament, rural M.P.s reflected the favourable initial attitudes of their constituents. Though nationalist members returned to Stormont in 1933, the level of criticism was inevitably muted by the extent of continuing Unionist party domination. In November of that year the *Belfast Telegraph* could declare that the government had been elected on the day that nominations closed. In the succeeding parliament, Spender observed that ministers needed the support of only eight of their own party members and could therefore 'carry almost anything'.[40] By then the Nationalist members had ceased taking their seats once more.

However, the smooth passage particularly of the early agricultural measures through the commons was also in part attributable to Brooke himself. As minister he quickly established a reputation as a skilled parliamentary performer. His comments were direct, concise, knowledgeable and in the descriptive phrase favoured most by his colleagues, 'lucid'. He was characteristically well-briefed, ready to explain and defend policy and in the words of one journalist, was consistently intent on 'meeting the house half-way'.[41] During the second reading of the milk and milk products bill, the first major measure for which Sir Basil was responsible, Lynn remarked

I have heard a good many bills introduced in my time and I have never heard a bill introduced in a better, a more lucid, a more comprehensive way than this bill.

Later he added that Brooke had 'tackled a number of difficult problems with great courage and if I may say so with great ability'.[42] By the mid-1930s, such comments were almost part of the ritual of parliamentary debate at Stormont. Though the house was never uncritical, many members regarded him with respect, even deference. Brown stated 'we have never had a better or more enterprising minister of agriculture'. Minford reflected on

the enormous amount of good he has done for the industry . . . I do not know any minister who has done such good for the province, . . . we are proud of him . . . he is . . . young, energetic and practical.

Dehra Parker remarked on Sir Basil's 'great reputation' in Great Britain, and stated that his measures were 'like a breath of country air'.[43] Other members representing urban constituencies expressed equally favourable opinions. To Midgley he was 'advanced and progressive', whilst Grant spoke of having 'just as much regard for . . . [him] . . . as any member of this house'.[44] Even Henderson who had initially described Brooke's appointment as one of the worst blunders made by the government, and suggested that his salary be reduced by £1,000, modified these opinions. He retracted his earlier 'hard statements', though they never entirely ceased, and complimented Brooke on doing a 'fairly good job', and being 'easy to understand'.[45]

Criticism in parliament and elsewhere was also tempered by the evidently beneficial effects of government measures on agriculture. Collectively these helped to increase production, or at least arrest earlier decline, and to improve the reputation of agricultural products from the province and thereby enhance their selling value. The post-war contraction in total average was partially reversed in the 1930s, the value of gross output increased by over £6 million between 1932–33 to 1937–8, and export values for food, drink, and raw materials rose by over 8 per cent in the same period. The livestock sector showed spectacular advances, with the number of pigs trebling and sheep and poultry numbers rising by 13 per cent and 16 per cent respectively between 1931 and 1939.

In the same period the province's per capita output in agriculture rose from being 48 per cent of the English level to 52 per cent. Though the tillage area fell, value of output increased; oats, flax and barley averages were all expanding strongly in the late 1930s, and yields were by local standards high for all major products. In addition, between 1926 and 1937 the total numbers employed in agriculture, the number of farm owners, and the number of full-time labourers all showed an increase. Average farm-size became slightly larger, and there is some evidence of a rise in living standards. Studies of farm income indicate the severity of the depression in 1932–3, and a substantial recovery by the mid-1930s, especially on holdings where the bulk of work was carried out by the family, serving long hours, paying attention to detail and specialising in dairying, pigs, poultry and sheep. Brooke also claimed that between 1932–3 and 1937–8 labourers' wages rose by up to 15 per cent. Overall, the department's policies were sufficiently effective to stimulate enquiries from many foreign governments seeking advice and information. Clearly in a difficult economic environment the 1930s had seen considerable progress in the province's agriculture, even though Sir Basil was not fully successful in achieving 'the keystone' of his policy, namely 'getting assistance strictly similar' to that in Great Britain.[46]

Northern Ireland undoubtedly benefited from the existence of an imaginative and competent local ministry, with power to adapt agricultural reforms, and to develop, albeit within strict limits, a regional policy in response to the area's distinctive problems. Its achievement has been described by one historian as a triumph of 'adaptability'.[47] The Babington report, published in 1946, likewise praised the overall correctness and effectiveness of departmental measures in the 1930s. Thus, for example, it described the pig marketing scheme as the 'prime cause of expansion' in that sector, the milk and milk products act as having 'had an important effect in maintaining the sale of milk' off farms, the fruit legislation as doing much 'to consolidate the industry' by raising the quality of fruit exports, and the Potato Marketing Association as having done 'useful work' and its continuance in the future was recommended.[48]

Brooke on occasion cited such achievements to illustrate the merits of devolved government. Though evidence regarding the efficiency of regional schemes in Northern Ireland might be evinced to justify administrative or governmental devolution, it does not necessarily validate the need for parliamentary devolution or indeed establish the indispensability of Brooke himself as minister. Sir Douglas Harkness expressed the view that though Unionists came to regard 'self-government as advantageous', from his experience he had 'grave doubt whether this has ever been the case'.[49] A recent analysis lays much stress on the vital role of Ministry of Agriculture officials and concludes that departmental 'policy was often achieved despite rather than because of regional representative institutions'.[50]

In any case, government policy was only partly responsible for any improvement in agricultural trends during the 1930s. The Babington report described the interwar expansion of Ulster grassland acreage as being due to the 'pressure of events . . . not due to conscious policy, . . . [and] . . . without scientific direction'.[51] Thus sheep numbers increased dramatically without being assisted by any government scheme. Pig production was stimulated not just by legislation but also by the availability of cheap fodder imports in the mid-1930s, and the disruption of southern exports to Britain caused by the Anglo-Irish trade war. This latter factor also helped in the short-term to cushion Northern Ireland store cattle exports against more severe depression. Despite the milk and milk products act, the rearing of dry cattle remained throughout more profitable than dairying, and the total numbers, profitability, and sale of cattle declined throughout the decade. Overall these trends would indicate that as Ulster farming became less self-contained, its profitability was determined less by government policy, than by such factors as the supply and cost of competing imports into Britain and the strength of the British market.[52] When in the late 1930s local producers pressed the ministry to establish a committee of enquiry into agricultural depression, Scott Robertson initially resisted on the grounds that it was caused by a down turn in the British economy and that therefore no solution could be found internally.[53]

The latter incident also underlines the increasing instability of Northern Ireland agriculture, and the fact that any agricultural recovery in the 1930s was relative, as the industry remained distressed throughout to a greater or lesser extent. The number of farmers remained stable because, unlike many of their sons, they accepted low living standards and hard work, convinced that they were better off on their farms than in the towns. Those with less than thirty acres were in most cases less well off than industrial wage earners. The large number of agricultural labourers was symptomatic of the lack of mechanisation and dearth of alternative employment. Their average income was well below the thirty shillings a week given to unemployed married men with two children. Wages and working conditions were such that particularly the younger sections of the workforce were keen to leave farming, and more would have transferred to industry had work been available. Even in the context of widespread economic depression, there was a net outflow of over 25,000 male workers from agriculture between 1925–38, resulting in localised shortages of qualified farm labour.

Despite the government's measures, farm incomes and profits remained depressed and as a result expenditure on drainage and fertilisers was neglected, and in many areas farmers and labourers were 'working with implements little in advance of those in use a century before'. Rural amenities were inadequate, sewerage often non-existent, water supply insufficient, and transport services unco-ordinated. In the early 1940s, the Ministry of Home Affairs estimated that 40 per cent of rural housing was either unfit for human habitation or overcrowded, and that over 60 per cent had neither gas nor electricity installed or available. Such conditions lay at the root of the rural depopulation which continued throughout the decade. There was no simple contrast of the type favoured by Brooke in his speeches during the early 1930s between the relatively affluent government-assisted northern farmer and his languishing southern counterpart. When such favourable comparisons were made by Craig in 1938 Spender felt that they were economically questionable and politically motivated.[54]

(2) Agricultural Crisis: the dismissal of the Pig Marketing Board

Brooke was himself under no illusions regarding the extent of agricultural progress in the 1930s, or the impact of his department's measures. Though regarding the latter as appropriate and constructive, he also felt that they were inadequate. In a memorandum which he submitted to cabinet in September 1938, he wrote,

Subsidies to the agricultural industry can only be at best palliatives, a useful means, perhaps, of tiding over difficulties until the real problem can be tackled. But we are in serious danger of giving doses and doses of medicine which merely deaden the pain, whilst the ailment increases in intensity and danger.[55]

The treatment which he now urgently prescribed was to lower production costs and possibly treble output through a dynamic and integrated programme of farm mechanisation, rural electrification and cheap loans for farmers. Any prospect of its immediate implementation was however removed by the intervention of war, though similar solutions were reiterated in the Babington report and other post-war surveys.

In February 1939, the *News Letter* suggested that such a policy was unlikely to receive a warm reaction from Ulster farmers.[56] This was not just caused by instinctive conservatism but also indicated a growing sense of unfilled expectation and of disillusionment with governmental regulation. The years immediately preceding the outbreak of war were the most difficult experienced by the department. In part this was due to the context of rural depression. In 1936–7, average incomes appear to have fallen almost to the levels of 1930–31, when farms 'did not pay an agricultural worker's wage to the operator.[57] Concern was expressed at the rising price of feed-stuffs and slackening of demand for some Northern Ireland products on the British market. There were indications of acute strain emerging in both the pig and fruit marketing schemes. In 1938, over 5,000 insured agricultural workers were unemployed, and in its annual review the *News Letter* recorded the widespread feeling that it had been a 'poor year . . . the schemes had not functioned as they were expected to . . . [but were] . . . rather a failure'.[58] Its greatest disappointment was with the level of prices, particularly for beef and mutton. In November, an Ulster Farmers Union meeting of delegates representing 100 branches resolved that 'the present plight and future outlook for the farming industry . . . was . . . never worse in living memory'.[59] There were calls for an enquiry into the causes of agricultural distress.

Such despondency was not shared by all. Sir Wilfred Spender after making enquiries into the level of farmers' bank deposits concluded that 'stories of acute general depression . . . are . . . greatly exaggerated'.[60] However, Brooke himself was quite pessimistic. In his September 1938 memorandum he considered the problems facing Ulster's producers. He included high transport costs, rising wages, mounting taxation and, in particular, low prices and the depressed state of the British market. As for the future, he was far from hopeful. The prospects for the industry he described as 'sufficiently gloomy as to cause very considerable concern', particularly if the problems of Europe were peacefully resolved, rearmament expenditure contracted, and, as a result, industrial unemployment spiralled. His proposals to increase rural productivity were thus designed 'to deal with the impending agricultural crisis', and he hoped that they would also serve to boost local manufacturing industry.[61]

Predictably, in these depressed circumstances farmers once more sought relief through the reduction or abolition of land purchase annuity payments. Delegations came to Stormont to press for this objective. It was raised at meetings between rural M.P.s, Brooke and the prime minister and was discussed by the Unionist parliamentary party.[62] In the country, tenants organised non-payment associations, receipts fell sharply in the final months of 1938, and Andrews was forced to issue instructions to the Land Purchase Annuity Board that consideration should be shown where there was evidence of acute distress. In Fermanagh, the county council embarrassed its chairman, still Sir Basil, by passing a resolution calling for annuities to be halved. The *Fermanagh Times* stated that 'in no part of Ulster has the outcry been so importunate'. Brooke himself complained to colleagues of 'the great deal of pressure' being put on him by the farmers.[63] Some of the former criticised his speeches at this time on the grounds that they fuelled discussion and roused expectations of government aid. But generally when addressing farmers, he appealed to their sense of honour, to the benefits of the union, and highlighted the threat that non-payment might pose to future government subsidies.[64] In the end, abolition remained beyond the financial resources of the Northern Ireland government and the campaign was thus doomed to failure and to frustration once more.

The context of distress also imposed additional strains on existing marketing schemes and aggravated simmering resentment at government regulations. Relations between the department and a number of boards deteriorated to the point of breakdown. One M.P. commented 'the bubbles are beginning to burst . . . the minister of agriculture is like the man who created Frankenstein, . . . [the boards] . . . are in pursuit of him, . . . They are out to devour him . . . politically'. Spender in less florid tones regarded it as 'unfortunate in the interests of the province that the various boards . . . seem unable to work in harmony with the ministry'.[65]

In 1937, discontent amongst County Armagh apple-growers reawakened. Against the background of bad harvest, producers sought the repeal of the fruit act, alleging that government regulation was 'absolutely ruining the industry', and local newspapers reported the formation of a breakaway Unionist party.[66] In the winter of 1938–9, similar pressures recurred when crops were decimated by severe frost and once more urgent representations were made to the prime minister. Sir James considered suspending their annuity payments, but was advised that this was impracticable as it would create demands for similar relief from other sectors.[67]

The most dramatic development in this period, however was Brooke's controversial dismissal of the Pig Marketing Board on 27 February 1939. His decision irritated the farming community in general. It contributed to friction within the party, even at cabinet level. It also helped sour Sir Basil's relationship with the house, providing new scope for criticism, and finally precipitated a division which was interpreted by the prime minister as a vote of censure in his administration. By this point it seemed that the Sir James's initial concern regarding the political risks involved in the marketing schemes had been more than justified. Certainly some informed opinion had come to regard the province's agricultural policy as an important contributory cause of the government's mounting unpopularity and its growing reputation for laxity and incompetence.

From its inception the pig marketing scheme had been uniquely unstable. In the course of 1936–7, it came under additional strains which brought it to the brink of collapse. The main cause was a rise in the cost of imported feed stuffs on which the industry was increasingly dependent, as its small-scale producers were unable to meet their own requirements. This precipitated conflict between farmers' representatives and curers over price levels. The ministry was concerned to find instances of curers refusing to buy pigs at the price agreed by the Pig Industry Council.[68] In this difficult period two Wiltshire factories closed down, the number of pigs cured in Northern Ireland fell and for virtually the first time since the marketing scheme came into operation their total numbers declined sharply. However, swift action by the board helped to restore confidence. By July 1937 the two curing plants had reopened, and two years later, a total of four was in operation. Meanwhile, the number of pigs in the province had recovered to reach record levels. Overall the achievements of the board had been impressive as measured by the growth of the pig population, and of curing capacity, and the generally high levels of prices. The degree of success it attained compared favourably with the experience of its British equivalent and was used in its defence during the parliamentary debates on its abrupt dismissal.[69]

On 7 March 1939, Sir Basil sought to justify in parliament his controversial decision to dismiss the board. One correspondent described the scene:

the house . . . [had] . . . the appearance of a theatrical first night. It was . . . a moment to delight the heart of a champion of democracy. Filling every seat, reclining on steps in the aisles and standing so thickly that the doors could not be shut, were citizens intent on the affairs of the state . . . [Brooke] rose, well prepared . . . Reading from a wad of notes, he spoke more tensely than is his usual custom.[70]

He defended his decision mainly on the grounds of administrative and financial malpractice by the board. He referred to rumours that had circulated from the autumn of 1938, of irregularities in the latter's activities. In the absence of any adequate investigation by the members themselves he had finally established his own enquiry, begun in September 1938, and conducted by two departmental officials. It completed its report five months later, and this provided much of the text for Brooke's half-hour speech.

The inquiry produced sufficient evidence to justify its own conclusion that the board's present administration and finances were highly unsatisfactory and that there were several irregularities in practice.[71] Much of its criticism centred on the chaotic and confused way in which its members had conducted the sale of live pigs, particularly to Great Britain. For example, it found that there was virtually no direct contact between the board and its mainland customers, that grading was lax and that inadequate consideration was given to prices, which were therefore too low. By contrast, within Northern Ireland the enquiry found that pigs were being bought by the board at unreasonably high prices. There was also evidence of serious malpractice at its network of depots and, in due course, a deputy-marketing officer appeared in court on a charge of corruption.[72] Analysis of the operation of droverage costs and feeding stuffs provided further evidence of inefficiency and malpractice. These allegations were broadly substantiated by a later enquiry, and were not uniformly contested even by board members at the time of their dismissal, one of whom wrote of its 'grave mismanagement and serious wastage'.[73]

Whatever the precise extent of malpractice involved in the dispute, both Sir Basil's comments and those of the three ex-Pig Marketing Board members who sat in the house revealed an absolute breakdown in the relationship between the ministry and the board. Brooke emphasised in his speeches the complete lack of cooperation that the department had received from the latter in the course of its investigations. He claimed that the board neither instituted any adequate enquiries of its own, nor at any stage produced remedial proposals, though throughout kept fully informed of his officials' activities. In fact he suggested that it thwarted their efforts by failing to make available to them auditor's notes, solicitors' correspondence and factory files. He also alleged that when the reports finally became available the board's chairman refused to discuss them with him, and that the day prior to its release, the board had signed a three year contract with its secretary-manager at an annual income of £1,500. This latter revelation, the house heard in the words of one reporter, 'with raised eyebrows and pursed lips'.[74]

For their part, the ex-board members spoke bitterly and at length on the manner of their dismissal. They protested at the speed with which Brooke and his officials had acted and at their cavalier, aggressive approach. On 18 February, the board had received copies of the ministry's report. Four days later at a meeting with Brooke and his officials, including Scott Robertson the membership was offered pre-drafted, typed terms demanding the dismissal of its secretary-manager and accountant, and the appointment of two officials as comptroller and auditor-general, to be responsible in future for administrative and accounting arrangements. Brooke was alleged to have stated, 'that is my dose. If you do not take that dose, here is the next',[75] indicating that a new board would be appointed. Members claimed that they would at this point have cooperated with the ministry had they been given two weeks in which to consider these proposals. Instead they were given two days, later extended to five.

When the two parties met again, on 27 February, the board refused to accept the ministry's conditions. As one of their spokesmen put it: 'members simply refused to do what was demanded of them'. It was also claimed that Brooke had declared

Since you as a board will not adopt the steps . . . I must get a board that will . . . There can be no question of continuing with the present administration a day longer than can be avoided.

He subsequently issued an order expelling them from office, and some ex-members stated that they first heard on the wireless the next day the news that a new board had been appointed. It was said that Dr J.S. Gordon had, after his 'instant' dismissal, 'slipped away into retirement a broken man, broken in health and in heart, like so much rubbish'.[76] Certainly within the department, senior officials regarded the clash with their former head as extremely upsetting.

The board members resented the fact that the ministry had acted as 'judge, jury, and prosecuting council', partly because they doubted its legal right to do so, and also because they had no faith in its impartiality and suspected its motivation. Thus, during the investigation, they had handed over to the officials only such material as they were legally obliged to provide, and kept their minutes deliberately brief in their determination not to prejudice their position. This distrust was rooted in the board's perception of the consistent trend of departmental policy over the five years of its existence. One ex-member stated tersely during the debate that there was 'one basic principle at stake . . . producer control'. Board members believed that their essential function was to represent the sectional interests of the producers who had elected them, but that the government had steadily eroded their power, so tragically weakening the influence of the farmer, whose prospects and confidence had been undermined in the process.[77]

Evidence of this alleged hostility was adduced. It included accusations of ministerial meddling in board affairs, its discriminatory allocation of curing licences, and, most crucially, the pattern of its legislation. Reference was made to the agricultural marketing act of 1934 and to the far reaching terms of the bacon industry bill, copies of which were given to M.P.s on the day before the board was dissolved. Overall it appeared to some members that dismissal was merely the final phase of government policy, that it had been waiting for the opportunity to strike, and had constantly been eroding board powers.[78]

Undoubtedly these claims had some validity. In 1934 the board had lost its powers to fix prices, with the formation of the Pig Industry Council. In part this new body was created in order to avoid further clashes between the Pig and Bacon Marketing Boards, but it was also symptomatic of changes in the nature of departmental policy. Officials found producer boards prone to be concerned solely with producer interests and thus developed a preference for mixed boards with their wider representation and less sectional perspective. Sir Douglas Harkness wrote:

This was the policy for which I had striven in the years before 1939, and it was in some ways the special contribution which Northern Ireland made to marketing development in this period.[79]

Brooke was similarly enthusiastic, once referring to the Joint Milk Council as the 'break-through . . . both sections of the industry talking together'.[80] Such a policy inevitably generated a sense of disillusion amongst farmers, as they had welcomed the marketing legislation in the expectation that they would thereby gain control of output and of the level of prices.[81]

Harkness recalled that after the formation of the P.I.C. 'considerable friction developed' between the ministry and the P.M.B. in contrast to their earlier 'close' relationship. He continued: 'There was hard bargaining between pig producers and curers on the council . . . and the producers did not think that the ministry gave them enough support'.[82] Members of the dismissed board indeed made this same allegation of government bias in favour of the curer. The Babington report may however give an insight into at least a part of the cause of their frustration. It stated that 'trade representatives on mixed boards tend to be better organised and instructed than producer representatives'.[83] It therefore recommended that in future schemes the ministry should build in structures to counteract this tendency.

The bacon industry bill was designed to rationalise and restructure the curing industry and also give guaranteed prices to pig producers over a three year period subject to the institution of a system of contracts. Certain limitations were imposed on the number of pigs that would qualify for support and the price levels were to be adjusted in accordance with variations in the cost of feed-stuffs. Once more the effect was to increase government powers and diminish those of the Pig Marketing Board. In January 1939, Spender noted 'the ministry wants . . . [the board] . . . to surrender . . . [its] . . . duties'.[84] One ex-member described it as useless to producers, complained about the 'few tattered rags' of power and control that it left to the board, and concluded that this measure was 'the real motive behind dissolution'.[85]

In fact Brooke had been firmly committed to the new legislation from April 1938, five months before the enquiry by his officials. The bill had been prompted partly by price-fixing and other difficulties with the existing scheme, but was essentially concerned to extend a Westminster measure to Northern Ireland.[86] In Britain, when bacon imports were reduced by quota in the early 1930s, the domestic industry failed to meet internal demands, and prices therefore rose. This benefited both the local United Kingdom farmer and the foreign producer equally, thus Britain paid more for her restricted imported supplies and received less. The marketing boards generally proved to be least effective for produce in which imports took a significant proportion of the domestic market. As a result, in 1938, the imperial government introduced a system of guaranteed prices in order to raise the efficiency and output of the British industry, and to permit a more flexible approach towards imports. Significantly, when the dust of controversy had long since settled in Northern Ireland the Babington report recommended a

return to the arrangements existing at the outbreak of the war, . . . [which] . . . represented the final evolution of the organisation for pigs and bacon marketing.[87]

It therefore advised that the P.I.C. and the P.M.B. be reconstructed and the bacon industry act fully implemented.

The Pig Marketing Board debates damaged Brooke's rapport with the house. The ex-board members, though exculpated at the time from all blame by Sir Basil, spear-headed the attack, calling as they had done publicly from the moment of their dismissal for an independent inquiry. From being generally supportive of the government's measures they became its voluble, articulate and knowledgeable critics. During the following months, they continued consistently to attack ministerial policy fighting what one contemporary described as 'a rear guard action . . . [of] . . . sniping guerilla warfare and propaganda'.[88]

They elicited considerable sympathy from some other members of parliament. Agricultural policy had of course never been immune from hostile parliamentary comment. Over the years this had been directed at a wide range of targets. Members had, for example, expressed irritation at measures reaching the house in a final and agreed form, or at too short notice, and had complained at the sheer volume of commons' time devoted to farming issues so, it was claimed causing neglect of urban and industrial problems.[89] Controversy had also been aroused by the nature of agricultural policy and its faults both of omission and commission. The delay in setting up an Agricultural Wages Board provoked anger. Healy claimed that the inadequate provision of labourers' cottages was 'in pursuance of the policy which . . . [Brooke] . . . expounded', even if it was not his departmental responsibility. The ministry was similarly accused by Nationalist members of religious discrimination in its appointment of boards. As the sheer volume and range of agricultural legislation proceeded, the level of criticism increased, and, on occasion, it assumed an ideological content. Thus, somewhat improbably, Brooke was described by Jack Beattie as a 'very extreme socialist'. J.W. Nixon claimed that he had turned the agricultural industry into 'something like what they had in Russia', and warned 'the day is coming, and will have to come when the black-shirt will clear . . . [them] . . . out'.[90]

Brooke's parliamentary clash with the P.M.B. members caused considerable confusion to those M.P.s not directly involved. 'Two series of attacks, both equally devastating, . . . most mystifying to the ordinary member',[91] as it was described by one of the latter. For a few M.P.s the whole episode served to confirm their fears and suspicions of the marketing legislation, and provided new opportunities to air old prejudices with regard to the department's innovations. The motivation behind their comments varied and the basis for their attack on the government frequently differed from that of the board. They focused much attention on assumed defects in the construction of the Pig Marketing Scheme. Mutually conflicting views were expresssed that it left the producers too dominant, the consumer too unprotected, the minister too weak, or parliament too ineffectual through having delegated too much power. Concern was also expressed at evidence of board recalcitrance, corruption and its alleged waste of public funds.[92]

With regard to Brooke himself, some praised his courage and devotion to principle, others admonished his high-handedness and attributed the scheme's defects to his neglect. The content of the debate was influenced by the context in which it occurred, a factor which did not favour Sir Basil. Thus there were references to the age and general incompetence of the government, the latter stimulated by the high level of unemployment, and the recent mishandling of public transport. Also in early March, the remaining members of the Butter and Cream Board resigned, alleging in a public statement, 'unjustifiable interference by the Ministry of Agriculture'.[93] The board, which represented cooperative creamery interests had been established to improve the market for butter and cream. Under this scheme all creameries were obliged to sell their products through board agents or obtain approval to do otherwise. When a large private creamery continued to ship cream independently, and was eventually fined £700, Brooke wrote to the board stating that he 'could not justify . . . [their action] . . . before parliament. As the board represented largely cooperative interests and as a private individual had been fined, it might be said that the board was partial'.[94] This intervention led to the resignation of some of its members, marked the end of good relations between the ministry and the Ulster Agricultural Organisation Society and helped confirm Brooke's image as impulsive and meddling. One M.P. spoke of his 'capacity for taking instant decisions', and another of 'the terrifying accounts' of what was going to happen once the Ministry of Agriculture introduced a scheme.[95]

'Let the house judge for it itself' was a somewhat overworked phrase used during the commons' debates on the P.M.B's dismissal. Throughout, the Unionist backbenchers were surprisingly silent, only two of them expressing a viewpoint, save the unspoken one of trooping into the lobby in support of the government when finally required to do so. A *Belfast Telegraph* correspondent commented: 'silence is becoming . . . [their] . . . mother tongue'. Despite Brooke's revelations of board iniquities and reassurances about the future of the industry, the opinion expressed was that some sort of independent enquiry was justified. The appeal of such a solution had been strengthened by recent precedent. In December 1938 the prime minister had appointed a committee of all parties in the house and the senate to enquire into public transport. This articulated parliamentary consensus was endorsed in a *News Letter* editorial.[96] Likewise Sir Wilfrid Spender, though convinced that 'certain abuses' had occurred, felt that the ministry ought not to have acted as 'prosecution, judge and jury', [97] and favoured a public sworn enquiry. He did appreciate, however, that by mid-March, the government would have lost in public esteem had it made this concession after having shown such strong initial reluctance.

However, the cabinet itself was by no means united. Andrews in particular stated with conviction that the 'Pig Marketing Board should have been given a better opportunity of presenting their case before an ultimatum was presented . . . to resign'. Throughout the dispute he endeavoured to persuade Brooke to hold a public sworn enquiry, and was given some support from J.F. Gordon, minister of labour, who had been impressed at 'the strong desire in many areas'[98] for such an outcome. But Brooke himself obdurately refused to accept Andrews' advice. Spender believe that Sir Basil misjudged the mood of the House having initially believed that he could convince members in the course of the debate that an enquiry should be rejected. During the cabinet discussion on 13 March, he persevered with his opposition, warning colleagues that he had been advised that two of his nominees (to the newly appointed P.M.B.) would resign if the duty of bringing order out of chaos had to be interrupted by judicial proceedings.[99]

The prime minister's response was vital. Without reservation he supported Brooke's position throughout. When Andrews sought to urge the necessity for an enquiry he found that Craig would not 'take the necessary time . . . to hear . . . [his] . . . representations'. Immediately before the parliamentary debates began, Sir James informed Andrews that they should be allowed to run their course and then the question could be shelved.[100]

As they proceeded he remained silent, beyond occasional interjections of 'Hear, Hear', to affirm his support for portions of Brooke's speech. Meanwhile, all three ex-board members rose and complained that they had found him 'unresponsive'. One stated 'The prime minister told us that for anyone who has a grievance, . . . [his] . . . door was open like Dr Barnardo's Home, . . . we have been hammering on that open door for six months and got no reply'.[101] Subsequently Spender noted 'as member after member . . . supported the demand of the late board for an enquiry . . . [Sir James] . . . was put in a very awkward position'.[102]

Nonetheless, that position, though not yet made public, remained unchanged. In cabinet, on 13 March, Craig expressed his opinion that the minister of agriculture had handled a difficult situation in a very competent manner. He spoke against a judicial enquiry, suggesting with the attorney general's concurrence, that such a response would require an act of parliament. Eventually, despite the repressed doubts that some ministers clearly felt, it was decided that a motion be put down in the prime minister's name approving Brooke's action in making the order, dated 27 February 1939, amending the Pig Marketing Scheme.[103] Despite being persistently pressed in parliament to say whether or not an enquiry would be held, Craig did not publicly reveal his position until a motion to this effect appeared in his name on the order paper for 23 March. Meanwhile, on Sir James's suggestion and clearly as a result of recent experience, the cabinet agreed to consider whether steps should be taken to exclude M.P.s, from the membership of marketing boards in future.[104]

As arranged Craig introduced his motion, and spoke passionately, from carefully prepared notes, against a judicial enquiry. To do otherwise, he suggested, would result in the bacon industry bill being delayed. He introduced a further argument which struck a more responsive chord, namely that it would be 'derogatory to this house . . . for any body . . . to be placed in a position of over-ruling what . . . [it] . . . has decided'. He also affirmed his belief that 'the vast majority of the farmers . . . [had] . . . ample confidence' in Brooke, and that after having gone 'into the matter meticulously . . . the minister had no choice' and had shown great 'courage'. He concluded

This motion is to show the Ulster people . . . [that we] . . . have complete faith in the manner in which the honourable gentleman carries out his arduous duties. I think nothing less is due to him.[105]

Not everyone agreed. In response Moore, the leading spokesman of the ex-board members, introduced an amendment in favour of an enquiry, and which declined to express any opinion on Brooke's actions. At this point, Craig rose once more and declared unequivocally:

No further enquiry is necessary, . . . the amendment . . . is tantamount to a vote of censure, and is regarded as such by the government . . . [Brooke's] . . . conduct is undoubtedly being questioned by three honourable members, . . . it is not one man's reputation that is at stake here, but it is a matter of the government of the country.[106]

Somewhat surprisingly, Brooke was not present in the chamber. Craig explained his absence from the proceedings. He stated that he had himself consulted the speaker with regard to procedure and had been informed that when a charge was made against a minister, he should not be present in the house. Accordingly, he had met Brooke 'coming in at the door . . . [and] . . . informed him of the decision, . . . It was his . . . [Brooke's] . . . intention to be in the house to reply'. The speaker had provided members with a similar explanation earlier in the debate. Some expressed doubts as to the wisdom of the decision, one describing it as 'contrary to common sense', as the issue was not one of personal integrity but public policy. Sir Basil had of course on two earlier occasions defended his position in the house at length.

In the debate which followed, four M.P.s joined with the ex-board members in demanding an enquiry. There were allegations of a 'cover up', appeals for 'new blood' and blunt statements that the present ministers were 'not fit to govern'. Nevertheless Moore's amendment was easily defeated. The drama, however, had not yet ended. Attention now switched to another amendment, which had been introduced earlier by James Brown, member for South Down. It had stated that 'No reflection [was] . . . cast on . . . [the] . . . honour and integrity' of the three ex-board M.P.s by the recent official enquiry. It was now itself amended to state that no such reflection was cast on any member of the old board. Before a vote could be taken, there were angry claims that Brown was acting in collusion with the front bench, and indeed two days previously he had introduced a motion in favour of a full investigation into all the boards. These accusations Dixon fervently denied.[107] Despite their protests, the ex-board members were now asked to leave the chamber, though not before making it clear that they would have voted against this amended amendment, had they been permitted to stay. Amidst scenes of Gilbertian supineness, the house at last divided, and the latter was carried with just one negative vote.

Thus an anomalous situation had been created. Ministry officials had found the old board guilty, amongst other crimes, of the peculation of public funds, and now the commons adjudged all of them to be 'men of honour and integrity'. On 25 April, Campbell asked Brooke directly whether the house had condoned corruption or the report disseminated libel. He received the reply that the new Pig Marketing Board was examining the situation and would soon produce its report.[108] This was the only additional enquiry held, and it did at least verify the findings of the ministry officials when published in September 1939.[109]

But in the end it is difficult to doubt the validity of Spender's judgement that a 'very difficult position'[110] would have been prevented, had Andrews' original advice been taken. Brooke himself came to accept that his department had treated the P.M.B. too harshly and attributed this in part to his failure to curb his own over-zealous officials.[111] That the final unsatisfactory outcome generated so little effective criticism in the house and so few votes in the opposition lobby is a measure of the numerical dominance, deferential nature, and essential mediocrity of the Unionist parliamentary party. The episode also casts a very poor reflection on the government, whose members supported and possibly connived at producing a compromise amendment which was totally inconsistent with the evidence produced and actions taken by one of its members, the minister of agriculture.

CHAPTER VI

The Political Impact of Brooke
and His Ministry

Sir Wilfrid Spender considered that the tense debate surrounding the dismissal of the Pig Marketing Board illustrated the total lack of a spirit of cooperation[1] within the administration. Certainly, there is ample evidence, by the late 1930s, to suggest that the activities of the Ministry of Agriculture had become deeply divisive at cabinet level and were generating greater tension between departments whilst at the same time significantly contributing to the government's mounting unpopularity. From early in the decade ministerial dissension was occasionally caused by the department's aggressive style, the financial cost and political risks involved in its schemes, and from time to time issues of principle, chiefly over the question of parity with Britain. The agricultural marketing bill of 1931, the milk legislation and the fruit and pig marketing schemes had each aroused discussion on one or other of these points, with Andrews consistently the minister most outspoken in his criticisms. He expressed concern regarding this programme, at different stages suggesting that the government was assuming too much responsibility, that too much power was being placed in the hands of officials or that ministerial actions threatened to create unemployment.[2]

The most serious confrontation between Andrews and Brooke prior to the P.M.B. dispute came in 1935 over Ministry of Labour plans to emulate Westminster, and extend unemployment insurance to the province's agricultural workers. Brooke stated that he was strongly in favour of this proposal but on condition that local benefits were lower than those in the imperial scheme and thus in line with Northern Ireland's lower wages, so ensuring that unemployment would not be made as attractive as employment. He also feared that the scheme would create pressures for an agricultural wages board which he regarded as impracticable until rural prosperity increased.[3] To Andrews the preservation of parity with Britain was a cardinal principle. He stated characteristically: 'It was the government's very definite policy since its establishment in 1921, that there should be equal standards and complete reciprocity in social insurance services between Great Britain and Northern Ireland'. He added, some months later, that to act differently 'would weaken the stand that the government has consistently taken'.[4] He himself had acted on this principle over issues as diverse as the school-leaving age, factory legislation and medical benefits for juveniles.[5] Andrews also regarded Brooke's fears as exaggerated and suggested that since benefits were based on need, Sir Basil's arguments implied that rural wages were below subsistence level. Both Craig and Pollock supported without reservation the Ministry of Labour position and the cabinet finally decided that there was no alternative but to introduce this measure on the same lines as Great Britain.

By the time of the next clash between Brooke and Andrews over the bacon industry bill, their respective positions had reversed. The Ministry of Agriculture did come under more pressure to form a wages board, particularly after Northern Ireland became the only part of the United Kingdom with no such machinery, and there was some concern that if no such measure was introduced cheap southern labour might displace the indigenous workforce in border areas.[6] When, in 1939, the department finally decided to act, however, Brooke justified the measure also by a strong appeal for strict parity with Britain. He explained to the house that it was particularly important to emulate Great Britain in the matter in view of the imperial government decision to extend the assistance afforded to the farming community. If no board was created he suggested that it would provide a 'basis for the suggestion that assistance to the Northern Ireland farmer is less justifiable than in Great Britain'.[7]

Over the establishment of a wages board, cabinet agreement had been a formality. This was not the case some months earlier, however, when new Exchequer assistance was extended to the pig industry under the bacon industry act in 1938. Brooke had then also argued for a policy of strict parity, determined to ensure that the province's pig producers received assistance on as favourable terms as in Great Britain, otherwise he informed his colleagues, it would be 'impossible for . . . [him] . . . to face the industry'.[8] He supported this case also by reference to the clauses relating to agriculture in the Anglo-Irish agreement. In addition, he suggested that such support was urgently needed as the imperial scheme would lead to a fall in pig prices on the British market, and on the grounds that the province's curing plants required rationalisation.

For his part, Andrews who had meantime succeeded Pollock, as minister of finance, was by the autumn of 1938 deeply concerned at the application of parity in this case. He feared that the enormous cost of this scheme, possibly over £750,000 would force Northern Ireland's imperial contribution into deficit and might generate criticism of the government not least from other agricultural sectors seeking similar assistance. The province's finances were already strained by falling revenue and the failure of the transport act, as well as growing unemployment. Also despite Brooke's reassurances, Andrews was concerned that the local scheme differed materially from that in Great Britain. Consequently he anticipated strenuous opposition from the British Treasury and suggested that a maximum upper limit be placed on any subsidy and a restriction imposed on the number of pigs that might qualify.[9]

Prolonged negotiations followed involving both the ministers of agriculture and finance, and the Treasury. In the spring of 1939 as the terms of an agreement began to emerge it became clear that Brooke and his officials had been compelled to make important concessions. Limits were imposed on the number of pigs that might benefit and on the total Exchequer contribution, which for the first year was much less than early Ministry of Agriculture estimates though more than Andrews had anticipated.[10] The scheme itself was delayed for one year, eventually coming into operation on 1 September 1939 only to be suspended by defence regulations in 1940.

The negotiations indicate that self-interest was the dominant factor in determining British government policy towards Northern Ireland farming. They also illustrate the growing departmental conflict within the Northern Ireland administration over the financial aspect of agricultural measures and their escalating cost. Habitual Ministry of Finance apprehension regarding this issue was heightened in the late 1930s by the deterioration in Northern Ireland's finances and worries that the province's imperial contribution might teeter into deficit. Spender believed that this could undermine his department's harmonious relationship with the Treasury and possibly therefore jeopardise relations even at governmental level.[11]

The exchange of memoranda between Brooke and Andrews during the negotiations also reveals an element of inter-departmental distrust. Sir Basil charged that the Ministry of Finance had prevented his scheme from being carried on British votes, a course which he claimed he would have preferred. Andrews responded by stating that this possibility had been blocked by the British Treasury, owing to differences between the Northern Ireland and imperial schemes. He also alleged that the Ministry of Agriculture preferred measures to be carried on Stormont votes, quoting from a statement by Scott Robertson that this gave greater freedom of action. Certainly Spender was convinced that through its actions the agriculture department was constantly attempting to escape the scrutiny of his ministry. This latter role he regarded as particularly vital in Northern Ireland given the lack of a strong political opposition in parliament. He considered that 'The only check that exists at all is the Ministry of Finance', and complained about those who thought that the imperial contribution was a source of unlimited financial help.[12]

Other aspects of the Ministry of Agriculture's polices caused acute disquiet. Sir Douglas Harkness characterised the general attitude of Northern Ireland government ministers as being 'against the extension of state activity and much in favour of economy'.[13] Not surprisingly, by the late 1930s, the apparently interminable nature of the agricultural programme with its apparently unquenchable capacity to absorb limited financial resources was a cause of concern, in particular at the department directly affected, the Ministry of Finance. In 1935, Spender wrote to Sir Ernest Clark: 'the main danger that I foresee at present is the growth of government in regard to agriculture'. Twelve months later, he complained that the marketing boards 'seem to be succeeding each other in rapid succession... my old conservatism and belief at any rate, in empire free trade make me rather alarmed'. At one point he suggested that Clark might be called in to advise on 'the soundness of government control',[14] at least, he may have hoped that the former might so advise Brooke during his visit to Tasmania in 1936–7. Andrews shared the uneasiness of his permanent secretary. At the time of the bacon industry bill one of the ministry's deepest fears was that if such assistance was given to pig producers it would lead to similar demands from other agricultural sectors.[15]

Brooke's memorandum, in September 1938, calling for increased agricultural output, mechanisation, rural electrification and cheap loans was greeted with less than enthusiasm at the Ministry of Finance. In cabinet, Andrews expressed concern regarding the financial implications of the proposals, and suggested that they must be thoroughly investigated. It was agreed to establish an inter-departmental committee, which the prime minister proceeded to appoint after some prompting from Scott Robertson.[16] When it eventually reported in November 1939, Craig considered that there was 'no question of giving effect to . . . [its] . . . major recommendations . . . at the present time'. Spender who was throughout highly sceptical, welcomed this inquiry into the Ministry of Agriculture's 'visionary ideas of the millenium', before the government announced its policy and committed itself to 'heavy expenditure and ridicule'.[17]

From the vantage point of the Ministry of Finance, the uneasiness aroused by the Ministry of Agriculture was as much related to its style as to the content of its proposed legislation. Spender's criticisms of its policies were partly because they conflicted with his political principles, and the fact that he was fulfilling his official responsibilities, but they also reflected a deep concern about the laxity, even the irresponsibility, of some of its activities and their likely impact on the government's popularity. To both Andrews and Spender, the department frequently appeared to be casual, impulsive and unnecessarily abrasive in its approach. This was the case not only over the dismissal of the Pig Marketing Board but also over other issues. These included, for example, the premature release of estimates before they were scrutinised by the Ministry of Finance, or submitted to parliament, or the issuing of public statements regarding future policy which thereby threatened to commit the government to actions which it had not yet agreed to adapt, or to raise popular expectations to levels which it might prove difficult to fulfill.[18] For these reasons Andrews was perturbed during the bacon industry bill negotiations by what he regarded as the unrealistically high figures being aired by the Ministry of Agriculture with regard to anticipated levels of aid for the pig industry. He also used his influence to ensure that the inter-departmental report regarding Brooke's September 1938 programme was not published.[19]

Brooke himself was by no means immune from these criticisms, apart altogether from his obduracy when the P.M.B. was dissolved. Spender regarded the department's habit of 'placating' members of the U.F.U. at least until the late 1930s and leading landowners as 'not altogether a healthy symptom' which could 'lead us into trouble with the Joint Exchequer Board'. Here he thought Sir Basil was extremely culpable, and regularly commented on loans made to persons of considerable private means, for purposes not contemplated by parliament. On one occasion he cited a grant of £1,200 to Lord Enniskillen given to 'improve the appearance of his demesne', and informed Brooke that he could 'not countenance' such a use of public funds. Meetings were held, and agreements drawn up in which Spender sought to ensure that loans were made less liberally and that the ministry was made fully aware of the terms on which they should be made available. In early 1938, Brooke defended giving drainage grants to large landowners as the 'wages paid . . . [did] . . . not exceed unemployment pay' and thus 'the land . . . [was] . . . drained for nothing'. Spender conceded that it was a 'difficult question'.[20]

Sir Wilfrid also criticised Brooke for the frequency with which he was not available to fulfill his ministerial duties in the late 1930s. Due to a visit to south

Australia in the winter of 1936–7 Brooke missed nine cabinet meetings and some cabinet business had to be postponed. It occurred at a time when the prime minister, the minister of home affairs and speaker of the House of Commons were all absent. It provoked parliamentary criticism. Referring to Sir Basil's absence, Henderson suggested that it was inappropriate as 'the people . . . [were] . . . almost on the verge of revolution'.[21] In early 1939, Andrews, who was acting prime minister, was somewhat disconcerted to find out that Sir Basil had gone to Monte Carlo without officially informing him, and without nominating anyone to act as minister in his absence. Some months later, Spender noted that Brooke would be unable to pay much attention to his agricultural duties as Craig had asked him to help organise a tank corps. Once more, the effect was heightened by the fact that the prime minister was unwell, the minister of home affairs unfit for his duties and the minister of labour was abroad. With only two ministers available, the cabinet secretary felt that cabinet meetings served little purpose, hence, Spender claims, matters were either held in suspense or dealt with departmentally.[22]

The content of Brooke's speeches also, on occasion, aroused deep concern at the Ministry of Finance. Spender felt that some of those made in the winter of 1938–39 fuelled speculation regarding the future of land purchase annuities, and heightened farmers' expectations of governmental relief.[23] On 22 December 1938, the *Northern Whig* reported that he had met representatives of the U.F.U. and had acceded to their demand for a committee of enquiry to investigate the causes of rural depression and advise on agricultural policy. Andrews was shocked when he received this information as the question had not been discussed by cabinet, and he feared that it might produce undigested proposals in conflict with British policy. He immediately contacted Craig, who claimed that it was also 'a surprise to him'. Andrews understood that the prime minister or his office subsequently advised Brooke against setting up a committee, told him to mark time until British policy was announced, and await his return from Ceylon in late February 1939.[24] Some weeks later, Sir Wilfrid wrote that 'an extraordinary situation' arose. He described how in early January, the committee was being formed, chairman and members appointed, and meetings scheduled. Andrews, now acting prime minister, was once more distressed. After discovering that Brooke had gone to Monte Carlo, he located Scott Robertson, who claimed that he was entirely responsible and apologised for acting against cabinet direction. Andrews told him to 'take no further action' and indicated his intention of 'having a talk with his minister'.[25]

When surveying the broad political scene in the autumn of 1938 Spender was profoundly dejected. This was partly because he had an acute sense that the government was losing ground with public opinion. This he attributed to the province's mounting unemployment, whose interwar levels when compared with Britain were at their worst in 1938. He also blamed the government's mishandling of public transport, which possibly cost the taxpayer £4 million.[26] In addition, whatever the economic impact of agricultural policy, Spender was convinced that politically it had contributed to the growing unpopularity of the local administration. He had always been acutely aware of the risks inherent in the marketing schemes not only because of fears that they might break down, but also concern that they might alienate non-farming sections of the electorate. In the mid-1930s he wrote, 'sympathy with the farmer may prevent an undue outcry as long as the general prosperity prevails', but he predicted very severe criticism of the schemes if a slump came and the public blamed them for causing inflation or depressing living standards. Several years later, it seemed to him that his fears had become reality. He reflected on the expensive mistakes made by the Ministry of Agriculture which had met with general dissatisfaction.[27] But he was particularly struck by the mendacity and ingratitude of the farming interest. He wrote: 'as soon as one part get subsidies . . . the rest look for help', adding later

It is extraordinary in spite of all the assistance given to the agricultural community, they are getting more and more dissatisfied with our governmental policy and criticising every measure which the government has introduced.[28]

By the late 1930s there was certainly every indication of widespread rural discontent. This was evidenced by the threat to form a splinter unionist party in County Armagh, the movement amongst farmers to withold land purchase annuities, the breakdown in ministry relations with the Pig Marketing Board and Butter and Cream Board, and the deterioration in its relationship with the Ulster Agricultural Organisation Society. As Spender pointed out, it was also reflected in the opposition of the major farmer representative organisations to ministry policy. P.M.B. and U.F.U. hostility to the bacon industry bill weakened Brooke's negotiating position when it was being considered by the cabinet. The U.F.U. Executive also condemned the dismissal of the Pig Marketing Board and opposed the formation of a wages board.[29] The initial expectation of its membership had not been fulfilled, and it became disillusioned by the dilatoriness of legislation and above all, alienated by the alleged anti-producer bias of government policy.

Partly due to U.F.U. intervention, agriculture became an issue in the 1938 Stormont election. The union drew up a questionnaire which it sent to all candidates to elicit their views on agricultural questions, and which Brooke felt obliged to respond to in detail. It also devised its own programme which included the reduction of land purchase annuities, concessions to farmers on transport costs, and the principle that marketing schemes should only be put into effect with the consent of the farming community which, it claimed, was the practice in England and Scotland.[30] The extent of government unpopularity may be gauged by the scale of independent unionist participation, challenging unionist party supremacy even in solidly unionist areas. It was described by the *Irish Times* as 'the first mutiny in 18 years'.[31] A number of independent candidates took up agricultural questions. Some attacked the effects of government legislation on the cost of living, The Progressive Unionists, the largest independent grouping, included in their election manifesto a commitment to the full programme.[32]

Much of the hostility directed against the department focused not on Brooke but on his permanent secretary, Scott Robertson. During the Commons debates on the dismissal of the P.M.B. an ex-member, Rowley Elliot, stated: 'I refused . . . to be dragooned by . . . [Sir Basil's] . . . chief lieutenant the greatest Hitler in Northern Ireland'. Similarly Rev. Robert Moore declared that he had been driven to the reluctant conclusion that while he [Scott Robertson] holds his present position . . . there can never be that harmony and cooperation between producers and their representatives and the Ministry of Agriculture that there should be.[33]

At the height of the fruit-grower's agitation, Wilson Hungerford, secretary to the Ulster Unionist Council, described 'the real feeling . . . in Armagh, I am afraid that Scott Robertson is making lots of trouble and is running his minister'.[34] Robertson's influence continued to be a cause of comment and controversy even after the outbreak of war.

Robertson was the son of a Scottish newspaper proprietor, who completed his higher education in England, specialising in chemistry, and after a brief academic career, joined the department. There he devoted his life to increasing the efficiency and improving the quality of Northern Ireland agriculture. He had little tolerance and less respect for the reasoning and intelligence of opponents. He had a dominant and abrasive personality. When he first became permanent secretary, four of his officials asked to leave the department. One of his colleagues remarked that personal popularity meant nothing to him.[35]

He undoubtedly made a profound contribution to the work of the ministry, a fact of which he was keenly aware. When he refused the offer of a C.B.E. in 1937 Spender claimed it was because he believed that he was deserving of a higher honour. He played a vital role in the negotiations with the British government from the milk scheme to the bacon industry bill, and served on a number of important imperial government committees. He helped formulate departmental objectives. Thus Spender refers to the mechanisation and elec-trification programme as 'Scott Robertson's policy', and the same description might be applied to the objective of getting all Northern Ireland pigs cured locally. For a civil servant, he adopted a uniquely high profile as when he proceeded to appoint the committee of enquiry into agriculture in 1939, knowing that it conflicted with cabinet direction or, more publicly, when he was a driving force behind the P.M.B. dismissal.[36]

Though Robertson made the greatest impact on public awareness, it is clear that other officials also made a significant contribution to the work of the department. Possibly their role was enhanced by the lack of a parliamentary secretary for agriculture and a resulting tendency to delegate the duties of that office to civil servants. Certainly Harkness later recalled with satisfaction his own considerable influence on legislation and the numerous committees, local and imperial, on which he served. He was in his own words 'a regular Pooh-bah'. Though after the war he became permanent secretary at the Ministry of Finance and titular head of the Northern Ireland civil service, he came to regard his years at Agriculture from the early 1930s, as with 'little doubt . . . the highlight of . . . [his] . . . career'. His promotion to more honorific positions later appeared as 'an anticlimax by comparison. . . . It seemed . . . [that he] . . . had exchanged the substance of power for the shadow'.[37]

However, the overwhelming impression of the relationship within the department between Brooke and his officials is one of cooperation and collective enthusiasm for shared objectives. Harkness, recollecting visits to Colebrooke with Robertson, wrote:

our great joy . . . was in winter, we were always provided with wonderful wood fires . . . There was a . . . very elegant but moderate sized dining-room. It had a charming circular club fender in front of the fire-place and after dinner Brooke, Scott Robertson and I would draw our chairs up to this piece of furniture, stretch our legs out to the fire . . . in true Pickwickian fashion, and proceed with our discussions on the misdeeds of the Pig Marketing Board and our reactions to them . . . sometimes we digressed into politics.[38]

Sir Basil frequently spoke of his officials with undiluted affection and pride, unreservedly supporting and justifying their activities. He praised them for being more in touch with the farming community than their colleagues in the United Kingdom, and claimed that 'the success of the various schemes . . . owed less to the boards concerned than the skill with which they had been devised' by his ministry, to suit local conditions.[39] During the commons debate on the dismissal of the P.M.B. he ardently defended Scott Robertson, with interjections of support from Craig. He stated that his permanent secretary had his 'complete confidence. I have worked in daily cooperation with him for five years', and that he had given 'whole-hearted service to Northern Ireland agriculture. I know of no one who could have secured for Northern Ireland greater assistance from the government of Great Britain'. Earlier, at the time of the election, Brooke passionately upheld the role of his civil servants.[40]

It is impossible to doubt the sincerity of these public statements, regarding his officials. Similar sentiments were repeated privately in his diary during the war. Even in the heat of the parliamentary debate his opponents did not impugn his motives for dismissing the P.M.B. One ex-board member stated 'I believe he thinks what he has done is in the best interests of agriculture'. There is some evidence that Brooke became less sure of this, believing that he ought on this occasion to have resisted the advice of his officials.[41] Spender, who closely scrutinised the department, records no suggestion of Robertson exercising any undue influence over his minister in this period, and gives instances of his advice being rejected by Brooke, the latter tending to be more flexible and pragmatic in approach.[42] Not only was Sir Basil committed to the policies of his ministry, but he himself tended to regard them, like his officials, as self-evidently good for agriculture and somehow, therefore above politics. On one occasion, he said of Healy and his colleagues that they had

never put anything in the way of the various marketing acts. They have always realised that these acts were only passed to help agriculturalists and were outside the realm of politics. I should like to say I am very grateful.[43]

Elsewhere he stated that he was 'more interested in agriculture than in politics', and reflected on the misfortune that in Great Britain politics and agriculture were 'mixed up'.[44]

Though Brooke identified with and defended agricultural legislation, he clearly did not himself originate it. Its timing and content were largely determined at Westminster, and its detailed local features defined by officials from his own ministry. This is not to denigrate the value or significance of his own contribution. He fulfilled his role in negotiations with the British government capably and confidently. Thus, some local industrialists were prompted to suggest that his services should be employed to seek contracts for Northern Ireland firms, an idea perhaps encouraged also by the visits of the duke of

Gloucester to Colebrooke in 1935 and 1938.[45] Douglas Harkness describes an agricultural conference, in 1936, at which Sir Basil 'displayed his full charm and friendliness. Everyone was delighted with him and I received many words of appreciation on the qualities of my minister'.[46] Within the department he helped give cohesion and unity of purpose to a potentially disparate team. In cabinet he argued his case cogently and determinedly, but was always willing to accept reasonable compromise.

Despite the fact that aspects of agricultural policy and of its application aroused bitter criticism at Stormont, his parliamentary abilities were widely respected and admired, and his sincerity unchallenged. Bitter verbal inter changes did not nullify his personal friendships. During the debate over P.M.B. dismissal, one ex-board member referred to Brooke as still his 'firm and fast friend' and almost two years later Brooke urged that Moore, the leading board spokesman, should succeed himself as minister.[47] Overall, despite its alleged errors and apparent risk-taking, the dynamism of the department was recognized. Its 'mistakes' one M.P. commented, were 'the result of its energy'.[48] This image of 'energy' and commitment, was shared by Sir Basil and was possibly lacking in his predecessor.

Beyond Stormont, Brooke helped to render more acceptable the otherwise abrasive image of his ministry. He was in his natural political element when talking to farmers or their representatives and establishing direct contact with rural communities. That his amiability was not rationed by the company he happened to be with, contributed to his effectiveness. Harkness wrote many years later that his 'main recollection' of the confrontation with the P.M.B. was 'the personal interest which Brooke took in the whole matter' and he regarded his role in dissipating rural hostility as vital. One newspaper editorial described a series of meetings in Fermanagh and Tyrone which both Sir Basil and his assistant secretary addressed in early 1939, as having been 'productive of excellent results, . . . [they went] . . . a considerable way to clear the air of suspicion and misunderstanding'.[49]

Though Spender had the most profound reservations about the province's agricultural policy and was far from uncritical of Brooke himself, he did nevertheless also pay tribute to his political qualities. He depicts him as a young, energetic and enthusiastic minister, who he suggested, would find it 'very disappointing', if he became aware of 'the value placed by the farming community on his activities'. In a private memorandum, written in 1938, Sir Wilfrid reviewed the performance of the government. He concluded that its sheer ineptitude was such that it might 'do irreparable harm to Ulster and to the unionist cause, . . . [and] . . . constituted a grave danger to the system of democratic government in the province'. He was scathingly critical of the cabinet, including Craig, whom he had come to regard as a liability, cocooned from reality by his wife, so ill that he ought to retire, and perhaps prevented from doing so by financial dependency on the premiership. Virtually the only exceptions in his dismal analysis of Northern Ireland's ministers and leading officials were Andrews, whom he considered to be over-worked and under-consulted, and Brooke.[50]

Brooke he described as being 'keen on his job', and capable of providing valuable advice beyond his immediate departmental responsibilities. There are some indications that his political influence did develop in the course of the decade. By the late 1930s he was the most frequent front-bench spokesman at meetings of the parliamentary Unionist party, though to a large extent this was due to the controversial nature of his ministry's activities.[51] Cabinet records, however, provide little evidence of him assuming a more dominant role. During discussions, he continued to speak almost exclusively on matters relating to his own department or on cognate questions such as transport or the linen industry. Possibly this is an illusion, however, caused by the brevity of the written conclusions, and in any case its significance might be overstated. Spender alleges that the cabinet system was breaking down towards the end of the decade with key decisions being made elsewhere.[52] This, he suggests, was mainly due to Craig's penchant for 'quick hasty decisions rather than . . . [going] . . . into a question with his colleagues', and the ill-health or absence of members.[53] A possible further factor was the propensity for its decisions to be leaked to the press.[54] In these more fluid circumstances, Spender states that Brooke was 'sometimes brought into consultation by the prime minister with the chief whip on matters relating to other departments'. He continues: 'his advice might be quite useful, if the facts were put before him but this is by no means always the case'. He later regarded Brooke's policy recommendations on transport as ill-considered.[55]

Meanwhile, Brooke's friendship with Craig appears to have matured and deepened. Sir Basil continued to give the prime minister unqualified loyalty. It was a sentiment expressed more frequently in his speeches as criticisms of the inadequacy of the government's leadership sharpened and as Stormont elections approached in the late 1930s. He also strongly attacked those calling for direct rule, stressing the dangers of an unsympathetic cabinet at Westminster and the continuing threat from the south. In April 1937, he asked the Fermanagh Unionist Association 'could they really say in their heart of hearts that they could find a leader who could inspire so much confidence or . . . that same feeling of pride'[56] as Craig. Some months later he described Sir James, with genuine conviction, as 'the man who made Ulster . . . and would never let Ulster down', concluding 'there is a devil of a lot of fight in the old gang'. He also defended the timing of the election, which resulted from a somewhat controversial decision taken on impulse and without consultation by Sir James, in mid-January 1938, after reading newspaper accounts of the Anglo-Irish negotiations and mindful of the new Eire constitution.[57] In essence it was a ploy to crush the independent Unionist 'wreckers'.

Similarly, Craig continued to make flattering comments about Brooke, particularly in speeches made whilst staying at Colebrooke during his periodic visits to Fermanagh. In April 1935, the somewhat ritualistic nature of these occasions was given added significance when he opened two bridges which spanned the Erne, linking the southern portion of the county with the North at Lisnaskea. They were named after Lady Craig and Lady Brooke, on his insistence, and their effect was to transform the prosperity of Brooke's political heartland. There are other indications that the relationship between the two had become particularly close. In Belfast, Sir Basil attended social functions patronised or organised by the Prime Minister, at which the attendance of other cabinet ministers was rare if not unknown. When Sir James moved into his new home at Glencraig, the Brookes were his first house guests. As the former's health failed, Brooke occasionally deputised for him at party meetings, or, unique amongst his colleagues, accompanied Lady Craig on semi-official engagements.[58] Writing to the latter in 1937, Sir James described having 'Pollock, Bates, Basil and Andrews in succession' to see him, thus being noticeably selective in his use of the more familiar form of address. Early the following year, when it was clear that Brooke would not be opposed at the election, Craig personally telegraphed him to state that he was 'delighted', and commented on his 'valuable services in parliament'.[59]

Though occasionally some of Craig's interventions in departmental affairs might be less than welcome he was generally supportive. In cabinet, he gave Brooke his backing on every occasion when it was required in the late 1930s.[60] He consistently backed Brooke's refusal of a judicial enquiry into the Pig Marketing Board, so rejecting the advice of Andrews and others. Instead he chose to regard the issue as one of confidence not only in Sir Basil but in the government itself. During the bacon industry bill negotiations, he fully supported Brooke's claim that Northern Ireland farmers should be granted subsidies on at least as favourable terms as those in Great Britain. When in 1938 Sir Basil abruptly announced that a committee would be formed to enquire into rural distress, Spender suspected that Craig, despite his protestations of surprise, had been consulted beforehand. Likewise, when Sir Basil made statements regarding land purchase annuities which caused concern at the Ministry of Finance in this same period, Spender claims that these had received Sir James's prior approval.[61] By contrast, in his 1938 memorandum, Sir Wilfrid complains that Andrews was over-worked and under-recognised, acting prime minister at least 'When anything unpleasant has to be done', and that though he carried the burden of three ministries, he was not consulted even on matters relating to his own department.[62]

In addition, Craig continued to delegate additional responsibilities to Brooke, which contributed to some of those absences from ministerial duties for which he was criticised. In 1936, the prime minister asked him to act as the representative of the Northern Ireland parliament to the Empire Parliamentary Association which was assembling in South Australia to mark the centenary anniversary of the state.[63] More significantly, in early 1938 Brooke and Milne Barbour were asked to accompany Andrews for his discussions with British ministers in London. The Anglo-Irish negotiations were then reaching fruition, Craig was unwell, and the three ministers were given what Spender describes as 'full powers to obtain favourable terms for Northern Ireland'. There followed the only serious confrontation with the prime minister in Sir Basil's political career.

The province was not directly involved in the early stages of the talks but both Hoare and Chamberlain had given strong assurances that it would be consulted and its interests safeguarded. As a result, Andrews regarded Craig's January election call as 'not quite fair to the electorate'.[64] During the months that followed the Northern Ireland cabinet adopted a firm position in the discussions, stressing the need for far-reaching concessions to revitalise the local economy, and the grave political problems that an unsatisfactory settlement might create. British ministers were sympathetic, eager to achieve Ulster's cooperation in implementing the agreement, and sensitive to her possible influence on opinion in the imperial parliament and in the country.

When in early March, De Valera made it clear that he would not accede to the Northern demand for free trade across the border, Andrews informed Hoare that nothing less would be acceptable and indicated that he could see no purpose in participating any further in the negotiations. Next day, on 5 March, Brooke assured his colleague that he was in complete agreement and would back him 'in any measure . . . [he] . . . thought fit, including resignation'. Subsequently the governor was sounded on his reaction to a possible resignation of the entire government and he stated that he 'would give the utmost support'. Blackmore was confident that if another election was held, it would focus British attention on the treaty and possibly precipitate a crisis when it was debated at Westminster. Likewise, Hoare is alleged to have said that he would take any step short of resigning to help Northern Ireland resist its terms.

Within two weeks, Spender writes, 'the whole situation changed',[65] when Craig intervened directly in the negotiations, after receiving a lengthy written appeal from Chamberlain. On 18 March Sir James met the latter, and without any prior discussion with his colleagues, privately assured him of his support for any agreement if Northern Ireland received adequate compensation.[66] Craig reluctantly agreed to attend a briefing session held next morning with Northern Ireland ministers and officials, less than two hours before their planned discussions with the British committee for Irish affairs. Andrews had insisted on the meeting as he was concerned that government policy was drifting, and though unaware of the firm commitments entered into on the previous day, he was anxious to clarify the precise position held by the prime minister. During its proceedings, Sir James read aloud a memorandum prepared by Spender, and approved by Andrews and Brooke, stating that no further concessions could be made. Brooke at once responded by saying that 'our cabinet could not for a moment accept the treaty and if it attempted to do so it would be thrown out'. The point was pressed and Craig entered a note confirming Sir Basil's observation and stated that he was in full agreement with the views in the memorandum. Both Andrews and Brooke stated unequivocally that they would rather give up office than surrender the position that they had held throughout the negotiations.

At their afternoon session with British ministers and officials, Craig confronted his ministerial colleagues with a virtual *fait accompli*. At an early stage he indicated his acceptance of the principle of the treaty and diverted the conversation towards what concessions and financial assistance could be given to Northern Ireland. Spender states that both Andrews and Brooke were 'astounded', and 'dumbfounded at this *volte face*',[67] only now beginning to appreciate the significance of the prime minister's earlier meeting with Chamberlain. Neither liked to refute him openly, but Andrews did pin-point the unfairness of the agreement as it stood. This apparently made a considerable impression on the home secretary who had been surprised by the lack of resistance from the Ulster delegation. It was subsequently decided that the Northern Ireland cabinet would submit a memorandum with specific proposals which would be considered by the imperial government.

By 25 March, memoranda and letters detailing a wide range of financial concessions desired from Westminster had been drafted, approved, and submitted. These included a request that whatever Exchequer assistance is given to an agricultural product in Great Britain shall be given on an equal basis from the United Kingdom Exchequer in respect of that product produced in Northern Ireland . . . Up to the present Northern Ireland has participated in the existing subsidies on the same basis as Great Britain but the principle of such assistance has never been admitted.[68]

Further discussions with British ministers followed in mid-April. Perhaps significantly Brooke was the only one of the three ministers who had been involved in the negotiations from the beginning of the year, not to take part, despite the fact that agricultural issues were being discussed. The imperial government paid most but not all that was demanded for the province's acquiescence somewhat cynically applying Craig's rather indiscreet advice 'not to give an Ulsterman all he wants'.[69] Andrews had earlier described the outcome as 'not a just one', and warned his colleagues that he might have to say so in the house, and he remained convinced that better terms could have been achieved had the prime minister handled the negotiations differently.[70] The final agreement was signed on 25 April, and published next day, though not before its contents had been leaked to the press soon after being ratified by the Northern Ireland cabinet five days earlier[71]

Arguably Craig's intervention was statesmanlike in that he adopted a more panoptic perspective than Andrews or Brooke, willing to sacrifice the local interests of the province to the greater needs of the empire. His officials were less magnanimous. Blackmore attributed his outlook to the inappropriate influence exercised by Lady Craig and Lord Glentoran, and claimed that Sir James was given an earldom for his services on this occasion. Spender was concerned about the role of Chamberlain's wife, Annie, in causing Craig's defection. He felt that the latter not only compromised Northern Ireland's position during the negotiations but convinced 'the English people that she . . . [was] . . . open to be bought if the price is high enough', and more ominously, led 'Chamberlain to the belief that even on the question of home rule Ulster had no strong views'.[72] These presumptions, he suggests, directly contributed to the intensity of the political pressures applied to the province during the early stages of the war. On this latter occasion Brooke showed that he was willing to make sacrifices for the greater needs of Britain and her empire.

That Craig's *'volte face'* should pass without challenge serves to illuminate once more the nature of Northern Ireland's political leadership, and specifically the extent of the prime minister's continuing ascendency within the Unionist government. Andrews, who had led the negotiating team until Sir James' intervention, did not resign and this must have helped determine Brooke's response. The former may have been persuaded to stay in office by Spender, who suggested to him that 'in regard to Eire the damage was beyond repair . . . [and that] . . . the best course was to do what he could for Ulster'.[73] It is also clear that he continued to feel a strong residual loyalty to Craig. In the autumn of 1938, unlike his permanent secretary, he was convinced that Sir James should remain as prime minister because 'he had a hold over the people of the province as Carson's successor which no one else had . . . [and] . . . a change was undesirable as long as . . . [he] . . . could carry the party with him'.[74] Considerations of this nature may well have influenced Brooke also. Though some evidence suggests that his confidence in Craig's leadership was shaken, his subsequent speeches still contained fulsome expressions of praise and fidelity describing him as the 'greatest leader in the world' and professing his 'unstinted loyalty and support'. He reiterated similar sentiments in his private diary during the war.[75] In addition, he may have been more hopeful than Andrews with regard to the prospects for significant concessions from the imperial government.

Spender writes that Brooke was as 'unhappy' as Andrews after the 19 March meeting, but that the prime minister pointed out what 'great benefits would accrue to agriculture by the new concessions, . . . as usual . . . Lord Craigavon had formed a very optimistic impression of what the British government was ready to give'.[76] In contemporary statements, though Sir Basil sought to distance the Stormont government from any involvement in devising the main articles of the treaty, he also reassured farmers that they were, due to the Treasury commitments it contained, in exactly the 'same position as . . . [producers] . . . across the water'.[77] In reality, the agreement did not alter their fundamental position. Thus when Brooke cited its terms during the pig subsidy negotiations in the autumn of 1938 to justify Ulster's claims to assistance on as favourable conditions as in Great Britain, it had no measurable effect. As one authority has concluded, the extent of British aid to Northern Ireland depended on the extent to which British interests were affected.[78] However, many years later Sir Basil considered that the terms finally signed were not without merit.[79]

The whole episode is of interest not only as an important instance of Craig delegating authority to Brooke and because it was the only major clash between the two politicians, but also because it exemplifies features of Brooke's unionism that he had revealed almost from the moment of his return from the western front. It was confident and aggressive in its resoluteness to protect the interests of the province as he perceived them, and in its willingness to stand up to the British government even to the point of resignation. It was acutely concerned with the attitudes of the Ulster unionist movement, and with the type of settlement it would be prepared to accept. In the last analysis his response indicates as well a deep, though not necessarily inexhaustible, loyalty to Craig, and a determination to preserve party unity which he expressed fervently in his 1938 election speeches. In addition there was a strong element of pragmatism, accepting that politics is, after all, the art of the possible. This was a *leitmotif* certainly of his early career.

Brooke's role during these negotiations is entirely consistent with his other political activities during these years. Reflecting on this period, he states that apart from promoting Northern Ireland's progress at his department his 'main concern . . . [was always] . . . our constitutional position, . . . defending it from those who verbally and physically attacked it'. He inevitably responded to the aggressive Southern propaganda of 1938–39, which accompanied the new Eire constitution, with its privileged status for the Roman catholic church and explicit claims to the six counties. He recalls being baffled and annoyed by the hostile attitudes towards the province then being expressed in England and the sympathy and prominence given to statements by nationalist politicians.[80] The revival of republican excitement coincided with, and may have encouraged, renewed I.R.A. activity which after strong measures had been taken in the south, spread to Britain. Unique amongst Ulster's cabinet ministers, Sir Basil visited northern British cities in the aftermath of terrorist violence, and delivered eloquent, passionate and moderate speeches in defence of the union, which were sympathetically reported in much of the English press.[81]

At Manchester, in January 1939, he reflected on the apparent lack of 'news value' in Northern Ireland's constant 'fidelity and friendship' towards Britain. He continued, by asking

Why must there be this persistent pressure on us to give up our position and a mode of government which satisfies us? . . . Why must we always be on our guard? . . . These are hard questions to answer. They puzzle the average northerner. They puzzle me. The Ulsterman is still more puzzled when he reads in his cross-Channel newspaper that it . . . [is] . . . his 'bigotry' or 'selfishness' or even 'stupidity' that is thwarting the realization of a United Ireland. I imagine that the Austrians or Czechs . . . must have felt . . . the same way when they read in the German papers that their 'unreasonable stubbornness' was preventing the realisation of the Pan-German Reich.

He repeated almost exactly a phrase that he had used during a speech in July 1921, when the state faced even greater external pressure: 'We ourselves, desire only to be left alone'. On this, as on other occasions, he declared that 'partition merely recognises the differences which exist between north and south, it does not create them, nor would its abolition remove them'[82] At no point did he question that the south was 'entitled to any form of government it desires'. Overall, Spender observed that Brooke 'put forward the Ulster case very fairly'. He himself believed that an effective way for the government to respond to southern propaganda would be to divert at least some of the money being invested in agricultural schemes to subsidising the resettlement of farmers who wished to transfer to the Free State.[83]

These speeches by Brooke and others depicting the perils of absorption by the south and warning of the need for Unionist vigilance to avoid 'losing control', did not prevent him, as minister, from cooperating with the southern authorities. Thus when the Free State sought to establish inspection huts for eggs from the twenty-six counties exported to Great Britain, via Londonderry and Belfast, he was agreeable. Aware of possible 'difficulty from the political aspect', he felt that the request should be acceded to without the northern government 'officially committing . . . [itself] . . . in any way'. Reluctantly and after some delay, the cabinet gave its approval.[84] He also permitted a Cork firm to establish a creamery in the South Down–South Armagh area, against competing schemes from within the province. However, when criticised he defended his decision by claiming that its owner was a 'staunch loyalist and good free-mason'.[85]

Retrospectively Brooke observed that his general attitude to the south and opposition to the Anglo-Irish agreement made him 'a target for republicans, . . . this I could understand'.[86] However, he had much earlier acquired an unenviable reputation amongst Irish nationalists due primarily to his role in the special constabulary and his emotive and much publicised speeches earlier in the decade. The latter continued to haunt him. They were constantly referred to in the nationalist press in the course of any news item on Brooke, despite, and no doubt because of the fact that his subsequent public statements were never again so intemperate or aroused so much controversy.

Presumptions regarding the narrowness of his unionism appeared to be confirmed by his platform appearances in the mid-1930s at meetings of the

Ulster Protestant League. Its honorary secretary defined the movement's objective as to 'keep Ulster protestant'. The dean of Belfast, referring to its leadership, stated in June 1934, 'we should bitterly condemn the intolerant spirit of men who would fain deny our Roman catholic fellow-citizens freedom to have their religious gatherings'. Healy defined its watchword as 'protestants employ protestants'. He described Brooke variously as its 'presiding genius', and as 'one of its leading spirits . . . in an intolerant and reactionary effort to stir up old animosities amongst the most ignorant and excitable classes'.[87] He also claimed that its activities helped foment the Belfast riots of 1935. In the house he alluded to one of the meetings some months earlier, at the Ulster Hall, during which someone shouted 'To Hell with the pope'. He proceeded to allege that the person involved, 'would probably not go half so far . . . [as Brooke] . . . in putting the implications of that expression into force', and that therefore he, [Sir Basil], was 'the more dangerous'.[88]

There is no evidence that Brooke was implicated in the league beyond addressing some of its meetings. The context for his speeches was more provocative than their content, which was uncompromising but not inflamatory. On such occasions in 1934–5, he expressed mainstream unionist opinions, opposing direct rule, defending partition, calling for party unity and eulogising the special constabulary. Though he threatened that if England placated the Free State, 'we will stand on our own legs again', he also stated 'we wish the south well, we do not intend to interfere with their concerns'.[89] Statements deploring protestants who sold their farms to Roman catholics or advising protestants only to employ protestants, were made by others. At one of these meetings, the *Irish News* noted that 'the proceedings were frequently interrupted by persons who apparently desired more virile speeches in the protestant cause'.[90]

Nonetheless due to such allegations as Healy's, Brooke felt obliged in August 1936 to deny that he had been banned or forbidden from speaking at the Twelfth demonstrations one month earlier, His absence from Orange platforms clearly had prompted such speculation.[91] Involvement with the Ulster Protestant League not only attracted unfavourable comment, but also indicated a lack of sensitivity on his part to nationalist opinion. In addition, some of his actions and attitudes in this period suggest that the controversial political assumptions that he had expressed with such candour in 1933–4, may not have changed. In October, 1937, Spender described with some uneasiness the sale of Kinawley police barracks in County Fermanagh. When 'a republican bid' was double that of any other, Brooke contacted Andrews and arranged for a higher, and by implication, unionist bid, which was accepted after the named closing date. It was, Sir Wilfrid states, 'a precedent that I should not like to see followed[92] Several years later, Brooke was active in the formation of an organisation within the county, the purpose of which was to ensure that protestant property remained in protestant hands.[93]

With the renewal of I.R.A. activity in 1938, Brooke's speeches strongly articulated unionist indignation and defiance. He declared that the campaign would merely stiffen Ulster resolve as it had done in the past, and spoke with nostalgia and pride of his own involvement in the 'B' specials. He had, on at least one earlier occasion, suggested that the province's children should be told of the heroic deeds of the Ulster Volunteers. He now unreservedly supported the implementation of those security measures applied with effect on previous occasions, the banning of anti-partition meetings, re-introduction of special constabulary night patrols, internment and the use of the special powers act. The latter he described as regrettable but necessary to 'protect... freedom', and prevent 'possible retaliation by our own people'.[94] Such a response showed little appreciation of the probable impact of this policy on non-unionist opinion, though these attitudes were undoubtedly shared very widely within the government and the party.

In May 1939, after the failure of the British government to apply conscription to Northern Ireland, he expressed his most bitter comments regarding the nationalist population. Speaking at the annual meeting of Fermanagh Unionist Association, he reflected on the general unionist 'mood . . . [of] . . . resentment, anger and hurt pride at the feeling of having been snubbed, after having made 'their offer of assistance to England'. Ulster was excluded he explained

because in their midst was a minority who whilst prepared to share in the benefits of empire, and trade with England, and to share in the benefits of their special services, they were either afraid or too despicable to take a hand in the defence of the country who defended them and were prepared to go to any length to prevent the loyal and brave men of this country from doing their duty.

In conclusion, he suggested that as 'trouble . . . murder and insurrection would not help the cause of England', and 'enforcing conscription would create a disturbance, . . . they could only swallow their resentment'.[95]

Similar feelings of disdain are again evident in his diary entry for Friday 1 September 1939. Brooke had been on holiday in Scotland when he received the news of Hitler's invasion of Poland. He described the atmosphere of 'world catastrophe, . . . impending disaster, . . . personal helplessness'. He continued 'Went home owing to war. Passed evacuated children. Masses of Irish on Glasgow boat, running away'.[96]

He himself, on arrival in Belfast, called at his ministry and then with Craig, before spending the weekend with his wife at Colebrooke. There he made enquiries about returning to full-time military service with the North Irish Horse. On Monday, 4 September, the matter was discussed with Sir James. He noted: 'The prime minister decided must continue as minister. Informed general'.[97] It was clearly a vital decision. It would have been impossible then for Brooke to have foreseen the political twists that within four years would bring him to the premiership, though he and his wife may have had some premonition of the personal tragedies that war might bring. Lady Brooke, in writing to *The Times* some weeks earlier urging conscription, concluded 'May I say . . . as mother of some of the possible future conscripts, it would be all to my advantage that . . . [it] . . . should not come to the province'.[98] Brooke recorded watching the boys playing croquet at Colebrooke and his wife commenting 'I wonder what will happen to them before the war is over.'[99]

CHAPTER VII

Wartime Minister of Agriculture 1939–41

'It is hard to believe there is a bloody war on. Why war? Where will it end?[1]' Brooke noted ruefully in his diary in October 1939. War certainly brought anguish and sorrow in abundance. Two of his sons were killed in action, the third was seriously wounded, and his wife suffered from prolonged and disabling illness. Yet these years also brought challenge and achievement. In early 1940, one local newspaper, somewhat given to over-statement, was already describing Brooke as 'The man the war made'.[2] The observation was perhaps premature, but not essentially inaccurate. A later study concluded that the war period was a 'triple triumph' for Sir Basil, during which, it claimed, he first mobilised farming to achieve maximum output, then helped ensure that the province's war production potential was more effectively utilised and, finally, 'filled the gap in leadership left by the death of Craigavon'.[3] Given his background, experience and capabilities, war was always likely to enhance Brooke's political stature. He had the energy and youth lacking in his colleagues. The persistent unwillingness of Craig and later Andrews to make the cabinet changes, increasingly regarded by others as inevitable, improved Sir Basil's personal claims to the premiership. War heightened the value of his social contacts at the highest level in Britain and gave renewed significance to his years of military service and later role in recruiting the special constabulary. It provided an environment which gave full rein to his pragmatic approach to administrative problems and to his facility, ably assisted by his departmental officials, for getting things done. From the outset, he radiated a deep commitment to allied victory and sought to instil a sense of urgency with regard to the war effort, both within parliament and beyond. In this objective, his awareness of the need for adequate publicity and capacity for communicating with people were an immense benefit.

At Colebrooke each week-end from the outbreak of hostilities he reviewed the military progress of the war. He did so despite the limited information available to him and a measure of discomfort at 'the idea of describing men who are fighting for their lives, as if it was a football broadcast'. His initial hopes of an early end to the conflict, centring on Hitler's peace proposals and later the prospect of combined action with the central powers against Russia, rapidly evaporated. Germany's early success in Scandinavia, the Low Countries and France, and Mussolini's imminent military intervention were recorded in sombre tones. However, he derived some comfort from Churchill's elevation to the leadership, noting that he was 'the right man at a very difficult time' and the hope, first stated in July 1940, that Hitler might invade Russia, if he was unable to establish air superiority over Britain.[4]

Though despondent, Brooke never despaired. During the Dunkirk evacuation he wrote admiringly of the 'courage and resolution' shown and added that though it.was 'a bitter pill . . . we have had disasters before without them being decisive'.[5] After the fall of France he observed 'I expect we shall get through'. Characteristically, he continued, 'I think that it should make the people realise that we are in the front line'. As in 1914–18, the experience of war impelled him to place local problems in a wider context. He noted: 'all our troubles are small compared to this [the Nazi] threat'.[6] The prosecution of the war effort was the essential touchstone by which he gauged the priorities of Northern Ireland government policy. This fact emerged clearly during the Anglo-Irish negotiations in 1940. It was also the essential spur to his own efforts at the Department of Agriculture.

Many years later, he recalled his realisation when war broke out that his 'responsibility [as minister] had multiplied overnight'. In his diary at the time he recorded his opinion, clearly influenced by earlier military experience, that victory would be 'won by economic pressure and blockade'.[7] However, the wartime potential of Northern Ireland agriculture for increased output seemed to be somewhat circumscribed, even though it remained the province's major industry, providing employment directly or otherwise for almost half of its population. In 1939, despite the ministry's achievements in the course of the decade, 80 percent of production still took place on small, under-mechanised, mixed farms, with much subsistence, a shrinking work-force and small reserve of labour. Due to interwar expansion of pasturage and dairying only one-seventh of total acreage was sown with food crops, mainly fodder for livestock, and flax. This was the second-lowest figure on record and represented just one-eighteenth of the United Kingdom total. These statistics, as well as the apparently tight physical restraints on how much tillage could expand suggested that Ulster's main contribution to the food campaign would be through the output of livestock and dairy produce.

An additional difficulty was that Ulster farming had become, particularly in the 1930s, extremely dependent on imports of feeding stuffs as well as of seed and fertilisers, supplies of which were likely to be disrupted in wartime. Similarly, five-sixths of the flax used by the linen industry was imported and increased output might be difficult to obtain, even with the inducement of high guaranteed prices, as the crop required considerable inputs of time, skill and labour, as well as suitable land. In addition, if feeding stuffs were scarce farmers would inevitably wish to grow crops which they could feed to stock. A further predictable problem was that the flax-processing facilities available in the province would be unable to cope with any significant increase in acreage.[8]

Nevertheless, there were some grounds for optimism in September 1939. Ulster's small farm structure was relatively flexible and had illustrated this in its response to the compulsory tillage orders issued at the end of the first world war. There was much virgin ploughing land which, if fertilisers were available, might withstand wartime cultivation. In addition, Northern Ireland agriculture would inevitably benefit from the imperial government's changed perception of the importance of agriculture in the context of war for the welfare of the nation and its consequent measures to maximise food supplies from both home and overseas sources.[9] Also the local Ministry of Agriculture had emerged by the late 1930s as the most dynamic in the Northern Ireland government. John Oliver as a young civil servant, recalls how it impressed him during this period as the department which 'knew its mind best'. He admired its close links with the faculty at Queen's University and the vital role played within it by agricultural scientists. He appreciated, in particular, the qualities of Scott Robertson, regarding him as an official who through his 'insight, understanding and energy . . . [was able to] . . . influence a whole course of events in public affairs, . . . [he] . . . knew what to do and how to do it.[10]

However, when war began the question of 'what to do' was complicated by the inadequate formulation and co-ordination of governmental plans to increase food output. The official war histories describe committees for this purpose being formed at Westminster from 1936 and British officials drafting defence orders relating to the province in early 1939, though they subsequently preferred to establish agency arrangements with the Northern Ireland ministries under the terms of the government of Ireland act.[11] However, Sir Douglas Harkness who was closely involved in the negotiations throughout discredits this notion that detailed pre-war plans were devised and agreed upon, and that, later, central government powers were delegated in an orderly manner. He recalled his personal impression of a meeting held after Munich, and attended by Chamberlain and other leading British ministers, at which Morrison put forward the case for taking immediate action to increase Britain's food output. He continues, 'there was a complete absence of decision' and the view expressed 'what fools we would look if we did this and there was no war'!

This lack of preparation he attributed mainly to the influence of those like Sir Donald Fergusson who 'thought that . . . there was comparatively little that the home industry could do after the neglect of so many years . . . [and thus] . . . even in the Ministry of Agriculture & Fisheries there was no great enthusiasm for agricultural mobilisation in the post-Munich year'. Thus, as a result, Harkness characterised the early months of the war as a period of considerable confusion, stating that 'for about three years the food . . . department had operated . . . and various plans had been formulated with which . . . [the Northern Ireland ministry] . . . was supposed to be acquainted. But when war actually broke out the Ministry of Food . . . [issued] . . . a whole series of orders under defence regulations . . . [which] . . . automatically applied to the whole United Kingdom . . . but . . . never thought of notifying us of what they had done . . . [These orders] . . . about which we knew nothing . . . caused the greatest embarrassment to us'. He concluded: 'This was symptomatic of our relations with the Ministry of Food in the first few weeks of the war'.[12]

Subsequently, Northern Ireland officials negotiated directly with their imperial counterparts and as a result the role of their department with regard to food production in the province was more accurately defined. The Ministry of Food, apparently with some reluctance, agreed to constitute the local Ministry of Agriculture as its agent. In order to co-ordinate plans more effectively one local official, usually Scott Robertson, remained more or less permanently based at Whitehall. There, he kept in constant contact with imperial departments and attended vital committees, including occasionally the Food Policy Committee of the war cabinet on which the secretary of state for the Home

Office permanently represented the Northern Ireland ministry.[13] Meanwhile, Sir Wilfrid Spender ensured that the considerable initial confusion surrounding the precise function of the Ministry of Finance in monitoring the expenditure of local ministries who were acting as agents for British departments was clarified by late September.[14]

Despite this early uncertainty, during the following months Brooke's ministry emerged with two predominant functions. Firstly, both through agency arrangements with the Ministry of Food and through delegation, it became a huge marketing organisation responsible for the purchase, sale and distribution to wholesalers and retailers of most of the principal articles of food produced in Northern Ireland. It also organised the shipment of any surplus to Great Britain and regulated the flow of vital imported goods. Though the United Kingdom government decided when and which goods would be controlled, local officials serving on imperial committees made some contribution to the formulation of policy, secured adjustments to schemes which were to be applied to the province and occasionally devised their own local structures drawing on the experience and the institutional framework which had been developed in the 1930s. Its second and more important function was that of directing and controlling the production of crops, livestock and livestock products in accordance with national need, deriving the necessary powers from a delegation by the secretary of state of the home department. In both these roles the creative opportunities for the Northern Ireland ministry were inevitably tightly circumscribed. Nevertheless, the overall success of its policies and the energy, tact and enthusiasm shown by Brooke in defending and explaining departmental policy in cabinet, parliament and the country, mollifying the various distribution and retail interests necessarily affected by the transformation in marketing, and directly exhorting farmers to increase their output, were undoubtedly of immense significance in enhancing his political prospects.[15]

The first major disruption of customary trading practices came on 13 January 1940, when the ministry became the sole purchaser in Ulster of cattle for slaughter, acting in its agency capacity and modifying the administrative machinery utilised in Britain. The details of the scheme were initially unclear. It was introduced after protracted and muddled negotiations with Westminster and the consequential delay in its implementation led to commons allegations that agricultural confidence in the province had been shaken. Meanwhile, local producer and retail interests were consulted and Brooke explained the new scheme to the Unionist parliamentary party.[16] The vital though belated, decision taken by the Ministry of Food to remove pre-war differentials and buy Ulster fat cattle at the same price as in Great Britain was justifiably described by Spender as 'a great triumph for the Ministry of Agriculture'.[17] Though Sir Basil wrote to and wired Morrison on this point, Craig's direct intervention, a rare occurrence, was almost certainly crucial. Harkness described the prime minister telling Morrison 'in the simplest terms . . . that we . . . were behind Britain in the fight against Germany, and that there was the feeling amongst [local] farmers that they should get the same price . . . as the British farmers'. Sir James concluded by saying: 'I just wanted to mention the position and leave it to you to decide'. Harkness, who was given no opportunity to speak, adds that the prime minister then 'rose to his feet and indicated to me to follow'.[18]

The subsequent satisfactory outcome contributed to the wartime increase in fat cattle numbers within the province, a sector hitherto unorganised, and helped ensure Ulster Farmers' Union co-operation with the scheme. Nevertheless the Northern Ireland ministry's method of grading animals, delays in farmers receiving payment for stock sold, and downward revisions in price levels during the following September caused criticism from producers which Brooke sought to mollify.[19] One other major difficulty which the latter had predicted during a commons speech in October 1939, was butcher resentment at the interruption of their normal trading methods. Brooke regarded their attitude as 'extremely selfish'. He urged that the province 'should be subject to the same limitations and restrictions as the United Kingdom', and that in any case, since it was an imperial scheme its essential principles could not be modified when applied locally. However, his own efforts at persuasion, even though reinforced by Craig, failed to prevent the butchers from at first refusing to purchase meat from the government.[20]

Despite these initial difficulties, the ministry succeeded in establishing sixty-seven collecting centres at which government staff weighed, graded and purchased over 160,000 cattle and 574,000 sheep during the first twelve months of operation. It also directly operated abattoirs and sold almost £3,000,000 worth of meat and other products to the province's butchers in accordance with their ration-card requirements. In addition it met the needs of the forces stationed in the six counties and shipped over £2,000,000 worth of livestock to Britain. Overall, the scheme worked smoothly. It functioned at a lower cost in Ulster than in any other region of the United Kingdom and as evidence of its efficiency Brooke could boast to the house in May 1940 that each animal was being used from 'head to hoof'.[21] His earlier inspection tour of purchasing centres and abattoirs had afforded him much satisfaction.

Meanwhile a parallel scheme relating to pig production came into operation on 15 January 1940. Thereafter the ministry purchased pigs directly at thirty scattered collecting depots, and became responsible for the purchase of all pigs in the province to be slaughtered for human consumption. They were bought at Ministry of Food prices, which varied with weight and grade, and were disposed of to curers at a price determined by the controlled price of bacon. Curers supplied bacon to the forces on ministry instruction and the latter purchased any bacon surplus for shipment to Great Britain.[22]

As a result of these initiatives the Pig Industry Council lost its pre-war price-fixing role and ceased to function. Its responsibilities had earlier been temporarily and inadvertently superseded, causing considerable official embarrassment and illustrating the lack of co-ordination and planning during the early months of the war. On 3 September 1939, the Board of Trade issued an order which apparently unintentionally set the price for pigs sold for slaughter not just in Great Britain but also in the province. It was several weeks before the Northern Ireland ministry actually received a copy of this instruction and this confirmed that the price arranged by the imperial parliament was higher than that earlier agreed by the P.I.C. Eventually the order was overridden by a second, operative from 2 September, and issued by the board at the request of the Northern Ireland ministry and the P.I.C. This adjusted the price downwards to the level already agreed locally, though not without generating friction between the ministry and some local producers, litigation in the High Court and a succession of difficult questions for Brooke in the house.[23]

After the introduction of bacon rationing, the government also took over the duties of the Pig Marketing Board. This caused concern in the commons and. amongst some civil servants as it was feared that the department might in the post-war period find itself owner of two bacon-curing factories in which the board held a controlling interest,[24] However, complaints with regard to the pig scheme centred above all on the low level of pig prices determined by the Ministry of Food, particularly after they had been reduced in September 1940. This decision was variously described by Brooke himself as 'our chief griev-ance', 'the real blot' and 'a profound mistake'.[25] However, despite pressure from his department and a U.F.U. delegation to Westminster, the price remained unchanged. Craig's direct intervention was once again sought by Sir Basil but the prime minister refused to act, stating that it was a 'technical question'.[26]

Due to the low level of price and the shortage of imported feeding stuffs, pig numbers in the province fell consistently throughout the war, so that by 1945 they stood at 40 percent of 1939 levels, though they recovered rapidly there-after. Nevertheless, in 1940, ministry payments to pig producers totalled over £6,000,000 and £4,000,000 was paid to curers for surplus bacon, subsequently transferred to Britain. These levels were higher than officials had anticipated, due to the justifiable anxieties felt by farmers with regard to future supplies of animal fodder at the outbreak of hostilities.[27]

From November 1940, the ministry also became the sole purchaser of milk sold off Ulster farms. The basis of the producer's price was that of 1938–9 and it was subsequently raised uniformly with the United Kingdom. The milk was sold to distributors at a charge which enabled them to receive a fixed margin in the liquid market and to creameries at a level which permitted them to sell butter at the controlled price profitably. This was the beginning of a minor revolution in the milk industry, which reflected an associated change in governmental priorities.[28] Gradually, the balance of economic advantage swung away from beef and towards liquid milk production. Later measures taken to stimulate the latter in response to inflated wartime demand had such success that milk rationing was never required in the province. Meanwhile Brooke was particularly concerned to encourage the production of high-priced manufactured goods both in order to raise price levels and as a means of improving the long term prospects of this agricultural sector. Though there were complaints once more at the low level of prices, the ministry paid a total of £2.75 million to producers during the first twelve months of the scheme and forty million gallons of milk was produced, five-eighths of which was for manufacturing purposes. Also, during the winter period 10–17,000 gallons of milk was sent daily from the province to Great Britain. Moreover, the foundations were laid in this period for a very dramatic expansion in milk output of improving quality as the war progressed.[29]

Meanwhile, from 12 February 1940, potato production was controlled under the potato control order. Its objective was to fix prices at a reasonable level for grower, distributor and consumer, and achieve orderly marketing and equit-able distribution. There had earlier been allegations of profiteering in the house. The scheme also included a system of licensing, and the operation of a ministry levy used in the disposal of surplus output. Apart from complaints about prices, criticism was levelled at the government's failure to construct processing factories in the province. However, Brooke defended this policy, suggesting that the volume of output did not justify their construction and that they would 'simply collapse' after the war.[30]

Finally, the Northern Ireland ministry also administered both the fertiliser and feeding stuffs (maximum prices) orders promulgated by the Ministry of Food. Under the terms of the former it controlled fertiliser supplies and licensed and inspected the 2,500 merchants involved in distribution. In early 1941, quotas were calculated and ration-books provided for each of 95,000 livestock owners. Allocations to individual merchants were subsequently determined by the requirements of those farmers registered with them.[31] In addition, the department also sought to ensure that the province received its legitimate share of feeding stuffs imported into the United Kingdom. This issue was a matter of the deepest possible concern to Ulster farmers given their absolute dependence on external supplies. Even in the first weeks of the war there were reports of shortages, panic-buying, escalating prices and hoarding. Suggestions were made in parliament that the government should introduce a rationing scheme and gloomy predictions made that if there was no relief local livestock would soon, 'die like flies'.[32]

At least in part Brooke privately shared these fears. In September he warned retailers that they would be prosecuted if they charged excessive prices. As the situation deteriorated during the weeks that followed he noted in his diary 'if no relief, must kill pigs', and later forecast 'chaos if things go on'.[33] By the end of 1939 the imperial government had reduced the provinces supply to 30 percent of pre-war consumption. In controversial circumstances Roland Nugent was appointed to the Northern Ireland ministry's staff and given feeding stuffs and fertiliser supplies as his defined area of responsibility.[34] This was no doubt in part a response to the recurrent allegations being made in the commons that the province was not receiving its fair share of available supplies. This claim was at first forcefully denied by Brooke, but in February 1940, the minister of food revealed at Westminster, in answer to a question by Dr Lyttle, that Ulster had received less than her legitimate entitlement. Soon afterwards, Sir Basil was forced to concede at Stormont that there had been 'an unfortunate interruption . . . a temporary period' when this had been the case.[35] Though supplies had by then recovered to two-thirds pre-war levels, Brooke was not hopeful with regard to the future and indeed over the whole period of the war, the volumes available in Northern Ireland appear to have been proportionately much lower than those allocated in Britain.

As the drive to produce more food intensified after 1940, government controls inevitably extended to include a range of additional products. Nonetheless, the wartime transformation in customary trading methods was already well under way in the course of Brooke's period as minister. During 1940, in the livestock sector alone total ministry turnover was in excess of £23.5 million. Brooke justifiably described the outcome as 'a revolution in customary methods of marketing, grading and slaughtering . . . carried out without serious opposition and with little dislocation'.[36] In the same period the total value of the department's marketing and commercial activities, arising out of war services, amounted to £35 million, the product of over one million separate transactions. Douglas Harkness, whose major responsibility as senior assistant secretary was to organise the state purchase of food, said of the first six months of the war that they were 'the most active . . . [he had] . . . spent in . . . [his] . . . public career'.[37] By May 1940, he regarded his 'initial wartime job' as completed since the 'reorganisation of . . . [the ministry] . . . on a war basis had advanced so far that the back of the problem had been broken'.[38] He therefore requested a transfer to the Ministry of Supply.

However, the most important function of the ministry during this period was that of directing and controlling the output of crops, livestock and livestock products whilst acting in its capacity as a food production department. It was the success of this aspect of departmental policy with which Brooke was most closely identified. In the context of war, increased food, feeding stuff and flax output became a vital necessity. For this purpose a compulsory tillage order was issued on 15 September 1939, under defence regulations, requiring producers to cultivate an additional minimum proportion of the arable land on their holdings, their precise obligation varying in accordance with their acreage previously under crop. Under pre-war plans, computed on the basis of tillage achievements in 1918–9, Northern Ireland was to plough up 150,000 acres more than had been cropped in 1939. This figure represented one-sixteenth of the target set for the whole United Kingdom. The Ministry of Agriculture, however, decided to aim for 250,000 acres. Brooke and his officials held throughout, in Harkness' words, 'a much more forceful view of what could be demanded from the home farmer' than was generally accepted at Westminster.[39]

In Northern Ireland the most effective and the predominant means of achieving an expanded arable acreage was to stimulate and direct production using price incentives as a lever. Unlike Britain, there was no attempt to dictate to farmers which fields to plough or crops to grow. Thus, in October 1939, Brooke informed the house that all staple crops would be purchased at fixed guaranteed prices, their precise levels were still being negotiated with imperial officials.[40] Sir Basil regarded 'price inducements . . . [as] . . . the best way' to raise output and constantly urged that they be guaranteed well into the post-war period thus 'making the present crisis a stepping-stone for the future further advance of agriculture', and instilling in farmers the 'confidence' that the industry would not 'be let down again'.[41]

In enforcing the tillage order, the efforts of departmental officials and inspectors were supplemented at a local level by the police authorities and by the forty year-old county committees of agriculture. To facilitate the food production campaign the latter were brought under the direct control of the ministry to whom a number of their functions was transferred under the agricultural emergency provisions bill. Sir Basil informed a generally sympathetic house that this legislation was 'a war measure . . . essential . . . [in] . . . the battle for freedom and democracy' and would 'enable the government to conduct the campaign on the same basis as in Great Britain'. He spoke of the need for 'direction from a single centre, just as in an army you need unity of command'.[42] The county executive officers and district tillage officers supervised the arrangements for the ploughing up of grass-land by visiting farms, determining quotas and seeking to ensure that adequate seed and feeding supplies were available as well as providing the ministry with information and advice.

In order to provide a means of proving that the terms of the tillage order had been complied with, an agricultural returns bill was passed, making it obligatory for farmers to furnish statistical returns relating to their holdings. In the house Brooke also justified this measure on the grounds that the information acquired would enable the department to allocate machinery and essential farm supplies more efficiently, that the scheme had operated in Britain since 1925 and that all returns would remain confidential. It passed in amended form, despite strong criticism from a vocal minority that it was an unnecessary imposition, as a voluntary system of returns had, it was claimed, worked adequately since the Famine. Fears were expressed that the legislation would become permanent and be 'the thin end of the wedge'.[43]

The ministry also sought to stimulate production by a variety of other means which cumulatively helped to raise its spending to record levels. To save labour, raise productivity and lower production costs, it took over the supply and distribution of agricultural machinery. There were, however, immense difficulties involved in encouraging mechanisation. Most farm equipment had to be imported, and initially the quantities sent over from Great Britain were substantially below local official estimates of essential requirements. Brooke requested Craig to write to Morrison on this issue and throughout eagerly encouraged, though without success, the establishment of a Ferguson tractor factory in the province.[44] Other problems included the lack of capital and conservative attitudes of farmers, which prompted Brooke to comment despondently after visiting Derrygonnelly, that 'they . . . [were] . . . really backward, not tractor-minded'.[45] Nonetheless, by early 1941, the number of tractors in operati n in the province was already four-and-a-half times pre-war levels. By the end of the war, Blake claimed, that 'to go south was to be transported in a matter of minutes from the twentieth to the seventeenth century. Within five years, Ulster farming had become substantially mechanised'.[46]

In Northern Ireland, unlike the mainland, producers became the private owners of tractors which were sold by the ministry under a purchase scheme announced in October 1939. They proved to be honest and prudent borrowers. To ensure the optimum use of the machinery available its distribution was controlled by the department, which also fixed charges for ploughing, reaping and binding, and stipulated the minimum acreage to be worked by each tractor. In addition, increased fertiliser consumption was encouraged through a variety of subsidies and grants. Their usage in any case increased with the expanding tillage acreage, high wartime price levels and growing awareness amongst producers of their efficacy. This trend, however, was not sufficient to prevent a fall in yields due to soil exhaustion after 1941.[47]

A number of pre-war schemes to encourage a contraction of grass-land and stimulate increased arable output, were maintained. Thus, under the agricultural development act producers continued to receive £2.00 per acre of old pasture ploughed up, and the application of lime and slag was still subsidised under the agriculture act. Also the scope of earlier land improvement schemes was amended in 1940 to include grants for drainage schemes and for the clearance of whin and scrub. It was later broadened still further to include almost all costs of improvement, losing in the process its links with unemployment relief. In addition, the ministry sought to encourage the cultivation of allotments, working in conjunction with the Northern Ireland central allotments committee and utilising once more the legislative framework devised in the 1930s.[48]

To induce increased flax production, the government again offered high guaranteed prices. For the 1940 crop it provided flax seed which, like other arable crops, was sold at a subsidised price, with loans available to farmers to facilitate purchase. Supplies were initially acquired from Canada and Holland, and subsequently from Britain and from within the province itself. Meanwhile, ministry scientists were successful in eradicating disease from locally produced seed. The department also sold heavily subsidised flax pullers for cash or on hire-purchase terms, in order to lower labour costs and as a means of preventing a recurrence of the disruptive strike action which occurred during the First World War. In addition, grants were available for the erection and extension of scutch mills and retting factories and workers in the former were brought within the terms of the agricultural wages act.[49]

Finally, and probably crucially within days of the tillage order, a ministry-orchestrated propaganda campaign was launched appealing on patriotic grounds for farmers to produce more and stressing also that it was in their own immediate commercial interests to do so. In this publicity drive both regional and head quarters staff co-operated and Brooke himself played a leading role. In September and October 1939, he visited each of the county agricultural committees, usually accompanied by Scott Robertson, whose primary departmental responsibility was food production. Sir Basil seemed well pleased with the response, noting in County Londonderry that 'all seemed anxious to help', and in Tyrone that one of his most voluble critics during his clash with the P.M.B. was now 'all oil'. He was similarly gratified by the strong spontaneous support given by the U.F.U. and the enthusiasm shown by representatives of the horticultural and allotments organizations.[50]

Nonetheless, the farming community was slow to respond due mainly to a combination of bad weather and uncertainty or dissatisfaction regarding price levels. In mid-December 1939, just 130,000 acres, little over half the projected tillage quota, had been ploughed. Brooke was clearly deeply concerned. As he travelled around the countryside, he frequently commented on the lack of any significant increase in arable acreages. During the king's speech debate he stated that 'some parts of the country . . . [were] . . . slow' and warned that this was 'illegal' and that 'such farmers would not be allowed to farm'.[51] In January 1940, he records leaving a meeting of county officers 'with a feeling of disquiet' adding 'we will have to act to get ploughing done'.[52] He had two months earlier expressed his concern in cabinet at the inadequacy of his department's publicity and now sent out a personal message to every farmer. This Blake described as 'masterly, . . . phrased in practical language that . . . [farmers] . . . would understand'. It warned of the dire threat to the province's livestock and poultry if feeding stuff production was not increased. It also appealed for 5,000 acres of barley, maize imports having fallen to pre-war levels, and for a similar acreage of flax also urgently required as available local supplies of yarn and fibre had become exhausted and Baltic imports had collapsed.[53]

The department hired a van, from a Belfast tobacco manufacturer, and this was used by Brooke, equipped with a loudspeaker, for travelling around markets and fairs to appeal personally for more tillage. Spender had reservations about this approach, remarking that 'it savours rather of a political campaign', but he added 'I suppose it can be justified under war conditions'. It also prompted some hostile comment in the house, but most of the members regarded it as 'amongst the best and wisest investments that the minister . . . [had] . . . ever made'.[54]

During January and February 1940, reports from county executive officers increasingly justified the expectation that the province would exceed even its amended target of 250,000 acres. No doubt the generally attractive price levels that had meanwhile been agreed upon by the imperial government, as well as the threat of legal action by the local department, contributed to this satisfactory outcome. Blake, the official historian, however, attributed it mainly to the success of Brooke's letter of appeal, subsequently an annual departmental practice, in instilling an increased sense of urgency amongst Ulster farmers. Thus, in late March, Robertson telephoned Colebrooke to inform his minister that 'we had 240,000 acres'; the final total was over 270,000 acres. To Brooke it was 'a wonderful performance' and he recorded that his cabinet colleagues were 'very pleased'.[55]

He had himself for some time been noting 'the good signs of ploughing' around the countryside. His diary comments indicate the extent of his personal commitment to the campaign and undiluted delight at its success. In early April, he remarked on the 'very good tillage' around Enniskillen and Omagh, adding that it was 'most striking and exhilarating. The farmers and officers of the ministry have done really magnificent work. All are to be congratulated'. After a visit to Londonderry with his family he records that they 'saw masses of ploughing, . . . visited a big farmer named Lynch, what a joy it is to meet a man like him'. It was as though his archetypal Ulsterman was a farmer, making the optimum use of his land in the service of king and country. On another occasion, he described as 'a fine show' a holding 70 percent of which had been ploughed using two donkeys.[56] Sir Basil's pride in the province's achievement was evident in the course of a national radio broadcast which he gave in March, entitled 'The plough versus the submarine'. He concluded his appeal for increased output by issuing a challenge. He stated that Ulster had 'aimed at 70 percent more than its share . . . as . . . part of our contribution to winning the war, . . . We are going to do it, . . . Have a shot at beating us'. Next month he told the visiting minister of supply, Leslie Burgin, that the wartime increase in tillage acreage was 'Northern Ireland's best story'.[57] He also noted in his diary with obvious satisfaction that Kingsley Wood had complimented him on his department's success and that representatives from the Treasury and Ministry of Food had said 'we had done a good day's work' and expressed enthusiasm for 'our methods'. In April 1940, he organised a province-wide tillage inspection tour by British pressman. Sir Basil always had a keen eye for publicity opportunities and undoubtedly was his ministry's most effective propagandist.[58]

During the autumn of 1940 it was decided in the context of deteriorating shipping prospects and after discussions with British ministers and officials to raise the province's tillage quota by a further 13 percent for the following season. The campaign was launched in December 1940, amidst a flurry of publicity, the official announcement of government objectives being made at Westminster on 28 December. In the course of the preceding negotiations the contrasting attitudes of the Northern Ireland and imperial departments were again evident. Sir Basil urged, without success, that a further addition of 2½ million acres to the arable land of the United Kingdom should be possible in 1941. K. A. H. Murray noted that this opinion was hotly contested by other agricultural ministers.[59]

However one evaluates the economic success and political impact of departmental policy in the 1930s, few have doubted its effectiveness during the war years in mobilising Ulster farming to achieve maximum output. One authority refers to Northern Ireland agriculture in wartime as 'stretched to the limit', whilst another claims that the province's producers 'made a larger proportional contribution to the home-produced food supply than any area in the British Isles'.[60] John Oliver recalled the 'striking progress' made by local farmers in this period and concluded that they 'performed prodigies of production'. This view is shared by Blake who praised, in particular, 'the direct and impelling forcefulness' of Brooke's leadership.[61] Sir Basil himself was certainly well pleased with the achievements of his ministry. The purchase, resale and distribution of food had, he felt, been implemented 'with remarkable smoothness and efficiency', whilst the success of the tillage campaign was clearly beyond all that he had hoped.[62] During 1939–40, Northern Ireland was the only United Kingdom region to exceed its quota. According to the department's own figures, the province's acreage represented a more than 40 percent increase on pre-war levels, twice the comparable figure for England and Wales, and three times that of Scotland.[63] Also remarkable is the fact that this rate of expansion was sustained in 1940-41.

Nonetheless, whatever the incentives offered to farmers or however dynamic the department may have been, there were inescapable limits to what could be achieved in Ulster, mainly imposed by the small cultivated acreage available and the physical realities of soil and climate. The expansion in feeding stuff production, particularly oats and root crops, could not compensate for the sharp fall in imported supplies to a wartime average of 40 percent late 1930s levels. Thus, though cattle numbers were stable, and poultry numbers actually increased, there was a dramatic decline in the pig and sheep populations. Also the tillage campaign failed to reach its projected acreage for wheat and barley, both of which were difficult to grow locally. Similarly, the 1940–41 target of 100,000 acres for flax was not reached until 1943-4. Meanwhile, between April–September 1940 the linen industry experienced a period of crisis, during which unemployment in this sector doubled.[64] By October of the following year, half of the province's spinning mills had closed down. Once more local flax production could not adequately make up for the fall in imported supplies, some of which were diverted to Scotland.

Attempts to increase domestic production were complicated, initially by confusion between the Ministries of Agriculture and Commerce regarding their precise responsibility for stimulating acreage. Also, despite the high price levels agreed with the Ministry of Supply in January 1940, farmers were reluctant to expand acreage. As Brooke stated, in the house, 'their natural anxiety . . . [was] . . . first of all for their stock'. He also pointed out that flax production was labour intensive and could cause soil exhaustion and concluded that 'from an economic point of view you must build your policy on a livestock policy'.[65] Though Sir Basil, his officials and the farmers themselves were generally satisfied with flax price levels, this view was not reciprocated either by Andrews and the spinning sector of the linen industry or some vociferous Unionist back benchers. Brooke noted that he was 'very annoyed at Andrews' attitude', adding that he 'seems always to play where his interests are touched'. Similarly, Spender observed, in 1942, that the difficulties in devising an effective policy for the industry 'were much greater due to the fact that both Mr Andrews and Milne Barbour were personally interested in the linen trade'.[66]

Despite these shortcomings in the tillage campaign, Brooke conceded in the 1960s that the 'ploughing up . . . [was] . . . a little overdone . . . [though] . . . it seemed highly essential in those critical days'.[67] This view was confirmed by a post-war government report on the Northern Ireland economy which concluded that wartime levels of agricultural output and productivity were poor and disappointing. This it attributed to the scarcity of feeding stuffs and the operation of compulsory tillage which in combination 'forced' the province 'into a relatively uneconomic type of farming'.[68] It pointed out that in this period though Northern Ireland increased its tillage acreage proportionately more than Great Britain, conversely it contracted more rapidly after the war than on the mainland. However, the report also stated that the value of Ulster's agricultural output at current prices rose more in wartime than elsewhere in the United Kingdom due mainly to the change in relative price levels. The Ministry of Agriculture bought much of the province's saleable agricultural output direct from the farmer at guaranteed prices which were uniform throughout the United Kingdom. Transport costs for local producers were reduced to that of bringing goods to collecting centres. As a result of this, as well as increased levels of employment and production, the total of farm incomes rose proportionately more than in Great Britain, wages rose faster, and local income per head caught up partially on imperial levels.[69]

Thus, in wartime, Ulster producers experienced increased prosperity, and enjoyed the security of profitable guaranteed prices and assured stable markets, having been relieved of much of the difficulty of competing successfully on the British market. However it is not clear how far Brooke himself as a practising farmer shared in the province's increasing agricultural prosperity. Colebrooke as always attracted much of his interest and energy. Virtually every weekend he returned there to relax from the pressures of office and also fulfill his social obligations within the local community. He retained his position as chairman of the county council, remained prominent in the Fermanagh Unionist Association, played an active part in parish if not diocesan affairs more from a sense of duty than personal piety, and indulged in his favourite sporting recreations. Farming the demesne remained an enduring pleasure, indeed passion, and perhaps became even more of a financial necessity in wartime.

On his estate the impact of the war was increasingly obvious, not only in the presence of soldiers bivouacked on the sheep park, but also in the changing pattern of its agricultural output.[70] The expansion of tillage crops such as barley and flax indicated that it was not immune from the effects of legislation introduced by his department. There was as well clear evidence of financial stress caused by the increased levels of wartime taxation. For this reason two of his sons were transferred from their English public school to schools in Wales, the numbers of labourers and domestic servants he employed was reduced, trees were reluctantly cut down as 'the only way to save Colebrooke[71] and clear his overdraft, and in 1940 one of his two motor cars was 'laid up' for the duration of the war. It may be that such pressures heightened Sir Basil's already considerable commitment to a career in politics, by increasing his dependence on his £2,000 yearly ministerial income. His diary, however, gives little hint that this was the case, and his son strongly denies any suggestion that financial inducement played any part in his father's political motivation. The fact that Brooke offered to resign from his position in the cabinet on at least three occasions between December 1940 and April 1943 lends support to this viewpoint. Nonetheless, Douglas Harkness firmly believed that his considerable income from government service was a not unimportant factor in sustaining Sir Basil's political involvement.[72]

Whatever the extent of his financial difficulties, in the course of his weekend retreats to Fermanagh and of his travels elsewhere in the province, Brooke was heartened during his final months as minister by the enthusiasm and high morale of the farming community. In December 1940 he noted that he had 'never had more satisfactory meetings with the county committees . . . than . . . this year, practically no criticism'. Whilst travelling around fairs and shows, he observed that farmers seemed 'satisfied'. Those he met he described variously as 'keen and appreciative' and 'extremely kind and pleased'.[73] The generally high level of producer co-operation with the department is illustrated by the very small number of legal proceedings which the latter found it necessary to institute against those failing to comply with the tillage order.[74] Brooke was also delighted with the very substantial improvement which had meanwhile occurred in the relationship between his ministry and the Ulster Farmers' Union. As Harkness later recalled, war provided the opportunity for 'both to bury the hatchet'.[75] Thus the farmers' representatives gave, in Beattie's phrase, 'hearty support' to the tillage campaign and overall seemed satisfied with price levels.[76] Strains did occur, caused particularly by the confused level of pig prices in September 1939, the department's system of livestock grading and most of all its wages bill and the findings of the wages board. Sir Basil regarded the U.F.U.'s response to the latter as 'selfish . . . they must understand that if agriculture gets assisted they cannot go on paying the low wages they have done'.[77] Nonetheless, despite disagreements on such issues their pre-war antagonism diminished remarkably quickly.

A significant factor in this increased co-operation was the extremely close personal relationship which developed between Brooke and Moore, president of the U.F.U. and one of the ministry's most virulent critics when the P.M.B. was dismissed. As an indication of this, in October 1940, Sir Basil described a letter from the U.F.U. relating to the flax production campaign as 'quite excellent, far better than anything I should have expected, . . . I think Moore must have been at the back of it and influenced them to play their part as patriotic men'.[78] Moore for his part enthusiastically informed the commons that 'there . . . [had] . . . been a constant two-way traffic' between the ministry and the farmers' representatives, continuing, 'sometimes the committee, [the war committee of the U.F.U.] asked to be received by the minister, and perhaps oftener the minister asked the committee to come and confer with him'.[79] Significantly, in early 1941, Brooke advised Andrews, the new prime minister, to appoint Moore as his successor at the Ministry of Agriculture.[80]

Thus when reviewing the year's progress in December 1940, Sir Basil wrote, with evident satisfaction 'The whole ministry has worked as a team, everyone full of enthusiasm and drive from Scott Robertson downwards, . . . I am very proud of the work that the ministry and the farmers have put through during the last critical eighteen months, and I think that, though criticism may be hurled at Ulster for other reasons, nobody can criticise her agricultural effort'.[81] Though, undoubtedly, many would have agreed with Brooke's verdict, Spender would have been less generous in his assessment of the performance of his ministry. To him, the war accentuated many of those aspects of its policy which he had criticised in the 1930s. He was concerned at its growing powers which he feared might prove difficult to reverse under peacetime conditions, and consistently sought more effective Ministry of Finance consultation and control over its expenditure. He regarded it as extravagant, and protested at its unwillingness to make savings on services which were a direct charge on the British Exchequer. This Sir Wilfrid believed would have helped 'to keep the esteem of the . . . Treasury'.[82] He complained that its grants and subsidies 'merely . . . [assisted] . . . that part of our population which is exceedingly prosperous . . . [and that] . . . people . . . [were] . . . being educated to do nothing unless heavily subsidised by the government'.

Both Spender and Andrews continued to criticise Brook's policy of providing large land-holders with grants to improve their estates under land improvement schemes. Sir Basil justified this on the grounds that 'food production . . . [was] . . . the primary consideration'.[83] He also alleged that such subsidies were available in England, and suggested that it was imperative to preserve the goodwill of the county lieutenants whose co-operation in the province's recruiting campaign was vital.[84] He may also have considered that the burden of taxation which they carried legitimised such expenditure, though in parliament the view was expressed that landlords were benefiting more from government regulation than farmers. The strength of Andrews' feelings on this question was underlined when he rejected a compromise suggested by Spender, describing it as 'an easy way out . . . [and] . . . lacking in courage on a matter on which he felt so strongly'. Eventually Brooke was forced to accept with reluctance a compromise the essentials of which were explained to the house by Andrews, on the former's insistence.[85]

Spender continued to be disturbed by the activities of some Ministry of Agriculture officials, notably Scott Robertson. They clashed initially over the precise powers of the Ministry of Finance in relation to the agriculture department after the latter had entered into agency relations with the imperial government. The matter was resolved in principle by a Treasury ruling in late September 1939, which upheld Sir Wilfrid's authority. In addition, Spender felt uneasy about the violent changes in Robertson's promotion recommendations and was alarmed by his appointment, in September 1939, of Sir Roland Nugent as an unpaid principal officer in the department.[86] Nugent had served in the Foreign Office and was currently a Northern Ireland senator. Similar concern was expressed by the prime minister and in the house, and eventually his service was terminated in the spring of 1940. Spender also received disconcerting complaints about Robertson's overtly political role within the ministry. One of his correspondents referred to the latter speaking on behalf of the government, and justifying its policy 'whilst his minister, whose duty it was to expound . . . and advocate it, remained silent'. This led to a reprimand from Sir Wilfrid who suggested to Robertson that though in war-time he might attend 'a meeting to explain a decision . . . it would . . . be wrong for any civil servant to . . . claim that he [was] . . . responsible for . . . policy. [He] . . . should . . . make it clear that any question of formulating . . . or defending . . . policy rests with the responsible minister'.[87]

There can be no doubt that Brooke continued to rely heavily on his permanent secretary. The latter played a vital role in defining and implementing ministerial policy and personally conducted most of its crucial negotiations at Westminster where he also sat on a number of important committees. He was Sir Basil's most consistent adviser on almost all aspects of departmental administration, and regularly briefed him for cabinet discussions and parliamentary debates, as well as for his infrequent visits to London. He also travelled around the countryside with his minister, accompanied on some occasions by other members of the Brooke family, to visit purchasing centres and abattoirs, talk to farmers and address county committees. He both explained and defended policy. On one occasion Brooke notes that Robertson was 'undefeated in cross-examination', and Spender refers to a strongly pro-department article in the *Northern Whig*, during the farmers' clash with local butchers, which he alleged was 'absolutely inspired' by the permanent secretary.[88] The latter was well aware of his own singular contribution to the work of the ministry. Thus he defended his claim to a special subsistence allowance, not granted to other officials of equivalent rank, as justified, owing to 'the much greater importance' of his work.[89]

However, his relationship with Brooke appears to have remained one based on partnership and mutual confidence. Both were totally committed to the maximisation of local food output in response to the war emergency, on the best terms possible. Brooke deeply admired Robertson's activities and eloquently defended him in the house. In December 1932, he described him as 'one of the greatest experts on agriculture in the British Empire'. In 1940, he urged on Craig the necessity of giving him an honour as 'he deserves it and so does the ministry', and soon after his transfer to the Ministry of Commerce, he wrote to 'thank him personally for all that he had done'. Robertson's request soon after Brooke had taken up his new duties, that he should cross to London to conduct negotiations with imperial ministers on behalf of his old department, suggests that the latter's confidence in his permanent secretary was reciprocated. As John Oliver observed Robertson would have had 'little time or patience with a weak minister'.[90]

Nonetheless, Robertson's role within the Ministry of Agriculture was a widespread cause of concern. Brooke himself records that Dixon was 'going around saying I am led by the nose by Robertson, I am the fool and he is the knave'.[91] Also in the house a vociferous minority reiterated a number of Spender's strictures on the activities of Brooke's department and of his permanent secretary in particular. Sir Wilfrid was himself extremely sceptical as to the motives of those involved, and believed that there was a strong case for closing parliament down altogether during the war period.[92] Predictably, M.P.s criticised ministry interference with customary forms of marketing, the price levels set for foodstuffs and the apparent shortages of essential supplies, and deprecated the extent to which the government's agricultural policy in wartime was determined at Westminster.

However, their most consistent cause of complaint was 'the unduly autocratic attitude towards both the public and . . . this house' which they attributed to the department.[93] Much of their comment was directed at Robertson who tended to be somewhat abrasive in manner, and insensitive to his ministry's public image. A number of his early speeches caused controversy in the commons, notably one appealing to the public on behalf of his department during its dispute with the butchers in January 1940, and another recommending that farmers continue with their farm work on Sundays. On 2 November 1940, a further cause of contention arose when in the course of his remarks at a U.F.U. lunch, also attended by Brooke, he outlined the main features of the ministry's new rationing scheme for feeding stuffs which was then imminent.[94] The house had received no preliminary notification of this and M.P.s protested their astonishment at hearing of the department's intention from press reports of its permanent secretary's speech to the farmers' representatives, particularly as the impending adjournment would preclude any adequate parliamentary discussion of this initiative. On 12 November 1940, Brown appealed on behalf of his colleagues for the 'right to be consulted when a vital step of this kind is contemplated'. He added: 'no other minister would . . . permit the permanent head of his department to make speeches of controversy and policy'.

In his reply Brooke defended his senior official, stating that the rationing scheme was complex and therefore required to be explained to the U.F.U. and that it had 'been the custom in . . . [his] . . . ministry . . . for . . . officers . . . to go out and explain what the schemes are'. However, he suggested that those interested in agriculture might form a committee to whom he would be 'only too glad to give . . . information', thus formalising the formerly *ad hoc* and infrequent meetings held between himself, sometimes accompanied by Craig, and the rural M.P.s.[95] One week later an eleven-man committee was formed, in the words of one of its members 'to protect the rights of agriculturalists, . . . the day has arrived when we will no longer be ignored'. Amidst taunts of 'Nazism' and 'Hitlerism', Brooke agreed to discuss the rationing scheme with the new body.[96] Spender predicted that the committee would cause 'great difficulties' and be 'very embarrassing' to the government. However, Sir Basil appears to have been well pleased with the outcome of the meetings he held with it. He records that its members had 'got hold of the most fantastic stories as to how rationing would be carried out, . . . after about an hour's discussion . . . and my giving them a promise that I would discuss with them the final scheme, . . . they left satisfied'. He was similarly satisfied with the results of the next meeting, two weeks later, having in the meantime discussed their comments and objections with the prime minister and with Robertson.[97]

Brooke viewed his frequent parliamentary appearances with conflicting emotions. He clearly relished the verbal 'cut and thrust' of commons debates and questioning, and enjoyed giving his critics 'one or two good cracks'.[98] Generally the latter were not especially well informed, and suffered from the speaker's constant willingness to stretch the rules of debate in order to protect ministers. Also back-benchers had to acknowledge the mounting evidence that local farming was increasingly prosperous, and that unlike almost all other sectors of the Ulster economy, was being fully mobilised for war production. As Sir Basil was obviously competent, alleged departmental failings were often attributed to officials or to interference by the imperial government. 'The difficulty', one member suggested, was in 'the ministry itself and not on the part of the minister personally'.[99]

Occasionally, Sir Basil complained that commons proceedings were, like those of the privy council, 'a waste of time', but more frequently he expressed disappointment with the attitudes of his parliamentary colleagues. Thus, during the tillage campaign, accompanied by Andrews, he suggested to Craig that the party whilst apparently supporting his ministry 'did all to oppose, . . . with Dixon making everything difficult'. He records stressing that he 'would not be responsible for any policy where we could not say that we had done our share'. He was also determined that on the issue of food rationing 'we must remain with Great Britain . . . otherwise our position would be very weak'.[100] However, not everyone accepted the necessity for the province to 'share' in the privations of the mainland. Sir Basil later recalled 'a body of opinion at Stormont . . . [which was] . . . outraged at the idea that Northern Ireland should have food rationing . . . as we were a food-exporting country'.[101] At the time he observed 'I am afraid no M.P. realises there is a war on. If Ulster stands out on this she is doomed. Her loyalty is skin deep'. He deplored 'the general attitude' of the parliamentary party and stated that he was 'very angry' with Dixon who 'did not want ration cards' in the six counties. He firmly rejected the prime minister's suggestion that the latter should join his ministry, 'presumably', Sir Basil observed 'to keep him quiet', and also resisted pressure from both Craig and Dixon to have a clause inserted in the census bill making it a war measure only.[102]

Nonetheless, Brooke clearly felt gratified by a growing awareness that parliamentary attacks on himself and his officials were gradually 'dying down'. He thus regarded the debate on his ministry's estimates, in May 1940 as having gone 'extremely well . . . [with] . . . very little criticism, . . . [we were] . . . congratulated by one and all'. This was mainly due to a deepening appreciation of the overall success of his department's policies and of its very considerable achievements, whatever doubts members may have shared with regard to the adequacy of its consultation with the house. Favourable comment was made on the success of the tillage campaign, surpassing a target which had seemed to one member 'an impossible task', and also on the general smoothness with which the purchase schemes had been implemented.[103] The latter had earlier been described as 'magnificent' with the points that had been criticised, mere 'pin-pricks'.[104] The ministry was praised for its apparent efficiency, alertness, and capacity for hard work. These characteristics it was thought had been demonstrated at the outset by its success in becoming an agent for the imperial government, and the close contact which its officials maintained with the latter, as well as by its close co-operation with the U.F.U, and timely purchases of foreign seed supplies. Even Robertson attracted some of the credit that was his due, but inevitably much praise was lavished on Brooke himself, even by some of the government's most ardent critics. Nixon said of him that he had 'worn himself to a thread' and Brown stated that he had 'brought to his position as large a contribution in energy, enthusiasm and ability as any one man humanly could do'.[105]

Inevitably, Sir Basil's performance as minister of agriculture was compared favourably with that of other members of the cabinet, particularly as public awareness of the ineptitude of some of his colleagues increased. Thus, Edmond Warnock, one of the government's most persistent critics, who resigned as parliamentary secretary at the Ministry of Home Affairs, in late May 1940, commented on 11 June: 'The minister of agriculture has made two blades of grass grow where none grew before, I exempt him from any criticism'. Some days later, he stated 'I left the government . . . because it has been slack, dilatory and apathetic. It has done little or nothing except for one man and that one man is the minister of agriculture, . . . a young, virile, able man who threw himself heart and soul into the task he had, and made a magnificent success of it'.[106] On 6 August he remarked 'It is always a great pleasure . . . to listen to the minister of agriculture because he does try to answer the points put to him, . . . too often we are fobbed off . . . It is a great pleasure . . . [to be] met with reasoned argument'.[107] He urged that Brooke be given new and increased ministerial responsibilities, privately suggesting that he move to Home Affairs.[108] Sir Basil who had himself a deep admiration for Warnock was somewhat embarrassed to be so 'exonerated' from his attacks on the government. He confided, 'it is most distasteful to me having differences made as between myself and other ministers'. Though he rejected the suggestion that he ought to change ministries, commenting 'I think I am as well where I am', he strongly sympathised with much that Warnock had said. In late May, he recorded having 'to reply . . . for the government to a very strong attack by' [the latter] and added, 'I think that I was effective, at least I was told by some that it was good, but it is very hard when one feels that more could be done'.[109] From this period onwards Brooke was confronted by a deepening and unavoidable dilemma. He was torn between, on the one hand, a profound and enduring sense of loyalty towards ageing colleagues and, on the other, a steadily growing conviction that cabinet change was vital if the province was to make an adequate combination to the war effort.

Colebrooke: "The great love of Brooke's life."

Three generations of Brookes, c 1892. Seated at the window are Brooke's grand-parents Sir Victor and Alice, standing are Uncle Ronald (left) and his father Douglas (right), his mother Isabella is nursing his sister Sylvia with Uncle Alan (left) and Basil (right), sitting in front of her.

The spoils of the hunt; Brooke in India 1909.

''There is nothing to do unless you play polo,'' Brooke in India 1909.

Brooke with his bride, Cynthia Sergison,
on their wedding day, 3 June 1919.

Sir James Craig inspects the county's constabulary at Colebrooke, in 1924, with Brooke on his right hand side.

Brooke, the rising young cabinet minister in the 1930s.

Brooke with his cabinet and some Imperial Unionist M.P.s in 1944. Front row:- M. Sinclair — Finance; Sir R. Ross — Imperial M.P.; Sir B. Brooke; Sir H. O'Neill — Imperial M.P.; W. Lowry — Home Affairs; F. Harland — Imperial M.P. Second row:- D. Campbell — Imperial M.P.; W. Grant — Health and local government; W. Stewart — Imperial M.P.; D. Parker — Parliamentary Private Secretary, Education. Third row:- B. Maginnis — Parliamentary Private Secretary, Commerce; Rev. R. Moore — Agriculture; Sir W. Hungerford — Parliamentary Private Secretary, Home Affairs; Lord Castlereagh — Imperial M.P.; Colonel Hall-Thompson — Education; Professor Savory — Imperial M.P.; Sir N. Stronge — Chief Whip.

Brooke exhorting shipyard workers to increase their efforts in 1943.

Brooke's cabinet, June 1945. Left to right:- Rev. R. Moore — Agriculture; W. Grant — Health; M. Sinclair — Finance; Sir B. Brooke — Prime Minister; E. Warnock — Home Affairs; Colonel Hall-Thompson — Education; H. Midgley — Labour. At back R. Gransden — Secretary to cabinet; W. McWilliams — Assistant Secretary.

Brooke meets Clement Attlee to discuss Eire's imminent withdrawal from the Commonwealth, August 1948.

Relaxing at home, 1947.

At Buckingham Palace with the Queen and her Commonwealth Prime Ministers in 1953.

Left to right: Mr. Mohammad Ali (Pakistan), Sir Godfrey Huggins (Southern Rhodesia), Lord Brookeborough (Northern Ireland), Mr. Holland (New Zealand), Mr. Nehru (India), Mr. Bustamante (Jamaica), Sir Winston Churchill, The Queen, Mr. Menzies (Australia), Mr. St. Laurent (Canada), Mr. Senanayake (Ceylon), Dr. Malan (Union of South Africa), Dr. Borg Olivier (Malta).

Brooke at the hustings, election 1949.

Brooke pursuing "the most pleasurable pastime in the world," September 1954.

CHAPTER VIII

Brooke, the Cabinet and the Strains of War, 1939–41

'Nothing is foreseen, every decision is postponed'.[1] This verdict passed by the *Manchester Guardian* on Asquith's government in December 1916 might be applied with equal force to the Northern Ireland cabinet after September 1939. If Brooke can be regarded, legitimately as the politician that the 'war made', the reverse was true of his ministerial colleagues. The context provided by their record of almost unmitigated failure greatly enhanced the political significance of his achievements as wartime minister of agriculture. In December 1939, Spender remarked, after twenty years experience as a senior civil servant, that there was 'one . . . factory in which we could claim that we or the Free State are the largest manufacturers namely the factory of grievances. I am not at all clear that this particular factory is not the most paying one in the province.'[2] Undoubtedly its output increased significantly during the early years of the war. Even the official war history characterised this period as one of apparent failure, disappointment and frustration for the Northern Ireland people, and concluded that 'the sense of inertia, of fumbling uncertainty was too much for them'.[3]

The cabinet was experienced but ageing with some of its members, like Craig himself, subject to prolonged and incapacitating illness. In Spender's opinion Lady Craig encouraged her husband 'to remain in office . . . from the point of view of finance and social ambition', against his own inclination and apparently unaware of the extent to which his health had deteriorated. He led the government in increasingly dictatorial and whimsical fashion. He regarded important appointments, such as that of regional officer for the Ministry of Information, as part of his personal patronage. Gransden, the cabinet secretary, and also Sir James' private secretary, was used to transact errands for the family household, a function which he deeply resented. Sir Wilfrid estimated that in his combined salary and allowances, Craig received more than the British prime minister. This bizarre situation was protected from parliamentary scrutiny by some rather unorthodox tactics. Thus, when the Ministry of Finance estimates came before the house, the chief whip provided backbenchers with questions and points of criticism in order to divert attention from, and reduce the time available to discuss, the details of the prime minister's income. In addition, it was arranged that Beattie should be detained in the commons bar whilst debate on the 'cabinet office' took place.[4] Nixon could only protest ineffectually that he was the only opposition member present.[5]

151

There is also evidence that during this period, the cabinet system continued to disintegrate. Thus, when Craig was called over to London in May 1940 to discuss such vital issues as recruitment, the formation of a local defence force and Anglo-Irish relations, only Glentoran received notification. Spender observed that the latter was more 'in touch with the prime minister than the members of the cabinet', adding that this was a 'very undesirable development'.[6] He also noted on a number of occasions Craig's preference that decisions should be given by individual ministers on their own responsibility or after consultation with him and indeed that there was a strong tendency on his part to reach decisions on important matters without consulting the ministers concerned at all. Sir Wilfrid advised Gransden that cabinet members should at least be informed, if necessary subsequent to a decision having been reached. The cabinet secretary, however, defended Sir James by suggesting that in war quick decisions are necessary and that the latter was acting 'as head of the government and not prime minister'. This, Spender concluded, was 'a new method of saying that . . . [Craig] . . . in wartime is a dictator and can override any decision arrived at in a cabinet meeting'. He continued: 'Gransden is taking advantage of the situation to remove all the constitutional checks'.[7]

Craig's evident response to the increasing gravity and number of attacks on his government was either to make extravagant claims regarding the success of its policies, or, more frequently, to attempt to buy off critics through 'concessions only justified by political expediency'.[8] The latter ranged from financial grants and subsidies and the allocation of government contracts to the setting up of parliamentary committees of enquiry and the creation of a ministry of public security. They fell short, however, of conceding what was increasingly sought, a change in the composition of the government itself and thus the volume of criticism ineluctably increased.

Warnock's resignation was in protest against the general inertia and incompetence of the government. He was convinced that Bates in particular was incapable of performing his duties, though, in the commons, he tended to attack the minister of commerce more strongly, apparently for tactical reasons. Spender regarded his response as 'not unjustified' and predicted that 'following on the lines of Mr Churchill', who had become prime minister two weeks earlier, Warnock would 'undoubtedly carry a very large weight of public opinion behind him'.[9]

Two weeks later Lieut-Colonel A. R. G. Gordon, parliamentary and financial secretary at the Ministry of Finance, also resigned. He explained to a half-empty house, expecting only routine business, that the government was 'by nature of its personnel, its lack of drive and initiative and utter lack of what war means, I here exclude certain members, . . . quite unfitted to sustain the people in the ordeal that we have to face. . . . It should resign and be reconstituted immediately'.[10] His resignation had been precipitated by a commons speech by the prime minister, on 11 June, during a debate on the 'defence of Northern Ireland'. Craig had claimed that within one week of his personal appeal the Ulster Defence Volunteers had been recruited, armed and placed on duty. The statement had been greeted with justifiable scepticism in the house. Gordon who said little at the time, regarded it as misleading, its 'figures . . . in complete variance with [those] . . . he himself was able to produce', and so believed that 'it would undermine the confidence of his men if he remained in the government a day longer'.[11]

Subsequently, both Warnock and Gordon threatened to move a motion of censure on the government, but at a party meeting agreed to a postponement, 'provided steps were taken to meet their wishes'. During the latter, Brooke sensed that 'a good many' back-benchers would have voted against the leadership.[12] Afterwards the two leading dissidents held discussions with Craig, who agreed to bring J. C. MacDermott into his cabinet as minister of public security. This concession ultimately proved to be inadequate. Thus, during the budget debate on 7 August, Warnock renewed his threat amidst widespread criticism of the government's failure to reduce unemployment and provide adequate civil defence and its apparent inability to do other than emulate British legislation and levels of taxation. Shortly afterwards, to placate his critics, Craig promised to support a motion of censure on the fraught issue of unemployment, provided that it did not directly criticise his administration. This was introduced by a Unionist private member, contained a ten-part programme designed to generate employment, and was debated on 10 and 17 September 1940. Once more the government was bitterly attacked, Beattie introducing an amendment, demanding its resignation and describing the prime minister as having reached his 'doting stage'.[13]

Within a fortnight, Warnock proceeded to introduce his long-awaited motion. He made a passionate plea for a change in the composition of the cabinet, stating that 'when a person becomes a member of the government of Northern Ireland . . . he becomes a tenant for life . . . Nothing but death, illness or promotion ever removes anybody'. When considering the competence of individual ministers once more he castigated, in particular, Milne Barbour and the Ministry of Commerce whose 'direction' he described as 'wrong, inept and palsied'. He concluded by stating that 'the prime minister might save his government but his responsibility . . . [was] . . . to maintain Ulster'. In response Craig was both defiant and inflexible. He suggested that the motion was tantamount to a call for a general election in wartime, and referring to the demand for cabinet change, he stated categorically, 'my answer is that I am not going to do it'.[14]

The motion was easily defeated. No doubt this was partly because, as one opposition member commented, the prime minister 'stood head and shoulders above . . . the party' and thus occupied 'the position of dictator'.[15] However, a further factor was Craig's preliminary agreement to establish a select committee on unemployment. It was, as Warnock remarked earlier, 'a favourite strategy'. Spender suggests that the chief whip adroitly used this lucrative bait to secure the support of certain private members. Both Sir Wilfrid and Gransden feared that its subsequent proposals might prove to be 'very embarrassing' for the government.[16] This view was shared by Andrews who protested that its creation could only defer the cabinet's difficulties for a few months. Nonetheless, since May, he himself had come to accept that, given the weakness of the government 'the times were too critical for him to take any strong action', and that unpalatable political compromises were necessary.[17] Craig himself was adamant. He regarded the concession as 'the only means of easing the dangerous political position, . . . the only practical course'.[18]

There were no by-elections in this period to enable an accurate assessment of how 'dangerous' the 'political situation' beyond Stormont had become. None-theless, there can be little doubt that the two ministerial resignations cumula-tively helped shake public confidence in the government. Thus, for example, the *Northern Whig* described Warnock's resignation as a 'sensation', though adding, 'It is doubted whether he is being quite fair to his former colleagues . . . since last September . . . the lethargy was at Westminster, not here'. However, soon afterwards when Gordon resigned, it stated 'the public is not convinced that . . . certain ministers are the best talent available. . . . More vigorous leadership is immediately essential lest worse befall us than a reconstruction of the government'. By the time of the September censorship motion it remarked that 'the sense of complacence . . . has been sharply disturbed at Stormont. Things are not right, and they know it and admit it now'.[19]

Other factors also contributed to the government's continuing decline in public esteem. These included the formation of a new and more dynamic British administration, thus rendering it more difficult to attribute local failure to imperial laxity, and leading inevitably to unfavourable comparisons between the quality of local leadership and that at Westminster. Also the deterioration in the allied military position in Europe made the fumbling efforts of Craig's cabinet appear all the more indefensible. In addition, there was ample and growing evidence that the latter was simply incompetent. Unfortunately, as parliamentary and public criticism of its performance rose, so its confidence and capacity for trenchant action diminished. The high levels of unemploy-ment, rising each month from the outbreak of war until February 1940 were widely regarded as a measure of governmental ineffectiveness. Also increasing concern was expressed regarding the inadequacy of the province's civil defences, particularly after the fall of France, as the pattern of German air-raids on mainland cities became clearer and as Northern Ireland's strategic importance gradually increased. When in response, Craig once again hastily suggested that an all-party committee be set up to advise on A. R. P. Bates fervently opposed, fearing that the extent of Ulster's inadequate provision would thus be exposed. For once Spender sympathised with his attitude.[20]

The latter was concerned also with many other aspects of policy failure, some of which attracted less public attention, but which were, nonetheless, arguably more grave. He was 'disturbed' by reports of nepotism in the recruitment of staff at food offices by the clerks of local authorities. He derided the Ministry of Commerce's inability to provide an adequate and less vulnerable power supply for the province outside Belfast harbour. When officials at that department suggested the creation of an electricity board with responsibility for the whole six counties he observed that there was 'no possibility of our government facing up to such a proposal', due mainly to doubts as to its ability to pass the necessary legislation through parliament.[21] Primarily for this reason, concealed behind a stated desire to avoid controversial legislation in wartime, it rejected the idea of a power link-up with the south, abandoned an education bill, and its plans to co-ordinate road and rail transport services in the province.[22] As a result of earlier procrastination over the latter, Spender had feared that 'the name of the government and of [his] . . . ministry would be . . . dirt in the Treasury and city', and consequently he had now to be dissuaded by Whitehall officials from tendering his resignation. However, perhaps his most deep-seated private worry was what he regarded as the acutely unsatisfactory relationship between local ministers, particularly Dawson Bates, and the British military authorities based in the province. This he predicted might ultimately result in an imperial government decision to impose martial law on Northern Ireland.[23]

In this political context Brooke's wartime achievements at the Department of Agriculture might reasonably be regarded as not just 'Northern Ireland's best story' but to a considerable extent the province's only success 'story'. Douglas Harkness considered that it was in this period that Sir Basil first clearly began to converge as a potential future prime minister.[24] At the same time, inflexible and incompetent leadership was generating growing frustration and disillusionment amongst Unionist back-benchers and junior ministers, and even in the party beyond Stormont. Thus the strains and stresses that finally propelled him to the premiership were already apparent though for the moment contained at least in part by Craig's commanding presence. Apart from Brooke's activities at Agriculture decisive government action was restricted almost exclusively to security matters, where the cabinet displayed its customary energy, and to those issues which, to a greater or lesser extent, forced themselves upon the attention of ministers.

In the formulation of policy in these areas also Brooke played a predominant role. He was particularly concerned about the province's security position, in part reciprocating 'the very strong feeling [in Fermanagh] that the position in the county . . . [was] . . . not good enough . . . [and that] . . . the wrong people . . . [could] . . . get about'. In February 1940 he was warned by the county inspector of a possible resurgence in I.R.A. activity. At the time he was somewhat dismissive of the threat, noting that it was 'of course quite possible' but that he had 'heard nothing else for the last twenty years'. However, he came to regard the danger more seriously. In June he recorded without comment his land agent's remarks that the 'I.R.A. . . . [were] . . . more active, . . . [with] . . . people . . . being asked to sign on and they will fight Great Britain'. In addition, Brooke was disturbed by a growing expectation that Germany would occupy Eire. On 15 May 1940, he advised Craig that the government should 'watch this possibility'. Such a step he believed would enable Hitler to 'threaten the western approaches to Britain' and he regarded the south as 'the easiest place, in view of I.R.A. activity', and because an invading force could take advantage of local 'hostility to England in the Eire population'.[25]

Thus, by mid-June 1940, Brooke was convinced of the need to institute a system of passports between north and south, strengthen the special constabulary, introduce a curfew order and 'in fact to take every step, even at the inconvenience of the civil population, . . . to prevent invasion from the Free State'. At cabinet, on 15 June, he records that he 'was as strong as possible on protection and made some headway'. He suggested a curfew and staggered police and special constabulary patrols along the border. His colleagues rejected the former as 'the time was not considered opportune', but all supported Bates' suggestion that an order be made under the special powers act requiring everyone over the age of fourteen to carry identification.[26] One week later, a further order was agreed requiring persons coming into Northern Ireland from anywhere other than the United Kingdom to satisfy police that their purpose was legitimate. Due to evidence that this had led to interference with those involved in peaceful business, this was revised, in early July, on

MacDermott's suggestion, those questioned now having to satisfy police that 'they would not upset peace and order'.[27]

These measures combined with the introduction of special constabulary patrols, and internment, which began on the first night of the war, may be regarded as justified by the absence of civil strife. The I.R.A. had become quiescent by the end of 1940. Yet Brooke himself was not entirely satisfied. He continued to feel that 'the police . . . [were] . . . not taking the war seriously enough'. This he found 'most aggravating, . . . really it seems to be pushing against the invisible weight', and he described Wickham as consistently adopting 'a *non possimus* attitude'.[28] Thus when a home guard was being raised in Ulster during the summer of 1940, he consistently urged that it be placed under direct military control, no doubt at least in part because he was disturbed by the apparent laxity of the police authorities.

The question of raising this force arose after Eden had launched the Local Defence Volunteers in Britain on 14 May. Subsequently, Craig pressed for the province's inclusion in the scheme and without consulting his colleagues announced that the 'B' specials should serve as its nucleus.[29] Later in cabinet he referred to the 'grave objections . . . of which . . . [members] . . . were fully cognisant' to such a body being established in Northern Ireland on the same basis as in Great Britain. It was a view which they unanimously endorsed. Sir James personally consulted the imperial authorities and it was agreed that his government should be 'entrusted . . . with the duty of making protective arrangements . . . corresponding to' those on the mainland. On 25 May the cabinet decided to initiate recruitment, subject to further discussions with the Home Office and War Office.[30] Special constabulary sub-commandants were to select suitable applicants who like the 'B' specials would be placed under the authority of the inspector general.

Some senior officials expressed doubts as to the legality of such a course of action. Their concern was shared by J. C. MacDermott who on 25 June took up his duties as minister of public security. Also in parliament the procedures adopted were condemned by opposition M.P.s as a means of 'creating a sectarian and political force', with 'political loyalty' a condition of joining.[31] A contemporary diarist suggested that in making 'admission . . . a party issue the government helped ensure nationalist hostility to conscription in May 1941'. When Churchill raised such issues with the Home Office and they, in turn, contacted Gransden, the latter justified the government's actions on the grounds that the force had to be raised at very short notice and that had the 'B' specials not been used it would have been necessary to vet each application.[32]

Brooke dismissed such considerations. Regarding the cabinet decision on 25 May he observed 'There is just a doubt as to the legal position. Are they in fact armed forces of the crown?: To my mind it is only a quibble'. Three days later he spoke enthusiastically of the scheme in the house. He claimed that the existing 'B' special establishment was in a better position to carry out anti-parachute service than the newly formed British force, because it was armed and had a tactical knowledge. He commented, in relation to the L.D.V.s, 'I do not see how it is possible to eliminate fifth columnists unless you have a force that is recruited locally by people who know they are taking men who can be relied on. . . . The organisation of the special constabulary . . . would be more likely to produce the right sort of men and prevent the wrong type being equipped and armed'.[33] Subsequently, Sir Basil directed his energies and influence towards having both the L.D.V.s and the 'B' specials placed directly under military command. He remarked that 'if they are going to be used in a military capacity when the flag falls, the sooner the organisation is going the better'. The idea was originally suggested to him, on 3 July, by his brother-in-law, Harry Mulholland. Sir Basil noted at the time, that he 'entirely . . . [agreed], . . . am seeing MacDermott in the morning'. Indeed he raised the matter repeatedly with the latter and with Craig over the next four months. He found the P.M. 'not very keen' and formed the impression that he was 'afraid of upsetting Wickham, [adding], the personal feelings of any individual do not matter in these days'. MacDermott was more sympathetic to the idea, though concerned that there might be 'difficulty . . . in getting the right man'. He also complained that the 'inspector general was insisting that none but himself should have command'.[34]

Eventually, to Brooke's delight, in late October 1940, MacDermott produced a memorandum which contained the suggestion that the two forces be placed under military control. The latter was acutely concerned about the ambiguous constitutional status of the L.D.V.s and alarmed in particular that the Northern Ireland government was raising this body, not for internal security, but for the defence of the realm, and was therefore as a consequence legislating beyond its competence. He urged the British government either to assume direct responsibility for the force or to devise a constitutional expedient which explicitly enabled the Stormont administration to do so. The imperial authorities, however, rejected both courses of action.[35] Thus the L.D.V.s remained a branch of the special constabulary, though defence regulations were drafted whereby they might be placed under military control in the event of hostilities, and members of the force were obliged to sign a new declaration 'agreeing in emergency to . . . be subject to military law . . . [and] . . . obey the army council'.[36] In effect, the British government had pressed unconstitutional powers on the local administration. This outcome Brooke accepted with reluctance. He remained convinced that 'the transfer to military command ought to be done now', but acknowledged that because the 'constitutional position . . . [was] . . . extremely complicated, . . . [it would be] . . . difficult to administer any other way than under present officers'.[37]

Though Sir Basil had no direct role in raising the L.D.V.s he was, meanwhile, on Craig's request, actively involved in a campaign aimed at stimulating military recruitment in the province. In late May 1940, Sir James stated that he was 'very concerned' at the low levels of enlistment then current. During the early months of the war volunteers had come forward at the rate of 2,500 monthly but this had fallen with embarrassing rapidity to less than 1,000. In September 1940, Craig was attracted by the suggestion that unemployment benefit should be withdrawn from those who were eligible for military service and had failed to offer themselves for service. However, for the moment, he was convinced that a tactfully presented recruiting drive could be effective in attracting young men, particularly in country towns, whilst avoiding the risk of an upheaval in Ulster, 'at a time when every effort should be directed to winning the war'.[38] On 3 June he telephoned Brooke asking him to assume this responsibility 'as soon as the War Office . . . [gave] . . . the word'.[39]

The selection of Brooke is an indication of the prime minister's confidence in his abilities. It was clearly a task for which the former was well-suited given his military background, his experience in recruiting the special constabulary and his more recent involvement with the North Irish Horse. Though he accepted with typical enthusiasm, Sir Basil himself would have preferred conscription but was also conscious of the risks of embarrassing the British government by forcing this matter. In early August he records having 'raised . . . [this] . . . issue with . . . [Sir James] . . . again, but . . . [did] . . . not succeed very well'.[40]

When first asked by Craig to stimulate recruitment Brooke noted that he was 'not quite sure what . . . [his] . . . work should be'. In fact any action on his part was initially delayed by the War Office on the grounds that equipment was in short supply. In June, a further postponement was caused by the local military authorities who considered that a campaign then 'would be of little value' probably because recruitment for the L.D.V.s was begun in the course of that month.[41] Eventually, a series of rallies was organised by Brooke in mid-July amidst a measure of controversy and criticism.

As a preliminary step Sir Basil had first written to his majesty's lieutenants and deputy lieutenants in the counties, asking for their co-operation and advice on where meetings should be held. Spender felt that this ought to have been done by Craig personally, as he feared that the recipients would resent such a request coming from a 'junior minister'.[42] Perhaps, significantly, a later letter, circulated to the H.M.L.s was drafted by Brooke and then 'sent to the governor for dispatch'. More controversially Sir Basil suggested that a leading Glengall Street official should be used for publicity purposes in the campaign. He did so because he regarded the latter to be 'very good at that sort of work, . . . [and] . . . the only man to co-ordinate all efforts . . . [as he knew] . . . everybody in the country'. At the time he expressed some uneasiness as to whether the involvement of the party bureaucracy would be appropriate, noting, 'I do not like the idea . . . of a political body running recruiting but there does not appear to be any other machinery'. His choice appears to have been confirmed by a War Office decision not to provide him with an assistant recruiting officer. Brooke recorded his opinion that this was 'rather short-sighted if they want men', adding 'I reported this to the prime minister and we decided to use Glengall Street'.[43] The role of the latter in the campaign was raised in the house, one member commenting that 'it does not happen across the water'.[44]

The first recruitment rally was held in the Ulster Hall, Belfast, on 15 July and the last, seven weeks later, at Cookstown, County Tyrone. Brooke himself spoke at a total of sixteen meetings, missing only the parades and speeches organised in Londonderry. On the platform he was supported by a range of military officers and local politicians, including on occasion, Craig and, more frequently, Henry Mulholland and Lord Londonderry. The latter appeared to some as a rather inappropriate choice, given his pre-war contacts with and apparent sympathy for the Nazi leadership. Brooke, however, regarded him with some admiration, observing that 'people run him down and blame him but', he continued, 'it certainly seems to me that he saw the position some years ago and it is a pity that they did not take his advice and either make friends with Germany or fight her'. When, on one occasion, Brooke was shown a letter to Londonderry from Goering, suggesting Anglo-German friendship, and a free hand for Germany in eastern Europe, he observed 'this may or may not be right'. In any case Sir Basil was impressed by Londonderry's wartime commitment to allied victory, remarking that the latter was 'obsessed by the war, and talks of nothing else and feels that all that should be done is not being done'.[45]

The effectiveness of the campaign is difficult to gauge. Brooke himself found that the response at meetings was variable. Some, he described as well organised and attended with up to fifty recruits volunteering on a single evening, whilst others were 'rather inferior', with few of 'the men we wanted to get at'. In the end he was 'not sorry it was over', and felt that it had been 'definitely hard work'.[46] Though, in July 1940, the number of fresh recruits was easily the highest for any month since the first rush of volunteers when the war began, this was not necessarily attributable to the campaign. The rate was influenced by a multiplicity of factors, including service needs, variations in unemployment level and the war situation itself. The upsurge was due, primarily, to the impact of Dunkirk and was of short duration. Thus, throughout 1941–42, the recruitment level remained disappointingly low, exceeding a rate of 1,000 per month on only three occasions. In the house, Warnock suggested that the rallies were not being very effective, and this verdict is, in essence, reiterated by Blake who writes: 'Those at the time who sought to trace a connection between recruiting figures and recruiting campaigns, in particular towns in Northern Ireland, found little to confirm the hope that rallies produced immediate results'.[47]

A further, at least partial, explanation for the campaign's marginal impact was the decision to use the Unionist party machine. This must have discouraged recruitment from the minority. In his support for this, despite reservations, and for the use of the 'B' specials as the foundation for the L.D.V.s, Brooke shared the insensitivity of his colleagues towards nationalist opinion. His attitude on both issues must have helped confirm his uncompromising political image, and certainly weakened the force of his appeal within weeks of the outbreak of war, that 'people . . . set aside the Orange–Green dispute and co-operate fully with the government. If this war goes against us the only flag that will fly over Belfast or Dublin . . . will be the swastika'.[48] He himself was aware that his presence in the campaign might inhibit nationalist volunteers. Thus, when arranging the rallies for Londonderry City, he decided after discussion with the local H.M.L.s and D.L.s not to 'go there . . . [as he was] . . . a bit too politically minded and might keep the other sort away'. To indicate the strength of feeling there the county lieutenants had advised him that if conscription were introduced the city 'would go up in flames'.[49]

Brooke's support, in October 1940, for the activities of the Defence League Association in Fermanagh might be adduced as further evidence for his apparent political paranoia. Its purpose was 'to secure the banks for making any loans to loyalists who want to buy farms'. Sir Basil regarded it as a 'very good scheme', and thought that it 'should be made all over the six counties'. He also approved of the Orange Benefit Society which he thought was 'well thought out and should be a great assistance to help Orangemen to start business or buy land'.[50] There is, however, some evidence to suggest that such organisations were responding in some measure to a genuine threat. Thus, Healy sought backing for a similar nationalist scheme, some months earlier, stating that 'setting catholics on the land . . . [was] . . . the best means of achieving control in Northern Ireland'. He suggested that 'people who live upon the land constitute a more permanent population than those who are in trade or the professions' and that if the southern government was prepared to make funds available 'the result could be achieved more quickly'.[51]

However, Brooke's attitudes and his influence on policy were more complex than the fact of his support for such schemes might suggest. For example, during his period at the ministry of agriculture, the percentage of Roman catholics amongst his staff appears to have been higher than for that of any other Stormont department. When Andrews, in late March 1943, expressed acute anxiety about the number of civil servants recruited from the minority, it was Sir Basil's department which caused him the gravest concern.[52] The latter may himself have felt some uneasiness about the position. He complained that other ministers had been disposed to exert pressure on him to accept a larger proportion than they themselves were prepared to take.[53] Nonetheless, when Brooke was given the responsibility in November 1940 of dealing 'with the question of Roman catholics in our service', Spender welcomed the appointment, as he felt it was 'quite intolerable that our ministry should decline to receive members of this faith . . . if it is the government's policy that they should be generally accepted into the service'.[54]

Similarly Brooke's response to the Anglo-Irish talks in 1940 confirms the impression that his role within the government was not readily predictable or easily categorised. Many years later Brooke disclosed that his major 'worry' in this period, apart from security, was the prospect of De Valera reaching an agreement with the British government, whereby he traded his neutrality for the ending of partition. Sir Basil wrote that 'at a moment of crisis in the death struggle Northern Ireland could have been sacrificed. I had an awful feeling that had we refused, we would have been blamed for whatever disaster had ensued'.[55] From late April he, like his colleagues, observed the Anglo-Irish trade negotiations with apprehension, concerned that Eire might receive preferential treatment compared with the province, and ultimately fearful that Ulster's constitutional relationship with Britain might be compromised.[56] On 2 May he received reassurance from Harkness that the south had been unsuccessful in gaining any significant concessions and this opinion Brooke himself confirmed during direct talks with London ministers in the days following. He met Lord Woolton, minister of food, whom he considered a 'very fine man' who would 'not give the position away' and who had been 'apparently firm [with Eire] and told them where to get off'. Sir Basil also met Osbert Peake, under-secretary at the Home Office, 'who . . . [would] . . . deal with any of our questions at cabinet level', and described him as a 'live wire . . . [who] . . . should be a big help'. On his return he dined with Craig and, in his own words, 'gave him all the chat about the Eire negotiations'.[57]

Within weeks, early optimism began to dissipate. On 22 May Brooke recorded that 'the prime minister has had to rush to London', and although not informed of the reason, he deduced that it was probably 'about the Eire position'. Spender who was at least for the present more aware of the circumstances of the visit observed that 'the European position is so serious that there is no knowing what sacrifices it would be necessary for Northern Ireland to make'.[58] He also expressed uneasiness that Sir James might use the occasion to extract financial concessions from Britain as he had done in 1938.

Between April–July 1940 Craig was subjected to a mounting campaign of cajolement, persuasion and political pressure, such as he had not experienced since the treaty negotiations almost twenty years earlier. His response was consistently inflexible and dilatory, reflecting his priority, the preservation of the union, and in the circumstances is unlikely to have enhanced the province's position at Westminster. His first talks in London began on 23 May on the same day that it was decided to evacuate Dunkirk and that the British Army left Boulogne. He met Chamberlain again on 5 June, when the fall of France was imminent, Britain's position apparently hopeless, facing, in Churchill's phrase, 'the abyss of a new dark age', and the invasion of Ireland sufficiently probable that the southern authorities felt it advisable to initiate a recruitment drive. On this second occasion Craig was asked to put forward some proposal that might encourage the Eire government to take more effective measures regarding Ireland's defence. He failed to respond. One week later both he and De Valera were asked to come to London for talks on defence. Once more Craig declined to participate unless the south abandoned its neutrality and he received assurances that constitutional issues would not be raised. On 16 June, the cabinet decided to proceed with talks. Next day Malcolm MacDonald met De Valera, to discuss the establishment of a council for the defence of all Ireland. It was anticipated that this might lead on to consideration of the partition question.[59]

Neither Craig nor his cabinet were kept closely informed regarding the progress of these negotiations. Nevertheless, there are some indications of a measure of disagreement on how they ought to react, particularly if the south abandoned its neutrality in a bid for Irish unity. Sir Basil's response apparently differed from that of his colleagues, though he appeared initially to be opposed to making any concessions. Thus, on 22 May, he dined at Government House and met David Gray, United States minister to Ireland. He records that the latter was 'busy trying to find out how the north could be persuaded to join the south'. He continues: 'I think we succeeded in convincing him that the differences are very real . . . a complete difference of ideals'.[60] Indeed, Gray informed Roosevelt two weeks later that he had been warned by both Brooke and Andrews that even if a settlement was devised which was acceptable to Craig, they were 'not interested'.[61] Again, on 19 June, Sir Basil strongly supported Sir James's response to a telegram from MacKenzie King urging north-south co-operation in defence matters. Brooke stated that the prime minister's 'reply was . . . effective namely that we are part of the United Kingdom at war, whereas the Free State are neutral . . . and that the matter of defence was one for the United Kingdom government'.[62]

Nonetheless, various sources suggest that as the crisis escalated Sir Basil's response was more flexible than these comments might indicate. From the outset he was deeply concerned, lest his loyalty to crown and empire might come into conflict with his life-long commitment to the union. Thus, on 5 June, he recorded that he was 'still anxious about the position with regard to Eire . . . [and] . . . convinced that heavy pressure will be put on us to join up. The argument being that De Valera will allow the British army to come into the south and the fleet to use southern harbours, but he insists on Ulster coming in'. He concluded that it would be a 'very difficult nut to crack'.[63] Two days later he expressed relief when Craig explained the further efforts by the British government to induce him to discuss defence matters with Eire, writing 'so long as they keep on that line and do not discuss the constitutional position, I think we have a good case for staying out. But', he added, 'I always fear that we may be asked to sacrifice ourselves if Eire offers to cancel her neutrality and allow British troops into the country'.[64]

One Sunday in June 1940, John Brooke recalled his father considering such a prospect. The latter spoke of the pressures being exerted on the Northern Ireland government and stated that 'if 'we were faced with the choice of losing our civilisation or accepting the unification of Ireland he would find it a very difficult decision. He regarded western civilisation as of greater worth than anything else, being absolutely convinced of the menace of Nazi Germany'. His son concluded: 'It was my opinion that day in those circumstances he would have to do his best to secure Irish unity'.[65]

This broad impression is supported by a conversation which Brooke had with Frank MacDermott, a southern senator and occasional visitor to Colebrooke, who was seeking to act as an intermediary between the northern and southern governments. He called with Sir Basil, on 25 June, 'to discuss a conference on defence'. The latter records: 'I told him that the south had to give some proof of its pro-British, pro-Ulster tendencies . . . namely declare war before any discussions could take place'. MacDermott adds that Sir Basil 'admitted privately that if the south were to join the war on Britain's side in return for post-war unification, Craig's cabinet would be split with his own vote favouring a new relationship with the south'.[66] Undoubtedly, such a reaction would have been a minority one within Craig's cabinet, though it would probably have received support from J. C. MacDermott, after his appointment as minister of public security.[67]

When the southern senator subsequently sought to interest De Valera and Frank Aiken in what he had regarded as the promising results of his talks with Brooke, he was dismissed, Aiken stating: 'get this into your head . . . there are no conditions under which we would abandon neutrality'.[68] Though disappointed, MacDermott had himself earlier stressed to Sir Basil the unlikelihood of the south actively participating in the allied war effort as 'the great majority of people in Eire thought that Great Britain would be beaten'.[69]

Meanwhile on 23 June, Pat Herdman, the son of a northern Unionist senator, and an acquaintance of Brooke's, who also had contacts with southern leaders, called at Colebrooke to say that Sean McEntee was 'anxious to discuss the defence of Ireland' with him.[70] That Brooke should have received such approaches in itself suggests that his more flexible political attitudes were appreciated by some Free State politicians. In reply, Sir Basil once more stated that 'we cannot discuss anything until they declare war', and added that he 'could not act behind the prime minister's back and would have to inform him of anything he told me'.[71] These terms Herdman appears to have accepted and was sufficiently encouraged by their conversation that he arranged a meeting with De Valera two days later. He then raised the question of Ireland's defence and whether Eire would be prepared to enter the war in order to end partition. To his amazement, the taoiseach once more virulently opposed any compromising of neutrality, stating that to do so would 'split [the south] from top to bottom'.[72]

Herdman returned north and reported back to Brooke, who recorded his impression that De Valera was 'afraid of his fifth column . . . the I.R.A., and therefore will not move'. Sir Basil was clearly both relieved and alert to the potential political value of this assumed insight. He immediately told Craig of 'all these conversations' and argued forcefully that we [the Northern Ireland government] were now in a strong position with the British government, having done our best to establish contact'. He added that after their meeting Sir James intended writing to Chamberlain that morning.[73] The prime minister's letter reflected his nervousness and uncertainty as to the degree of progress so far made in the Anglo-Irish talks and attempted to exploit, and it would appear elaborate, on the information with which he had just been provided by Brooke. He wrote of 'my friend, . . . an absolutely reliable source' who had met De Valera and suggested to him that 'if he would declare himself as willing to come in with Britain, I would be glad to meet him anywhere at any time over mutual civil defence, provided no constitutional questions were touched upon'. Mr De Valera's answer was 'quite impossible', as he could not 'abrogate his position of neutrality on account of the strength of his fifth column'.[74] Craig thus repeated the phrase used earlier by Brooke.

However, neither this letter nor Sir James's strongly worded and defiant telegram to Chamberlain after he had received the British government's written proposals to the Southern government, prevented the negotiations from continuing. On 1 July, Brooke records that Craig received a letter from O'Neill who had just met Churchill and been informed that 'there might be discussions with De Valera and that we might be asked to make constitutional change'. Sir Basil added, despondently, 'I have always feared this. We must resist as long as possible'. On 6 July, similarly, Spender noted that the situation was 'critical' and expressed fears that martial law might be imposed as a preliminary to an Anglo-Irish agreement.[75] In fact, that same day Churchill informed his cabinet colleagues of De Valera's 'flat refusal' to accept the British terms and of his own intention to inform the Northern Ireland government that the negotiations had ended and had not been successful. Soon afterwards, Brooke wrote with both relief and satisfaction 'De Valera wants unity with neutrality, an impossible wish. I think this . . . finally cooks his dish. Churchill, I think understands that we can make no more moves in this direction'. Brooke was full of praise for Craig's commons speech next day, which stressed the impossibility of discussing defence with De Valera, so long as he insisted on neutrality. In Sir Basil's opinion the prime minister's remarks were 'well delivered and . . . very convincing'.[76]

Nonetheless, Brooke might well have identified with the sentiments expressed later by Spender that Sir James 'was always guided by his desire to ensure the prosperity of the province, . . . whereas . . . [he, Sir Wilfrid] . . . followed Lord Carson's line, thinking far more of the general effects upon the empire'.[77] Certainly, Brooke had shown during this 'moment of crisis in the death struggle' a greater willingness to compromise and to act in the national interest, than his leader or his cabinet colleagues. Just as he had suggested in early 1916 that he would prefer home rule to civil war in Ireland, so now he had indicated that in the final analysis, the defeat of the Axis powers must take priority over the preservation of the union.

Later, in 1940, in private discussions with British ministers and officials he defended partition on the same grounds as he had done with Gray earlier in May. He informed Hore-Belisha that the boundary was not a 'cause of differences but merely acknowledged that there was such a difference', and perhaps prompted by the failure of the recent negotiations, he added that 'if the south had the same loyalty as Canada, Australia or New Zealand there never would have been partition'.[78] Nonetheless, there is a hint of more flexible attitudes in a conversation Brooke held with Herbert Morrison, in September 1946. They considered the prospects for Irish unity and the relevance of projected population trends within the province which indicated that the Unionist party would eventually lose its majority. Morrison recorded that he found Sir Basil 'as always, reasonable and co-operative'. The latter stated that if the partition question was 'raised there would be a storm in Ulster'. He continued: 'if and when . . . [it is] . . . raised, Ulster would be insistent about two things, the entry of Ireland into the commonwealth before a United Ireland was established . . . [and] . . . some provision whereby the Roman catholic priesthood would no longer improperly intervene in state affairs, a change which would enable Ulster to tone down its own protestant preachers who – the prime minister admits – are sometimes a nuisance owing to their liveliness in politics'.[79] Brooke's own account of this discussion was, however, more emphatic in tone. In this he claims to have stressed that 'our population would not affect the situation in our life-time, . . . under no circumstances would it be possible to even contemplate union at the present time'.[80]

Perhaps fittingly, Brooke described with uncritical enthusiasm, Craig's last significant speech in the commons, on 29 October 1940, in which he attacked a motion in support of Northern Ireland uniting with the South. Sir Basil noted that the prime minister's reply was 'magnificent' and that 'proposers and seconders were so knocked about by the speeches from the government and opposition side that they did not even push for a vote'.[81] Less than one month later, at 9.15 pm, on the evening of 24 November, Gransden telephoned Colebrooke to inform Brooke that Sir James had died some three hours earlier.[82] He received this unexpected news with a profound sense of loss as well as a measure of fatalistic acceptance. Lady Craig described her husband as having been 'comfortable all through the day, reading and dozing, . . . [they had] . . . listened to the 6 o'clock news together on the wireless', she then left the room briefly and on her return found that 'he had gone from' her.[83]

On 26 November, in the commons, recalled from its Christmas recess, Andrews rose amidst cheers and paid eloquent tribute to the province's first premier and his own close colleague, stating prophetically: 'no one can adequately fill his place. Those of us who follow him can only pray to be given strength . . . to follow his noble example of public spirited integrity and unselfish devotion to duty'. In his comments Brooke described Craig as a 'born leader, a man of the greatest integrity whom friend and foe trusted . . . Ulster can never repay the debt it owes to him and might never appreciate all he meant to her'. He recorded similar sentiments privately. In his diary, he described Sir James's death as 'a terrible loss for the country',[84] and, in a letter of condolence to Lady Craig, wrote 'I myself feel stunned at the loss of a great leader and friend. I have had the good fortune to serve under two great men, the prime minister and Lord Byng, . . . both alike, completely loveable'. He continued, 'nothing can express the very deep feeling of gratitude that one has had the privilege of working with such a man. You will understand. . . . I wish you could have heard the public and private opinions expressed by M.P.s today'.[85]

Spender's private observations were much less fulsome and reflected his own deepening anxiety at the inadequacy of recent Unionist leadership. He noted that, 'In later years . . . [Sir James's] . . . health prevented him from giving matters due attention and engaging in long discussions with his colleagues and this led to his adopting short cuts on decisions. During the last two years he [had] . . . been inclined to give decisions or advice to ministers across the water which . . . [were] . . . less than sound. Death,' he concluded, 'had thrown off all the weight of illness and cares which had hung so heavily upon him during the last few years of his life'.[86]

Meanwhile, at noon on 25 November, Andrews informed the cabinet that he had been asked by the governor earlier that morning to assume the premiership. He stated that though aware of the heavy responsibilities involved, he felt it his duty to accept, adding that 'in doing so he appreciated that normally the leader of the party which had the majority in the house would be entrusted . . . with the duties of prime minister, and accordingly his acceptance was contingent on the choice of a leader by the Ulster Unionist party'. He indicated that, meanwhile, he would carry on if he had the full support of his colleagues, aware that 'whatever decision they reached would be in the best interests of Ulster'. All present offered him their full support. Andrews then invited his ministers to continue in charge of their respective departments, and suggested that for the present he would combine the offices of prime minister and minister of finance. Later that afternoon the cabinet, Brooke included, spent two hours looking for a suitable site for Craig's grave and arrangements were made for his funeral which was strictly private 'for reasons of public security'.[87]

In the press and elsewhere this orderly transfer of power was regarded with a measure of relief but also with some criticism. The *Northern Whig* remarked that earlier 'fears of constitutional difficulty were without foundation', however, it suggested that Andrews' conditional acceptance of the premiership was 'carrying his ideal of popular leadership rather further than . . . [was] necessary'.[88] Likewise, Brooke, after making private enquiries, concluded that it was 'wrong procedure . . . if the king's representative asks him to form a government, it is not a question for the party'.[89] Spender passed no judgement on the procedural propriety of Andrews' decision but observed that it was 'inconvenient . . . [and] . . . another example of the weakness of the democratic machine'. He was all too soon also convinced that the seven-week delay before the party elected him as leader prejudiced the new prime minister's political authority at the very outset of his term of office. On 7 December, he remarked that in this interim period, it was 'important that Andrews should not antagonise opinion amongst unionists, . . . and some of these [were] . . . taking the opportunity to press demands upon the government almost in terms of blackmail'. Just over two weeks later he reflected on 'influences . . . at work which . . . [were] . . . almost of a blackmailing character, both in regard to nominations to new posts and . . . demands upon the Exchequer. The fact that there is no new minister of finance makes the position much more difficult for the officials of the ministry'.[90]

Few at the time questioned the fact, as opposed to the nature, of Andrews' succession in 1940. To most observers he appeared to be both an inevitable and a deserving choice. His claims were based predominantly on his seniority and his experience. From 1937 he had served not only as minister of finance, but had for several years also acted as prime minister when Craig was ill or absent, and had intermittently assumed responsibility for the Ministries of Commerce and of Labour. Thus, he had carried in recent years the major burden of government office and had also been, since the formation of the state the prime architect of the step-by-step policy with Britain. He was an earnest, honest, reliable minister, trusted and liked by Craig, cabinet colleagues and, indeed, the whole unionist movement. On hearing of Craig's death the governor took soundings within the party, though not all, perhaps not any, of the cabinet was canvassed. No formal votes were taken, and no formal letters were exchanged.[91] When approached the new premier had no difficulty in forming a government, and the *Northern Whig* predicted that his ratification by the party was 'almost a foregone conclusion'.[92]

However, Andrews' appointment was generally received with resignation rather than enthusiasm. Some expressed doubts as to his capacity to provide the decisive and inspired leadership necessary in wartime. He was just one year younger than Craig and his age had prompted Warnock several months earlier to suggest that he be removed from cabinet office.[93] He himself suggested to Spender that he might be regarded as 'too old' by the party, and if so, he was 'quite ready to stand down' but he considered that 'except for this reservation his nomination would be confirmed'. Sir Wilfrid was, however, also concerned about his health and for this reason hoped that he would soon appoint a minister of finance.[94]

It has also been suggested that Andrews would not have been Craig's own choice as his successor. St John Ervine, the latter's somewhat unreliable, official biographer, refers to Brooke as 'a young member of . . . [Sir James's] . . . cabinet, who he had hoped would succeed him'. John Brooke confirmed that his father had himself believed that the ageing prime minister was 'grooming' him for the leadership.[95] One recent historian suggests that Craig may have believed that Brooke's 'family name would give some added prestige amongst British ministers'. The same source also considered that in any case Sir Basil's 'abilities far outshone those of his cabinet colleagues'.[96] This was widely recognised both in Britain and within the province. At the beginning of the war the *Belfast Telegraph* described him as 'Ulster's busiest minister and the most talked of man in the cabinet'.[97] During December 1940–January 1941, the *Northern Whig* commented that 'his progressive pre-war policy, although subject to much criticism . . . [had] . . . been acknowledged to have been beneficial'. It added that there had been a 'veritable revolution in agriculture since the war' in the course of which Brooke had shown 'energy and drive', 'force and courage', running his department 'ably and intelligently' and was, overall, 'an excellent success'.[98] Certainly his claims to promotion, even to the premiership, had been enhanced since September 1939.

Andrews had likewise been impressed by Brooke's performance at agriculture, describing him in a letter to Morrison as 'a most energetic and successful minister'. Moreover, he also believed that Sir Basil had a claim to the premiership.[99] The former remarked, with evident relief and satisfaction, to Spender that he 'had the support of Brooke who might otherwise be considered'. Sir Wilfrid, who had ruthlessly dismissed the claims of some other possible contenders, responded by suggesting that Sir Basil 'would be all the better for some training at the Ministry of Finance, before he undertook the responsibilities of prime minister'.[100] Sir Arthur Kelly recalled that some leading civil servants favoured Brooke's succession in 1940.[101]

It may also be the case that Craig would himself have preferred Brooke to succeed. Though he, unquestionably, had the deepest respect for Andrews, their relationship was exclusively on an official, rather than a social plane, and even on the former level was not entirely satisfactory. In the late 1930s Spender was constantly irritated by the fact that Andrews always seemed obliged to act 'as prime minister when anything unpleasant . . . [had] . . . to be done', and that, though he was also serving as minister of labour and minister of commerce he was 'sometimes not even consulted . . . [by Craig] . . . on matters relating to his own department'.[102] Andrews himself occasionally expressed feelings of annoyance and frustration. For instance, during the transport negotiations in 1940, he complained in cabinet of 'the unfair attempt to saddle . . . [him] . . . with the whole responsibility' for the government's lack of progress, and stressed that 'after all . . . [he had] . . . only been acting in accord with . . . [their] . . . wishes'.[103] It may also be significant that, shortly after Craig's death, when Sir Basil mentioned to Andrews the informal contacts he had had with the South during the Anglo-Irish talks, he found, clearly to his surprise that the latter 'had not been informed . . . [of them] . . . by the late prime minister'.[104] It is also noteworthy that when Pollock died in April 1937, Milne Barbour, rather than Andrews, was Craig's first choice as his replacement at finance, but he declined the position on grounds of age and business interests.[105]

Throughout this period Brooke continued to enjoy a close relationship with Craig. On a social level, he helped him entertain visiting dignatories at Stormont, and Sir James, though much less active, made a final trip to Fermanagh in July 1940, organised, at his request, by Brooke, 'to meet the leaders of the county'.[106] He also gave Sir Basil every support and encouragement at agriculture. This, the latter deeply appreciated, though without necessarily responding favourably to all of the prime minister's suggestions. Sir Basil found him 'comforting' when he complained of the lack of party support for the tillage campaign, and in agreement that Glentoran was 'talking rubbish' in opposing rationing. On other occasions he described Sir James as 'understanding and helpful' and again, after seeking his advice on a departmental issue, noted 'what a wise man the old man is'.[107] Craig from time to time supported Brooke in difficult negotiations, and when requested spoke in his defence in the house, or interceded on behalf of his ministry at Westminster. In addition, the prime minister continued to delegate responsibility to Brooke, most recently over the organisation of the recruitment drive. Also during the Anglo-Irish talks, though Brooke was not initially kept as closely informed as Glentoran, Sir James clearly valued Brooke's contacts with the south, and did act on the information that he had provided when writing to Chamberlain. He expressed his admiration for his minister in words of undiluted praise commenting: 'I say from my heart, thank God we have a man like him at present. I do not know anyone who could have carried all these things through with the same energy, skill and confidence'. On a later occasion he stated 'no one has a more arduous task, . . . when I see the burden that is on his shoulders with all the work of his department . . . I wonder how he is able to stand up to it'.[108]

Whether or not Brooke was justified in feeling that he was being groomed for the leadership, or whoever Craig would have preferred as his successor, it seems virtually certain that the latter gave no clear indication as to whom he felt ought to succeed. It is impossible to say whether this reticence was due to fear of causing party division in the context of war, or his failing capacity to make decisions; whether this uncertain outcome was influenced by the fact of his sudden death or reflected his considered opinion as to what the proper procedure should be. Arthur Kelly recalled suggesting to Sir James that in the context of the increasing aerial bombardment of Britain some provision should be made for the future leadership. The latter replied 'are you asking me to name a successor?', and added, emphatically, 'I will not do that'! He then indicated that in his view, when a successor was being appointed, a party meeting should be held, and a new leader elected, and that the governor should then send for the successful candidate and appoint him as prime minister.[109]

Whatever Craig's attitudes and feelings were it is noteworthy that Brooke's own comments relating to Andrews' succession, both at the time and since, do not suggest either the slightest expectation of preferment or the smallest trace of disappointment at the outcome. He gave Andrews, as the latter recognised, his unswerving support, noting in his diary, 'there are some murmurings against him, but we must back him for all he is worth'.[110] He did, however, strenuously urge on the new prime minister the absolute necessity for cabinet changes.

Though he had continued to revere Craig, even though this sentiment may have been weakened by the débâcle of the Anglo-Irish negotiations in 1938, Sir Basil had become increasingly concerned at the ineffectiveness of the government's performance. He sympathised with the 'general complaint . . . [at its] . . . inactivity' and was at least in part aware that the back-benchers were becoming dangerously alienated from the party leadership.[111] His defence of its record in parliament against the criticisms of Warnock and others sprang less from conviction than duty. He considered that the prime minister's response in mid-1940, of appointing MacDermott as minister of public security, was 'all right as far as it goes', implying that more far-reaching changes were necessary, and added that he did not 'like this being done after the pressure we have had'.[112]

Thus, on 26 November, Brooke suggested to Andrews that 'for psychological reasons if for no other, we must make cabinet changes'. The new prime minister was clearly uneasy at this prospect, as, next day, he asked Sir Basil 'did . . . [he] . . . think that the appointment of parliamentary secretaries would fit the bill'? This option the latter rejected. He records, four days later, 'I again urged my point that he must reconstitute his cabinet', but sensitive to Andrews' position, he continued, 'I see his difficulty with two old colleagues and I told him that if it would make things easier for him he could put me on one side as well as the others. This he refused to do'. Just over two weeks later, Brooke commented once more: 'The prime minister discussed some of his appointments with me. I am convinced that he will have to make radical changes in his cabinet. The sooner . . . [he] . . . makes his alterations the better; every day makes it more difficult'.[113]

Similar pressures for reconstituting the government were meanwhile being exerted from other directions. A number of back-benchers had for long urged that this was necessary and there were strong expectations within sections of the parliamentary party that it was imminent. Spender observed a number of members discussing the issue in the corridors at Stormont and deduced that they were 'obviously intending to press their claims'. One, he noted, had already arranged an interview with Andrews on the subject.[114] Also sections of the unionist press were increasingly insistent on the need for change. On 18 December, the *Northern Whig* suggested that, though criticism of the government was inhibited by party loyalty, 'a fairly substantial minority' of unionist opinion outside the house favoured cabinet reconstruction and that it 'would find a surprising amount of support'. Brooke's promotion to the Ministry of Finance, it 'regarded as certain', adding that 'it would meet with nothing but approval'. Later after considering more closely the interim report of the commons committee on unemployment, it went further, stating that Andrews 'should meet . . . [the commons] . . . with a reconstituted cabinet pledged to tackle the problem . . . on the lines formulated by the . . . committee'. It became increasingly critical of Barbour, considering the report to have been 'a virtual condemnation of . . . [his] . . . ministry', and suggesting that he should retire or be moved 'to some less onerous post'.[115]

Throughout, Spender was closely informed of Andrews' intentions regarding the appointment of his new cabinet. Despite his obvious reluctance, the latter does initially appear to have had significant changes under consideration. He was at first 'anxious' that Brooke should move to the Ministry of Finance, and Sir Wilfrid was delighted with another of the prime minister's suggestions believing that his nominee would 'prove a strong support for the government'.[116] However, on 13 January the prime minister told Spender of 'certain changes he was making in his original plans'. He had considered introducing into the cabinet ministers who were not members of the Northern Ireland parliament. Such a course Warnock had earlier suggested in the house citing Churchill's actions at Westminster as a precedent. However, Andrews explained that 'the Northern Ireland constitution made this practically impossible' as a minister had to obtain a seat within six months of his appointment and since 'the selection of candidates was left entirely to the localities there was practically no possibility of getting them to accept someone from outside the constituency'. He then indicated the changes which he had decided to make. He explained that he had 'found it necessary to move one of his ministers who had been subjected to a great deal of criticism and was promoting him. This made it necessary to make a rearrangement of his original intention, especially as he had already promised one ministry to a certain individual'. The outcome of these somewhat perverse considerations was that: Glentoran became minister of agriculture, apparently in fulfilment of a pledge by Andrews, Barbour was 'promoted' to become minister of finance and Brooke, therefore, was transferred to commerce.[117]

When Spender told his wife 'the news of the cabinet reshuffle' he made it clear that he would have 'liked Sir Basil . . . as his minister for choice'. Overall, Sir Wilfrid had been utterly perplexed at the 'suggestion of moving a minister upwards because of criticism, . . . like promotion to the House of Lords' and reflected, as he often did, on the 'weakness of our parliamentary machinery'.[118] Brooke, however, was relieved. He had forewarned Robertson on 3 December of 'possible changes in the cabinet'. When his name was being suggested for finance, he commented that he was 'not keen' and 'would rather stay where [he] was'. Eventually, on 9 January Andrews telephoned to request that he take commerce instead, a decision which had apparently been made at least one week earlier, and Brooke noted 'I agreed, as I would much rather have it'.[119] Wilson Hungerford became his parliamentary secretary. Spender had pointed out to Andrews, that if the former had been made a minister, Beattie would have replaced him as chairman of the commons select committee on unemployment and stressed that this would have been 'very unfortunate' as he was so 'ill qualified'.[120] Meanwhile, Brooke had used his influence with Andrews to have Moore appointed as minister of agriculture, urging that 'a good man was needed' and that he was 'the best man', the only M.P. 'who . . . [knew] . . . the principles of the various schemes and the war administration, . . . any other would for some time be a cypher'. In the end he accepted Glentoran's appointment with resignation, commenting that 'he should do all right'.[121]

Thus, Brooke's advice as to the necessity of cabinet change was ignored; Glentoran was the only new member appointed. Spender can have found little reason for satisfaction either. In his personal memorandum of August 1938, he had devastatingly exposed the incompetence or at least unsuitability of most of the surviving ministers, and, in May 1940, observed that 'there . . . [was] . . . no excuse for the retention of men unable to do a reasonable day's work'.[122] In the end, for whatever reason, Andrews had stuck on his original suggestion of mollifying criticism by increasing the number of parliamentary secretaries. As a result there were almost as many members of the government in the house, as private members. In the spring of 1941 this 'old guard' faced problems which were formidable and which ultimately proved to be beyond its capacity. These included restive back-benchers, a growing threat of aerial attack, a simmering scandal involving the Unionist-controlled Belfast Corporation and above all unemployment. Already in mid-January, after a commons debate on the latter, the *Northern Whig* observed ominously that the prime minister 'did not attempt to defend the government on its record . . . [but instead] . . . answered irrelevance with irrelevance. Is it not time there was an end to this trifling'?[123]

CHAPTER IX

Minister of Commerce and Production 1941–43

There was some uncertainty as to the wisdom of appointing Brooke as minister of commerce. William Scott later recalled the 'doubts as to whether he could adapt himself to the frequent and difficult negotiations with industrialists and unions'[1] which the post entailed. In the house Beattie alleged that he had been 'misplaced by the government', and Henderson with typical candour, remarked that he would not 'know . . . a scrapped shell from a turnip'.[2] The *Northern Whig*, by contrast, sought to reassure its readers, commenting 'we welcome [Brooke's appointment] as a positive stroke of genius on the part of the prime minister. The foresight, energy and enterprise that have characterised . . . [his] . . . work . . . will find ready employment in the commercial field'.[3] Sir Basil himself welcomed the challenge. In retrospect, he remembered being 'tipped for the Ministry of Finance, . . . [but] . . . was not at all keen about that', adding 'commerce . . . was much more in my line. The problems as at agriculture were all geared to the war effort'.[4] He enjoyed the sensation of getting things done. It may be, as one official who knew him intimately suggests, that he was even more contented in his new position than he had been at his former post.[5]

He entered into his new duties purposefully and expeditiously. Before the end of January, he had arranged the first of his visits to London to meet the heads of the supply departments, answered his first questions in the house, and delivered his first public speeches as minister of commerce.[6] He described himself later as 'very fortunate' in having Scott as his permanent secretary.[7] The latter was extremely able, had already served in the position for some fifteen years and was highly regarded by British ministers and officials. Sir Basil sought to strengthen his departmental team by asking Harkness to transfer with him from agriculture. He joined commerce in February 1941, but to Brooke's disappointment returned to his old ministry one year later. In his own account Sir Douglas states that he 'was not greatly interested in the commercial and industrial side', his training was exclusively in agricultural matters, and besides he disclosed to a somewhat sceptical Spender, in December 1941, that he believed 'the activities of the Ministry of Commerce . . . [were] . . . likely to be less important in the future'.[8]

Also Brooke had for the first time a parliamentary secretary, Wilson Hungerford. Immediately after his appointment, Sir Basil clearly defined the latter's area of responsibility, and, leaving no room for ambiguity, outlined his own approach as minister. He records 'I told him that in my opinion politics took second place, and that the thing was to get the job done. I give all decisions and all communications with outside ministries and with the prime minister'.[9] He sustained a dominant role in the relationship. Reviewing his period at commerce Spender noted, 'Sir Basil Brooke kept the strings very much in his own hands. Hungerford has not been given any major part in the transactions of the ministry'.[10]

Brooke's new position was a predictably unenviable one. That he should have preferred it to finance showed political courage, a profound commitment to the war effort and an apparent lack of personal ambition. Commerce was a small, junior ministry, dealing, in Harkness's phrase, with 'odds and ends'.[11] The inadequacy of its performance was widely regarded as an important cause of the government's diminishing popularity and of the province's high level of unemployment. This view was shared by Spender who described Milne Barbour's ministry on the eve of Craigavon's death as 'not very effective in getting things done'.[12] As a consequence Scott recalled its low morale in early 1941, stating 'our manpower was not being used . . . [and] . . . productive capacity remained to be mobilised . . . [after] . . . months of exasperating and frustrating discussions'.[13]

This was graphically illustrated when, two weeks before Brooke's appointment, Harold Wilson, then a secretary at the imperial manpower requirements committee, completed a report on the utilisation of Northern Ireland's resources. It revealed that after 'fifteen months of war, far from being an important centre of munitions, the province had become a depressed area'. It had 'not seen the construction of a single new factory', and orders with existing firms outside shipbuilding, had been on an 'exceedingly meagre scale'. Overall, it suggested Ulster's contribution to the economic war effort had been negligible, despite the availability of suitable labour, its continuing immunity from aerial attack, uncongested ports and unstrained transport network. As a consequence, unemployment which had almost halved in Britain, had increased in the province to almost 72,000 by November 1940, a level roughly equal to that found in Great Britain in 1932, the worst year of the depression. This was despite voluntary recruitment, and the emigration of some 14,000 workers to Britain over the previous twelve months, though these factors were partly offset by an influx of southern labour. The overall result, Wilson claimed, was that thousands of workers felt 'disappointment and disillusionment'. Others detected also a growth of extremism of all kinds including juvenile delinquency, though Brooke himself doubted that there was evidence to support this suggestion.[14]

Though the report ignored the contribution of Northern Ireland agriculture and made insufficient allowance for seasonal factors in influencing unemployment, it was clear that the province's economic potential was being seriously under-utilised. The causes of this were wide ranging, not easily resolved and, in some aspects, beyond the competence of any local agency. Unemployment levels were exacerbated by the absence of conscription which was described by G. H. Ince, secretary to the production executive of the war cabinet, as 'the outstanding reason for the availability of labour' in the province. A further major factor was the relative collapse of the linen sector, due mainly to dwindling raw material supplies. The industry's workforce contracted by almost 10,000 during the first fifteen months of the war, causing an escalation of female unemployment at a time when it was declining rapidly amongst male workers.[15]

The lack of war contracts was partly related to the structure of the Northern Ireland economy. Of an insured population of 330,000 in 1939, only 10 percent was engaged in engineering, shipbuilding or allied trades and many of these were in small firms, with little diversity of output and unsuited to mass production.[16] Local industry also suffered from a shortage of machine-tools and already from a shortage of some types of skilled labour. Further, a deterrent to the construction of new plant was the inflated production costs and inconvenience involved in transporting raw materials and finished products to and from the province. Overall, the supply departments preferred to use established, large, mainland firms and, where necessary, to create new capacity at mainland locations.[17]

In his conclusion, Wilson also attributed the under-utilisation of local resources in part to the conservatism of local management, the uncooperative attitude of trade unions, and the ineffectiveness of the Northern Ireland government. With regard to the latter, he criticised particularly the dilatoriness of the Ministry of Labour in applying its emergency powers to enforce dilution, and so ensure the optimum use of skilled workers through labour transfer, and as well the inadequacy of its retraining programme. In addition, he commented on 'the failure of the defence departments to mobilise the area for munitions production'. He pointed out that the imperial government had no representative in Northern Ireland, that the province was not itself represented on vital mainland bodies such as the Production Council, Labour Supply Board, Economic Policy Committee or Industry Capacity Committee, and that in the major dispersal scheme then in operation in Great Britain 'there was no provision made' for establishing units in Ulster. Thus he recommended the increased use of available local capacity and the building of new factories and indicated the need to reconsider 'the relationship between the two governments'. In his view 'some measure of devolution [was] necessary'[18] if Ulster's capacity was to be adequately developed.

Overall, Sir Basil regarded the Wilson report as 'an able and lucid statement' of the position. He wrote 'there is much to be done before we can say that Northern Ireland is playing its full part in the present struggle'.[19] He defined his own function as 'to make the production track as straight and as wide as possible and to see that local obstructions where they exist are removed'. His ultimate goal was the full utilisation of the province's human and physical resources in the war effort. Despite the immense difficulties involved there were some grounds for optimism. From a political viewpoint the virtually unrelieved failure of his predecessors made it difficult to appear unsuccessful by comparison. Also in these circumstances he could generally rely on strong support from Andrews, who at the outset acceded to Brooke's request that he be given 'a free hand, otherwise', Sir Basil claimed, he could 'achieve nothing'.[20] The prime minister expressed the opinion that if unemployment were to rise to a level of perhaps 100,000, it 'would have terrific repercussions on the government'.[21] Thus one week before the party meeting at which he was elected leader, he telegraphed Morrison, stating: 'most important that I shall be able to make a pronouncement indicating imperial government intention to establish a major enterprise here, . . . would be most grateful for your cooperation'. Morrison's response was sympathetic but not specific. Several weeks later Andrews wrote once more urging that 'the position . . . [was] . . . really quite impossible to defend'.[22] However, though the prime minister sympathised with Brooke's objectives it could not be assumed that he would support those measures that his minister might regard as necessary for their achievement.

In addition, the timing of Brooke's transfer to commerce was fortuitous. As Blake notes, by late 1940, 'production in the province was getting into its stride',[23] so much so that in the seven months to June 1941 unemployment fell by some 30,000. Mainland productive capacity was becoming more fully utilised and as a result the flow of contracts to local firms increased. At the same time, concern to exploit the province's redundant resources more effectively was felt at the very highest level in Britain. This was primarily with a view to increasing total war output, but also, because the contrasting level of unemployment between Northern Ireland and Great Britain was regarded as politically undesirable. The Wilson report was symptomatic of this growing imperial interest. A copy was sent to each of the production departments who were then obliged to submit memoranda for consideration by the production executive of the war cabinet.[24] Also, Churchill wrote to Bevin in January 1941 stating that his 'attention . . . [had been] . . . drawn . . . to the little use being made of the resources of Ulster', and adding, 'I hope that you are concerting measures to ensure that fuller use is being made of . . . [its] . . . capacity'.[25] He suggested that the situation required investigation. Thus, when Brooke made his first visit as minister to London, accompanied by Scott, in early February, he found Bevin in full agreement with the sentiment that 'it was a tragedy that . . . [the province's] . . . labour resources and productive capacity were not being used', and that 'workers displaced through the limitation of supplies had become unemployed instead of being absorbed in the munitions industry'.[26]

The solution which Brooke and his ministry consistently sought, and which was fully supported by Andrews, was the diversion of suitable work to Northern Ireland, as Wilson had suggested. Sir Basil pressed for the placing of munitions contracts with local firms, the establishment of new factories and dispersal of production units to the province, and increased supplies of machinery suited to its economy. As distress in the textile industry deepened he later suggested the transfer of home trade production from British firms, so freeing mainland labour for war production.[27] However, the emerging reaction of imperial ministers to Northern Ireland's unemployed capacity, in the spring of 1941, was not one of undiluted sympathy and support for these ideas. Bevin, having completed his enquiries by April, concluded that, after all, 'substantial use . . . [was] . . . being made of' the province's resources. He stressed that unemployment amongst men was decreasing rapidly, falling by 42 percent in the two months from 13 January 1941. This was especially the case in the munitions industries, where labour requirements were continuing to expand with the growing volume of contracts. He also drew attention to some of the difficulties involved in directing more work to Ulster.[28]

These were given further emphasis when Brooke attended the Imperial Production Executive on 8 April 1941, to consider 'the causes of . . . [Northern

Ireland's] failure to make . . . [a] . . . full contribution'. Particular stress was laid on factors for which the Northern Ireland government was in some degree culpable. These included the lack of adequate dilution in the province, the under-utilisation of the machine-tools and skilled labour which were available, the concentration of electrical power in one vulnerable station and the fact that deliveries on war contracts had been disappointing. Sir Andrew Duncan, minister of supply, told Brooke bluntly that 'it was up to Northern Ireland to display some initiative of their own' on these questions, if they wished to offset British government orders and investment. He considered that his own ministry had 'if anything' been 'over-generous' in the volume of contracts it had placed in the six counties.[29] In early May, Churchill reiterated these sentiments in a letter to Morrison. He noted that Ulster still did 'not appear to be making its utmost contribution'. After concluding that the supply departments were making as much use as was possible of her resources, he repeated Duncan's phrase that 'it was up to . . . [the province] . . . to display some initiative'. He asked the home secretary 'to consider what steps might be taken to encourage that initiative' on the points raised earlier, and enquired 'meanwhile could not another experiment in the loan of surplus manpower to this country be made?'. Morrison sent a copy of this letter to Andrews stating that he would 'like to be in a position to assure Mr Churchill of progress on these problems'. He added 'I am sure you do not feel any great difficulty in agreeing to further transferences of labour'.[30]

Though Northern Ireland ministers encouraged labour migration by denying benefit to those who refused work in Great Britain they strongly opposed this approach as a solution to the unemployment problem. They resisted partly because it could be interpreted as being symptomatic of the failure of local government policy. Also it was clearly unpopular with both unionist and nationalist communities. Brooke stated that to impose a scheme of enforced labour transfer or industrial conscription 'would arouse as much agitation as military conscription', and on another occasion noted privately 'nobody likes to leave their own country. We must make every effort to get work here for them'.[31] In any case much local unemployed female labour was not mobile either because of age, or family commitments or through being casually employed within the province.[32] Brooke regarded Churchill's letter with deep irritation commenting 'the responsibility is entirely theirs and not ours. They have refused to accept our cooperation'.

He helped the prime minister prepare a reply which in his own words 'put the ball firmly in their court'.[33] It stated that the Northern Ireland government 'shared . . . [Mr Churchill's] . . . concern', but that it had 'not been taken into the councils of the [supply] departments . . . [its] . . . services . . . had . . . not been used'. It continued 'If it is not possible to bring work to Ulster, I, [Andrews] must be able to announce that the imperial departments do not see their way to increase orders sufficiently to absorb . . . all available labour'. Nevertheless, despite his role in formulating this somewhat taciturn response, three weeks later Brooke himself wrote to Andrews stating 'there exists amongst British ministers dissatisfaction with Northern Ireland's war effort . . . however unpalatable the remedies, we should face them'.[34] In the course of the next two years he not only sought to increase the flow of war contracts to the province, and to improve the institutional framework between the two governments but he also tried to remove those grounds for imperial criticism which he regarded as justified. This latter process aroused controversy, precipitated cabinet conflict and almost caused his own resignation.

Churchill's 'initiative-seeking' letter in early May, commented critically on Ulster's 'power supply concentration in one vulnerable station'.[35] This was a reference to the fact that most of Northern Ireland's generating capacity was located at the corporation plant on the Harbour estate in Belfast, an exposed and inadequately defended site which had narrowly escaped destruction during the recent German air-raids. This problem had previously been mentioned in the Wilson report, by Ince and by Beaverbrook who had stated when Brooke attended the production executive in April, that it was 'the main objection to placing further orders in Northern Ireland'. In response Sir Basil had indicated his intentions to 'put the matter right'.[36] In fact within days of taking office he had asked Hungerford to examine the electricity position, and this enquiry had confirmed his view that it was 'really serious' and that 'nothing [had been] done since the war'.[37]

Much of the blame for this attached to the corporation. It had been advised by the Northern Ireland government, acting on a report produced by British electricity experts in June 1939, to increase immediately generating capacity, and to do so by constructing a new power station outside Belfast. The councillors responded with customary negligence and inefficiency. They failed to place a contract for any new generating set until September 1940, and this they intended to locate at the harbour site regarding it as appropriate 'if strengthened in some measure'.[38] Spender described them as having shown 'no sense of responsibility for their function and the war'. But he also censured the Ministry of Commerce which he thought 'remiss in letting the matter lie for fifteen months', thus he later alleged, displaying 'their usual tendency to run away from firm action'.

By contrast, the scheme which Brooke first laid before cabinet in late April 1941, Sir Wilfrid regarded as 'drastic' and likely to result in 'great political difficulties'.[39] He also considered that in submitting it Sir Basil had 'shown outstanding qualities and courage'. The former proposed that all Northern Ireland's electricity generation and distribution should be amalgamated under unified control, so relieving the corporation of its traditional duties in this regard; and, less controversially, suggested that the Ministry of Commerce should establish a new power station at Islandmagee and expand existing capacity elsewhere. The cabinet postponed consideration of the former because of the controversial issues involved, refusing in Spender's words to 'grasp the nettle fearlessly'.[40] However, Brooke was given approval to proceed with a new station at Ballylumford, to expand production at Larne, and to initiate negotiations with the Treasury regarding finance. In addition Sir Basil, possibly acting on Beaverbrook's suggestion, asked for and received his colleagues' reluctant assent to the opening of negotiations with the south, in the hope of obtaining additional supplies. Though Andrews spoke of 'political difficulties' regarding the latter and expressed doubts as to the power actually being available when required, it was difficult to deny Brooke's claim, particularly in the context of the blitz, that 'circumstances justified it'.[41]

From mid-August to late November the cabinet considered Brooke's now detailed proposals for setting up a seven-man Electricity Supply Board responsible for generation and distribution throughout the province. Sir Basil argued for this approach partly on economic and financial grounds, suggesting that it was the most efficient solution to the problem and also would enable the substantial British Treasury loan, by then agreed, to be expeditiously repaid. He recounted for the edification of his colleagues 'the sins of the corporation', stating on one occasion that to hand all electricity provision over to its control would be 'mid-summer madness'. He added later 'I prefer the parable of the talents, to take away from the unfaithful servant the talent that he has misused'. He also claimed that his policy would bring political advantages. 'I am confident', he stated, 'that the government will gain in prestige through taking a strong stand, . . . there is more to lose from drawing back than going forward'. 'Opposition', he suggested, 'would come from the less desirable elements in public life'. As an indication of this confidence he stated that he would welcome the opportunity to explain and defend his policy at a party meeting or a secret session of the house. In addition, he repeatedly stressed his earlier commitments to imperial ministers guaranteeing adequate and safe electricity supplies. At one meeting he expressed the fear that machine-tools might be transferred back to Britain if the problem was not resolved to their satisfaction. At another he produced a letter, which he had previously arranged for Beaverbrook to send, indicating the prospect of more war contracts which would create a further 4,000 jobs, if his proposals were adopted. The work in sight, he urged 'might absorb all the unemployed by next summer'.[42]

In presenting these arguments, Sir Basil was throughout strongly supported by his own officials. Spender observed that 'it was not until . . . [Brooke] . . . went to commerce that any attention was paid to the strong representations of the staff of that ministry'. Sir Wilfrid himself not only favoured the proposals but doubted 'if the government . . . ever had a stronger case for forcing . . . [the council] . . . to accept its terms'. Nonetheless, from the outset he was far from confident that the cabinet would 'dare stand up in Parliament to the opposition of Belfast corporation'. Such fears were justified. Soon afterwards he was deriding the government's 'qualities of timidity' and persistent policy of appeasement.[43]

In cabinet Andrews raised a series of objections to Brooke's proposed scheme. He suggested that it was inconsistent with Craigavon's policy of avoiding contentious legislation in wartime. He protested that the councillors had managed their electrical installations efficiently in peace-time. He raised a number of financial objections, including the need to compensate the corporation if the plan was adopted, the dangerous possibility that the new electricity board would raise its charges to Belfast consumers, and that its creation would arouse public expectations of reduced charges. In any case, he stated, merger would not of itself increase generating capacity. In essence, however, it was clear that his fundamental concern was, what he described as, 'the grave political repercussions'[44] likely to result from Brooke's proposals. In private conversations with Spender during the autumn of 1941, Andrews indicated that he was 'very anxious not to have any trouble with the corporation at present'. He explained that in his opinion the position of the Northern Ireland government was stronger than it had been for years. He therefore feared 'to upset the country',[45] particularly as a by-election was due to be held in the Willowfield constituency in December. Such considerations were obviously strengthened by the corporation's consistently hostile response to the merger proposals from the moment they were first mooted, whatever the financial inducements sanctioned by cabinet and offered by Brooke.[46] The councillors countered by suggesting that they themselves should take over Ballylumford, the Larne extension, and the government's financial obligations to the Treasury. In addition, Sir Basil's scheme was strongly criticised by the leadership of the Orange Order and by a number of cabinet ministers. Dawson Bates, for example, feared that it would further complicate his department's delicate relationship with the corporation, and expressed the view that public opinion was not 'educated to a sufficient appreciation of the situation' for merger to be practical politically.[47]

Though Brooke could also 'see political difficulties', he believed that there was 'no alternative' to his proposals. By mid-November he accepted the inevitability of 'a serious row over electricity', but stated: 'I have given undertakings to ministers on the other side and we must not shrink the responsibility'. Later diary entries indicate both his concern and commitment. He noted 'few of my colleagues, I am afraid, realise how serious the situation is', and several days later, remarked that 'At this time it seems fantastic to consider local politics. . . . The government should not be run by the corporation'.[48]

By late November, pressure on the cabinet to find a solution was increasing daily. The new plant at Ballylumford would soon be operative without the ministry having made any provision for its management and control, and it was becoming a matter of urgency to devise some means for the repayment of the Treasury's 50 percent loan. Eventually, on 25 November, agreement was reached. The merger scheme was rejected as 'not practicable at the present time', and the corporation's counter-proposal, which Andrews had regarded as a 'possibility', was also discarded.[49] Instead a compromise suggested by Bates and supported by Glentoran was accepted whereby under a defence regulation order, the Ministry of Commerce would have authority to direct and control the electricity generated by Belfast power station which was used by factories involved in war production. It was a response which Brooke had considered with his officials and had rejected five months earlier. He now reluctantly gave his agreement, though underlining that legislation would still be required to enable the ministry to operate Ballylumford and Larne power stations and to make provision for meeting the government's financial obligations to the Treasury. However, as he noted in his diary, and it is confirmed by Spender, 'even to go so far I had to tell the prime minister that the only solution that I could see, now that I was committed to the other side and the corporation here, was to drop me from the government'.[50]

Brooke correctly anticipated that devising the necessary order would result in 'another battle with the cabinet'. His first draft was rejected by his colleagues, Andrews complaining that it went further than Bates had suggested. Several days later suitably modified and diluted, it was adopted, though its announcement was deferred until after the Willowfield electors had gone to the polls. Under its terms Brooke favoured appointing Harkness as Belfast electricity controller but owing to very severe criticism at a party meeting of such a position being filled by a civil servant, the draft regulation had to be belatedly and hastily amended once again.[51]

In cabinet discussions over the subsequent enabling legislation Brooke continued strenuously to oppose growing pressure from Andrews and his ministers to hand Ballylumford over to the councillors. He described it as 'the easy way out, . . . quite wrong, . . . it looks as if we are knuckling down to the corporation'.[52] He was also concerned to preserve at least the prospect of an ultimate merger. But Spender believed that the government's 'position . . . [was] . . . so shakey' after the by-election defeat, that he doubted whether the cabinet would even be willing to proceed with Sir Basil's intended bill. However eventually in June 1942, Sir Basil received his colleagues' approval for his legislative proposals.[53] These defined the functions of the electricity controller, and provided for government ownership of Ballylumford and Larne power stations, and for repayment of the Treasury loan. Despite Spender's predictions that these terms would be more 'difficult for parliament to swallow' than the original merger scheme, both he and Brooke were surprised at how very easily the bill passed through the house. Sir Basil noted that even 'the opposition agreed it was necessary'.[54]

Nevertheless Sir Wilfrid considered that the government had emerged with 'grave discredit . . . [as] . . . they . . . [had] . . . not the courage to stand up to any criticism . . . no matter what the grounds for the decision at which they had arrived'. He records that 'the prime minister . . . [was] . . . so upset by the whole incident that he . . . [was] . . . considering every possible measure of appeasement of the people'. Indeed the episode does appear to have contributed to the hesitancy and ineffectiveness of his subsequent leadership. Spender felt much sympathy for Brooke who he considered had 'a very good case', but was 'compelled by his colleagues to adopt a half-measure', which was 'difficult to justify'.[55] Still, at least one crucial aspect of these events had delighted Sir Basil. Ballylumford power station had been 'brought into operation in record time', and as a result, the province had 'an ample power supply' sited at a less vulnerable location.[56]

Meanwhile, another equally intractable but vital matter was absorbing much of Brooke's time and energy: the urgent need to improve the structural relationship between his own department in particular and the imperial ministries. In Northern Ireland, as in other United Kingdom regions, an area board of the Ministry of Supply had been established to coordinate, supervise and encourage war production. In addition, each of the supply departments had their own area officer in the province, placing orders directly with Ulster firms. 'Not one' Brooke noted, 'had any connection with the Ministry of Commerce'. This governmental machinery was cumbersome, had singularly failed to inspire the confidence of local industry, and almost certainly had contributed to Ulster's productive capacity not being developed 'at anything like a reasonable rate'. It was severely censured in the Wilson report. Earlier, it had been criticised in memoranda written by Stormont ministers, as well as by the chairman of the area board himself, who had stated, in November 1940, that 'none of . . . [its] . . . members could be satisfied with the general output position or could consider that the organisation as it existed was the best'.[57] The reorganisation of area boards throughout the United Kingdom and formation of a production executive of the war cabinet prompted Andrews, on 8 January 1941, to ask Morrison 'if a member of the imperial government could act as spokesman'[58] for the province on the new executive. Though this request was rejected, British officials accepted that Northern Ireland should have an opportunity to have a say on economic policy and expressed their support for closer liaison between the two governments.

This prospect was pursued by Brooke almost from the moment of his appointment. In December 1941, he recalled his earlier astonishment, when he found that 'we [the Ministry of Commerce] were really taking no part in the organisation of war industries and, although we were held responsible, were unable to do anything about it'.[59] The need to improve the level of coordination between the two governments had been brought home to him during his initial visit to Britain ten months earlier. In the course of discussions with Sir Andrew Duncan, he became aware, apparently for the first time, of the former's difficulties regarding contracts placed in the province caused by 'tardy deliveries and failure to maintain scheduled time-tables'. The minister of supply himself expressed the view that the Northern Ireland government 'should take a more active and direct part in securing a better utilisation of . . . productive capacity'. In response, strongly encouraged by Andrews, Brooke suggested that the Ministry of Commerce might act as agent for the Ministry of Supply, thus emulating the structural relationship which had worked so effectively with the Ministry of Food and Fisheries.[60]

Protracted correspondence and negotiations followed and eventually, after a second visit by Sir Basil, the Ministry of Supply agreed that Scott should act as its regional representative in Ulster, a capacity in which he already served for the Board of Trade. Duncan stated that he had 'the greatest confidence in Mr Scott . . . [and] . . . would give him a free hand to place contracts'.[61] At the time, Brooke considered that 'this is in substance what we wanted, but I think will be difficult to explain politically'. For this reason Andrews was disappointed but Spender expressed 'great hope that things will now improve'.[62]

Sir Basil, however, came to regard the new arrangement as only a partial solution and soon afterwards was considering whether his ministry might not similarly represent other imperial supply departments in the province. He observed; 'every day it becomes apparent that we should run our own show here'. When in mid May 1941, a proposal was mooted by the imperial government in favour of strengthening the powers of the regional area board, Sir Basil at once expressed strong objections to Bevin, chairman of the production executive of the war cabinet, and eventually put forward his own counter-proposals. He wrote to the latter:

the [Northern Ireland] government should become more directly responsible for developing production here, . . . we appear to be only half in the war in the industrial sphere . . . given the responsibility of carrying out a production programme under your direction, I feel that my department could increase production simply by personal contact and powers to deal on the spot with the constant union difficulties . . . after twenty years of rather intimate government they like to be nursed.[63]

Bevin had earlier declared himself to be 'perfectly satisfied with his liaison with the Ministry of Commerce'[64] and favoured the continuation of the Area Board. Nonetheless, he invited Brooke to appear before the production executive, on 1 June, to present his case.

At this meeting, Sir Basil drew attention, both verbally and by memorandum, to the obvious contrasts between Northern Ireland and each of the other

United Kingdom regions. He commented on the fact that it was separated from the mainland by sea, and that it did not have conscription but most importantly, from the viewpoint of his argument, he stressed that it did have its own government, with executive authority over such matters as electricity, labour, transport, security and health. Indeed, as he stated, 'all the factors on which the production programme depends'. He alleged that the area board had been ineffective, and had caused confusion, overlapping, and divided responsibility, and urged that it be replaced by a production committee appointed by his own ministry, 'to deal with all matters affecting production' within the province. The present arrangement, he suggested, was 'not fair to the government of Northern Ireland'. In conclusion, he acknowledged that his proposals would require to be discussed in detail with the ministries concerned, but desired that they should first 'be approved in principle by the production executive'.[65] In this immediate objective, Sir Basil was successful, and was predictably delighted. He commented that it was 'a feather in our cap. . . . I hope that useful results will follow'. He had earlier remarked to Bevin that 'although . . . [he] . . . could not promise increased production, at least . . . [he] . . . could say it would not be any worse'.[66] Morrison seemed equally satisfied with the outcome, informing the war cabinet that it 'seemed likely to prove a satisfactory arrangement' and expressing to Andrews his expectation that it would 'enable Northern Ireland to increase its contribution to the war effort'.[67]

The area board held its last meeting on 18 June and, subsequently, a Production Advisory Committee (later called Production Council) was appointed by the Ministry of Commerce, chaired by Brooke, with a membership similar to the old area board. It included representatives from the supply departments, the relevant Northern Ireland ministries, and local industry, as well as two experts to advise on labour and industry problems. Initially the new body met frequently but its large size made this impracticable. Thus, in mid-1942, a production executive composed of officials was formed, with Scott acting as chairman.[68]

Blake considers that this organisational structure proved its competence. By recognising the Ministry of Commerce as the effective agency for Ulster's war production and giving it the powers necessary, he writes, 'executive authority was now associated with the power of determining policy'. The machinery, he also claims, was 'clearer', with the Production Advisory Committee efficiently harmonising the efforts of the supply departments and the Northern Ireland government. Also through Brooke and Scott its work was synchronised with that of the other Stormont departments and important local committees.[69]

However, Brooke himself continued to be dissatisfied with the degree of cooperation which he received from the supply departments, in particular from the Admiralty and the Ministry of Aircraft production. Though the regional representatives of both these ministries were located in the same building as the Ministry of Commerce, so facilitating closer liaison, both still preferred to operate independently within the province, largely for reasons of security. They failed to keep Sir Basil informed of contracts placed locally. He was not forewarned when, in September 1941, the Ministry of Aircraft Production appointed as their local area officer, Mr Smiles, ex-chairman of the now defunct area board. Sir Basil noted ruefully that his duties were 'identical' with that of his own ministry, later adding 'it is a backward move . . . and will start again the difficulties we had with the . . . board'.[70] Vainly and with growing exasperation, he urged that Smiles be transferred to the staff of the Ministry of Commerce. The most striking instance of this lack of collaboration came in February 1941, when the M.A.P. embarked on the construction of Langford Lodge, a vast aircraft repair base for the U.S. Army/Air Force, without Brooke either being consulted or receiving any preliminary instruction.[71]

Thus when reviewing the administrative machinery on 29 May 1942, in a letter to Oliver Lyttelton, Brooke expressed the view that though it had generally made for 'close cooperation and smooth working. . . . [he was] . . . by no means satisfied that the present arrangements were the most efficient'. He suggested that 'the most satisfactory method . . . would be for each department to appoint [him] as their agent' or, alternatively, that their local representatives join the staff of his ministry. In his diary, he indicated the strength of his feelings on the issue, stating that he must have 'complete control . . . [and would] . . . not agree to carry on under present circumstances'.

Eventually, Brooke's importunity bore results when in June 1941, the Ministry of Aircraft Production agreed to emulate the Ministry of Supply by making the Ministry of Commerce their agent, transferring Smiles to the staff of that department. Soon afterwards, Lyttelton could justifiably congratulate Brooke on having 'the various threads in his hand with the single exception of Admiralty work'.[73] After almost eighteen months of negotiation, he had become the effective political head of virtually all the machinery of war production in Northern Ireland. Sir Basil himself was delighted. During his final months as minister, he considered that the level of coordination between the British supply departments and the local ministries responsible for essential services left 'little to be desired'.[74]

Brooke's eventual success both in resolving the problem of Northern Ireland's vulnerable electricity supply and in helping to devise a more integrated administrative structure with the imperial departments did not, however, guarantee that local under-utilised capacity would be developed. As he wrote to Lyttelton somewhat despondently in May 1942, his principal difficulty remained 'to secure anything like adequate work' for the province.[75] Throughout this period Brooke continued to seek the construction of new munitions factories, the diversion of more contracts for existing heavy industry with requisite machinery and supplies, and as an increasing priority, the transfer of home trade textile production so freeing mainland labour for war production. With these objectives, Scott remained in London much of the time, and maintained constant contact with the supply departments. His efforts were frequently reinforced by Brooke who, on at least sixteen occasions as minister, made a round of the Whitehall offices, usually keeping upwards of twenty separate appointments. It was an exercise which he regarded as vital and appears to have genuinely enjoyed. During one visit he recorded in his diary 'we have got to fight hard' to get work and later recalled with relish his verbal clashes with Beaverbrook as he pressed the claims of Ulster industry.[76] On occasion, he also used his British contacts as an additional lever with which to achieve his objectives within the province itself. He did so in his conflict with cabinet colleagues over the electricity supply question and also in his tussles with local management.

Though these activities were far from unsuccessful, there remained immense obstacles in the way of attracting anything approaching sufficient orders to utilise surplus local resources. Despite the improvements in governmental machinery, it continued to be difficult to secure immediate decisions from the considerable number of different British departments with whom the Ministry of Commerce had dealings. The problem was not diminished by the constant structural changes which occurred within the imperial government's administration, and to which Northern Ireland ministers and officials had necessarily to accommodate themselves. In addition, the pattern of supply department demand was constantly changing as the grand strategy of the war developed, and as quantities of certain stores accumulated.[77]

Beyond this there were other more specific difficulties. When in early 1942, acute flax shortage threatened to raise Northern Ireland's unemployment figures by a further 20,000, it appeared self-evident that textile orders should be diverted from firms in Scotland and Lancashire to the province. Thus Brooke sought a production executive directive to this effect, and was strongly supported by Andrews.[78] However, as Lyttelton, wrote to Sir Basil, though such a policy was 'attractive . . . [it was] . . . difficult to find practicable opportunities' for its application. In some instances, to have channelled orders to Northern Ireland would have instantly created fresh or additional unemployment on the mainland, by inflating existing pockets of labour surplus or making immobile workers redundant. In the weaving sector local production costs were higher than in Britain. In Lancashire, a vigorous campaign was launched against the diversion of cotton yarn to the province illustrating the additional political difficulties with which British ministers were confronted.[79] Brooke's case was weakened by the fact that the linen industry had traditionally produced a luxury product and had not met service demands prior to the war.

Similarly, there were considerable problems in the way of attracting new factories, or additional war contracts and supplies for existing Ulster firms. Disappointment at the level of success impelled Andrews, in February 1942, to write bitterly to Beaverbrook of the 'strong general complaint that Northern Ireland is not helped to anything like the extent she should be'.[80] Possibly, as Brooke and Spender suspected, fear of invasion or the prospects of an Anglo-Irish agreement served to deter the supply departments from locating more war production in the province during the early stages of the war.[81] By late 1941, the volume of new factory construction and plant extension had already slackened significantly throughout the United Kingdom. To have transferred output from established, even if congested, British locations then would at least in the short term have disrupted production. In any case, by that time, there was virtually no unemployed skilled labour or surplus machine-tool capacity available in the province.[82] Also, the experience of the Belfast blitz dissolved any residual illusions of Northern Ireland's invulnerability to aerial bombardment. It caused extensive industrial damage, so disrupting contract schedules, and lowered the morale of the workforce. Brooke noted in mid-April that the 'men . . . [were] . . . living too near vital targets'. He continued if we have a series of blitzing, there will be no labour . . . left to carry on'. Hence, during the following months as a matter of urgency he had hostels constructed to accommodate 2,000 essential war industry workers on the outskirts of the city.[83]

Perhaps the most vital obstruction in the way of attracting further war work was the inadequate performance of some of Northern Ireland's major firms. Already, in December 1940 and January 1941 Spender had commented that the local aircraft industry was 'giving us a bad name across the water' and was 'a great disappointment'.[84] Though many years later Brooke reflected on how 'Ulster industry rose to the demands of the war . . . Management and workers welcomed, indeed clamoured for, a chance to help',[85] this was not his view at the time. From his earliest visits to Whitehall and his attendances at production executive meetings, he was left in no doubt as to the total dissatisfaction felt towards major local industrial producers by the supply departments. He was confronted by a litany of complaints of their dilatoriness in fulfilling orders, the lack of dilution, the under-utilisation of machine-tools available, and accusations that management was more concerned to increase potential post-war capacity than to fulfill their wartime contracts in a responsible way. Brooke records being told 'resolve these and . . . [he] . . . would get work'.[86]

In a wide range of ways Brooke sought to improve the province's unenviable industrial record and to imbue both management and workforce with a greater sense of urgency. With this objective he personally visited factories frequently, and organised visits by others. Once, accompanied by the governor, he recorded that their concern was 'to let workers see that the job that they are doing is of great importance'. On another occasion, he himself told a group of linen operatives that they were 'doing as useful work as those engaged in shell factories'. He undoubtedly enjoyed this direct contact with the labour force. He describes a local trade union leader bringing to his office thirty women workers, who were seeking employment. He notes that he 'gave them tea, and told them that . . . [he] . . . would do everything possible to get alternative work . . . [adding] they impressed me very greatly'.[87]

He had a profound belief in the efficacy of propaganda and made extensive use of the media. During a production and savings drive, initiated by Beaverbrook, in mid-1941, he devised the slogan, 'it all depends on me', and on another later occasion 'have you declared war on Hitler?' He recorded characteristically of one broadcast that he had tried to 'bring in the personal touch as much as possible'. He was delighted with his resultant 'fan-mail' which included a congratulatory letter from Morrison. However, throughout, he retained a healthy scepticism as to the likely impact of such activities and there was no shortage of evidence testifying to its limitations. Thus he decided against asking Bevin over for a speech-making tour of the industrial workforce when advised that he would not be listened to, a fate that had already befallen a number of military dignatories.[88]

Arthur Kelly described Brooke as being 'more than ordinarily interested in questions of . . . cooperation between management and workers in war production factories'.[89] This Sir Basil sought to foster mainly through his Production Advisory Council, on which both local management and trade union leaders were represented and which was regarded by the government as the main forum for the discussion of labour problems. In addition, the later production executive, composed of ministry officials and area officers, devoted much of its time to analysing and seeking to improve labour relations. Because of the existence of these bodies, particularly the former, both Sir Basil and the prime minister resisted trade union pressure from late 1941 for an employer-union conference.[90] For further support, Sir Basil appointed William Grant, parliamentary secretary at the Ministry of Labour, as his labour adviser, to help resolve local disputes, and an ex-M.A.P. official, E. H. Cooper, to promote improvements in industrial organization.[91] Also, Sir Basil frequently requested the supply departments to send over their experts to analyse and make recommendations with regard to local production problems.

In disputes, Brooke generally strove to protect the position of the recognised trade union leadership as against the shop-stewards. During the strikes of October 1941, he observed 'we must back the officials'. His readiness to meet the latter almost resulted in the withdrawal of the employer's representatives from his production executive in mid-1942.[92] In addition, he encouraged both the cabinet as a whole, and the Ministry of Labour in particular, to assume a more active role in resolving industrial unrest. The effectiveness of his own department in this field was acknowledged by W. P. Kemp, a director of Short & Harland, who commented that 'your intervention . . . has served its purpose, . . . it has encouraged the other ministry [of Labour], to take a more serious and urgent view of the matter'.[93]

A further constant problem which also absorbed Brooke's interest was that of ensuring the optimum usage of Northern Ireland's labour resources. Scott observed in February 1941, that 'although . . . [dilution] . . . is rather outside his bailiwick, he [Sir Basil] is very definitely of the opinion that our government should play an active part'.[94] In the succeeding months his responsibilities in this vital area steadily increased. In mid-June 1941, Andrews asked him to serve as chairman of the cabinet manpower committee. Its function was to consider means of securing the fullest possible utilisation of the manpower available in Northern Ireland,[95] and it immediately held a census of the labour and machines-tools used in local war industry. It began somewhat inauspiciously. After its first meeting, Sir Basil stated that he was 'not very pleased with the attitude of Labour. They did their best to pluck every suggestion. Difficulties must be overcome if production is to increase'. However, he continued, 'they agreed that labour supply officers were our region because we are in charge of production machinery'.[96]

The necessity for creating such an organisation had been stressed by Bevin during the production executive meeting attended by Brooke two weeks earlier. Their function was to strive to increase output, soothe labour relations, and to accelerate dilution so releasing skilled workers and reducing production costs. The urgency of their introduction increased as the local shortage of skilled labour became more acute. The initiative behind the scheme came from Brooke, and it was accepted by a reluctant cabinet in February 1942.[97] Their resistance was partly because of hostility to a 'more pronounced industrial control than before'. Andrews, in particular, was concerned that employers would resent any increased pressure to recruit labour through labour exchanges. Brooke also records that there was a 'good deal of talk from the linen people at the possibility of inspectors taking all their skilled men'. He continued: 'This may be necessary, I told them so'.[98]

Cabinet agreement was in part a response to the conclusions of the Denholm report, a wide-ranging inquiry into the use of labour at the province's war producing factories, conducted by imperial Ministry of Labour officials acting on Brooke's request. It expressed sympathy with management, suggesting that effective planning and efficient use of machine-tools were extremely difficult given the uneven flow of orders from supply departments and often inadequate quantities of vital raw materials on occasion made available. However, it also commented critically on the lack of dilution and the general break-down in industrial relations, remarking on the 'lack of cooperation and goodwill amounting almost to suspicion amongst employers, management and employees'.[99]

'Dilution', the replacement of skilled workers by those who were semi-skilled or unskilled, was particularly difficult to enforce in Northern Ireland, especially whilst there was still surplus skilled labour available and there were therefore widespread fears that it would simply transfer those at work in increasing numbers onto dole queues. In such circumstances it was extremely difficult to convince trade unions that it was necessary for the completion of contracts in hand, especially as the unions were eager to take full advantage of their enhanced wartime bargaining position. That more was not achieved was generally attributed by British officials to governmental ineffectiveness. Thus one of them commented in April 1943, 'I understand the power both to direct labour and . . . to issue essential work orders extends to Northern Ireland . . . the trouble is not that there are no powers but that the present minister of labour does not exercise them'.[100]

The criticisms of Northern Ireland industry mentioned in the Denholm report were not universal. At Mackie's engineering works, for example, successful dilution had enabled the extensive use of female labour, the firm had an impressive, almost strike-free record, and a management which appears to have been solicitous of the needs of its workforce and which was very highly regarded by British ministers and officials as well as by Brooke and his ministry.[101] However, particularly at the two local industrial giants, Harland & Wolff and Short & Harland, problems relating to the lack of dilution, inadequate output, strained labour relations and dilatoriness in the fulfillment of contracts were not satisfactorily resolved whilst Brooke was minister, and their performance continued to be a cause of acute concern to imperial departments throughout these years.

After a post-blitz visit to Harland & Wolff shipyards with Morrison in July 1941, Brooke noted, 'The directors claim that it is all one happy family. I only wish I could think the same . . . a lot of grouses'.[102] His ministry found the firm generally uncooperative, uninterested in the welfare of its labour force and hostile in its attitude towards other engineering works. Officials criticised its reluctance to sub-contract, and alleged that it poached labour from neighbouring engineering works.[103] Brooke claimed that Sir Frederick Rebbeck was 'bitter in his jealousy of Mackie's'. He was increasingly convinced that the root cause of the firm's failings was incompetent management, though prepared to concede a certain lack of objectivity due to 'personal resentment'[104] of its managing-director. Far from acting as 'umpire' between the Admiralty and the latter as he later claimed, he repeatedly and constantly pressed for Rebbeck's demotion or replacement.[105]

This course of action was given very serious consideration when the imperial government sought to accelerate escort vessel production as a matter of urgency in the spring of 1943. The firm's performance was as a result closely scrutinised by a cabinet sub-committee set up to enquire into the shipbuilding facilities in Northern Ireland.[106] Its members regarded the quality of the ships it produced as generally satisfactory. However Bevin, whose attitude towards Northern Ireland became noticeably more hostile after the conscription crisis, regarded its output as significantly inferior to comparable British yards.[107] This he attributed to insufficient dilution and lack of managerial drive. He claimed that if the firm was properly organised, production could be raised by the equivalent of adding a further 7–8,000 men to Admiralty shipyard labour in England. Though other factors were cited, including the psychological and physical disruption caused by the blitz, and the fact that the firm produced a large proportion of 'difficult' vessels and did extensive ship repair work, both of which dragged down productivity figures, the consensus of opinion was that much blame attached to Rebbeck. It was alleged that, though he was capable, he had concentrated too much on the reconstruction of damaged yards after the air-raids, had been weak in his handling of labour, had played the various supply departments off one against the other, and had altogether too many interests and was thus unable to give the yard sufficient attention. He was described by the first lord of the Admiralty as 'unreceptive and inaccessible'.[108]

Rebbeck attributed much of the criticism of himself, and of his firm, to the deterioration in his personal relations with Brooke, and the alleged bias of Lord Linlithgow who, he told Spender, had wished to close down the yard even before the war.[109] Sir Wilfrid also noted that Andrews 'never forgave Harland & Wolff for not making him a director in succession to his uncle Lord Pirrie'.[110] However, though the management structure was modified, increased authority being given to the Admiralty's regional controller, despite Brooke's entreaties, Rebbeck remained. This was mainly owing to the difficulties involved in finding a satisfactory replacement, and also because to have removed him would probably have required government purchase of the firm's assets. Even in February 1943, local reports suggested that its absenteeism levels were twice those of the worst British yards.[111]

At Short & Harland's aircraft factory there was also overwhelming evidence of incompetent management. Lack of dilution during this period resulted in an acute shortage of skilled labour at dispersal plants with a gross over concentration at the factory's main extension, thus impairing Stirling output and inflating production costs.[112] Wages paid by the firm were higher than at smaller Belfast engineering firms though negotiated with the same unions. The company's strike record in this period was incomparably the worst of any major war producing factory in Northern Ireland, whether gauged by the frequency of stoppages, their duration or the numbers involved. Government officials were concerned at the extent to which alleged managerial inefficiency had become a subject of public comment, and had contributed to the loss of trade union respect and confidence. Labour representatives from the firm complained of a shortage of tools, unsuitable premises, and under-production. They reported structural defects in aircraft parts including claims that wings and fuselages were dangerously out of line. Low morale was reflected in poor discipline, the misuse of tools, destruction of materials, and extremely high absenteeism levels.[113] There were also some reports of disloyal elements having infiltrated the workforce and deliberately sabotaged the war effort. A Mass Observation report referred to 'a considerable area of fostered dissatisfaction . . . in Short & Harlands'.[114] In addition, both management and unions were accused of using the war emergency for their own advantage. Overall, in late 1942, a well-informed British official estimated that the firm was not working, at more than 65 percent efficiency and that 'any amount of people [were] drawing pay for loafing about'. He continued 'I believe they [the management] are afraid of their workers'.[115] Other reports estimated that production at Shorts was three times slower than at similar British firms with the workforce on average taking three times as many hours to produce each aircraft.[116]

Scott attributed many of the firm's difficulties to the fact that it was young and inexperienced and that 'the handling of men . . . [was] . . . not their strong point'. He believed that its problems were exacerbated by the rapid growth of its labour force, drawn from 'all and sundry', and the impact of dispersal, which further exposed its lack of competent management.[117] From September 1942, Llewellin supported the contention that Mackie Brothers should be put in charge of all aircraft production in the province in order to accelerate Stirling production which still languished behind projected target figures. His ministry had already decided not to expand Shorts but rather to concentrate on increasing its efficiency.[118] Andrews was described as being 'not altogether in favour' of this, and stressed the 'need for very great care'. By contrast, Brooke was enthusiastic. He had long been critical of the company's management and suggested to the prime minister that 'the urgent need for heavy bombers dwarfs all other considerations'.[119]

In the end this drastic option was rejected largely due to fears of further disrupting production at the firm, and of aggravating its tense labour relations. However in March 1943, the Ministry of Aircraft Production did decide to take over all Short Brothers' shares and, as a consequence, the management at Short and Harland's was reconstructed. Dramatic improvements in productivity appear to have resulted. In February 1944, Scott claimed that the number of days lost through bad time-keeping had fallen by as much as 3–400 percent in some shops. Cripps, several weeks later, informed the commons that the number of aircraft delivered by the company had shown an increase of 69 percent during its first twelve months under new management, whilst the size of its workforce had actually decreased.[120]

However, such a welcome prospect lay in the future. When reviewing the achievements of his two years as minister in mid-1943, Brooke's overwhelming impression was one of frustration, even dejection. Certainly, he could look back with deep satisfaction at the success of some aspects of his policy. He regarded relations between the Northern Ireland ministries and the supply departments as 'excellent', and the electricity supply problem had been resolved satisfactorily, even if the administrative structure was not as he would have wished.[121] But he was profoundly disappointed by his failure to eradicate unemployment which proved to be both durable and volatile.

During 1941 he had felt optimistic that the problem might be eliminated. The statistics showed an encouraging, steady fall, as orders from the supply departments increased and growing numbers were absorbed in the construction industry, building aerodromes, bases for British troops and air-raid shelters. Substantial output in the textile industry was maintained as linen exports were still permitted prior to lend–lease, the industry's dollar earning capacity being welcomed.[122] In addition, during the first two years of war approximately 23,000 men enlisted, and 28,000 workers transferred to Great

Britain, though an unknown number returned, particularly as a Home Office official noted 'if bombs fell in their vicinity whilst over here'.[123] Thus, by August 1941, adult male unemployment had been reduced to 5 percent and of these almost one-third were regarded as unemployable either on health grounds, or because they were I.R.A. suspects or had dubious industrial records. The remainder included those frictionally unemployed and 1,400 involved in retraining schemes.[124] Thus in October, with some justification, Brooke described the figures as 'very satisfactory' and soon afterwards observed 'we have finished the first stage . . . no more skilled men on the books . . . [it is] now necessary to use available labour'. He was 'hopeful that during the coming year we can reduce it further'. This sentiment was echoed in the king's speech.[125]

In early 1942, however, linen exports were controlled and this factor alone, along with diminishing Ministry of Supply contracts and raw material shortages, threatened virtually to double the province's unemployment levels. Also the aerodrome construction programme was almost completed by May 1942, and the resulting contraction in its workforce was mainly responsible for an increase in the male register of some 50 percent by the following November.[126] These developments were at least partially counteracted by Ministry of Commerce success in winning contracts in Britain. The problems of the textile sector were eased by the production of utility clothing and parachutes, and by imports of Courtaulds' fibre. Nonetheless the state of the local spinning firms was described by Brooke as 'deplorable' and 'in inevitable decline'.[127] A number of new factories were constructed mainly producing torpedoes and ball-bearings. Between July 1941–July 1943, the total numbers employed in the shipbuilding, engineering and aircraft industries increased by 26,000. Smaller engineering firms, which initially had 'failed to give of their best', meanwhile organised themselves into groups, for the purpose of doing contract work on a cooperative basis. Cumulatively the success of the Ministry of Commerce was not unimpressive. Overall, Blake considers that 'the establishment of an effective production council and its executive was . . . a turning point', as prior to this sometimes contracts were not always accepted and factory projects not developed.[128] Employment was also boosted by large-scale building work associated with the arrival of American troops, including the construction of a 'virtual new town' at Langford Lodge, to serve as a depot for the Lockheed overseas corporation.[129]

Still, as Brooke noted despondently two weeks before becoming premier, 'Even today . . . despite strenuous efforts . . . a substantial volume of manpower [is] unused'. Though unemployment had continued to fall in the course of 1942, 19,000 people were still on the register in April 1943, 5 percent of the insured population, and this despite 40,000 workers having transferred to Great Britain over the previous three years. Sir Basil proceeded to analyse the damaging repercussions which flowed from these statistics. He considered that they had contributed to the 'tardiness' of dilution, as 'the lack of constant pressure of work has always made it extremely difficult to justify'. Training schemes were 'almost nugatory' in their impact due to the lack of demand for those trained. Machine-tool utilisation and the extension of night shifts left 'much to be desired', once more 'impeded by this general feeling of lack of urgency [which is], bound to exist as long as the flow of work is insufficient . . .

for the capacity available'. He declared that 'the only way to instill and maintain the Dunkirk spirit as long as military conscription does not apply is to ensure the location here of additional production units'. He also believed that 'the general drive for accelerated and expanded production' was still being impaired by the 'lack of cooperation' and 'unhelpful attitudes' at Harland & Wolff and the 'intractable managerial, labour and production problems' at Short & Harland.[130] As a result of the latter, unflattering references to Northern Ireland's industrial production continued to be made at Westminster, much to Brooke's irritation as he considered them to be based on inadequate information, and likely to have further 'undesirable repercussions on the morale of workers'.[131]

Despite the pessimistic phrasing of his April memorandum, however, Brooke was convinced that 'Ulster [had] pulled her weight, [and that] had we been able to start as soon as England we should have very little to complain of'. He had also begun to detect 'a much better spirit of cooperation than [he] had ever seen before'[132] at his production council. It was soon clear that some of his most 'intractable' problems were actually nearing solution. Thus by August 1943 when sending his regular up-dating report to Morrison his perception had changed and his tone had become noticeably more optimistic. Though unemployment continued to cause him 'anxiety' he viewed the future with more confidence than he had done six months earlier. He considered that 'definite progress' had been made at Harland & Wolff and that at Short & Harland the previously endemic managerial problems and low level of worker morale had been 'smoothed out' by the new management. There was also, he believed 'an improving machinery of industrial relations . . . [and] . . . undoubtedly now a certain pride of achievement amongst most workers and management'.[133]

This does not appear to have been self-delusion. Scott, who was still permanent secretary at commerce, was similarly optimistic. In July 1943, he could report 'no unused capacity of substantial size left. The rate of production is satisfactory, and altogether the sense of frustration previously existing has gradually disappeared'.[134] Much of the credit for this he attributed to Brooke himself, later recalling that Sir Basil devoted his 'single-minded attention to pressing forward with the war effort . . . and quickly won the respect and trust of management and workers'. He continued, 'as the department tends to be the lengthened shadow of its head, the new regime led to the first installation of a sense of urgency, of responsibility and of purposefulness throughout the whole team'.[135] British officials were also quick to express their appreciation for the qualities of the new minister. As early as May 1941, Sir Basil was said to be 'tackling the situation with great urgency' and his activities were used to justify Home Office predictions that the 'Northern Ireland authorities would strain every nerve to put their house in order'.[136] Lord Beaverbrook likewise expressed his 'tremendous admiration' for Brooke's 'work . . . during the war'.[137]

At the same time, Brooke clearly enjoyed the personal confidence of his prime minister, though in contrast to his relationship with Craig, contacts on a purely social level were rare. Almost certainly Andrews stayed at Colebrooke on just one occasion, when invited by his host to address the Fermanagh Unionist Association in early 1941.[138] Nonetheless, despite this and their frequent political differences, Brooke on more than one occasion expressed his liking for Andrews, describing him in such phrases as 'charming' and 'really very nice' and, with perhaps a hint of condescension, 'a very good little man'.[139] The latter generally gave Sir Basil every encouragement and was kept closely informed of his activities at the Ministry of Commerce. The prime minister also frequently sought Brooke's opinion on issues of varying gravity including whether or not the Northern Ireland government should officially respond to Herbert Gough's calls for Irish unity, the cabinet change consequent on MacDermott becoming attorney general, and later over how to respond to the Unionist back-bench revolt in January 1943.[140]

In recognition of the changing functions of Brooke's department and of his evolving role within the government, Andrews expanded the title of his ministry to 'Commerce and Production' in February 1942, possibly on Sir Basil's own suggestion, at a time when Beaverbrook's duties as minister of production along with those of other imperial departments were being redefined. In addition, without any formal announcement, Andrews made him deputy prime minister. The first clear indication of his changed status came when Sir Basil, in his leader's absence, answered commons questions on behalf of the government. Spender was not entirely happy with either of these developments. With regard to the former, he felt it unwise for the government to encourage the impression that it was 'responsible for reserved services in Northern Ireland when at the most it . . . [could] . . . only endeavour to secure the cooperation of the British government'. As a result of the latter 'change of policy', he feared that 'the position of the minister of finance . . . [had] . . . to some extent been undermined'.[141] He recalled that though for a time Lord Londonderry had claimed to act for the prime minister in Craig's absence, later Pollock and subsequently Andrews had always presided over the cabinet in such circumstances.

Nonetheless, Sir Wilfrid also records his 'high opinion of Brooke's judgement' and he consistently welcomed and encouraged the delegation of greater responsibility to him. Thus when the government was creating a committee for postwar reconstruction, he regarded Brooke as the only cabinet minister who was 'obviously suitable' to act as its chairman, though he considered that he 'had more than enough on his hands . . . dealing with war problems that were much more important'. He did not sympathise with Gransden's view that the proposed administrative structure threatened to place too much power in Sir Basil's hands. Sir Wilfrid also 'cordially supported' the idea of transferring transport services from home affairs to commerce. He himself urged that Brooke be given greater responsibility for government services during a blitz emergency thus utilising his military experience. He also welcomed Sir Basil's appointment as chairman of the Home Defence Executive, if he was 'able to give sufficient time to his duties', adding 'I don't expect that with Brooke there will be much danger of unnecessary delays in reaching a decision'.[142]

With regard to the latter, responsibility for improving the unsatisfactory relationship between the Northern Ireland government and the military authorities was a function increasingly delegated to Brooke, thus involving him in 'every vital area of security and production'.[143] Spender considered the situation to be so unsatisfactory that unless more effective cooperation could be achieved, he feared that the province would 'be involved in martial law', with the civil service taking over responsibility from ministers. Unfavourable reports by army personnel prompted George VI to raise the lack of mutual cooperation with Andrews in December 1940.[144] Officers criticised the inefficiency and 'softness' of the local administration, a claim which seemed justified by Dawson Bates' apparent refusal to reply to military correspondence and the fact that despite high unemployment the assistance of troops was vital in clearing street debris after the Belfast blitz.[145] For their part government ministers complained of the lack of consultation and high-handedness of the military authorities.[146] This was due certainly in part to fears by the latter that sensitive information might be leaked.

It was against this background that Andrews asked Brooke in early May 1941, to act as chairman of the newly established Home Defence Executive, a committee composed of forces' representatives and civil servants, and formed possibly on Gransden's suggestion. Its purpose was to secure greater coordination between civilian and military authorities and devise plans for possible invasion. It began somewhat inauspiciously. Spender commented critically on its initial concern with vague generalities rather than particular points, whilst Brooke was reported to be 'much perturbed at the rather flippant manner of the discussions of the civil servants present, [and] regretted such a lamentable exhibition had been given to the service members'. He indicated his intention of meeting the former to express his displeasure. Later meetings did however deal with specific issues of mutual concern, and Spender was soon convinced that it 'served a useful purpose in bringing the civil administration into touch with the fighting forces', and that its chairman was 'successful in bringing home to our ministers a greater sense of responsibility for coordinated action'.[147]

Meanwhile Brooke was given responsibility for looking after the requirements of the American troops in Northern Ireland. No doubt this was in part because it coincided with his departmental duties and because of his military background and contacts. It was also an extension of his overall role within the government of helping to entertain not just military personnel but visiting royalty, politicians and officials. On 9 June 1941, Andrews asked him to preside over a meeting with American officers to discuss their labour, material and transport needs.[148] These subsequently included the establishment of a naval base at Londonderry which at peak employed 3,000 local construction workers.[149] On 7 January 1942, the prime minister telephoned Sir Basil to inform him that he had been summoned unexpectedly to London. Two days later, the former attended a committee of the war cabinet, presided over by Attlee and briefed by Alan Brooke who disclosed details of the imminent arrival in Ulster of large numbers of United States troops. Sir Basil also records discussing this dramatic development with his uncle at the time and being 'asked' by Churchill 'to see personally that the hospitality accorded to the Americans was of the very highest order'.[150] The latter had earlier told his colleagues that 'everything possible should be done for . . . [their] . . . comfort'.[151]

Brooke, who had watched with avid interest the improving prospects of American military intervention, had a profound sense of the historic significance of the occasion when the vanguard of several thousand divisional troops and their mechanised equipment arrived soon afterwards. He noted 'we are the first to welcome American troops. I think it is a great honour'. With genuine enthusiasm, he sought to meet their considerable physical needs and to satisfy their hospitality requirements. The task was not without its difficulties. In September 1942, he noted 'the Americans still look on us with suspicion' and next day records travelling to London for discussions with British officials on 'the colour question'.[152] Nonetheless, a Mass Observation study of 'The Americans in Ireland', three months earlier had concluded that 'the morale of ' American troops in Ulster . . . [was] . . . high'.[153] Early the following year, Andrews asked him to organise the anniversary celebrations of their arrival, and subsequently to arrange ceremonies commemorating the formation of the Russian Red Army. The latter he carried out with something less than total conviction noting in his diary that he 'would not trust the Russians as far as [he] could see them'.[154]

The delegation of such duties to Brooke was entirely appropriate. He greatly enjoyed military company. When in London he delighted in meeting Alan Brooke, sometimes accompanied by other generals. At Colebrooke, he personally welcomed and frequently entertained the British and later American troops who bivouacked on the estate, despite the inconvenience and damage caused by their artillery practice and bomb-throwing exercises. Each weekend he continued to write private war memoranda, analysing the grand strategy, weighing up developments in each theatre of the conflict and seeking to predict future events. He wrote with enthusiasm of R.A.F. bomber raids on Germany, was repelled by indications of French collaboration, and absorbed by the shifting tide of battle in North Africa and Eastern Europe. His comments varied from the bland to the incisive. When Germany invaded Russia, an event which he had long predicted, he observed that it was 'all to the good, may kill a certain number of Germans'. When the allies attacked Libya he immediately welcomed the prospect that it would 'place us in a better position to attack Italy'.[155]

Overall, Brooke had a passionate interest in the war and commitment to allied victory rooted in his own military experience and background and in his political convictions. Inevitably this was further stimulated by his own family's involvement in the conflict and in particular when his sons took up their commissions. He encouraged the latter in their service careers, using his influence on their behalf. Though in early 1942, he noted apprehensively 'it is difficult to say how much more we shall see of them before they are engulfed in the present conflict', he later recorded how 'very proud of the three of them', he was.

In the house he constantly sought to instill something of the sense of urgency with regard to the war which he himself felt. Despite the disappointingly high levels of unemployment, he was conscious of having a good rapport with its membership. When his ministry's estimates were being debated in June 1942, he noted that 'everybody was most complimentary and satisfied that all was being done that was possible'. Earlier he had remarked of the debate on the king's speech that 'the government . . . [was] . . . fairly heavily attacked . . . but on the whole it was a very fair attack and they were quite polite about my efforts'.[156]

Undoubtedly Brooke's identification with the war effort, his energy and his ministerial competence were widely recognised, commented upon and favourably compared with his government colleagues. Herbert Shaw observed that Andrews was 'a much lesser man than his predecessor and [did] not enjoy anything like the same veneration among Ulster unionists', adding that he was, 'head, moreover, of a weak cabinet in which Sir Basil Brooke seems to be the only really effective minister'.[157] This view was shared even by some of the government's most strident parliamentary critics. J.W. Nixon declared that there was 'no one in the world more keen than [Brooke] . . . about the winning of the war'. He referred to the other cabinet members as 'too complacent' having earlier stated 'I do not believe in my heart that the cabinet ministers save the minister of commerce . . . realise the terrible plight that the British empire is in at the present time'. John Beattie said of Sir Basil that he was 'a live wire', later stating that the 'Ministry of Commerce was in its infancy not many years ago although it should have been the leading department of the government . . . but since the honourable gentleman became minister . . . I must say he has made this a live ministry'.[158]

Likewise, Unionist backbenchers expressed similar sentiments. James Brown, who was described by Spender as the 'most violent critic'[159] of the administration, said of the minister of commerce that he was 'industry and alertness personified', and later that 'his activity leaves nothing to complain of'. Hall-Thompson stated in early 1942, that no ministry had 'shown more energy and enthusiasm, and deserves more thanks from the general public than . . . Commerce'. Lieut Colonel Gordon who had earlier resigned from Craig's cabinet said of Brooke 'he deserves every credit for what he has already achieved . . . he has managed to establish on a sound basis the production of Northern Ireland'.[160] The significance of such statements was more than transitory. It was after all the attitude and actions of these members and their back bench colleagues in the succeeding months which primarily determined the fate of the Andrews' government and which finally propelled Brooke to the premiership.

CHAPTER X

The Premiership

In the 1960s, reflecting back on his period as deputy prime minister and minister of commerce, Brooke recalled: 'Involved as I was in my many duties, I became aware of stirrings of unrest on the political front', Andrews leadership was 'being challenged by some back-benchers, . . . a crisis threatened'.[1] He was alluding to the events which led to the fall of the Andrews' government, arguably the most dramatic political development in Northern Ireland's history during the first forty years of its existence. The causes of this fall generated considerable bitterness at the time and cast a shadow over Brooke's early years as premier. There was a strong presumption, shared by Andrews himself, that Sir Basil had manoeuvered against his leadership and so positively contributed to the collapse of his administration. This verdict has been reiterated by recent historians though the events themselves have never been adequately analysed. It is an allegation which Brooke virulently denied both in the 1940s and consistently thereafter. This was the most crucial phase in Sir Basil's early political career. It is imperative to establish the reasons for the fall of the Andrews' government, including the precise role played by Brooke, and to assess the verdict of one authority that it was 'regrettable that Andrews' term was so brief' as Ulster would have been 'more prosperous and peaceful' had he survived.[2]

Arguably Andrews had been unfortunate in becoming premier when almost in his seventieth year. By this time his health had already begun to fail, a process accelerated by the strain of war. His verbal indiscretions due to deteriorating hearing were said to be a cause of 'consternation' in official circles.[3] His tenure began when the war position was bleak, 'a dark and dangerous hour',[4] and when Ulster's productive capacity was severely under-utilised by imperial supply departments. From the outset doubts were expressed as to whether he was 'strong enough' to meet the demands of the office.[5] In family background, personality and experience he was ill-equipped to provide the leadership necessary in the supreme crisis. His performance inevitably compared unfavourably with Churchill's role in Britain. He did not have the physical strength or ability, or, perhaps, even the inclination or time to mobilise and inspire his government and its supporters. He said himself 'I never relish speaking in a personal vein'.[6] In moments of crisis he often appeared to be preoccupied with political appearances, and trivial questions rather than substantive issues. Spender observed that Andrews had 'no idea of the war position,. . . [it is] . . . very difficult for a man of his upbringing and outlook to realise . . . the relative importance of matters of local interest and those of European concern'.

Even in the late 1930s Sir Wilfrid had foreseen the danger that Andrews' political career might suffer not only from the physical strains caused by the excessive governmental burden which he then carried but also from too close an identification with Craig's increasingly unpopular leadership. Andrews himself, when reflecting on the roots of his political problems as premier, suggested as a poignant factor this 'legacy of unpopularity'.[7] However, in his choice of cabinet he did nothing to diminish the negative force of his inheritance. Also, arguably, by his decision not to accept the premiership until elected party leader, he helped further to compromise his already weak position as during the resulting period of uncertainty he had little choice but to curry favour with the Unionist parliamentary party.

The new government does not appear to have benefited from any 'honeymoon' period. It lost its first by-election, in late March 1941, in Craigavon's old seat by a wide margin on a high poll. Whatever the idiosyncracies of the constituency, the *News Letter* had believed 'the issue . . . to be . . . perfectly clear, . . . Is North Down behind the Ulster government or is it not'?[8] This statement had been echoed by Andrews, two days later. Likewise, in the commons, though the cabinet was given a guarded welcome, Unionist backbenchers provided Andrews with little cause for comfort. In early 1941, a retired British official observed that 'for some time there has been murmuring on the Unionist back-benches, though no attempt at revolt could survive Lord Craigavon's frown. Now however, the back-benches might conceivably carry a vote of censure, without perhaps realising how heavy would be the responsibility they would thus assume'.[9] Spender noted that they 'were not inclined to give any support . . . whenever they can find an excuse for abstaining', and observed that during one early division all pro-government private members left the chamber and government members alone supported the motion against the opposition. Overall, there was little evidence to support Andrews' claim that the back-benchers were more kindly disposed towards his cabinet than they had been towards Craig's.[10]

From the outset the prime minister adopted what he himself referred to as a 'policy of conciliation' and which he initially believed to be 'bearing fruit'. Gransden later described it less sympathetically, stating that 'whatever might have been the attitude of Mr Andrews as minister of finance his policy as prime minister . . . [was] . . . one of appeasement'.[11] To a growing number of observers, the government appeared weak, ineffective, even incompetent. Throughout it showed a characteristic tendency to procrastinate until forced to act, Andrews himself apparently always prepared to rationalise inactivity. Lacking strong leadership its policies were consistently defensive, directionless and vacillating. Overall, it failed to inspire party loyalty, to command public respect or to retain, let alone enlarge, its electoral support. During the course of the next two years, the cabinet itself suffered from diminishing morale, and growing fractiousness, particularly amongst its junior members, and as a Home Office report noted, ineluctably backbench criticism 'tended to increase'.[12]

Andrews was immediately confronted by problems directly resulting from the neglect and prevarication of Craig's government of which all his own cabinet had been members. Early in 1941, the commons committee on unemployment, whose creation he had fervently opposed, began to produce interim reports. These amounted to a 'serious indictment of the government',[13] criticising in particular the wartime contraction of the linen industry and inadequate levels of land drainage in rural areas. Andrews' defensive and hasty response was characteristic of his premiership. Prior to their publication he was reported to be 'very much worried', fearing that his 'government was going to be held up to contempt'. He spoke of the need to forestall the committee's findings and to 'be able to state what aid would be given when the report was debated' in the house.[14] Hurriedly, therefore, in early January, a cabinet subcommittee was set up and a package of aid to the linen industry agreed. Soon afterwards a drainage commission was established and new land grants introduced. Finally the cabinet decision to dissolve the committee was approached with intense circumspection. Spender, who had regarded its completed reports as 'a waste of stationery',[15] deplored this tendency to play down to criticism. It was a recurrent theme in his comments over these two years.

Neither the confidence nor the prestige of the government was enhanced by the German air raids in April–May 1941 which merely served to exacerbate its problems and confirm its defensive, hesitant posture. Government apprehension at the prospects of a blitz had increased in preceding months with growing awareness of the devastation which it had caused in Britain, and of Northern Ireland's lack of preparedness and vulnerability.[16] However, in the time available little could be done to supplement inadequate anti-aircraft protection, to provide shelters for the 50,000 houses in Belfast without provision, or make up for the shortage of civil defence materials, some of which had earlier been returned to Britain in the mistaken assumption that the province would remain immune from aerial bombardment.[17]

Thus when the blitz did come Northern Ireland was appallingly unprepared. Though government statements spoke of 'splendid morale'[18] and W. D. Scott encouraged Andrews to appeal publicly on the lines of Lincoln's Gettysburg address, 'It is for us the living to be dedicated here to the unfinished work',[19] fear and panic had already reached epidemic proportions amongst the population of Belfast. In late April, 100,000 people fled from the city, overwhelming evacuation plans and reception areas, and causing Brooke acute concern about public health risks even in an area as remote as Fermanagh. Dawson Bates had to inform cabinet of the rack-renting of barns, and, in some areas of up to thirty people crowded together in small houses. In addition, tens of thousands of 'ditchers' were streaming out of the city nightly, to return at dawn, On impulse, the cabinet ordered 3,000 huts to accommodate them, a response which conflicted with imperial practice and was censured privately by the Ministry of Health and publicly in the *Evening Standard*. Though more trenchant measures of blitz preparation followed, they came too late to prevent very bitter attacks in the commons, particularly on the Ministry of Public Security. Beattie's intemperate remarks led to a one-week suspension from the House.[20] In an attempt to mollify the back-benches, MacDermott addressed the party on civil defence, and the cabinet, finally, and with great reluctance, agreed to the parliamentary demand for a secret session.[21]

The extent of continuing public fear was highlighted when, after an air-raid alert on 25 July 1941, at 2.00 am, 30,000 people fled from the capital.[22] No bombs actually fell. Both MacDermott and Spender believed that 'there was more panic amongst the people of Belfast than in the cities of Great Britain which had been subjected to worse bombardment'. The former even suggested that 'opposition demonstrations might take on organised forms and that he expected an attack on Stormont buildings by our population'.[23]

The experience of aerial attack contributed to the reopening of what was for the government a highly sensitive issue and one on which Brooke held strong opinions. At a long and difficult cabinet meeting in mid May, MacDermott urged the introduction of conscription. He regarded it as an essential means of restoring communal discipline, and achieving equality of sacrifice, and stated categorically that unless such a step was taken 'he would not be able to carry on'.[24] Brooke fully supported him, having four weeks earlier raised the question at the Home Office, and on 4 April, impressed on Andrews that 'we must welcome it'. Also on 4 April, Blake states somewhat misleadingly that the prime minister had himself 'reopened' the conscription question in a letter to Morrison.[25] Andrews, however, though implying support for its introduction, was typically cautious and more concerned with public appearances than with ending voluntary enlistment. He stated:

my colleagues and I are placed in a very real difficulty . . . Our people are left in doubt as to the real position. It has never been made clear that the decision [not to apply conscription] was the decision of his majesty's government. I should feel indebted to you if you would take the opportunity of having our position set forth clearly.[26]

Independently and probably unaware of any of these developments, on 12 May, Bevin suggested to the war cabinet that the extension of conscription to Northern Ireland should be given 'further consideration'. 'Subsequently, with his colleagues 'generally in favour', it was decided to ask Andrews for 'an expression of views'.[27] On 21 May, Andrews responded that his government was 'emphatically of the opinion that conscription should be applied', having consulted his party and cabinet and later the Ulster Unionist standing committee and council.[28] His unequivocal reply may also have been influenced by the governor's advice to 'strike whilst people's feelings are hot', given to him in conversation one week earlier, and the presumption that in the aftermath of the blitz opposition would be less intense.[29] However, no attempt was made to verify this either from the police or army or from nationalist leaders. Brooke was one of four ministers and two officials who accompanied the prime minister to London on 2–4 May for discussion on the details of its application, the principle having been accepted.

On 27 May, however, the British war cabinet decided against extending conscription to Northern Ireland. This was due to accumulating evidence of opposition from southern Ireland, the United States and Canada, as well as from within the province itself. Evidence of the latter was provided mainly by a memorandum drawn up by Colonel Wickham at Morrison's request and by a campaign orchestrated by Nationalist M.P.s and senators with Catholic Church support, culminating in a rally held in Belfast on Sunday 25 May attended by up to 10,000 people.[30] There was however a further factor. Andrews had returned home alone on the Saturday evening, other Northern Ireland government ministers remaining in London on business. He was clearly impressed by the events of the weekend, and, on the morning of 26 May, contacted the home secretary to indicate that the strength of opposition would be greater than anticipated and that though his government would like to see conscription applied 'the real test . . . must be whether it would be for the good of the empire'. This is likely to have influenced the attitude of the British government when next day it agreed a statement, later cheered at Westminster, stating that 'it would be more trouble than it was worth'.[31] Andrews privately expressed the opinion that 'the best course had been taken' and, when Churchill, perhaps more speculatively, reopened the question again in early 1943, he once more opposed, fearing that it would cause political disturbance and boost the I.R.A.[32]

This sudden change in the attitude of the imperial government towards extending conscription bewildered informed opinion in the province. The P.M. had apparently acted on his own initiative. Spender later recorded that he could 'not follow exactly the reason for the sudden *volte face* by the British cabinet' and earlier records show that both Glentoran and Gransden were similarly perplexed.[33] MacDermott appears not to have been consulted by Andrews. Brooke certainly was not, and only gradually became aware of the circumstances in which the decision was made. In late March 1942, Sir Basil, in the course of pursuing more war contracts for the province, was genuinely shocked when Bevin complained to him that 'we [Northern Ireland] were asking for a privileged position, because we had not had conscription and that was the fault of . . . [our] . . . government. We had got cold feet'.[34] Brooke fervently denied the suggestion and informed Andrews who wrote 'expressing surprise that [Bevin] . . . should have used this argument to prevent work coming here'.[35] Two years later, however, Brooke checked the conscription file, possibly prompted by other accusations similar to Bevin's, and noted 'it seems to me that having decided on conscription, Andrews on his return home, . . . had been told of possible riots . . . and though he had told Churchill that the government was prepared to face any difficulties, on his return he . . . telephoned British ministers and rather left the responsibility of the decision in their hands. This they were not prepared to accept'.[36]

At the time, Andrews suggested to a disbelieving Spender that the episode had 'strengthened Ulster's position across the water'.[37] Brooke's later comment would seem a more accurate assessment: 'I think this action has made it extremely difficult for us on the other side, especially with Bevin . . . one of the prime movers on the conscription issue. We should never have gone forward so far unless we had been quite determined to carry it through'.[38] These events must have served to reduce the credibility of the Stormont government at Westminster and raise serious doubts as to the quality of its leadership. Within Northern Ireland, statements by Wickham and Gordon in particular suggest that the final outcome was in the best interests of public order, and broadly welcomed by both communities. Nonetheless, the government had failed to achieve its publicly stated objective and its political opponents might have reasonably claimed the victory.

Somewhat surprisingly, Andrews had stated in mid October 1941 that although when he assumed office the government's position was 'very shaky, . . . [and] . . . independents could count on being successful in any political contest . . . now . . . the position of the government was stronger than it had been for many years' and he was, therefore, 'very anxious not to do anything that would upset the country'. Such an assessment was an illusion probably caused by a combination of his political insensitivity and narrow range of social contacts as well as serious defects within the organisation of the Unionist party. It could no longer be sustained after the Willowfield by-election defeat four weeks later and the associated increase in unionist press criticism of the administration. Within days of the result, Andrews was said to be 'very anxious about the political position of the government'. These anxieties proved extremely durable. In May 1942, he telephoned Spender, his somewhat embarrassed confidante, to discuss the weakness of his administration stating that he 'was satisfied . . . that if there was a general election now the government would cease to have a majority'. It was a view widely shared by influential opinion within the province.[39]

The gravity of this assumption was heightened by the knowledge that the Northern Ireland parliament was due to expire on 1 March 1943. Until late June 1942, Spender was convinced after talks with leading British officials that the imperial government would not agree to a prolongation unless the composition of the cabinet was changed and another formed, as in Britain, 'on a more national basis'. Andrews may have shared these fears. Spender refers to the P.M.'s desire to prepare for the election and quotes him as saying during the electricity negotiations that it was something that 'he had to think of'.[40] His government agreed to ask for a prolongation of parliament in mid-February 1942 but not until five months later did the war cabinet record its willingness to do so. Its only condition, that the Northern Ireland house should pass a resolution indicating its approval, was in fact welcomed in the province. The local cabinet had earlier agreed that such a parliamentary procedure would help 'to establish the principle that the 1920 act could not be amended without [local] . . . parliamentary consultation'.[41]

This fresh evidence of the government's political vulnerability from late 1941 reinforced the cautious instincts and reactive nature of Andrews' policies. Thus party whips sought to avoid by-elections, as a result leaving some constituencies without adequate representation for prolonged periods. Appropriately, the matter was raised in the house by Midgley. Spender observed with disapproval cabinet reluctance to increase the salaries of permanent secretaries, due to political considerations, the declining proportion of civil servants on honours lists and the general tendency for party leaders and ministers, with the stated exception of Brooke, to use the civil service as a 'whipping boy'.[42] When Andrews attributed government unpopularity to lack of courtesy on the part of the officials, Sir Wilfrid felt this indicated 'a complete lack of appreciation of the true situation, people expect the government to govern, not play down to the baser interests of self-seeking people and public bodies'.[43]

Such criticisms had validity. The government did seek to avoid potentially difficult or unpopular legislation. With regard to transport, war might have been regarded as an opportunity to coordinate road and rail services. Andrews opposed this as he felt that people would not tolerate interference with free competition, and he was said to be 'very reluctant to quarrel with the Transport Board', in marked contrast to 'the very determined attitude' he had adopted towards it as minister of finance.[44]

The political context also helps account for protracted cabinet discussion in 1942 about the 'infiltration' of Eire workers. Some importation of southern labour was essential particularly for heavy industry, where the local labour force was insufficient. As a result the Ministry of Labour was actively involved in cross-border recruitment. The process did involve security risks as a significant proportion of the labour was employed on highly sensitive construction work, or at quarries where explosives were available. There is also some evidence that imported labour lacked any strong commitment to the war effort. Andrews, however, justified the stricter controls eventually introduced in September 1942, mainly as a means of stifling parliamentary and public criticism caused mainly by the comparatively high level of local unemployment and the fact that large numbers of Ulster workers had been obliged to transfer to factories in Britain to find employment.[45] When the proposed restrictions were being scrutinised by reluctant imperial ministers, Spender commented that it was 'a matter for regret that the prime minister did not have any near relatives serving in different parts of the world which would help bring home to him the frightful crisis with which our empire is faced'.[46] Ironically, at this time the Dublin authorities were themselves giving serious consideration to the control of north-bound emigration, fearing the economic and political consequences of the simultaneous expulsion of thousands of southern born men and women from Ulster when the war ended.[47]

Another matter which positively demanded the attention of Andrews' reluctant and embarrassed government was the activities of the predominantly Unionist Belfast Corporation. A much publicised Home Affairs inquiry in June 1941 indicated that the latter had been guilty of extensive corruption and abuse of patronage. At first the department hoped that the councillors might be induced to reform themselves, and under strong government pressure they did convene their own committee of enquiry, However, in April 1942, the corporation rescinded the crucial sections of its far-reaching proposals, so creating what Bates described as 'an extremely serious state of affairs'.[48]

From mid-1941, there had been growing public support, particularly from Belfast ratepayers, for the dissolution of the council. The corporation's response was increasingly perceived as 'defiance pure and simple' and governmental inaction as evidence of collusion between ministers, Unionist M.P.s and councillors which 'prevents the proper steps being taken'.[49] This assumption had considerable justification. The government's position was acutely difficult. Corporation members were extremely influential in Belfast Unionist associations and within the party organization. Indeed Spender suspected that 'lower elements . . . especially those associated with the local authorities . . . [were intent on gaining] . . . control of the party machine' and that it would be 'very difficult to rid . . . [it] . . . of the dirt that [had] crept in'.[50] Thus Bates regarded dissolution as 'out of the question', mainly because, if attempted, the government would find it 'impossible to hold office'. He therefore recommended the appointment of city administrators, who would act as an executive, and be guided by the elected councillors 'who would continue to define policy, thus preserving the facade of democracy.

Andrews remained as he had been during the electricity negotiations, 'anxious not to have any trouble with the corporation'.[52] He suggested that even this compromise measure 'would distract from the unity of effort . . .

needed to win the war',[53] contravene the principle of introducing no controversial legislation in wartime and possibly prejudice litigation involving council members currently before the courts. With extreme reluctance and after prolonged delay he and the cabinet adopted Bates' recommendations. However, amidst threats from some Unionist members that the party would be broken up, and from Belfast Unionist associations that they would splinter and wither, as well as continuing pressure from the corporation, the government relented. On the prime minister's suggestion, the cabinet agreed, though not unanimously, to support two amendments which significantly weakened the original Belfast county borough administration bill by specifying the period for which city administrators would be appointed and restoring to the council some of its powers of appointment.[54] However, when the second of these was moved at the committee stage, it was criticised by Midgley with devastating effect, and, Spender records, this 'caused so much anxiety in the cabinet that it was hastily resolved to withdraw it'.[55] Overall the latter regarded the episode as a 'shattering blow' to the government and a 'complete victory to the corporation'.[56] There can be no doubt that the legislation caused very deep divisions within the government, and served to alienate some influential elements within the party who opposed the bill, whilst failing to satisfy those who believed that firmer action was justified.

The handling of industrial disputes was a further major area of wartime responsibility which provoked adverse comment about the Andrews' government and aroused serious doubt about its competence. In part criticism was directed at the machinery for resolving disputes created under the terms of the conditions of employment and national arbitration order which came into effect in August 1940. This order, aimed at the prompt settlement of trade disputes reported to the Ministry of Labour, the department responsible, prohibited strikes and lockouts and established a National Arbitration Tribunal. Trade unionists claimed that the latter was slow, inflexible with regard to wages and, in common with the defence regulations generally, favoured the employers.[57] The charge of bias was denied by J. F. Gordon, the labour minister.[58] However, MacDermott, attorney general from October 1941, described the machinery as 'clumsy and slow', complained that some of the cases which came before him were 'months old' before a strike had occurred, and that such delay 'tempted . . . [workers] . . . to take matters into their own hands'. Andrews' reply indicated that there was 'room for improving the existing machinery'.[59]

A more fundamental criticism, expressed by local management and a number of officials and politicians, was that the Northern Ireland government was, in Bevin's phrase, 'weak and complaisant'[60] in its attitude towards labour, and that this had directly contributed to a deterioration in industrial discipline. There was evidence to justify such charges. Thus, for example, amidst controversy, in late 1941 and early 1942, the Ministry of Home Affairs intervened on two occasions to reduce fines imposed on workers involved in illegal action over demarcation, who had subsequently petitioned the governor. During a carters' strike in October 1941, the government was initially reluctant to permit naval personnel into the docks to collect essential equipment and the delay caused to flax deliveries prompted one telegram from a linen firm to Andrews enquiring: 'does the Ministry of Labour realise there is a war on'?[61] Several weeks earlier a manager at Short & Harland's complained at Ministry of Labour inaction when confronted by workers who refused to go to dispersal factories. He informed Andrews that the workers

know their action is winked at by those in authority. It is necessary for the government . . . to state that the same regulations are in force regarding dispersal factories [in Northern Ireland] as those which are in force in England. Until then we will have no peace in industry. The workers are as good as any in the kingdom but they must not be allowed to enforce mob rule.[62]

From the spring of 1942, Brooke had forseen a major confrontation with labour and 'urged the P.M. to be strong, any weakening would be taken advantage of'.[63] In October, the worst strike of Andrews' premiership occurred. It originated in the consistently volatile dispersal unit of Short & Harland's, at Balmoral. The immediate cause was an attempt by management to implement a Ministry of Production instruction regarding Sunday work. It spread rapidly, within two weeks affecting 10,000 workers in the aircraft industry, the shipyards and other engineering firms, and the number of strikers was still rising.[64]

On 15 October Churchill telegraphed Andrews stating that he was 'shocked at what was happening', adding gravely, 'It is very hard for Northern Ireland to . . . carry such a burden'.[65] Imperial ministers were further distressed, not least because of possible repercussions on the mainland, when they learnt next day that the Stormont government had set up, without conditions, a court of enquiry. Morrison thought it a dangerous concession to an illegal strike, contrary to all British practice, and in any case 'a dilatory method of dealing with an urgent matter'.[66] Andrews had partly justified an enquiry on the grounds that it 'would let the public see the facts and . . . the strikers . . . see the error of their ways'. However, the strike was ended mainly through the direct intervention of trade union officials from Great Britain acting on the invitation of the Northern Ireland government.[67]

Its root causes were complex but although the failings of management and irresponsibility of the trade unions were generally accepted as contributory factors, inevitably much blame also attached to the government. Ormeau Unionist association wrote to the P.M. stressing the 'need for prompt action' in industrial disputes and castigating 'the policy of drift'. Much criticism focused on the Ministry of Labour whose record in other areas, particularly dilution, had similarly attracted adverse comment. One of Brooke's labour inspectors observed that 'it did not exhibit the same strength of character . . . in dealing with employees . . . as Mr Bevin'.[68] Spender claims that 'the general impression' amongst officials in the department was that it showed 'deplorable weakness' particularly in the early stages of the strike.[69] It was a view which he fully endorsed.

By early November 1942 MacDermott had become deeply despondent over the whole question of labour relations and industrial discipline. In a lengthy letter to Andrews he suggested that the time had come to repeal the order making it an offence to strike, as it was now 'painfully evident . . . [that] . . . it will not deter mass strikes'. He warned that 'numbers acting in concert can defeat the law', and this threatened 'to bring the rule of law into contempt and to weaken the whole fabric of organised society'. He also observed that the

Ministry of Labour no longer expressed any opinion to him as to the expediency of instituting proceedings against strikers. He deduced from this, and no doubt from the sequence of past departmental appeals to him not to press the order that the ministry 'finds prosecutions for strikes increasingly embarrassing'. This was a further reason, he suggested, for implementing his recommendations. However his worries went deeper. He predicted the likelihood of more mass strikes and concluded that, 'the strain of war is likely to increase and I doubt if we as a community have the discipline or sense of responsibility to meet it without further trouble'. He therefore advised, as he had done in the aftermath of the blitz, that conscription be earnestly sought.[70]

Churchill was to justify reopening the conscription question several months later on similar grounds. He referred to 'young fellows of the locality . . . [who] loaf about with their hands in their pockets' and how this deleteriously affected 'not only recruiting but the work of . . . Belfast shipyards which is less active than other British shipyards'.[71] Andrews dismissed the idea as 'not falling within the realm of practical politics'.[72] However, on MacDermott's insistence that matters should not be left to drift, a ministerial conference was held in early December, which appears to have been unproductive. Brooke commented that it 'wasted considerable time'.[73] Meanwhile, the prime minister suggested to the minister of labour that he seek Bevin's advice on 'some step to get . . . hold of difficulties . . . before they boil up'. He also stressed that Bevin 'keeps this matter very much in his own hands' and he had 'never seen why [Gordon] should not deal with such matters to the same extent'. In his reply the latter had defended strongly his ministry's reluctance to use its emergency powers on the grounds that to do so would weaken the existing voluntary negotiating machinery. In his view this was 'too high a price', and, in addition, the trade unions 'would resent it'.[74] In labour disputes, during early 1943, this same approach continued and the department's emergency powers and machinery remained unchanged.[75] So also did the tensions within the government and the criticism of its performance which these circumstances engendered.

There was of course a more positive aspect to government policy. In early December 1941, Gransden observed that 'the new prime minister held very different views from those he had expressed as minister of finance'. He was referring to Andrews' emerging opinion that the government should spend money more liberally on social services, set aside resources for post-war reconstruction and assert its independence of Treasury control to a greater degree. Spender had sensed a change of outlook from the moment of Andrews' appointment, and later dismissed this aspect of his policy uncharitably, as 'getting credit from the electorate by the distribution of government funds'. He disapproved strongly of the prime minister's special pleading with the Treasury, aimed, he felt, at getting better terms for the province than were available on the mainland and he regarded it as both damaging to Northern Ireland's reputation at Westminster and unjustifiable as conditions locally were less severe than in Britain.[76]

As the timing of Gransden's remark suggests, this feature of his policy became more marked as Andrews' consciousness of the political weakness of his administration and of the changing aspirations of the electorate increased. In Northern Ireland as elsewhere, war stimulated expectations of social improvement, a development associated with high tax levels, the huge imperial contribution, heightened awareness of unequal services when compared with Britain and the publication of the Beveridge report. The condition of the refugees who fled in panic after the blitz served to illuminate the extent of poverty in Belfast. Later, as the United Kingdom progressed steadily forward to safety and final deliverance, interest in post-war policy and planning was stimulated. Days after the Willowfield result, Andrews reflected ruefully on his disadvantageous position. Whereas the opposition could promise the electorate 'millions of money', he was restrained by his government's relationship with the Treasury. He stated then that he must give 'a categorical answer . . . of the government's intentions', and later that 'steps must be taken to restore the confidence of the people'.[77]

Andrews' policy, however, was based on conviction as well as expediency. He was firmly convinced of the need for increased public expenditure and regarded opposition criticism on these grounds as legitimate. On several occasions he outlined to Spender and to the cabinet the extent to which housing, health, education and poor relief provision in the province lagged behind Britain, citing as evidence the mortality rates for expectant mothers and infants, both of which had risen in the interwar period.[78] Implicit in Andrews' attitude was the conviction that the British government had not treated the province entirely fairly and a profound frustration at the trammelled nature of his own authority. He stated that he was 'not going to stand for the continuation of the present position in which officials of the Treasury were able to veto expenditure which our government thought essential'. In addition, he felt that the size of Ulster's wartime imperial contribution 'justified our paying attention first to local needs' and that 'he must be able to distribute some on behalf of the government'.[79]

The changing emphasis of Andrews' policies was also forced upon him by influential young members of the Unionist party who in Gransden's words made the matter 'very urgent' and 'pressed from outside in a somewhat startling way'. In conversation, correspondence and memoranda, which were discussed by cabinet in mid-1942, Maynard Sinclair, Brian Maginess and Wilson Hungerford urged very forcefully the necessity of producing detailed plans for the post-war period, and of announcing them as 'publicly and speedily as possible'. This they suggested 'would arouse enthusiasm and capture the imagination of a great majority of the people' and 'was essential for the future of the province as well as of the party'.[80]

The tangible results of this aspect of government policy were somewhat meagre. On 30 July 1942, the prime minister made a speech in the commons on post-war policy. It was made, as he explained to the chancellor later, in response to 'a very definite and sustained demand . . . pressed upon me that I should give a real lead on social problems in future years'. It contained a commitment to improved housing, cheap electricity, and expanded educational services and referred to plans being prepared on a range of issues including transport, local government and industry. He stressed that this 'ambitious' programme was 'our domestic concern . . . for our government and parliament to carry out', and concluded that 'if foresight, energy and courage could solve [post-war problems] . . . they will be solved'.[81]

The speech had been carefully timed. It was made in response to a pre-arranged question just before the third reading of the Belfast county borough administration bill and also on the eve of the summer recess thus effectively denying the house an opportunity to discuss it until September. The tactic was dismissed by Midgley as 'cowardly, mean and despicable', and by Spender as 'rather a smart course'.[82] The latter had felt so concerned at the content and publicity surrounding this unilateral statement of future policy that he had sent a draft of the speech to the Treasury. In return, he received a departmental comment so strongly worded that Sir Wilfred correctly surmised that it conveyed the views of the chancellor himself, an impression confirmed when Kingsley Wood wrote to Andrews.[83]

In correspondence and later discussions both chancellor and officials criticised the entire lack of consultation preceding the speech, particularly as they regarded 'parity of services as the sheet anchor of . . . [their] . . . financial relations with the province'.[84] Its timing was regarded as incomprehensible and its content as unwisely specific. In conversation with Maynard Sinclair, Wood also stressed that the post-war period might be one of hardship, shortages and high taxation and thus to suggest that plans would be ready for implementation was 'misleading'. Andrews' statement was variously described at the Treasury as a crude 'attempt to bolster up his political position by promising the moon', a 'dangerous lapse into the homes for heroes tone . . . we were to eschew this time' and a bid to establish the principle that 'whatever tune Northern Ireland calls the imperial government will pay the piper'.[85]

Andrews, who had taken great exception to the chancellor's letter, in his reply drew attention to the powerful political pressures acting on his government, and urged that he sought merely to bring the province's inadequate social services into line with those in Britain and was only asking for 'a reasonable degree of latitude' for his government. Conflicting interpretations have been placed on Wood's response. In this, the latter recognised that 'the major responsibility' for post-war reconstruction lay with Andrews' government, and admitted the delicacy of his political situation but stressed that though Ulster might legitimately claim the right to make up 'leeway', she could not claim 'preferential treatment' and once more underlined the need for prior consultation.[86] Andrews deduced from this response that he had gained 'extended financial powers . . . from before', in its recognition of 'leeway' and its definition of his government's functions.[87]

The chancellor's letter has been described by one authority as Andrews' 'crowning achievement', because in accepting the province's right to establish all its social services on an equal basis to those in Britain the former had 'in effect invited Ulster to put up a case for making good leeway'.[88] This interpretation, however, is mainly based on Andrews' own statements and was not shared at the time by Milne Barbour, Maynard Sinclair or by officials at the Ministry of Finance. Spender regarded Woods' letter as 'very temperate . . . [and] . . . a generous statement of the claims of Northern Ireland for special treatment', but believed it merely 'confirmed existing arrangements'.[89] This view was also accepted at the Treasury for whom the prime minister's speech had been a source of surprise and irritation. When British officials negotiated, in 1946–8, a new post-war financial agreement with Northern Ireland, necessary because of imperial legislation in 1941 and 1946, the precedents cited and applied were the agreements of 1926 and 1935–6, with no reference being made to this wartime correspondence.[90]

In his controversial speech, Andrews had stated, 'we intend to make preparation at once, . . . I have entrusted . . . the minister of commerce with the duty of making the necessary arrangements for the consideration of those urgent problems that will arise at the end of the war'. This was a reference to the Brooke committee set up some weeks earlier as a direct result of cabinet discussion of the memorandum produced by Sinclair and others.[91] It consisted of all the permanent secretaries and the parliamentary secretaries with Brooke as chairman. Its function was to expedite departmental examination of post-war problems, co-ordinate Northern Ireland's plans with those in Britain and make policy recommendations. However, a post-war reconstruction committee, the Planning Advisory Board, had already existed for three months. It had been formed with cabinet approval by the Ministry of Home Affairs, was chaired by Lindsay Keir and its purpose was 'to advise on matters of principle' in the preparation of a plan for the post-war period.[92]

Brooke dismissed the policy-making structures of the earlier body as 'wishful thinking' and observed 'we will be working on parallel lines unless one of us is disbanded'. He concluded that both bodies 'could not go on as at present organised'.[93] In early September, at cabinet, Bates defended the prior claims of his advisory board and this was accepted by a majority of his colleagues.[94] Though an attempt at compromise was made, the Brooke committee was left with no clearly identifiable function. Days later on Brooke's suggestion, it went into 'cold storage', and soon afterwards disbanded. Sir Basil commented 'I refuse to preside over any committee unless the machinery is in good working order' and reflected on the 'hopeless muddle' of post-war planning. To Spender it was 'another instance of the government's tendency . . . to try and damp down parliamentary criticism of dilatoriness . . . by taking action in advance of the British government and without knowing their procedures and policies'.[95] Not surprisingly when post-war reconstruction was eventually debated in the house, some backbenchers expressed very frankly their doubts as to the government's ability to make good its policy commitments both on the grounds of its age and alleged past incompetence. Sir Wilfrid was initially relieved at the restrained tones of Andrews' own contribution which he described as 'perhaps the best . . . he has ever made'. Later he learnt that the P.M. had 'not been altogether pleased' with it himself, as 'owing to the strike position he had very little time to edit it'.[96]

On the day that his committee placed itself in 'cold storage', Brooke recorded in his diary that though he personally liked Andrews, 'I find that I disagree with him on many matters'.[97] No doubt at the time post-war policy was uppermost in his mind. Brooke had throughout stressed the necessity for close collaboration with British ministers. After Andrews' July speech he expressed appreciation of Spender's attempts at damage-limitation in relations with the Treasury.[98] He clearly felt deeply frustrated with the confused plethora of bodies which had been devised, and, immediately after becoming premier, created as a priority new planning structures.[99]

Quite apart from this, however, and his near resignation over the electricity question, his differences with the P.M. were frequent and ranged over vital areas of government policy. With regard to labour he encouraged Andrews on a number of occasions to adopt a stronger approach, as he did also in relation to local management. In September 1942, after advising him that 'we should take a stronger stand', he continued: 'I am afraid he did not agree . . . but I cannot follow his argument'. During the October strike, he shared MacDermott's despondency, writing, 'we cannot win a war of this sort without discipline and there does not seem to be any'. Earlier he had supported Bates' Belfast county borough administration bill and referred to their 'successful battle' to gain cabinet approval. He opposed both of the amendments subsequently suggested by Andrews stating 'I don't think it is right to pander to those who want corruption by giving councillors powers to appoint men to jobs', and adding later 'my own view is we must do the right thing irrespective of the party'.[100] On the conscription issue, Brooke favoured throughout a determined policy to have it applied, partly to 'be on a par with the rest of the U.K'. and also for the more pragmatic reasons that it was 'complicating our labour position' and was 'so often used by the imperial authorities on production questions'. He regarded the final decision not to apply it as 'probably wise' having earlier predicted nationalist opposition 'varying from passive resistance to actual rioting'.[101]

His views also conflicted with Andrews' over a range of lesser issues. Though aware of the security risks involved in importing southern labour, Brooke remarked 'it is, of course, a danger but . . . the war effort is essential and if we are short of men we must get them up'. He was constantly concerned to improve the level of government and military cooperation. Differing attitudes were highlighted when, in mid-1941, the R.A.F. requested the use of the Senate as an operations room. Andrews hesitated, fearing that this could raise important constitutional questions and even undermine the position of parliament, and initially offered the entrance hall at Stormont instead. Brooke regarded the Air Force suggestion as 'a bombshell', but added 'we should put no obstacle in their way'.[102] Quintessentially he was more inclined than the P.M. to regard Britain's treatment of Northern Ireland as fair and reasonable. Thus when Andrews sought an increased Treasury grant for an extension to Ballylumford power station, Sir Basil opposed as he felt that it could not be justified. Similarly, when the prime minister complained about the poor quality of the province's coal allocation, fearing disturbances if it was distributed in Belfast, Brooke remarked, 'He needs to be careful, we cannot ask for special treatment, I think we have got good concessions'.[103] Overall, on these and other issues, Brooke favoured a stronger, more assertive style of government than Andrews. In essence, he viewed all policy in the context of the war and his attitude was determined by his perception of what would best serve the war effort. On one occasion he referred to Andrews as 'merely pandering to criticism',[104] a tendency with which he expressed little sympathy. Apart from over the electricity question, there is no evidence that he seriously considered resignation until the spring of 1943. After the Willowfield result he records a conversation in which it was suggested to him that he should 'quit', and his reply that 'I cannot leave the ship if it is in a bad way', adding 'unless a big issue of principle is involved'. He was certainly conscious of the government's growing unpopularity. When speaking on behalf of the Unionist nominee at Willowfield he had found the audience 'not very enthusiastic . . . but quiet until the candidate got up when there was a series of interruptions. It ended up rather a noisy meeting'. When Andrews consulted the party soon afterwards to explain the 'difficulties of the position', Sir Basil doubted 'that they were very impressed. The whole party seems rather shaky'. He accepted without question the view of a local journalist that the government 'would not get a show if it went to the country'.

In considering the causes of the government's unpopularity, Brooke consoled Andrews by suggesting that 'what was really wrong was people wanted a change, just as they wanted a change in England'.[105] Undoubtedly such an explanation had some validity. It was mentioned in a political analysis produced by the Home Office in April 1943, and was accepted by Andrews himself. Longevity of service went beyond the government, causing one critic to observe that 'the bureaucrats are worse hangers-on to office than the cabinet'.[106]

However, the causes of disaffection went deeper as Sir Basil himself was well aware. There were accumulating doubts as to the competence of what was often termed the 'old guard'. This was due in part to their age and health. Much criticism focused on Milne Barbour who was widely regarded as too old, weak and ineffectual for the responsibilities of his office. In the late 1930s Spender had written very critically of his performance as minister of labour, and continued to worry whether he was strong enough to defend adequately the interests of his department. However he had since developed a deep respect for Barbour regarding him as conscientious, straight and someone who 'shared the ideals' of his officials.[107] Sir Wilfrid had no doubt that cabinet changes were necessary but considered that there were other more legitimate targets. He was consistently critical of Gordon's handling of labour questions. Glentoran and Grant he thought, might be replaced on health grounds alone. He suspected the former of always being ready to do 'a quick one on the Treasury and described him unflatteringly as one of those men of average intelligence who believes that the state has an unlimited purse'. He recognised his immense influence in the government but regarded it as generally misdirected towards encouraging Andrews to play down to lower elements within the party.[108]

However Spender's most acid remarks were reserved for the minister of home affairs, Dawson Bates, whose department caused him 'great anxiety'. He believed that 'most of the criticism of the government on real grounds' was attributable to Bates, and admitted to feeling a certain personal animosity to him.[109] In wartime he felt it was indefensible for a minister with his responsibilities to continue to live in Portrush, seventy miles from Belfast, and accumulate over 30,000 miles yearly in a large official car. He censured his persistent inattention to duties and prolonged absences, noted that officials had great difficulty in getting a real decision from him and wondered how long it could last. They clashed acrimoniously over finance. Spender particularly resented Bates' hutting order for blitz refugees and his efforts to raise special constabulary pay above British levels. He also accused him of a persistent lack of courage in standing up to local authorities, especially Belfast Corporation.[110] However, even his diluted measure establishing city administrators aggravated not only the government's but Bates' own personal unpopularity. A commons' vote of censure alleging corruption on his part coincided with the second reading of the bill. With regard to the latter, Brooke felt that Bates 'made a very good case . . . as far as I could see there . . . [was] . . . no foundation for these attacks'. It was not until early 1943 that Sir Basil came to regard Bates as a political liability.[111]

There seemed no shortage of evidence of the collective incompetence of the 'old guard'. There was the continuing high level of unemployment. As Spender commented when comparing Bevin's difficulty in finding labour with Northern Ireland's labour surplus, 'Gilbertia could hardly provide a more extraordinary situation'.[112] There was also continuing industrial unrest for which the government was regarded as at least partly responsible. Possibly the *News Letter* was also correct in detecting a 'swing to the left' amongst working people in the war period and a receding awareness of constitutional issues.[113] The extent of government unpopularity was aggravated further by defective party organisation and propaganda. There was in addition, the uneasy feeling that the province was, in MacDermott's phrase, 'only half in the war'.[114] This was even more obvious to an informed observer. A Mass Observation report, dated June 1942, states

The lack of war urgency and relative lack of anxiety . . . is most striking [in Ulster], . . . rationing or transport difficulties are still the source of . . . irritation and resentment. . . . Even the blitz . . . is regarded . . . as almost an insult and a grievance; . . . anyone who is keen on the war effort is liable to feel uncomfortable, . . . a . . . feeling of guilt at being there, . . . perhaps the most curious shock . . . is seeing men lying about . . . on the grass outside the City Hall, or sleeping . . . in the backs of cars, . . . anyone who behaved in a peacetime way in London or Liverpool would at once be noticeable and might even cause a riot.[115]

Not surprisingly, in these circumstances when Andrews spoke of applying 'foresight, energy and courage'[116] to resolve post-war problems, his words had a somewhat hollow and unconvincing ring. Admittedly the cause of some of these features lay beyond the competence of the Northern Ireland government. Unemployment was in part due to insufficient British war contracts. The Mass Observation report stressed the importance of conscription in accounting for 'Ulster apathy', commenting that 'by studying . . . the situation [there] one is able to see the enormous part which conscription has played in influencing Britain's psychology'.[117] Though Andrews' role was far from passive, the decision not to apply it was an imperial one and reflected the continuing internal political realities within the province. Nonetheless, a growing and influential sector of public opinion in Northern Ireland attributed their feelings of dissatisfaction to errors of omission and commission on the part of the local government. In Spender's view it had encouraged complacency leading the public to 'believe that they were making sacrifices even greater than in England and Scotland'. He thought it 'deplorable' that it 'did not seem to realise the urgent necessities of war . . . [or] . . . make the people respond as they did in 1914 'to Carson's appeal. They had failed to offer 'leadership and sacrifice'.[118] Brooke likewise felt that there was 'a great deal in what . . . [the government critics] . . . say'. In December 1941, after the Willowfield defeat, he echoed Spender's sentiments commenting 'I think that Andrews must come in with a declaration that he is out to win the war and nothing else matters'.[119] However neither fully appreciated how tenuous the political position of the government had become, particularly in parliament.

It is, of course, true that any backbench revolt which might seriously threaten the existence of the government seemed highly improbable. Though the parliamentary party had produced a significant volume of criticism, particularly from the late 1930s, the whips could feel reassured by the fact that out of thirty-eight government supporters in the house, sixteen held offices of profit under the crown and the number of private members was depleted in wartime by those serving in the forces.[120] Also, as Spender observed, there was a dearth of decisive leadership to articulate and mobilise effectively unionist resentment. Attacks launched by non-Unionist M.P.s were frequently phrased in such bitter and violent tones that it was 'difficult for reputable party members to go into the lobby with them'. John Beattie was widely regarded as a spokesman for Sinn Fein.[121] His vote of censure on the government failed to find a seconder in December 1941, and his later attack on the prolongation of parliament was so fierce that 'those who were going to support his amendment . . . decided not to speak'.[122] His role was such that at times Spender even suspected that he might be acting in collusion with the government front bench. The American consul observed that if he had made similar speeches in the south, he would have been arrested.[123]

Nevertheless, there are clear indications of growing disaffection amongst Unionist M.P.s. Parliamentary party meetings became more tense, and even normally routine business could cause acrimony. On 15 December 1942, for the first time members failed to agree on a nomination for the Senate. Party officials favoured Gerald Browne, a 70 year old ex-Hansard editor, whose elevation they had disclosed to the press before the members had met. Many backbenchers and junior ministers supported Dr Carnwath who had published a very critical report on Belfast housing. Browne was victorious at a second meeting, after it had been decided that only Belfast members should vote. Spender felt that the incident caused deep resentment amongst the rank and file who felt tricked by the party whips.[124] Though territorial representation was the norm in Senate appointments, such an expedient had never before proved necessary.

Also party meetings had traditionally provided ministers with a forum in which to defend and explain government policy and this continued to be the case. However, they appear to have become more reluctant to do so, due in part to the sensitivity of some legislation, and no doubt to their declining confidence and morale. Bates was coerced into consulting the party over the Belfast county borough administration bill. After the Willowfield result, Glentoran strongly opposed Brooke's suggestion that Andrews should consult the party to discuss the political situation.[125] Though this was eventually discussed on three occasions in late 1941 and early 1942, Brooke came to feel that Andrews likewise was eager to avoid calling party meetings.[126] Their infrequency was used by Brown, one of the government's most virulent backbench critics, to justify putting down private motions. He argued that the latter had become necessary 'merely . . . to ventilate grievances'.[127]

Despite appeals by Glentoran that members should give 'every assistance and help' to the chief whip, there is also evidence of declining party discipline in the house.[128] Though the vote of censure on Bates was defeated by twenty votes to four only eight backbench Unionists supported the government. This was far from satisfactory as a three-line whip had been issued and some members were in the house but failed to enter the lobby. During the second reading of the Belfast county borough administration bill, Brooke described the P.M. and Glentoran as 'very jubilant' when it was evident that 'the government would have support'. However, the bill passed by just twenty-three votes to ten and fourteen of its supporters were government members; thus a majority of the private members who voted, opposed it.[129] The government's nervousness and vulnerability were further illustrated by the speed with which it capitulated to Midgley's criticisms of one of the amendments at the committee stage.

The latter incident illustrates that though the composition of the house changed little the arrival of the two newly elected independent members did sharpen the level of critical comment. These combined with Unionist back-bench critics and others in attacking familiar targets such as the composition and competence of the cabinet, the inadequacy of the war effort, and high unemployment levels. In October 1942, they were joined by Dr Lyle who became M.P. for Queen's, a constituency for whose representatives Glentoran felt a profound contempt.[130] In his maiden speech Lyle articulated the growing commons' interest in post-war reconstruction, and must have helped confirm doubts as to the ability of the government to fulfill its commitments. Two months later, he introduced a motion, supported by precise and devastating arguments, calling for the establishment of a Ministry of Health. After citing mortality statistics he declared that in 'the slaughter of innocents . . . the Ulster government had out-Heroded Herod'.[131] Spender records that members listened in 'tense silence' during his attack on Bates 'which though quietly expressed was the most serious allegation . . . [Sir Wilfrid] . . . had ever heard against . . . a minister'. Brooke remarked that it was 'a dirty debate' and that the 'house [was] deteriorating in its general attitude'. Delicate negotiations followed involving Lyle, Andrews and Glentoran, in a desperate effort to persuade the former to drop his motion. The compromise finally accepted was that the prime minister would establish a parliamentary committee on health services.[132]

Soon afterwards Andrews was reported to be 'very alarmed' at the committee's activities, fearing that it would produce 'violent criticisms' of government inaction. He advised officials 'to take immediate action to torpedo' its recommendations by producing proposals for immediate negotiations with the Treasury, which would permit the government to make payments to local authorities so enabling all the province's social services to be brought into line with those in Britain. He also expressed himself as willing to meet Churchill and 'tell him that he could not carry on unless the chancellor agreed'.[133]

The Treasury negotiations began in mid-January 1943. Throughout Spender kept Capt. C. P. Petherick, the Ministry of Finance official directly involved, apprised of local political developments 'so that he might fully appreciate the importance which the P.M. attached . . . to his mission'. He similarly kept Andrews informed of any favourable results, so that they might be used to bolster his political position, and indeed reference to changes in the derating system was included in the king's speech in February.[134] However, in the meantime the extent of Unionist back-bench disaffection had become clearer, revealing the gravity of the government's political position. Private members held a secret meeting during the week-end of 9–10 January, with Norman Stronge, Glentoran's successor as chief whip, being subsequently informed of their deliberations and conclusions. The precise details of what they agreed are unclear but certainly they sought the introduction of younger men into the government, particularly as the preparation of comprehensive post-war policies was increasingly regarded as a matter of urgency. Brooke states that their demand was 'for the P.M. and cabinet to retire before the next election'. Spender records that thirteen backbenchers called for the resignation of Andrews, Bates and Barbour, adding that since their discussions were leaked to the press, it was 'perhaps a more serious crisis than any that had preceded it'.[135] Crucially both sources agree that, from the outset, the objective was a change of leadership and not just the replacement of some ministers.

The gravity of the 'crisis' was deepened by a general acceptance that the public had lost confidence in the government. One Home Affairs official stated that even 'if the present cabinet was able to introduce the millennium the electorate would still desire to have a change'.[136] The *News Letter*, which was sympathetic to Andrews, suggested that the backbench meeting was 'a reflection of a widespread feeling in the constituencies of which the two last by-elections gave unmistakeable evidence'.[137] Four weeks earlier Spender observed that unionist press comments on the need for 'young blood', though expressed in guarded terms, were 'significant pointers to the prime minister'.[138] *The Times* likewise reported that judging from recent by-election results 'the electorate . . . [was] . . . behind the demands for revision'.[139]

In addition, it is clear that within the government a number of junior ministers were deeply concerned at its lack of effective leadership and general incompetence. As minister of public security, MacDermott cannot have formed a very favourable impression of the government, and was certainly disappointed with the level of cooperation that he had then received from colleagues. He had also been obliged to carry much of the burden of criticism for the lack of adequate blitz preparation. In November 1941, he became attorney general. Andrews was said to have been disappointed with his performance as minister. He undoubtedly had a reputation for being 'somewhat discursive' and had found it difficult to establish a working relationship with Wickham, the ageing inspector general.[140] In his new position, his dissatisfaction with the government increased. In particular, he was critical of the defective machinery for resolving labour disputes, the ineffectualness of the Ministry of Labour, and the worsening strike position which he believed threatened to erode respect for law and order. He was also concerned about the prime minister's increasing unpopularity, Experience in his new position confirmed his earlier view that communal discipline could only be sustained by means of conscription and convinced him that stronger leadership was essential. Many years later he could clearly recall his deepening conviction that Andrews' appointment had been an error and that Brooke was 'the man', who could provide the government with the necessary energy and drive.[141]

W. B. Maginess, parliamentary secretary at the Ministry of Commerce, clearly shared MacDermott's doubts regarding Andrews' suitability for the premiership. In June 1942, he and Wilson Hungerford had informed the P.M. that his 'policy of appeasement was in their view one of the matters which had lowered the prestige of the government and that their continued support was dependent on more resolute leadership and a better appreciation of the war effort'.[142] They were convinced that as an absolute priority detailed post-war policies should be devised and publicised. Andrews' July speech and the confusion leading to the disbanding of the Brooke committee of which both were members, were unlikely to have dispelled earlier doubts or assuaged these criticisms, certainly as far as Maginess is concerned.

In January 1943, even the *News Letter* reflected on 'how little thought seems to have been given to the political future' by the government.[143] This aspect of policy is likewise unlikely to have impressed Maynard Sinclair. He was parliamentary secretary at the Ministry of Finance, a courageous and able minister, socially adept and instinctively liberal in his attitudes who was for the moment too young to challenge for the leadership himself.[144] He had cooperated with his two colleagues in preparing memoranda for cabinet on post-war policy.[145] He had later regarded Spender as entirely justified in sending the Treasury a draft of Andrews' speech. Soon afterwards, he met the chancellor in an effort to explain the political pressures acting on the prime minister, and came away believing that a sympathetic letter from the latter to Kingsley Wood would enable the matter to be closed.[146]

Again, in early December 1942, Sinclair had strongly disagreed with the P.M.s response to Dr Lyle's commons' motion favouring the creation of a Ministry of Health. He wrote to Andrews supporting the immediate establishment of such a department, and regarded his subsequent decision to set up a parliamentary committee as likely to bring discredit on the cabinet as it 'could only be regarded as a method of postponing a decision which could be given at once'. Earlier, he had courageously supported the Belfast county borough administration bill, despite his constituency association passing a resolution calling for his resignation for doing so. His position was made more difficult owing to the total unpredictability of government policy.[147] He informed the prime minister that he would oppose his amendment restoring to the corporation the power to make appointments. From his conversations with Spender, in June 1942, it is clear that he already believed in the necessity not just for cabinet changes but for Andrews' replacement.[148]

The prime minister's handling of the corporation question also severely strained the support for the government of William Lowry, parliamentary secretary at the ministry of home affairs. He had been very keenly committed to the Belfast county borough administration bill, urging the cabinet, in May 1942, that city administrators should be appointed immediately, and that there was 'no possible excuse . . . for . . . delay'.[149] When Andrews proposed his two amendments, the former considered resignation. He summarised his position in a sporting analogy, stating that 'the government had asked him to act as their jockey in a very important race and requested him to spare neither whip nor spur, but half-way through . . . they had suddenly asked him to change his mount'. In addition he had a totally unsatisfactory relationship with his minister Dawson Bates, whom he once described as 'our greatest unconscious humourist'. One Home Affairs official claimed that 'any decisions he might arrive at' with the parliamentary secretary were 'always discredited' by his superior. After becoming minister himself Lowry scrupulously avoided having any direct contact with his predecessor, delegating these duties to members of his department.[150] Nonetheless, for the moment he retained a residual loyalty for his cabinet colleagues.[151]

Thus amongst junior ministers there was a deep and widespread concern at the general incompetence of Andrews' leadership, and the threat that this represented to the future of unionism and preservation of law and order in

Ulster, as well as fears that it might prejudice the relationship between the Northern Ireland and imperial governments. Given the extent of this disaffection it is clear that even without the action taken by the backbenchers, some form of political crisis was looming in early 1943. One week before the private members met in early January MacDermott came to see Brooke to discuss 'the great agitation' in the country against the prime minister and ask him to meet Sinclair and Maginess. Sir Arthur Kelly also recalled at this time a number of junior ministers, led by these two parliamentary secretaries, coming to see him regarding the lack of 'punch in the government' and seeking his advice on how to proceed.[152] Likewise, Spender, after long 'very confidential' talks with Sinclair observed that the backbench meeting had, in fact, made the position of those ministers who felt the need for cabinet change more difficult because the former had 'raised the issue on personal grounds . . . [and] . . . made a direct attack on the prime minister'. Sir Wilfrid himself supported the replacement of those government members who were obviously incapable, but he did not favour a change of leadership as he was convinced that it would be difficult to form an alternative cabinet. However, he notes that neither Sinclair nor Brooke viewed 'the situation in quite the same light'.[153]

In the aftermath of the private members' discussions Brooke expressed a range of reactions. On the one hand he records feeling 'very sorry for the prime minister' and stated the opinion that he was having a 'very rough deal'.[154] Many years later, he was extremely critical of the backbenchers remarking that 'if they had gone to Andrews and voiced their complaints instead of holding secret meetings the crisis might have been avoided; at the very least, Andrews would have been spared much of the heartache he had to endure'.[155] On the other hand he also believed that 'the political situation . . . [would] . . . have to come to a head', that Andrews ought to 'retire at once' and indeed that it was 'difficult for any of us to remain'. He felt deeply despondent about the future of unionism in the province.[156]

When MacDermott came to see him on 4 January, Sir Basil refused to 'discuss . . . [his] . . . feelings towards the P.M.', stating that 'the only thing . . . [he could] . . . discuss was the actions and interests of the country and the party'. He stressed that 'they should tell . . . [Andrews] . . . what action they proposed to take before they took it in fairness to him'. He continues 'It is extremely awkward for me as I don't want to be disloyal, . . . I must see to it that the P.M. is not placed in a difficult position'.[157] Ten days later when Sinclair came to discuss the 'crisis', Brooke again emphasised that 'he must on no account take any action without informing the P.M.'. Soon afterwards the former met Andrews, 'expressed his criticism of . . . [him] . . . in the frankest possible manner' and offered his resignation. He, however, agreed to retract it, on the premier's request, 'whilst questions of reorganisation . . . [were] . . . under discussion'.[158]

Meanwhile, Spender was confident that Unionist headquarters would, as in the past, succeed in getting 'the government around a very difficult corner', by causing 'dissension in the ranks of [its] critics' and taking advantage of the lack of obvious leadership amongst the backbenchers. But he did expect party officials, as on previous occasions, to make concessions and assumed that Milne Barbour would be asked to resign. In fact, on 13 January the latter agreed 'to leave himself in the prime minister's hands', after talks with Glentoran and Stronge.[159]

However, from the outset, the *News Letter* noted 'in official circles . . . little disposition to attach importance to'[160] the backbench meeting and indeed, it was soon obvious that Andrews intended to fight the malcontents. On 12 January, he held a cabinet on the crisis, without an agenda or recorded conclusions, where he indicated that he would meet the private members and then the full party, and would stress that he had the full confidence of the British government and defend his ministers including Bates.[161] Three days later, after confronting the backbenchers, he seemed confident, commenting to the press 'I don't look very worried, do I'?[162] By the eve of his meeting with the parliamentary party, Spender who had gradually modified his earlier opinion, expected him to replace any junior ministers who had been openly hostile. Such a step the former considered likely to cause further divisions within the movement, though he felt relief that Barbour might now be reprieved.[163]

On 19 January, forty-four M.P.s and senators met for two hours at Glengall Street, the unionist party headquarters. Eight of those who participated, whilst protesting their 'loyalty' and paying tribute to the years of service rendered by senior members, spoke of the need for a 'new team' or a 'change of leadership'. Otherwise, they predicted electoral disaster for the party. Amongst them was, William Dowling, the backbench spokesman, and Henry Mulholland, the speaker of the Commons, who had already written to Andrews suggesting that he retire.[164] It included also three junior ministers J. C. MacDermott, Dehra Parker and Brian Maginess. MacDermott spoke of the 'ample evidence of hostility to the government, . . . a change [was] essential'. Curiously, in view of his attitude later, Lowry defended his colleagues. Andrews who had apparently hoped that he would not be asked to make cabinet changes, spoke for half-an-hour. After further pro-government speeches, a resolution was passed unanimously stating 'that the present is not an opportune time for discussing the administration, that the subject requires careful . . . consideration, and that . . . the prime minister should not be asked to make a further statement on the matter until a party meeting is convened by him for the purpose'.[165]

Thus an impasse had been reached with the case for change being forcefully expressed, and the prime minister making a reply which had failed to placate his critics. The resolution placed upon Andrews the onus of making the next move. On 26 January, he told Brooke that he was 'trying to make up his mind on the resignation question' and expressed a sentiment with which Sir Basil agreed, to the effect that his decision 'must be for the good of Ulster'.[166] Meanwhile speculation regarding the political future was rife in the press, amongst politicians and officials, including the governor, and in the country. There was a widely held view that the prime minister should at least make changes in his cabinet.[167] To Brooke the situation was 'most unsatisfactory' and he reflected on the general lack of 'confidence in the present regime'. He had not spoken at the party meeting but it confirmed his opinion. He recorded that he was 'surprised at the number [of backbenchers] who thought there should be a change. Even some of the parliamentary secretaries spoke strongly'.[168]

He discussed the issue with Andrews on at least four occasions over the next four weeks. Sir Basil was sympathetic, and sought to allay any fears the P.M. might have had with regard to intriguing, but offered advice which was as consistent as it was apparently unwelcome. He told him on 2 February that 'as far as [he] could see there were three alternatives. One was that the backbenchers should withdraw, *in toto*, their remarks about him; the second was that the P.M. should resign; and the third that the government should resign'. Privately he believed that, given the attitude of the private members, Andrews had no real choice but to resign. He also offered to resign himself as deputy prime minister, regarding it as necessary out of 'fairness to the prime minister' and himself, so that 'it could not be said that whatever recommendation . . . [he made was] . . . self interested'. Two weeks later, on 16 February, Sir Basil repeated these views when Andrews reopened discussion on the political situation, but concluded 'we do not seem to be making much progress'. On this occasion, he notes 'I told him that I could not possibly continue if the backbenchers were opposed to the government'.[169]

The prime minister ignored both Brooke's advice and his threats. Immediately after the party meeting on 19 January, the *News Letter* had reported 'indications' that on the issue of cabinet changes Andrews' 'attitude was stiffening' and, predicted, with less than enthusiasm, that he might seek a vote of confidence at the annual conference of the U.U.C.[170] On that same day Glentoran told Spender that 'a move was afoot amongst the Orange lodges to support Mr Andrews as prime minister on the grounds that he was a strong supporter of the working classes', a reference to his involvement in the Ulster Unionist Labour Association. Sir Wilfred also noted that Andrews was 'anxious to put forward a lot of names for political honours', so 'drastically' cutting once again nominations from the civil service. He claimed that this bait helped influence the attitude of one of Belfast's morning newspapers.[171] At the same time through his own speeches around the province and the king's speech, with its reference to strengthening the special powers act, commitment to increased grants for local authorities and support for the Beveridge report, Andrews was clearly bidding to increase support for his government.[172]

Meanwhile, on 23 February, the Unionist backbenchers, having just returned for a new parliamentary session, were told at a brief meeting that no decision regarding cabinet changes would be made before Easter, and, in the meantime, the P.M. appealed for their support. To Spender this was a political blunder which would, he believed, make it more difficult for Andrews to effect those replacements which were 'very desirable and indeed inevitable'. This view was shared by Gransden and by Wickham who regarded Dawson Bates' prolonged illness as an opportune moment for him to retire in a graceful way.[173] The latter's credibility suffered further due to large-scale I.R.A. prison escapes from Belfast and Londonderry which were assisted by the collusion and incompetence of wardens.[174] Andrews' hesitance merely seemed to exacerbate doubts as to his suitability for leadership. Earlier the electorate had dealt a further 'severe blow' to the government in a by-election in West Belfast where the unionist vote fell by over 30 percent from 1935, whilst the total nationalist vote actually increased. Meanwhile, 34,000 man-days were lost through strike action in February and the docks were paralysed by a dispute the following month. Within the party, backbench hostility continued unabated. The Young Unionist Association was scathingly critical both of the composition of the cabinet and of the whole moribund party organisation which it regarded as dominated by an indolent, ineffective geriatric clique, who in the words of Maurice May had 'lost the confidence of the unionist electorate'.[175]

There were also indications of divisions within the government itself. In late February, the *Sunday Dispatch* published an article by the marquess of Donegall which claimed that the cabinet was 'split from top to bottom', particularly over the issue of cabinet restructuring, with Andrews' obstinacy being supported by Bates and Glentoran. The P.M. was incensed and considered taking legal action.[176] His sensitivity was no doubt a measure of the accuracy of the account. Brooke observed at this time that 'the government was not working as a team' and that 'everyone [was] looked upon with suspicion'.[177] He once more discussed resignation with Andrews but agreed to remain at his post when requested to do so by the prime minister. However, he again stressed that 'when so many of the parliamentary party was in opposition [he] considered it a very bad thing for any government to' stay in office. Perhaps tempting providence, he also told him that if 'I had been told by my supporters what he had been told, I would not have stayed on for a minute'.[178] Sir Basil also discussed the crisis with MacDermott and Lowry and told them that as he had no confidence in the government, he 'really ought to resign . . . but on the other hand I cannot create a crisis'. His advice to them was 'that the right thing to do was to wait until the prime minister had seen the backbenchers'.[179] Meanwhile, in early March, newspapers reported that three junior ministers had resigned but had been prevailed upon by Andrews to continue to serve. MacDermott also recalled the prime minister refusing to accept his resignation at this time. When the former indicated that this might cause him future embarrassment, he was told that he could feel free to criticise the government.[180]

A further party meeting was arranged for 19 March, apparently indicating that Andrews was ready to reply to demands for changes in his cabinet. On this occasion he stated categorically at the outset that he would not tolerate any interference in the selection of ministers, that the present team was the best available at a critical time, and concluded by saying that he would leave the decision in the hands of the party. A vote of confidence in the prime minister was then moved and challenged by Edmond Warnock who commented that though the former had 'his good points . . . drastic measures must be taken . . . [including] . . . changes in the government'. Finally the original motion was reluctantly withdrawn and another, seconded by Glentoran was passed unanimously. It stated that 'having heard the statement by the prime minister, we request that he should reconsider the question of changes in his cabinet'. After Andrews had replied briefly to his critics the three-hour proceedings were concluded for the first time in twenty-two years of party meetings, by a rendering of the national anthem in a vain attempt to recapture a lost unity.[181]

Brooke described the meeting as 'very outspoken as before. The M.P.s asked the prime minister to make the change but this merely acknowledges that this is his right as indeed it is . . . [and] . . . in no way withdrew their criticism'. He added 'I must ask Andrews what his plans are and tell him that it cannot go on'.[182] In Spender's view, the prime minister had simply miscalculated the mood of the party. He wrote 'I imagine [he] expected that members would acquiesce in his firm line . . . [but] . . . he has found that criticism of the cabinet cannot be dealt with in this way and that it will be essential for him to make some changes if he is to retain his leadership'.[183]

Though Spender's analysis is probably accurate, the prime minister did not share his deductions. Andrews was driven to introspection but not to any change in his unyielding response. Days after the party meeting, he spoke to Sir Wilfrid of his 'very special difficulties', and of how his father had been correct in supporting nine county partition as 'Northern Ireland was too small for its own government, . . . people go to the prime minister over trifles'. He also asked Sir Wilfrid about the number of catholics in the higher branches of the civil service stating that 'we could only take . . . those who are loyal', and that 'any such senior appointment would mean the end of the government'. Spender was able to reassure him but regarded it as unwise for the prime minister to concern himself about such matters.[184]

Meanwhile Andrews sought to rally his support by making a round of the local Unionist associations in the country and seeking a vote of confidence at the annual meeting of the U.U.C. That he would succeed in the latter was never in doubt, and as Spender noted he would then 'have to decide his attitude towards those members of the government who . . . [had] . . . been criticising the constitution of his cabinet'. He was distressed when informed by Gransden that the prime minister would ask his critics to resign and probably replace them with older men. Both Sir Wilfrid and the cabinet secretary were convinced that this would 'inevitably' split the party.[185]

On 25 March, Andrews explained his intentions to Brooke indicating that he would 'wait until after the meeting of the council and then see the M.P.s'. Both then and subsequently Sir Basil regarded his response as wrong, believing that it was 'a great error of judgement' and that his 'leadership was at fault'.[186] At the time, he immediately suggested to the prime minister that 'the M.P.s were the only thing that mattered as they were the machinery for implementing policy'. Three days later, he wrote a letter to Andrews, with his wife's assistance, which 'emphasised again that votes of confidence from the associations were of no value unless he got the M.P.s to withdraw their opposition'.[187] On 2 April, he discussed its contents with the prime minister for one and a half hours, once more arguing that going to the associations would 'not help' but 'would drive a wedge' between the constituencies and their parliamentary representatives. He repeated that 'unless . . . [Andrews] . . . could get the M.P.s to withdraw [he] could not continue'. The latter promised to let Brooke know when he intended to call a party meeting. Sir Basil commented: 'I rather felt he did not want to do so'. Meanwhile, he told MacDermott that he 'could not go further with the prime minister'.[188]

The Ulster Unionist Council met on 16 April, with its largest attendance on record. Brooke records that there were some 'pretty hot speeches'. The News Letter referred later to 'plenty of plain speaking' and indeed the mood of the meeting was the subject of conflicting interpretations in its correspondence columns. Certainly a resolution of 'unabated confidence' in the prime minister was passed by acclamation.[189] Andrews later informed Churchill that out of 750 delegates there had been just two or three dissidents.[190] Possibly, as Kelly suggests, he now genuinely believed that the crisis would pass, given this support from the council, the resolutions from the local Unionist associations, and the assumed support of a majority of the party at Stormont. The Belfast Telegraph however issued a clear warning that his position was not secure, stating that if the vote was regarded merely as a mandate for the old guard, then the signs were that disunity would be a 'continuing business'.[191]

After the meeting Spender noted 'one point which caused . . . [him] . . . a little anxiety, . . . the prime minister seemed to indicate that there would be no change in the composition of his cabinet'.[192] He recalled ominously that certain of the junior ministers had pledged to resign unless such changes took place. This point had not been missed by the junior ministers themselves. Andrews had, in fact, stated categorically that

so long as I remain prime minister I must be left free to choose my colleagues as every prime minister in the world is free to do. I will not simply for the sake of change replace men who have given, and are still giving valuable service to Ulster.[193]

On 19 and 21 April, Maginess, Sinclair and Parker discussed their position with Brooke, all three of them 'eager to push in their resignations right away'. Sir Basil's advice was that they should 'hold [their] . . . hand' until the party meeting. This suggestion they appear to have accepted. Meanwhile on 20 April, Brooke impressed on Andrews that he 'must call a . . . meeting at once'. Next day he was able to tell MacDermott with whom he was in close contact, that the prime minister had agreed to summon the Unionist M.P.s without the Senate, whose attendance on earlier occasions Brooke had opposed. Possibly these threats of resignation by government members had forced Andrews to recall the parliamentary party. Once again, Sir Basil 'put his resignation in . . . [the prime minister's] . . . hands, in order to let [himself] have an opportunity to speak.[194] At preceding meetings he had remained silent during discussions on the political crisis. This 'suggestion' subsequently leaked to the press leading to Brooke denying that he had resigned but adding 'it depends what the party does at Wednesday's meeting'.[195]

The meeting took place on 28 April amidst widespread rumours that as many as six ministers had resigned and fervent official denials that this was the case. Even cabinet ministers complained of being 'totally ignorant' of what was happening, and that Mr Andrews had 'not given any information'.[196] However, it was widely accepted that matters would now come to a head and evident that Andrews' U.U.C. resolution had done nothing to ease his position or silence the demand for changes in his cabinet. On the contrary, as the *News Letter* observed, the divisions had 'become sharper'. It declared: 'never was there a time less suitable for petty intriguing or the pursuance of personal aims'. Spender canvassed support for a compromise solution whereby Andrews would retain the leadership but would replace weak colleagues. He concluded 'I am afraid that my initiative is not likely to find favour'. But he foresaw one 'benefit, . . . there presumably will be the makings of an alternative cabinet'.[197] As for Andrews himself, any earlier euphoria had clearly evaporated as the party meeting loomed nearer, and he made a final belated effort to preserve his position. After cabinet on 28 April, he approached Brooke who records that

He wanted me . . . to compromise, I agreeing to help him form a new government. I was quite unable to agree because the only constitutional way is for me to go if I disagree with the prime minister and he refuses to take my advice on the handling of the crisis.[198]

Later that day thirty-three Unionist M.P.s gathered at Glengall Street, each pledged to secrecy regarding the proceedings of the next three and a half hours.[199] Though senators were not invited, J. H. Robb, leader of that house, was at one point consulted and conveyed the views of the upper chamber. The meeting began with a brief statement by Andrews on the political position. In strong fighting phrases he defended his colleagues, insisted once more that he must be free to appoint his own ministers, and stated that he would continue to serve as leader if a majority were prepared to follow him. A further twenty-four speakers followed of whom twelve were on record as favouring change. The first was Brooke who had not hitherto spoken publicly on the crisis. He noted:

I made my position clear and explained that I told the prime minister on 16 February, that there were only three ways of handling the position. One, was to convince the M.P.s by argument that they were wrong. . . . Two, that the members of the government should resign and leave him to form a new government. Three, that he should have to resign himself. I explained that to my mind the M.P.s were the only people who mattered in this dispute and that votes of confidence would not convince . . . [them] . . . that they were wrong.[200]

Subsequently, at least two compromise proposals were put forward and rejected. The minutes refer to a suggestion that 'all members of the government hand in their resignation and that the prime minister and Sir Basil Brooke be asked to reform the government'.[201] A number of ministers stated that they would place their resignations in Andrews' hands if it would ease his position. Some critics, however, were not satisfied and demanded a change of leadership. Crucially Sir Basil himself again rejected the suggestion. He described being urged by 'different people, including Lord Glentoran' but that he 'turned the suggestion down flat'. He added: 'it strikes me that anything said against the prime minister shows that there must be a lack of confidence [in him] and, although I did not say it, it seems obvious that the suggestion underlying this idea is that . . . [Andrews] . . . is not competent to select his own colleagues'.[202] An alternative proposal was put forward by MacDermott who suggested that the prime minister should remain in office until the estimates had passed through the commons, and then hand over to Brooke. The minutes record only Andrews' rejection.[203]

Though no formal vote was taken, as the meeting proceeded Andrews probably appreciated that he might not even secure the support of a majority of those present and was apparently so advised by Glentoran. It was transparently clear that even if he were successful, a considerable number intended to persist in their opposition, six members of the government would resign and the party would be irretrievably split. Spender observed that some members hesitated to give the prime minister their support when they realised how deep a division it would cause in the party and how detrimental it would be to the unionist cause. Sir Wilfrid considered that the outcome was a considerable 'shock' for Andrews, as it was also for Glentoran who finally conceded that he 'knew when he was beaten'. The latter was probably the 'seasoned campaigner' privately consulted by Andrews in an adjacent room on whether it would be worthwhile to fight on in order to preserve the leadership. When the premier received no encouragement, after about three hours discussion, he finally decided to resign. Before the members assembled, a resolution was proposed that 'the party should go forward unitedly and that any disagreement that had been shown should be healed up now'.[204] No vote is recorded and the proceedings were adjourned until the following Monday. Andrews left Glengall Street with

Brooke. Next day he reported to the governor. No formal letters were exchanged.[205]

A period of delay and confusion followed. In part, perhaps this was inevitable for, as the assiduous Spender noted, 'there was no provision in the order of procedure for the post of next prime minister',[206] and he therefore advised Kelly to consult officials in Britain on what should be done. It was generally assumed that Andrews would advise the governor to send for Brooke, and that he did so is stated in the Ulster Unionist Council's annual report for 1943.[207] At the time, Sir Wilfrid wrote 'there is no definite knowledge of whom . . . Andrews . . . is proposing to suggest, . . . I fancy it would be difficult for any minister other than Brooke to form a cabinet'. He added that if Sir Basil failed 'it would mean a general election'.[208] The Communist party was so certain of Brooke's succession that it sent him a telegram demanding Beattie's inclusion in his government. Similarly the *News Letter*, on 29 April, reported that Andrews would resign and recommend Brooke as his successor. However, next day it bore the headline 'Andrews still premier' and quoted as evidence the bland court circular, issued the previous evening from Government House, which simply stated that 'Andrews, the prime minister of Northern Ireland, had an audience of the governor today'.[209] Spender deduced that 'the latter had merely asked . . . [the prime minister] . . . to continue in office until his successor . . . [had] . . . formed a cabinet'. He continued, 'it is quite obvious . . . [that Andrews] . . . has suggested to the governor that he should send for Brooke', and that Sir Basil 'was unable to make any contacts with those whom he is preparing to approach before he has been invited by the governor to undertake the task'.[210]

Certainly, Brooke himself heard nothing on 29 April. Even the next day, he records 'no decision as to P.M. has yet come through'. However, the same diary entry continues 'Commander Henderson rang to say that the governor wished to see me tomorrow at 11 am, presumably this is to ask me to form a government'. Also Gransden called to discuss the adjournment of the house, and suggest that Brooke put down a vote of confidence motion in the new government. On 1 May, over lunch at Government House, the governor 'invited [him] to form a cabinet'.[211] Immediately, he returned to Colebrooke, to catch a 1 lb. 6 oz. trout in the Narrows. However for some the confusion persisted. Barbour continued to complain that he felt 'uncomfortable' and 'knew nothing'. Even when it had been substantiated that Andrews had resigned, he was uncertain whether this meant he had also resigned, or ought now to resign, or alternatively would remain in office until his successor was appointed. Spender, for once, could offer no definite answers.[212]

It seems improbable that Andrews did after all advise the governor to send for Brooke when tendering his own resignation. If he had done, one might have expected him to mention the fact in his explanatory letter to Churchill, written on 30 April. It merely states 'You are probably aware that I have asked . . . the governor to accept my resignation . . . which he will no doubt do within the next few days'. A Home Office report, bearing the same date, adds 'it is understood that Sir Basil Brooke will have an audience during the week-end',[213] likewise giving no indication that Andrews had recommended Brooke. Though Spender considered that Andrews had accepted the 'new position far more cheerfully than seemed possible in the first instance', in fact the crisis had generated considerable personal bitterness. Thus when Brooke wrote to Andrews expressing regret at their recent 'differences of opinion', he observed after receiving the latter's reply 'he thinks that I have manoeuvred against him, which is, of course untrue'.[214] Their conflicting interpretations regarding these events seem also to have arisen when Sir Basil met the governor. Apparently Andrews had a good relationship with the duke of Abercorn, having earned his gratitude by preventing him from being replaced some time earlier.[215] Sir Basil recorded after his audience with his grace that 'he had not got a clear picture of . . . the cause of the crisis before'. Earlier Brooke had suggested that the governor was 'annoyed that the papers have made statements [regarding the succession] which . . . [had] . . . no authority from him'.[216]

It is also significant that the previously friendly relationship between Andrews and Gransden cooled markedly, due to the fact that the cabinet secretary had contacted Brooke on 30 April, in order to discuss parliamentary procedure, before the latter had been to Government House.[217] In addition, a number of well informed contemporaries did not believe that Andrews suggested Brooke's name to the governor. These include MacDermott[218] and Spender himself, who in early May recorded 'certain developments of the cabinet crisis are only now beginning to emerge. I gather that when Andrews handed in his resignation, he suggested to the governor that he should invite Lord Glentoran to form a cabinet but the latter was unsuccessful in doing so and that it was subsequently that the governor asked Brooke to become prime minister'.[219] Brooke's son also believes that Andrews suggested Glentoran but continues 'I believe that Abercorn took soundings and did not ask Glentoran'.[220] A recent account suggests that 'a section of the party . . . thought that . . . Lord Glentoran should seek support. He was unwilling to let his name go forward but the small element of uncertainty led to the delay of the official announcement. The governor sounded representative opinion'.[221]

Andrews certainly felt profoundly unhappy about the manner in which at least one of his colleagues had been treated, and expressed this to Churchill on 10 May, stating 'I deeply regret that Lord Glentoran is not included in the new government'. He added with dubious accuracy, 'I feel sure that he would have been included had he not sacrificed himself in standing loyally behind me'.[222] This section of his reply, which it was thought would remind readers too much of the quarrelsome characteristics of many British citizens, prompted imperial officials to decide that his letter ought not to be published. Glentoran did of course retain the presidency of the U.U.C. until his death in 1950, when Brooke succeeded him.[223] The position gave him effective control of the party organisation outside parliament.

An additional cause of Andrews' hurt and disappointment, which he indicated to Kelly, was his own exclusion from Brooke's cabinet.[224] He had told Sir Basil that he would be willing to serve under his leadership. He believed that he still had a contribution to make, given his prolonged ministerial experience, particularly in the circumstances of war. Though he assured Churchill that he would remain in parliament and with his late government colleagues endeavour 'to be helpful',[225] the absence of departmental responsibility was bound to leave an immense gap in his life. He found little solace in becoming a companion of honour as he cared little for honours, though Spender, apparently erroneously, assumed that he had been offered and had rejected a peerage.[226] Almost certainly he did derive some consolation from Churchill's widely publicised tribute to his political achievements, expressed as his son remarked in 'such an exceptional way'. Overall, Kelly thought that Brooke had been right to exclude Andrews as the latter's presence would, he believed, have been 'embarrassing'.[227] In any case Sir Basil decided to appoint almost a completely new and therefore inexperienced cabinet, chose not to select a deputy and warned the ministers at their first meeting that 'no one was to consider himself permanently in the job'.[228]

It is impossible now to judge with assurance whether earlier similarly extensive cabinet replacements could have saved Andrews' premiership. Certainly the optimum time for change was when the latter formed his new government after Craigavon's death, rather than the spring of 1943. By mid January of that year the recalcitrant backbenchers, a number of junior ministers and Brooke himself already believed that a change of leadership was required and not just revisions in cabinet composition. The conviction had taken root that a crucial source of the government's ineffectiveness over the previous two years lay with the prime minister himself.

Andrews' handling of the final crisis can only have confirmed these deepening doubts as to his suitability for the highest office. He showed a surprising unwillingness to make the changes urged upon him, particularly in view of his government's almost unbroken record of concession to external pressures. Not until his last full day as P.M. did he make a suggestion to Brooke which appeared to envisage immediate and extensive cabinet restructuring. Prior to that, according to the observations of Spender and Gransden, the only change which he actively and consistently sought to implement was a purge of his junior minister critics, a course which they both strongly opposed. When he wrote to Midgley, soon after the Willowfield by-election, suggesting that they should now 'work together on those matters in which . . . [they were] . . . mutually interested',[229] it was not to offer him a seat on the cabinet, but on Brooke's Production Advisory Committee.

In part the motives behind Andrews, inflexibility might be regarded as entirely honourable. The *News Letter*, on the day of his anticipated resignation, wrote that he had 'sacrificed himself on the altar of loyalty'.[230] Next day, he himself explained to Churchill that he had refused to replace 'colleagues who had served Ulster faithfully for many years and who in . . . [his] . . . opinion . . . [were] . . . the best available at the moment to continue to do so'.[231] During the commons motion of censure on Bates, Andrews defended his minister partly on the grounds that the latter had enjoyed the confidence and respect of Carson and of Craig and indeed of his own father.[232] Spender similarly recognised this motive noting that 'it . . . [was] . . . a pity that Mr Andrews had allowed his friendship for his colleagues to cause him to hesitate in making changes'. On an earlier occasion, however, he underlined the fact that such a course was not necessarily laudable, stating 'Andrews seems to regard loyalty to his colleagues as being more important than ensuring that the destinies of the state are guided by those who are able to do so'.[233]

Spender also indicates that a multiplicity of other factors influenced Andrews' judgement. The former suspected that Dawson Bates was not replaced owing to his serious and continuing financial problems, and out of consideration for the fact that as minister responsible for security he had for so long run the risk of I.R.A. attack. In addition, as early as June 1941, when considering Bates' ministerial incompetence, Sir Wilfred referred to Andrews' 'fear . . . to make cabinet changes', and, with considerable prescience, concluded that they were unlikely to occur 'unless parliament forces the hand of the cabinet'.[234] Substance is added to this imputation of political weakness by evidence that Andrews recognized the inadequacies of some of his colleagues, and may not after all in all honesty have regarded them as 'the best available'.[235] He expressed to Spender his concern that the prestige and influence of the Ministry of Finance might have suffered as a consequence of Milne Barbour's appointment and indeed he appears to have agonised over promoting him in the first place. Likewise, in March 1943, he confided to Sir Wilfrid that he was not satisfied with the 'dilatory' and inefficient administration of the Ministry of Home Affairs.[236] Andrews' relationship with Bates may have been less amicable than it appeared. A British official observed in 1941, that 'though [they were] outwardly friendly . . . I am told [they are] in fact by no means so!'[237] Spender claimed that when he was asked to retire the latter categorically refused to do so,[238] and later concluded that if all [Andrews'] ministers had acted as responsibly as Barbour, 'the present position would never have arisen'.[239] Gransden implied that Bates was not alone in objecting to leaving his post. One unnamed cabinet member is reported as saying that he did 'not intend to retire . . . except by the hand of God'.[240]

Andrews' inflexibility may also have been partly caused by the manner in which the issue of government restructuring was initially raised by the backbenchers: their use of secret meetings, producing a list of named ministers to be replaced including himself, and the further indiscretion of leaking the proceedings to the press. He regarded cabinet appointments as very much a prerogative of the prime minister. When appointing MacDermott's successor he expressed the opinion that he had 'full powers' to do so, and other ministers must accept it as a 'fait accompli'.[241] In addition, more than one contemporary commented on the stubbornness of Andrews' administration comparing it unfavourably with that of his predecessor. One M.P. suggested in mid-1942, that the province was 'travelling in seven-league boots towards dictatorship'. Even Spender observed that in the summoning of Ministry of Finance officials and issuing of directives to them, Andrews seemed to be emulating the führer.[242]

Finally Andrews' reaction to the crisis would suggest a considerable measure of simple political miscalculation. Persistently he seems to have believed that he could silence his critics by a resolute, inflexible stand. Brooke describes his ultimate failure to do so as 'a terrible blow' to the prime minister.[243] In his responses, Andrews relied too heavily on Glentoran's advice. He regarded him as one who 'knows Ulster's ways as few do' and whose 'advice is always sound'.[244] MacDermott more perceptively described him as 'not one of the party's wise men',[245] a viewpoint shared by Spender. To the latter the whole crisis underlined the extent to which the U.U.C. and Unionist headquarters had ceased 'to represent the people', and had 'got out of touch with the electorate'.[246] After all, the absolute necessity for cabinet change at least was accepted by senior ministers such as Barbour and Brooke, high-ranking officials including Spender, Gransden and Wickham, and influential sections of the unionist press, as well as those backbenchers, junior ministers and young unionists whose strident demands are so closely identified with the government's fall.

It may be that Andrews never had a true appreciation of the nature of the pressures which forced his resignation. In his explanatory letter to Churchill, he outlined the cause and scope of the revolt. He stated that:

a number of the members of the Unionist party in the house . . . [desired] . . . a change of leadership on the grounds that I . . . [had] . . . refused to accede to demands that I should ask for the resignation of certain colleagues.

He continued;

In the Northern Ireland parliament the numbers are so few a small group could make my life as leader . . . very difficult and in the interests of party unity . . . I feel that the course I have taken was . . . the right one.[247]

He stressed how 'gratified' he had felt at the vote of confidence he had received from the U.U.C. His son, who indicated that his father used to 'tell [him] every day of his problems', similarly claimed that:

the real reason . . . [for the revolt was] . . . to have new faces in the government. . . . My father refused to change two . . . senior ministers to save his own position, . . . he preferred to sacrifice himself for party unity at Stormont, even when in the country he had the confidence of the people.[248]

Andrews also believed that Brooke had manoeuvred against him, a presumption which contributed to the legacy of bitterness and division bequeathed by these events, and to Brooke's difficulties during his first years as premier. It was an interpretation given some credence in the press. The *Manchester Guardian* referred to Brooke as having 'led the revolt'.[249] The doubts of some historians as to the objectivity of his advice and actions appear to be confirmed by his comment many years later that he 'always strove to reach as far as . . . [he] . . . could in anything . . . [he] . . . attempted and strove to extend whatever talents . . . [he] . . . had to the maximum'.[250] In addition, in an untypically ambiguous passage, Spender wrote in late January 1943 of 'the . . . impression being conveyed that most of the criticism of the cabinet was due to certain aristocratic quarters who thought that Andrews was too radical'. From the newspapers, Sir Wilfred considered:

there is some indication this is the course of action being followed and there is little doubt where the inspiration is coming from. . . . It means that certain elements in the cabinet are engaged in a campaign against certain other elements who as far as I know have in no way attempted to undermine the prime minister's position.[251]

This may be an oblique reference to Brooke which unfortunately Sir Wilfrid does not refer to or illuminate elsewhere.

Brooke at the time and subsequently dismissed all such allegations as being without foundation, and stressed that his accession 'cost . . . [him] . . . more worry and problems than anything else in . . . [his] . . . long life'.[252] His career was not marked by overriding political ambition. In the weeks after Craigavon's death, he stated clearly his objections to being made minister of finance, the natural stepping stone to the premiership. He enthusiastically accepted the Ministry of Commerce, arguably the least attractive position in the government. Also he unhesitatingly supported Andrews' succession, so earning his gratitude, and urged on him the necessity of strengthening his administration by making changes in his cabinet.[253] He even offered his own resignation to facilitate the process. Once more he had offered to resign over the electricity question in 1942.

Such behaviour would suggest not only a lack of political ambition but perhaps even the lack of complete commitment to a career in politics. Many years later, Brooke referred to becoming premier as 'perhaps the pinnacle of . . . [his] . . . achievement', and observed 'I cannot say that I was ever an ambitious man in the sense that I put success before anything else'.[254] It is improbable that politics played so central a part in his life as it did for Andrews. He enjoyed a wide range of interests, most of which centred around his estates and his life as a country gentleman. In December 1941, whilst indulging in his favourite weekend sporting pastimes, shooting and fishing, he noted that it was 'better than worrying about electricity'.[255] His keen and active interest in farming continued as he sought to raise Colebrooke's output in response to the wartime emergency. He remained, with some reluctance, chairman of the county council and played a leading role in the Fermanagh Unionist Association.

At the same time he encouraged and followed with pleasure and pride as well as some sense of foreboding the emerging military careers of his three sons. On 26 March 1943, he recorded in his diary 'It's a sad day, the War Office reported that Julian had been killed in action'.[256] He had received the news whilst attending a conference on the dock strike at Stormont and 'with characteristic fortitude . . . put the telegram in his pocket, left the room for a short time to break the news to Lady Brooke, and continued to deal with the business in hand without informing his colleagues'.[257] On 25 April, the day before the vital party meeting, he attended a memorial service on the estate which, he noted, 'neither Cynthia nor I were very keen about . . . but the whole parish wanted . . . to show their sympathy, . . . it was very touching, . . . naturally, an upsetting experience'.[258] Meanwhile in 1941, Lady Brooke had herself suffered her first prolonged period of serious illness.

However, war brought pleasure as well as pain. It may well be true to say that during these years nothing gave him greater pleasure than his regular meetings with Alan Brooke, sometimes joined by other generals. He delighted in joining their discussions on grand strategy, or listening to the latest informed gossip on the level of German casualties, or hearing his uncle expostulate on Stalin's enigmatic personality. After one such meeting, he observed, 'I don't think I had ever been so interested in my life', and after another, he stated categorically that it was 'the most interesting dinner that . . . [he had] . . . ever attended'.[259] The exhilaration which he derived from these occasions recalls his remark to Macready, twenty-five years earlier: 'I am a soldier, not a politician'.[260] It is noteworthy that his social life revolved around his family, landed society, military personnel, but rarely politicians.

This no doubt partially accounts for the fact that Brooke entirely failed to anticipate the timing and scale of the revolt against the government. Many years later, he recalled that his work at the Ministry of Commerce 'occupied all [his] time, [he] lived, ate and thought it, and in a way . . . enjoyed it. Then suddenly [he] found himself in the middle of a . . . political crisis'.[261] It is undoubtedly true that he was absorbed by the responsibilities of his department. When previewing the new year in December 1942, his ambitions centred on reducing unemployment and on hopes for allied victory.[262] Though he had been concerned for some time about the government's inept performance and diminishing popularity, he was genuinely surprised, in January 1943, at the degree of hostility displayed towards it by both private members and junior ministers. As the extent of the crisis became clearer, and some suggested that he himself might replace Andrews, he privately recorded his doubts as to the desirability of the premiership and some uneasiness regarding his own suitability for the office. When, on 14 January, *The Times* observed that in unionist circles his name was being 'freely mentioned as the ultimate successor to the prime minister', he noted 'I might be alright as a departmental chief, . . . I don't know that I would have the political acumen to make a good prime minister'. Shortly afterwards he stated that 'no-one with any ambition would do it as to my mind the political position here from the unionist point of view is as bad as it could be'.[263]

His role during the crucial weeks which followed was passive rather than active. He was acutely aware of the delicacy of his position, observing that 'as the obvious successor, I was open to the accusation of conniving at Andrews' downfall'. He claimed that his responses were 'all directed to keeping the party together and preventing the downfall of the government'. He undoubtedly had throughout his career a strong sense of cabinet responsibility and of loyalty to his colleagues. Many years later he observed with justification that he 'at no time had . . . any contact with those in the backbenches who were organising the revolt . . . [and] . . . in fact . . . was not even aware of their efforts until the crisis had developed beyond the point of no return'.[264]

As for the junior ministers, it is significant that it was they who established contact with Brooke. They did so in order to discuss their concern at the unpopularity and ineffectiveness of the government and seek advice on how to proceed. The talent of the dissidents weakens the credibility of any claim that they were used or manipulated to engineer a change of leadership. Many years later, both MacDermott and Kelly in recalling the events of these crucial weeks shared the view that Brooke did not intrigue, or canvass or conduct any personal campaign though he was, of course, aware that others were considering him as an alternative prime minister.[265] The *Belfast Telegraph* likewise described him as 'someone who had no personal ambitions throughout all this business'.[266] When he was approached Brooke did not minimise the gravity of the crisis nor did Spender whose advice was similarly sought. Brooke stated repeatedly that those involved must inform Andrews of their views and intended actions. He also consistently advised the junior ministers that they should not act impulsively but allow the prime minister time to respond to their criticisms.

Meanwhile he gave Andrews clear, though for the recipient unpalatable advice, having already privately came to the conclusion that 'there was no alternative but for [the prime minister] to go'. From the beginning of February, he advised him 'to face the party, and if he could not persuade them, he must ask us to resign, so that he might reform the government, and failing that he must resign himself'.[267] Andrews did not act on this advice but instead attempted to rally his support through resolutions and speeches outside parliament. His tour of the constituencies was described by the American consul in Belfast as 'not . . . so much in the party interest as in the maintenance of his own position'.[268] It was a response which Brooke regarded as both inappropriate and divisive. On 28 April, after almost three months of apparent inflexibility and on the eve of the critical party meeting, Andrews suggested that Brooke help him to reform the government. Sir Basil's refusal both then and later when the members had assembled, sealed the fate of the government. That the suggestion should have been made was indicative both of Andrews' dwindling confidence and also of the lack of confidence felt by the parliamentary party in their leader.

Brooke's rejection of it, and his role in encouraging the junior ministers to offer their resignations simultaneously with his own, on 28 April, might be interpreted as acts of political ambition. Alternatively they might be regarded as an acknowledgement on his part that in the interests of the war effort and of party unity more than cabinet re-selection was required. In September 1942, he had advised Andrews that 'the only thing is to do the best for the war, and not to worry about other people's feelings'.[269] Brooke probably believed also that he could provide more effective leadership than Andrews. If this was his view it was shared sufficiently widely within the party for him to be able to form a competent cabinet which Spender thought, despite being little-known, would 'be able to carry out its duties very effectively',[270] and which proceeded to win a convincing vote of confidence in the house. It was, Sir Wilfrid felt, 'a very satisfactory beginning for the new government'.[271] This final outcome was not the product of Sir Basil's overweening personal ambition and manipulative skills. Rather, the previous administration collapsed through the weight of its own incompetence.

As leader, Brooke had much to offer the unionist movement, including comparative youth, a distinguished record of ministerial service, military experience, and useful contacts in Britain. He had also a genial, affable personality. Kelly said of him that he 'could have sold sand to the Arabs', and MacDermott described him as 'on easy terms with all men'.[272] His early years as premier were not however easy. A Mass Observation report noted in mid-1944,

Ulster does not escape the terrible implications of modern life . . . In common with other democracies there is a restlessness in regard to the whole pace and procedures of politics and established parties. The long domination of the Unionist party is being threatened . . . Some of the forward-looking members of the Ulster government are very uneasy, . . . and the present prime minister diplomatic, intelligent, lively Basil Brooke is considered by some of his party too advanced and too liberal. There have been considerable background movements to replace him, and the solidarity of the Unionist caucus shows, for the first time in twenty years, signs of a crater.[273]

Conclusion

Many elements went into the 'making' of Brooke as prime minister. Clearly his ideas and attitudes were deeply influenced by his class and family background, as well as by his deep roots in Fermanagh. The pattern of his early years conformed closely to the classical Anglo-Irish mould, attendance at public school in England, followed by military service, before assuming the responsibilities of his estate, the final progression being unexpectedly delayed by the intervention of war. It is not easy to assess the cumulative impact of this experience. Possibly prolonged exposure to the carnage of the western front eroded his religious belief.[1] Probably his earlier direct contact with strikes and riots in South Africa helped shape his perceptions of how the threat of civil disorder might best be counteracted. Certainly service with the Hussars heightened his awareness of and appreciation for the empire. Also the protracted separation from his county and from Colebrooke for most of twenty years sharpened his commitment to both.

He reached full political consciousness in the context of extreme political crisis in Ireland, with Fermanagh cast in its familiar historic role as one of the march-land areas under British rule. In these circumstances, Brooke instinctively identified with the aggressive conservative–unionist traditions of his family, taking a leading role in assisting his usually lethargic fellow-citizens to organise themselves for their mutual self-defence. This spontaneous response was vital in laying the strongest of possible foundations for his later involvement in politics. By his actions he not only won the admiration and trust of the unionist electorate in Fermanagh and elsewhere, but also earned the respect and gratitude of the party's leadership in Ulster, particularly that of Sir James Craig. Nonetheless only gradually in the course of the decade after the great war does his interest in and commitment to a political career become manifest.

As a minister he revealed a number of desirable qualities: energy, confidence, accessibility, an ability to communicate and to delegate, social poise, adaptability, knowledge – especially of agriculture – and, with regard to his general perspective, a surprising degree of pragmatism even in relation to constitutional issues.[2] These attributes contributed to his rapid political rise. They enhanced the value of other initial advantages, including his relative youth, aristocratic background, long and proven record of service by the late 1920s, and his close relationship with Craig. Also, as he himself was always the first to acknowledge, his ministerial success owed much to the talents of senior civil servants both at agriculture and commerce and to the encouragement and guidance provided by Lady Brooke. A further crucial factor in accounting for his final dramatic elevation to the leadership was the evident incompetence of his ageing ministerial colleagues and the consistent unwillingness of both Craig and Andrews to respond positively to the mounting pressures for cabinet change. The long-anticipated outcome was a spontaneous and far-reaching revolt within the Unionist party and an associated widespread demand that Brooke be made premier.

After becoming prime minister Brooke displayed characteristics which he had first clearly demonstrated at a local level in the early 1920s and again later whilst serving as a junior member of cabinet. He retained his simple tastes and modest charm both of which help to account for his rejection of an earldom towards the end of his career on the grounds that he had been 'ennobled enough'.[3] A close cabinet colleague considered that Sir Basil's greatest attribute was his ability to communicate'; he inspired 'absolute trust . . . social barriers did not exist in his outlook'.[4] An eye-witness recalled vividly the resulting spontaneous affection shown by Belfast crowds towards Lady Brooke after the memorial service held in honour of her husband at St Anne's Cathedral in August 1973. It was, he considered, an indication 'of the united feeling of love that the people of Ulster had for Lord Brookeborough. The real memorial service was held outside the cathedral with the people, not inside with the top brass'.[5]

Throughout, Brooke also constantly affirmed his commitment to the union, though during both world wars he showed a willingness to accept compromise, in early 1916, to avoid civil war in Ireland and, in 1940, as a sacrifice necessary if nazism in Europe was to be defeated. In addition, he had an abiding concern with matters of security. Both attitudes were intimately associated in his mind with feelings of suspicion towards the minority. From the vantage-point of his admirers, the greatest triumphs of Sir Basil's later career were the courage and resolution with which he responded to the 1956 I.R.A. campaign and, above all, the clauses which were included in the Ireland act, seven years earlier, at his request. The latter enshrined the principle of self-determination for Northern Ireland and so apparently safe-guarded the province's constitution. He himself wrote with obvious satisfaction, at the time: 'We have got what we wanted . . . Ulster is safe'.[6]

Overall, despite his initial worries about nationalisation and of imminent pressures to force the province to join Eire after the Conservative defeat in the general election of July 1945, Brooke's own courageous and essentially pragmatic approach helped to ensure close cooperation with Attlee and his cabinet. Far-reaching social reforms were implemented locally despite strong resistance from right-wing elements in the Unionist party, some of whom favoured dominion status. Attlee himself later recalled the 'cordial relations' which his ministers enjoyed with their Ulster colleagues and 'particularly with the prime minister, Sir Basil Brooke'. He continued, 'although the Northern Ireland government is Conservative and . . . [its] . . . members predominantly in opposition to Labour, . . . the legislation of the Labour government has been paralleled in Northern Ireland'.[7]

During the early 1970s when the system of government which Brooke had bequeathed, progressively disintegrated, there was a predictable tendency amongst some unionists to regard his premiership almost as a golden age. It was identified as a period of decisive and energetic leadership, steady industrial consolidation, though without unemployment ever being eradicated, and strong and stable institutions both at party and governmental level. One leading local Unionist politician then remarked that: 'had . . . [Sir Basil] . . . taken office in 1963 . . . Ulster would not have been sold out to face the tragedies we are undergoing today'.[8] Another, reflected on his 'great gift of maintaining unity, since his leadership there has been no-one who has been successful in maintaining meaningful unity'.[9] Brooke himself would have been delighted by such a tribute. In periods of acute internal party conflict he frequently expressed the conviction that 'unity was the only thing that mattered', and stated that his sole 'object . . . [was] . . . to re-establish unity and not to create dissension'.[10] The degree of success which he achieved in this objective is a measure of his capacity for leadership and force of character.

Perhaps the most eloquent posthumous assessement of his qualities was contained in a peroration delivered by Reverend Samuel Crooks. In it Sir Basil was described as 'a leader and inspirer of the Ulster people . . . [who had shown] . . . resolution, courage, vigilance, and endurance'. It continued, 'we shall pray that the memory of his virtues and his achievements may remain as part of our heritage, inspiring generations to come to emulate his magnanimity and patriotic devotion'.[11]

However, many even within the ranks of his own party would reject such a positive evaluation of Brooke's career, and of his premiership in particular. His last diary entry is revealing. It is dated 21 February 1963, one month before he relinquished the premiership. In it he refers disdainfully to the 'delinquents' (his Unionist party critics in parliament) who had sat 'most of the afternoon' at Stormont and who had 'eventually produced a resolution calling on [him] to dismiss Danny [Glentoran] and, if not, calling for [his own] resignation'.[12]

More negative appraisals of his leadership gain credibility from popular recollections of him as an old, apparently misplaced, patrician figure, who it seemed had lingered too long in office, so repeating an error that he had himself recognised in Sir James Craig and vowed not to emulate. Such interpretations inevitably acquire additional force from the provinces endemic political instability since the late 1960s. In 1973 one of his leading political opponents concluded that Brooke's 'unremitting way of politics contributed to a great extent to the present strife' in Northern Ireland.[13] By then such views were shared by *The Times* which stated that his 'refusal to bring the Roman catholic minority into active participation in public affairs . . . [was] . . . a serious blemish on his political record . . . His mind [was] prejudiced to an extent that damaged the political development of the province . . . [Northern Ireland's] sectarian strife . . . is in part attributable to the immobility imposed in his long period of political leadership'.[14] Amidst considerable controversy this opinion was repeated and amplified at his memorial service by Rev. Dr Arthur Butler. He commented that Brooke 'was not a political visionary. He did not appear to think of long-term solutions to our problems. It can be argued that if he had thought differently and acted differently Northern Ireland would not be in the state in which it is today. . . . Throughout his time as prime minister the barriers between protestant and Roman catholic were virtually unbreached, . . . a root cause of our unhappy situation'.[15]

Thus, Brooke's critics might consider that though he has not been honoured by a memorial cast in bronze or cut in stone, one can still be found ingrained in the unenviable features of the province itself, its interminable political tensions and sectarian violence; in truth, *'si monumentum requires, circumspice'*. On such a view it might seem an appropriate as well as tragic irony that his son, John Brooke, then minister of state for finance should have delivered the final speech from the dispatch box at Stormont prior to its suspension on 28 March 1972. In his valediction, he quoted from a poem by Rudyard Kipling, written about Ulster in 1912, the year in which Sir Basil's active political career might be said to have begun. The latter fully identified with the sentiments that it expressed:

The dark eleventh hour draws on and sees us sold.
To every evil power we fought against of old . . .
The blood our fathers spilt, our love, our toil, our pains,
Are counted as for guilt, and only bind our chains.
Before an empire's eyes the traitor claims his price.
What need of further lies? We are the sacrifice.[16]

Brooke's successors to the premiership have passed conflicting verdicts on his talents. Brian Faulkner said of him: 'one could not have asked for a more loyal or courageous chief. Lord Brookeborough had the ability to concentrate on things that were important, the details he left to others. He got through his work effectively'.[17] However, the most influential and certainly the most damaging reflection on Sir Basil's career was that provided by Lord O'Neill. Though he wrote of the former's 'immense personal charm'; and noted that he was 'good company' and a 'good raconteur', he added, 'those who met him imagined that he was relaxing away from his desk, what they didn't realise was that there was no desk'. He concluded that he was 'a man of limited intelligence, . . . quite impossible for him to have been a minister in London'.[18] This view has virtually become an established orthodoxy. It was quoted in *The Times* obituary which was in turn a source used by the Rev. Dr Butler. A recent authority reiterated O'Neill's assessment and, citing him as evidence, commented that Brooke was 'a lazy man of limited ability', who as prime minister, 'proved his limitations and his partisanship'.[19]

In relation to his overall career such an assessment is both inadequate and inaccurate, relying too heavily on sources that are far from being objective and, with regard to his early years in office, it is unhistorical. Senior officials including those at agriculture and commerce as well as cabinet colleagues and party members testified frequently and eloquently to his talents as a minister. His critics would, of course, allege that his career was flawed throughout by his distrust of the Roman catholic minority and obsessive commitment to the union and the empire and conclude that he constantly failed to rise to that higher level of leadership which does not 'simply pander to its own supporters, but dares to chip away at their prejudices'.[20] In later years Brooke himself conceded that he was less 'ecumenical' than others, adding in his own defence, 'it must be remembered that I lived through . . . the most troubled of times' in Ireland's history.[21]

Undoubtedly, the violence and upheaval of the First World War and of its immediate aftermath profoundly influenced his emerging political consciousness as for so many of his generation. Any narrowness of vision which he acquired then was reinforced subsequently. This was due in part to the disillusioning reality that the nationalist community in the province persisted in its unwillingness to accept, identify with or fully participate in the institutions of the state. Brooke also found it distressing that these attitudes were fomented and fostered by successive southern governments. In the 1930s irredentist claims on behalf of the Free State became markedly more strident, culminating in article II of the 1937 constitution which stated that 'the national territory consisted of the whole island of Ireland'.[22] The use of violence to 'peg out the territory just as Hitler was doing' (in Czechoslavakia), was also considered.[23] Yet, concurrently, the taoiseach Eamon De Valera, whole-heartedly and single-mindedly cultivated catholic, republican and Gaelic values within the twenty-six counties and in pursuit of these was prepared to justify sectarian discrimination in public employment.[24] In the words of one eminent historian 'he made the mistake of implying that the only true Irishmen were catholics'.[25] With obvious justification the *Irish Times* in August 1973 concluded that 'In assessing Lord Brookeborough . . . it is salutary for his critics, especially in the Republic, to ask themselves if, in [his] lifetime those who aspired to unity of the people of Ireland themselves did much to frame conditions which favoured such an outcome'.[26]

Such developments were antipathetic to Brooke, to the traditions of his class and indeed to the mores of the whole Ulster unionist community with which he so fully identified. They served to justify and perpetuate the order of political priorities which he had articulated and acted upon in the early 1920s. Brooke was born into the landed gentry and became a soldier by instinct and inclination but he was driven into politics primarily from conviction – the need to defend and preserve the union which was then threatened. During the following decades the threat to its survival remained and the necessity to defend it therefore did not diminish.

Bibliography

A. MANUSCRIPT SOURCES

(a) NORTHERN IRELAND

1. Fermanagh:
Letter books of Fermanagh Unionist Association, (Unionist headquarters, Enniskillen)

2. Public Record Office of Northern Ireland, Belfast (P.R.O.N.I.):
Cabinet conclusions, (Northern Ireland), 1921–1943, (CAB 4/1–550)
Cabinet secretariat, subject files, second series, (particularly CAB 9A, 9B, 9C, 9CD, 9E, 9F, 9J, and 8G, relating to the Ministries of Finance, Home Affairs, Labour, Civil Defence, Agriculture, Commerce, also Parliament and prime minister's department)
Departmental files, (particularly COM 61, 'NE' National Emergency files, AG 16, 'A' Policy files, and FIN 18, Treasury division, 'A' Registry files)
J. W. Blake papers, (CAB 3A, 'The official history of Northern Ireland', official papers and copies of official papers')
Brooke papers, (D 3004, D 736, D 998)
Books of survey and distribution, (D 1854)
Castle list of Irish House of Commons, 1783, (T 3035)
Sir Ernest Clark papers, (D 1022)
Craig papers, (D 1415)
F. H. Crawford papers, (D 640)
Falls and Hanna papers, (D 1390)
Fermanagh County Council, minutes, (LA 4)
Dr. J. S. Gordon papers, (D 2734)
T. E. Grove papers, (T 808)
Sir Douglas Harkness papers, (not yet catalogued)
Harcourt's list of the different interests in the Irish House of Commons, 1777, from the Gilbert collection, (T 2833)
Rev Mr Henry, Topographical descriptions, (T 2521)
Jeremiah Jordon papers, (D 2073)
Liddle papers, (D 1402)
Hugh de Fellenberg Montgomery papers, (D 627)
Major Moutray papers, (D 2023)
Spender papers, (D 715, D 1633) (diary D 715/1–24)
Unionist Clubs Council minute book, (D 1327)
Ulster Unionist Stormont parliamentary party, minute book of meetings, (D 1327)

3. Queen's University, Belfast:
R. M. Henry collection

(b) REPUBLIC OF IRELAND:

1. Genealogical Office, Dublin:
Brooke family pedigree, (MS 178)

2. National Library of Ireland:
Melville papers (MS 54)

3. State Paper Office, Dublin (S.P.O.):
Crime Special Branch, R.I.C., reports by inspector general, district inspector, divisional commissioner and county inspectors
Crime Special Branch, R.I.C. files
Dail Eireann papers
North East Boundary Bureau papers
Provisional government and Free State cabinet files
Provisional government and executive council minutes

4. University College, Dublin:
Mulcahy papers, (F 7)

(c) BRITAIN:

1. Army Records Centre, Hayes, Middlesex:
Records of Captain Sir B. S. Brooke

2. The British Library, (Reference Division), Newspaper Library, Colindale Avenue, London

3. Tom Harrisson Mass Observation Archive, Brighton:
Files and diaries relating to Northern Ireland

4. House of Lords, Record Office:
Beaverbrook papers
Lloyd George papers
Lord Wakehurst papers

5. Imperial War Museum, London:
Diary of Sir Henry Wilson

6. Liddell-Hart Centre for Military Archives, London:
Alanbrooke papers

7. Public Record Office, London (P.R.O.):
Sir John Anderson papers, (CO 904/188)
Cabinet conclusions, memoranda and committees, (mainly CAB 21, 23, 24, 27, 65, 66, 67, 123, 129 including respectively registered files 1916–1959, cabinet minutes to 1939, cabinet memoranda to 1939, committees to 1939, war cabinet minutes 1939–1945, memoranda 1939–1945, files of the lord president of the council, and memoranda from 1945)
Papers of the Irish Boundary Commission, (CAB 61), 1924–1925
Crime Special Branch, R.I.C. reports by county inspectors and inspector generals, (CO 904/48–115)
Crime Special Branch, R.I.C. intelligence notes, (CO 903)
Colonial Office, files, (CO)
Foreign Office, files, (FO)
Home Office files, (mainly HO 45, HO 184)
Ministry of National Insurance, registered files, (PIN 18)
Prime minister's office, (PREM 3, 4)
Sturgis diary, (P.R.O. 30/59/1–5)
Stephen Tallents papers, (CO 904/23–31)
Treasury files, (T 160)
War Office files, war diary of 10th Hussars, (WO 95)

8. Royal Military Academy, Sandhurst:
Registers and reports

9. Somerset House, (Probate Office), London:
Will of Sir Arthur Douglas Brooke

10. Winchester College:
Magazines and Reports

(d) UNITED STATES:
The National Archives, Washington
Reports by P. W. Buhrman, American consul general, Belfast, to Department of State

B. PARLIAMENTARY PAPERS
(a) UNITED KINGDOM:
Official report, 3rd and 5th series, *Parliamentary debates*, House of Commons
(b) NORTHERN IRELAND:
Northern Ireland House of Commons papers (1931–1943)
The *Parliamentary debates*, official report, House of Commons
The *Parliamentary debates*, official report, Senate
Report of the agricultural aid committee, 1923, (Cmd 17, government of Northern Ireland)
Eleventh general report of the Ministry of Agriculture, 1931–1934, (Cmd 180, 1937, government of Northern Ireland)
Report of the conditions of employment and wages of agricultural workers in Northern Ireland, 1938, (Cmd 199, government of Northern Ireland)
Report of the investigators appointed by the Ministry of Agriculture to enquire into the administrative and financial arrangements of the pig marketing board, 1938, (Cmd 205, government of Northern Ireland)
Report on the general administration, organisation and financial arrangements of the pig marketing scheme, 1939, (Cmd 208, government of Northern Ireland)
Report of the agricultural inquiry committee, 1947, (Cmd 249, government of Northern Ireland)
Twelfth general report of the Ministry of Agriculture, 1934–1950, (Cmd 295, 1951, government of Northern Ireland)

C. OFFICIAL PUBLICATIONS
Blake, J. W., *Northern Ireland in the Second World War*, (Belfast, 1956)
Land owners in Ireland, return to owners of land, (Dublin, 1876), compiled by the Local Government Board
The *London Gazette*
Murray, K.A.A., *Agriculture*, (London, 1955)
North-Eastern Boundary Bureau, *The handbook of the Ulster question*, (Dublin, 1923)
Quarterly army list
Report of the Irish Boundary Commission, 1925, with an introduction by Geoffrey J. Hand, (Shannon, 1969)
State Paper Office, *Intelligence notes, 1913–1916, preserved in the State Paper Office*, ed. Breandan MacGiolla Choille, (Dublin, 1966)
Shearman, Hugh, *Northern Ireland, 1921–1971*, (Belfast, 1971)
Ulster year books, 1926–1956, (Belfast, 1926–56)
Ulster Unionist Council, *Annual reports*

D. NEWSPAPERS AND PERIODICALS
Armagh Guardian
Belfast News Letter
Belfast Telegraph
Daily Mirror
Enniskillen Advertiser
Fermanagh Herald
Fermanagh Times
Impartial Reporter

Irish News
Irish Times
Lisbellaw Gazette
Manchester Guardian
News of the World
Northern Whig
Sunday Dispatch
Sunday News
Sussex Daily
The Times

E. SECONDARY SOURCES

Atlee, C. B., *As it happened,* (Surrey, 1984)

Beckett, J. C., *The Anglo-Irish tradition,* (London, 1976)

Belfast and Ulster directories, 1921–40

4th earl of Belmore, *Parliamentary memoirs of Fermanagh and Tyrone, 1613–1885,* (Dublin, 1887)

Bew, Paul, Gibbon, Peter and Patterson, Henry, *The state in Northern Ireland 1921–72,* (Manchester, 1979)

Bodkin, M., 'Notes on the Irish parliament in 1773', in *Proceedings of the Royal Irish Academy,* xlviii, (1942–43)

Bowman, John, *De Valera and the Ulster question, 1917–1973,* (Oxford, 1982)

Bottomley, P. M., 'The North Fermanagh elections of 1885–1886', in the *Clogher Record,* viii, no. 2

Brooke, R. F., *The brimming river,* (Dublin, 1961)

Bryant, Arthur, *The turn of the tide, 1939–1943,* (London, 1954)

Buckland, Patrick, *The factory of grievances,* (Dublin, 1979)

Buckland, Patrick, *A history of Northern Ireland,* (Dublin, 1981)

Buckland, Patrick, Ulster unionism and the origins of Northern Ireland, (Dublin, 1973)

Budge, Ian and O'Leary, Cornelius, *Belfast: approach to crisis: a study of Belfast politics 1603–1970,* (London, 1973)

Burke's landed gentry of Ireland, ed. L. G. Pine, (London, 1958)

Burke's peerage, baronetage and knightage, ed. Peter Townsend, (London, 1970)

Burke's Irish family records, ed. Hugh Montgomery-Massingberd, (London, 1976)

Callwell, C. E., *Field Marshal Sir Henry Wilson: his life and diaries,* (London, 1927)

Carroll, Joseph, *Ireland in the war years, 1939–1945,* (Newton Abbot, 1975)

Churchill, W. S., *The aftermath,* (London, 1929)

Churchill, W. S., *The second world war,* ii, (London, 1949)

Clark, Wallace, *Guns in Ulster: a history of the B special constabulary in part of Co. Derry,* (Belfast, 1967)

Cole, John, *The Thatcher years,* (London, 1987)

Colvin, Ian, *The life of Lord Carson,* i, (London, 1934)

Cook, Chris, *Sources in British political history,* i–v, (London, 1975–8)

Crotty, R. D., *Irish agricultural production: its volume and structure,* (Cork, 1966)

Curran, J. M., *The birth of the Irish Free State, 1921–1923,* (Alabama, 1980)

Dane, Mervyn, *The Fermanagh 'B' Specials,* (Enniskillen, 1970)

Deutsch, R. R., *Northern Ireland, 1921–1974: a select bibliography,* (New York, 1975)

Dewer, M. W., Brown, John, and Long, S. F., *Orangeism: a new historical appreciation, 1688–1967,* (Belfast, 1967)

Donaldson, Francis, *Edward VIII, the road to abdication,* (London, 1978)

Ervine, St John, *Craigavon: Ulsterman,* (London, 1949)

Falls, Cyril, *The birth of Ulster,* (London, 1936)

Farrell, Michael, *Arming the protestants,* (London, 1983)

Farrell, Michael, *Northern Ireland, the Orange state,* (London, 1976)

Faulkner, Brian, *Memoirs of a statesman*, (London, 1978)

Fisk, Robert, *In time of war*, (London, 1983)

Flackes, W. D., *Northern Ireland, a political directory, 1968–79*, (Dublin, 1980)

Flackes, W. D., *The enduring premier*, (Belfast, 1972)

Fraser, David, *Alanbrooke*, (London, 1982)

Gibbon, Peter, *The Origins of Ulster unionism*, (Manchester, 1975)

Harbinson, J. F., *The Ulster Unionist party, 1882–1973*, (Belfast, 1973)

Harkness, David, *The restless dominion*, (London, 1969)

Harkness, David, *Northern Ireland since 1920*, (Dublin, 1980)

Hazlet, Sir Arthur, *The B Specials, a history of the Ulster special constabulary*, (London, 1973)

Hepburn, A. C., *The conflict of nationality, in modern Ireland*, (London, 1980)

Hill, Rev. George, *An historical account of the plantation in Ulster*, (Belfast, 1877)

Hunt, William, *The Irish parliament, 1775*, (Dublin, 1907)

Isles, K. S. and Cuthbert, N., *An economic survey of Northern Ireland*, (Belfast, 1957)

Jackson, H. A. and Wilson, E. R., (ed.) *Winchester College registers, 1901–1946*, (London, 1956)

Johnson, D. S. 'The economic history of Ireland between the wars' in *Irish Economic and Social History*, i, (1974)

Johnson, D. S., *The interwar economy in Ireland*, (Dundalk, 1985)

Johnston, E. M., 'Members of the Irish parliament, 1784–1787', in *Proceedings of the Royal Irish Academy*, lxxi, (1971)

Jones, Tom, *Whitehall diary, Ireland, 1918–1925*, iii, (London, 1971)

Jupp, Peter, *British and Irish elections, 1784–1831*, (Newton Abbot, 1973)

Lawrence, R. J., *The government of Northern Ireland*, (Oxford, 1965)

Leigh, M. S. (ed.) *Winchester College registers, 1884–1934*, (Winchester, 1940)

Kennedy, David, 'Catholics in Northern Ireland 1926–1939', in *Years of the great test 1926–1939*, ed. Francis McManus, (Cork, 1967)

Livingstone, Peadar, *The Fermanagh story*, (Monaghan, 1969)

Lodge, Edmund, *Lodge's peerage, baronetage, knightage and companionage*, (London, 1912)

Lyons, F. S. L. *Culture and anarchy in Ireland, 1890–1939*, (Oxford, 1979)

Lyons, F. S. L. *Ireland since the Famine*, (Suffolk, 1982)

Maltby, Arthur, *The government of Northern Ireland 1922–1972, a catalogue of breviate of parliamentary papers*, (Dublin, 1974)

McColgan, John, *British policy and the Irish administration, 1920–1922*, (London, 1983)

Macready, F. N. C., *Annals of an active life*, 2 vols., (London, 1924)

Meehan, C. P., *The fate and fortunes of Hugh O'Neill, earl of Tyrone and Rory O'Donel, earl of Tyrconnell*, (Dublin, 1885)

Miller, D. W., *Queen's rebels; Ulster loyalism in historical perspective*, (Dublin, 1978)

Moody, T. W. *et al.*, *A new history of Ireland, 1534–1691*, iii, (Oxford, 1976)

Murphy, Desmond, *Derry, Donegal and modern Ulster, 1790–1921*, (Derry, 1981)

Murray, K. A. H., *Agriculture*, (London, 1955)

Nowlan, K. B. and Williams, T. D., (ed.) *Ireland in the war years and after, 1939–1951*, (London, 1969)

O'Carroll, J. P. and Murphy J. A., *De Valera and his times*, (Cork, 1983)

Oliver, John, *Working at Stormont*, (Dublin, 1978)

O'Hara, P. J., 'Financial returns, for the seven years 1930–1937, on eleven farms in Northern Ireland', *Journal of the Ministry of Agriculture*, vl, (1938)

O'Maologáin, P. O., 'An early history of Fermanagh', in *Clogher Record*, ii, no. 3, (1959)

O'Neill, Terence, *The autobiography of Terence O'Neill*, (London, 1972)

Savage, D. C., 'The origins of the Ulster Unionist party, 1885–1886', in *Irish Historical Studies*, xii, no. 47, (1961)

Scott, Rev. John, *A review of the principal public characters in the House of Commons in Ireland,* (Dublin, 1789)

Scott, Rev. John, *A parliamentary representation of Ireland, (Dublin, 1790)*

Scott Robertson, *Pig breeding and marketing in Northern Ireland,* (Belfast, 1934)

Shea, Patrick, *Voices and the sound of drums,* (Belfast, 1981)

Shearman, Hugh, *Northern Ireland 1921–71,* (Belfast, 1971)

Steven, Leslie, *Sir Victor Brooke, sportsman and naturalist,* (London, 1894)

Stewart, A. T. Q., *The Ulster crisis,* (London, 1967)

Treadwell, V. W. 'Extracts from the 1622 survey of the plantation of Donegal', in *Donegal Annual,* ii, no. 3 (1953–4) and iii, no. 1 (1954–5)

Vaughan, Louis, 'Byng of Vimy, an appreciation', in *Army Quarterly,* xxxi (October 1935–January 1936)

Vincent, John and Stenton, Michael, *McCalmount's parliamentary poll book of all elections, 1832–1918,* (Brighton, 1971)

Walker, B. M., 'Party organisation in Ulster, 1865–1892', in Roebuck, Peter, (ed) *Plantation to partition,* (Belfast, 1981)

Walker, Graham, *The politics of frustration,* (Manchester, 1985)

Whitmore, F. H. D. C., *The 10th (Prince of Wales Own) Royal Hussars and the Essex Yeomanry, during the European war, 1914–1918,* (Colchester, 1920)

Whyte, John, *Church and state in modern Ireland, 1923–1970,* (Dublin, 1973)

Williams, Jeffrey, *Byng of Vimy,* (London, 1983)

Williams, J. G., 'An economic survey of small holdings in Northern Ireland' *Journal of the Ministry of Agriculture,* iii, (1931)

Wilson, Thomas, (ed.) *Ulster under home rule: a study of the political and economic problems of Northern Ireland,* (London, 1955)

Young, W. R., *Fighters of Derry, their deeds and descendants,* (London, 1932)

F. THESES

Barton, B. E., 'Sir Basil Brooke, the making of a prime minister' (Ph.D., Queen's University, Belfast, 1986).

Elliot, Sidney, The electoral system in Northern Ireland since 1920, (Ph.D., Queen's University, Belfast, 1971).

Greenlees, Sandra, 'The structure and development of agriculture in Ulster, 1900–1939', (M.Phil., New University of Ulster, 1976).

Harbinson, J. F., 'A history of the Northern Ireland Labour party, 1891–1948' (M.Sc., Queen's University, Belfast, 1972).

McColgan, J. J., 'Irish government administration: British administrative policies in Ireland, 1920–1922', (Ph.D., University College Dublin, 1978).

Magill, P. F., 'The Senate in Northern Ireland, 1921–1962' (Ph.D., Queen's University, Belfast, 1965).

O'Halpin, Eunan, 'Emergency legislation and the instruments of power in Ireland, 1916–1920', (M.A., University College, Dublin, 1980).

Phoenix, Eamon G., 'Introduction and calendar of the Cahir Healy Papers', (M.A., Queen's University, Belfast, 1978).

G. INTERVIEWS

Mr. J. L. O. Andrews, Comber, 7 August 1979

Sir Harold Black, Belfast, 9 November 1979

Lord Brookeborough, Ashbrooke, 23 February 1985

Miss Noreen Cooper, Enniskillen, 29 July 1979

Sir Douglas Harkness, Belfast, 4, 11 June 1979

Sir Arthur Kelly, Belfast, 21, 28 April 1979

Lieutenant Colonel George Liddle, Enniskillen, 5 August 1980

Lord J. C. MacDermott, Belfast, 11, 14 May 1979

Miss Emara MacNeill, Helen's Bay, 12 May 1979

Notes to Chapters

INTRODUCTION

1. Brooke's unpublished memoirs in the Brooke papers. D 3004/D/46, Public Record Office of Northern Ireland, (P.R.O.N.I.), (hereafter cited as Brooke memoirs). These are also extensively quoted in the calendar of the Brooke papers. The memoirs are disappointingly brief, stop in 1918, and contain only the writer's recollections of childhood, schooling and military service. There are no references to political events or to Brooke's own political attitudes. Nonetheless, for the study of contemporary political events the most valuable surviving Brooke papers are classified under D 3004, (P.R.O.N.I.). Unless otherwise indicated, all the government files and private papers cited in these footnotes are held at the Public Record Office of Northern Ireland.
2. John Vincent and Michael Stenton, *McCalmount's parliamentary poll book of all elections, 1832–1918,* (Brighton, 1971), part I pp 87, 88 and part II pp 111, 112. See also B. M. Walker, 'Party organisation in Ulster, 1865–1892', in Peter Roebuck, (editor), *Plantation to Partition,* (Belfast, 1981), p. 208; P. M. Bottomley, 'The North Fermanagh elections of 1885 and 1886', in the *Clogher Record*, viii, No. 2 (1973), p. 176; the letter-book of J. W. Dane, secretary of Fermanagh Conservative Association in D 1390/26/7, 'Political papers of Messrs Falls and Hanna, solicitors', passim; and D. C. Savage, 'The origins of the Ulster Unionist party, 1885–1886', in *Irish Historical Studies*, xii, no. 47, March 1961, passim.
3. The best source for these developments is Crime Special Branch, R.I.C., handwritten confidential monthly reports by county inspectors (hereafter cited as county inspector's reports), and, filed with them, those of the inspector general, January 1893–September 1914, in co 904/48–95, Public Record Office, London (P.R.O.). Some of the inspector general's reports, however, (mainly for the early 1900s) are in boxes 3, 4, in the State Paper Office, Dublin, (S.P.O.). See also Crime Special Branch, R.I.C., weekly reports by the divisional commissioner on political feeling in Belfast and the northern division, March–September 1893, (S.P.O.), box 5, (hereafter cited as divisional commissioner, weekly reports); and Crime Special Branch, R.I.C., monthly reports by the district inspector on secret societies in the northern division, 1887–1895, (S.P.O.), box 6, (hereafter cited as district inspector, monthly reports).
4. Thus F. S. L. Lyons, in *Ireland Since the Famine* (Suffolk, 1982) a meticulous study of Irish history up to the 1970s, made only three brief and inconsequential references to Brooke in the course of almost 800 pages.
5. Patrick Buckland, *A history of Northern Ireland,* (Dublin, 1981) p. 82.

CHAPTER I

1. P. O. O'Maologáin, 'An early history of Fermanagh', (edited version of the history by John Dolan), in the *Clogher Record*, ii, no. 3 (1959), p. 462; also Rev. George Hill, *An historical account of the plantation of Ulster*, (Belfast, 1877), pp 145, 146. Many of the early English settlers in Fermanagh came from East Anglia.
2. R. F. Brooke, *The brimming river*, (Dublin, 1961), p. 182; and the Brooke family pedigree, MS 178, (in the Genealogical Office, Dublin).

3. See extracts from patent rolls and Ulster inquisitions, in Hill, op. cit., p. 324; W. R. Young, *Fighters of Derry, their deeds and descendants,* (London, 1932), p. 94; 4th earl of Belmore, *Parliamentary memoirs of Fermanagh and Tyrone, 1613–1885,* (Dublin, 1887), p. 94. See also W. D. Flackes, *The enduring premier,* (Belfast, 1962). This is a short, unpaginated pamphlet consisting of interviews with Brooke, conducted by Flackes, (a *Belfast Telegraph* journalist) in 1962. They were also published by the newspaper in the spring of that year.

4. Hill, op. cit., pp 176, 499–527.

5. Cyril Falls, *The birth of Ulster,* (London, 1936), pp 216, 217.

6. Hill, op. cit., p. 324.

7. See 'Book of survey and distribution' for County Donegal, entry for barony of Kilmacrenan, compiled c. 1680, in D 1854/1/23, from the Annesley manuscripts.

8. V.W. Treadwell, 'Extracts from the 1622 survey of the plantation of Donegal' in the *Donegal Annual,* iii, no. 1 (1954–5) p. 44; also Hill, op. cit., p. 524.

9. See the articles of complaint, of the earl of Tyrconnell, in C. P. Meehan, *The fate and fortunes of Hugh O'Neill, earl of Tyrone and Rory O'Donel, earl of Tyrconnell,* (Dublin, 1868), p. 135.

10. Hill, op. cit., p. 514.

11. V. W. Treadwell, 'Extracts from the 1622 survey of Donegal', in *Donegal Annual,* ii, no. 3 (1953–1954), pp 512, 513.

12. See copy of Basil Brooke's will, in the T. E. Grove papers, T 808/15061–15077, 'Notes on County Fermanagh'. The 'Book of survey and distribution for County Donegal' refers to the 'castle and town called Donegal belonging to Captain Henry Brooke', in D 1854/1/23.

13. Genealogical Office, Dublin, MS 178, op. cit. Also see chancery bill, drawn up by Basil Brooke, Henry's son, in D 3004/A/1. This gives details of his father's career, and was drawn up in 1680. Also see *Burke's peerage, baronetage, and knightage,* edited by Peter Townend, (London, 1970), pp 370, 371, (hereafter cited as *Burke's peerage).*

14. 'Book of survey and distribution for County Monaghan', in D 1854/1/8.

15. Peadar Livingstone, *The Fermanagh Story* (Monaghan, 1969), p. 70, also pp 66, 93; and Hill, op. cit., p. 335. Genealogical Office, Dublin, MS 178, op. cit.; also *Burke's peerage*; op. cit., pp 370, 371.

16. Chancery bill drawn up by Basil Brooke, dated 1680, in D 3004/A/1; also transcript of the exchequer bill, drawn up by Thomas Brooke, dated 1681, in the Grove papers, op. cit., T 808/15061–15077, 'Notes on Fermanagh; and undated and incomplete articles of agreement between Thomas and Basil Brooke, in D 3004/A/1.

17. See description by 'Falkland', (Rev. John Scott), in *A review of the principal public characters in the House of Commons in Ireland,* (Dublin, 1789), pp 63, 64.

18. *Burke's Irish family records,* edited by Hugh Montgomery-Massingberd, (London, 1976); pp 514, 515.

19. R. F. Brooke, op. cit., pp 14–19.

20. See Harcourt's list of the different interests in the Irish House of Commons, compiled in 1777, in the Gilbert collection, transcript of list in T 2833/2; *Burke's peerage,* op. cit., pp 370, 371; also the list of members of the Irish House of Commons, in 'Note on the Irish parliament in 1773', by M. Bodkin, in *Proceedings of the Royal Irish Academy,* xlviii, (1942–43); pp 145–232.

21. See 'Castle list of Irish House of Commons', dated August 1783, in T 3035; and list of Irish House of Commons members, by Henry Dundas, compiled in 1793, in the Melville papers, National Library of Ireland, MS 54.

22. *Landowners in Ireland, return of owners of land,* compiled by the Local Government Board (Dublin, 1876) pp 249–53.

23. Extract from the 'Book of survey and distribution', for the barony of Magherasteffany, written in 1641, reproduced in the *Clogher Record,* ii, no. 3 (1959), p. 524.

24. Account of County Fermanagh, dated 1739, written by Rev. Henry, in T 2521/3/1, 'Rev. Mr Henry's topographical descriptions, Co. Fermanagh, 1739'; also survey of Colebrooke, dated c. 1727, by William Starratt, in D 988/21/1, 'A survey of Henry Brooke, esq., his estate in County Fermanagh', and note by Henry Brooke on cover of Starratt's survey.

25. See contract with William Farrell, Dublin, for the construction of Colebrooke, dated 1820–1822, in D 3004/B/8.

26. Quoted in Livingstone, op. cit., p. 187.

27. *Impartial Reporter,* 24 February 1874, 15 November 1883.

28. David Fraser, *Alanbrooke,* (London, 1982), p. 38; also F. S. L. Lyons, op. cit., p. 119.

29. David Fraser, op. cit., p. 38.

30. Cyril Falls, op. cit., pp 216, 217. The family is frequently referred to as 'the fighting Brookes', see Arthur Bryant, *The turn of the tide, 1939–1943*, (London, 1957), p. 17; and Flackes, op. cit.
31. David Fraser, op. cit., p. 38.
32. R. F. Brooke, op. cit., p. 14; also W. R. Young, op. cit., p. 95; Flackes, op. cit.
33. Brooke memoirs, op. cit., in D 3004/D/46.
34. See diary of Arthur Brooke, vol. II, in D 3004/D/2; also David Fraser, op. cit., pp 38, 39.
35. R. F. Brooke, op. cit., pp 21, 22.
36. *Burke's Peerage*, op. cit., pp 370, 371.
37. David Fraser, op. cit., p. 539.
38. Sir Winston Churchill, *The second world war*, vol. 11, (London, 1949), pp 233, 234.
39. Brooke memoirs, op. cit., D 3004/D/46; Flackes, op. cit., David Fraser op. cit., p. 39.
40. *Burkes landed gentry of Ireland*, edited by L. G. Pine (London, 1958) p. 112.
41. Genealogical Office, Dublin, MS 178, op. cit.; also *Burke's peerage*, op. cit., pp 370, 371.
42. Livingstone, op. cit., p. 120; also Belmore, op. cit., passim; and Peter Jupp, *British and Irish elections, 1784–1831*, (Newton Abbot, 1973), pp 180 and 182, section on Enniskillen.
43. Burke's peerage, op. cit., pp. 370, 371; also Edmund Lodge, *Lodge's peerage, baronetage, knightage, and companionage*, (London, 1912), pp. 363–5; and Belmore, op. cit., p. 56.
44. Ibid., pp 61, 62, 65; William Hunt, *The Irish Parliament, 1775*, (Dublin, 1907), p. 7.
45. This is referred to in 'Castle list of the House of Commons', dated August 1783, in T 3035.
46. 'Castle list of the House of Commons', dated August 1783, in T 3035.
47. Hunt, op. cit., p. 7. Hunt states: 'In the last session he opposed on every material question'.
48. 'Castle list of House of Commons', August 1783, in T 3035, op. cit.
49. Belmore. op. cit., p. 72.
50. See list of the House of Commons, by Baron Bolton, secretary to lord lieutenant, dated 1784, in E. M. Johnston, 'Members of the Irish Parliament, 1784–1787', in *Proceedings of the Royal Irish Academy*, lxxi (1971), p. 172.
51. See 'Falkland', (Rev. John Scott), *The Parliamentary representation of Ireland*, (Dublin, 1790), pp 35, 36. He was defeated by Lord Cole, whose family 'purchased Lord Belmore's interest' in the county to secure victory, p. 36.
52. Belmore, op. cit., pp 87, 88, 89; Livingstone, op. cit., pp 199, 201; also *Parliamentary Debates*, (Commons, Westminister) vol. lxxx, col. 112, 2 May 1845, also vol. lxxxiv, cols 738, 796, 6 and 9 March 1846.
53. *Belfast News Letter*, 15 August, 5, 16 September 1845 (hereafter cited as *News Letter*).
54. Leslie Stephen, *Sir Victor Brooke, sportsman and naturalist*, (London, 1894), pp 4–5.
55. See letter, dated 26 February 1853; in D 3004/E/4, press cuttings of Sir Arthur Brooke.
56. Quoted in an article entitled 'The Ulster boys and the struggle for Northern Ireland', dated 6 March 1938, and signed 'Dr J. M.' in D 3004/C/1.
57. Brooke memoirs op. cit.
58. Stephen, op. cit., p. 3; and David Fraser, op. cit., pp 39, 40.
59. Sir Victor Brooke to Hugh de Fellenberg Montgomery, 2 February 1879, in D 627/428/4, the papers of Hugh de Fellenberg Montgomery.
60. Stephen, op. cit., pp 20, 21, comment by Professor Huxley.
61. *Impartial Reporter*, 10 April 1884; and *Fermanagh Times*, 1 January 1885; also Livingstone, op. cit., p. 183. Sir Victor may have been concerned that the operation of the custom might cause a decline in protestant land-holding.
62. Stephen, op. cit., p. 2.
63. *Fermanagh Times*, 26 November 1891. This newspaper was established as a conservative rejoinder to the liberal *Impartial Reporter*, its first edition was dated 4 March 1880.
64. Flackes, op. cit.
65. Patterson to Montgomery, 29 February 1866, in D 627/250. Patterson, Montgomery's local sub-agent, was describing the response of some local landlords to the Fenian threat.
66. Sir Victor's private papers contain a list of leading subscribers to the association, in D 3004/C/1.
67. *Fermanagh Times*, 10 December 1891. Sir Victor's first speech as a member of the order was printed beside his obituary.
68. *Enniskillen Advertizer*, 22 July 1875.
69. Account of 'The Ulster boys and the struggle for Northern Ireland', dated 6 March 1938, and signed 'Dr J. M.' in D 3004/C/1.

70. *Fermanagh Times,* 26 November 1891. In the United States, Sir Victor and Douglas called with the Roosevelts. When Alanbrooke met F. D. Roosevelt, in June 1943, the latter 'remembered them well', see Arthur Bryant, op. cit., pp 407, 630.

71. This is mentioned in J. Whiteside Dane to Lord Erne, 22 October 1885, in D 1390/26/7. No Archdale came forward, and a member of the Crichton family refused the candidacy; also *Fermanagh Times,* 15 October 1885.

72. *Impartial Reporter,* 3, December 1885, also 29 October and 5 November 1885.

73. *Fermanagh Times,* 5 November 1885.

74. Ibid., 10 December 1885.

75. *Impartial Reporter,* 10 December 1885.

76. *Fermanagh Times,* 20 May 1886, also 11 January, 1 April 1886.

77. *Fermanagh Times,* 22 July and 7 October 1886.

78. See Sturgis diary, entry for 30 July 1920, vol. I, in P.R.O. 30/59/1. Sturgis was an alert Castle official whose diary covers the period from July 1920–January 1922.

79. Eunan O'Halpin, 'Emergency legislation and the instruments of power in Ireland, 1916–1920', (unpublished M.A. thesis, University College, Dublin, 1980), p. 188, (Sir N. F. Warren Fisher was permanent secretary, Treasury and head of civil service, 1919–39).

80. Sir Victor Brooke to Douglas, 18 April 1887, in D 3004/C/1; and Sir Victor Brooke to Hugh de Fellenburg Montgomery, 2 February 1879, in D 627/428/4.

81. *Fermanagh Times,* 28 November 1907, obituary of Sir Douglas.

82. Brooke memoirs, op. cit.

83. *Fermanagh Times,* 28 November 1907; also see papers relating to Sir Douglas's role within the county in D 1390/24, 26, 'The estate papers of the Brooke family', in the 'Political papers of Falls and Hanna, solicitors'.

84. *Fermanagh Times,* 15 December 1892, and 28 November 1908.

85. Undated letter in Sir Douglas's correspondence, addressed to 'Harry', almost certainly written in the late 1880s, in D 3004/C/1.

86. See 'Minute book of Fermanagh county grand lodge 1845–1909', in D 1402/1, the papers of Lieu. Col. George Liddle, passim. Also see *Fermanagh Times,* 20 August 1908. Sir Douglas was district master of Brookeborough district.

87. See letter from Dudgeon to Sir Douglas, 20 October 1893, in D 3004/C/1. Dudgeon represented the South Fermanagh Unionist Association at the revision sessions, and became Sir Douglas's election agent.

88. *Fermanagh Times,* 19 January, 14 March and 1 August 1895.

89. Dudgeon to Brooke, 26 February 1894, in D 3004/C/1.

90. Trimble to Montgomery, 16 January 1893 and 12 March 1894, in D 627/428/207 and D 627/428/235.

91. *Fermanagh Times,* 14 March 1895: see also District inspector, monthly report, May 1894, State Paper Office, Dublin, box 6.

92. See Montgomery's correspondence on 14 and 18 March, and 4 April 1894, with Trimble and G. L. Falkiner, I.U.L. in D 627/428/238, 239, 243.

93. Dudgeon to Brooke, 22 February 1894, in D 3004/C/1.

94. District inspector, monthly reports, April and May, 1894, in State Paper Office, Dublin, box 6.

95. Dudgeon to Brooke, 20 October 1893, also Sir Douglas's printed electoral manifesto, dated 9 July 1895, in D 3004/C/1.

96. *Fermanagh Times,* 11 April, also 14 March 1895.

97. Dudgeon to Brooke, 17 July 1893, in D 3004/C/1.

98. See analysis of election results in ibid., also similar figures given in *Fermanagh Times,* 21 November 1895.

99. District inspector, monthly report, May 1894, in State Paper Office, Dublin, box 6.

100. *Fermanagh Times,* 27 September 1900.

101. Jeremiah Jordon to Brooke, 11 July 1895, in D 3004/C/1.

102. Obituary in *Fermanagh Herald,* 30 November 1907. This was the county's main nationalist newspaper.

103. *Fermanagh Times,* 28 November 1907, 5 December 1907.

104. Minutes of county grand lodge meeting, November 1907, in D 1402/1.

105. *Fermanagh Times,* 28 November 1907. See also F. S. L. Lyons, *Culture and anarchy in Ireland, 1890–1939,* (Oxford, 1979), pp 118, 119, for a penetrating analysis of the attitudes of the Anglo-Irish gentry.

106. See breakdown of South Fermanagh electorate dated 30 October 1894, and prepared for Jeremiah Jordon by his election agent, in D 2073/2/6, in 'Jeremiah Jordon, family and political correspondence, 1894'; also *Impartial Reporter,* 12 August 1882, which claimed that not a single Roman catholic lived in the townland of Brookeborough.
107. Jordon to Brooke, 11 July 1895, in D 3004/C/1.
108. See B. M. Walker, 'Party organisation in Ulster, 1865–1892', op. cit., p. 208; also P. M. Bottomley, 'The North Fermanagh elections of 1885 and 1886', op. cit., p. 176; the letter-book of J. W. Dane, op. cit., in D 1390/26/7, passim; *Fermanagh Times,* 28 May, 10 September, and 3 December 1885. There was a strong tendency amongst conservative to rely on the organisational framework of the Orange Order, tenant loyalty and church influence.
109. See county inspector's reports, December 1892–May 1893, in P.R.O. CO 904/48; also divisional commissioner, weekly reports, dated 2, 16 March 1893, in State Paper Office, Dublin, box 5.
110. County inspector's reports, May, August 1893, in P.R.O. CO 904/48.
111. See ibid., in P.R.O. CO 904/86, 87 passim.
112. See ibid., P.R.O., CO 904/91, 92, passim.

CHAPTER II

1. Brooke memoirs, op. cit.
2. Ibid.
3. *Sunday News,* 14 January 1968. The paper ran a series of weekly interviews with Brooke, conducted by Ken Nixon.
4. Brooke memoirs, op. cit.
5. Sheelagh Mulholland to author, 9 July 1979.
6. See 'Notes on my life', vol. 1, 'Childhood, soldiering in peace, First World War, 1883–1918', in Alanbrooke papers, (Liddell-Hart Centre for Military Archives, London) (hereafter cited as Alanbrooke memoirs) section 3, The memoirs are brief and unpublished.
7. Account of Alanbrooke's childhood by Lady Hilda Henrietta Wrench, (his sister), in Alanbrooke papers, (Liddell-Hart Centre for Military Archives), section 10.
8. Sir David Fraser, *Alanbrooke* (London, 1982), p. 44.
9. Sir David Fraser, op. cit., p. 44.
10. Alanbrooke memoirs, op. cit., ii, 1919–39. See also Arthur Bryant, *The turn of the tide, 1939–1943,* (London, 1957), p. 416. He refers to their 'close' friendship. His study is based on the Alanbrooke papers.
11. Ibid., op. cit., i.
12. Brooke memoirs, op. cit.
13. *Sunday News,* 14 January 1968.
14. Brooke memoirs, op. cit.
15. *Sunday News,* 14 January 1963; also see genealogical details of Brooke's mother, in D 998/25/3. 'Bundle of papers and correspondence mainly of Sir Basil and Lady Brooke, 1880–1920'.
16. Brooke memoirs, op. cit.
17. Sir Victor Brooke to Hugh de Fellenberg Montgomery, 2 February 1879, in D 627/428/4.
18. Alanbrooke memoirs, op. cit., i.
19. Brooke memoirs, op. cit.
20. Ibid.
21. See *Winchester College registers, 1884–1934,* edited by M. S. Leigh, (Winchester, 1940), and *Winchester College registers, 1901–1946,* edited by E. R. Wilson and H. A. Jackson, (London, 1956), passim. Also see Winchester College magazines, 1901–05; and Brooke memoirs, op. cit.
22. *Sunday News,* 14 January 1968.
23. Brooke memoirs, op. cit.
24. From registers and reports for 1905–1908, kept at Royal Military Academy, Sandhurst.
25. From records of Captain Sir Basil Stanlake Brooke, M.C., kept at Army Records Centre, Ministry of Defence, Hayes, Middlesex (hereafter cited as Brooke army records). These contain little not available in the *Quarterly army list,* (January, 1919).

26. Brooke to mother, 29 December 1908, in D 3004/C/2. This box contains Brooke's letters to his family at Colebrooke, 1908–1918.
27. Brooke to mother, 10 February 1909 and 28 August 1910, in D 3004/C/2.
28. See entry for 27 February 1909, in D 3004/G/5, 'Album and diary . . . recording hunting and other experiences of Sir Basil Brooke, February 1909–December 1910'.
29. Brooke to mother, 22 July 1901, in D 3004/C/2.
30. These complaints are, however, mentioned, see Brooke to mother, 10 June 1910, also 13 May 1910, in ibid.
31. *Sunday News,* 14 January 1968.
32. Brooke to mother, 22 April, 5 August and 6 October 1910, in D 3004/C/2.
33. Brooke to mother, 6 May 1910, also 23 November 1909, in ibid.
34. See will of Sir Arthur Douglas Brooke, dated 18 October 1907, with codicil, dated 2 November 1907, (Probate Office, Somerset House, London).
35. Brooke to mother, 5 August 1910, also 23 September 1910, in D 3004/C/2.
36. Brooke transferred on 4 January 1911, see Brooke army records, op. cit.; and Brooke memoirs, op. cit.
37. *Sunday News,* 14 January 1968, also Brooke to mother, 20 July 1911, in D 3004/C/2.
38. Alanbrooke memoirs, op. cit., i.
39. Brooke memoirs, op. cit.
40. Sir David Fraser, op. cit., p. 49.
41. Brooke to mother, 20 July 1911 and 3 April 1912, in D 3004/C/2.
42. Brooke to mother, 3 June 1912 in ibid.
43. *Fermanagh Times,* 1 August 1912.
44. Brooke to Sheelagh, (his sister), 14 August 1915, in D 3004/C/2.
45. *Fermanagh Times,* 19 November 1908.
46. *News Letter,* 19 September 1912. Carson spoke at length of Fermanagh during the 1641 insurrection and Williamite wars. Also see Brooke's recollections of covenant day, in *Belfast Telegraph,* 27 September 1962.
47. *Sunday News,* 14 January 1968, also W. D. Flackes, op. cit. He recalled helping W. C. Trimble drill the Enniskillen Horse.
48. See minute book of Fermanagh county U.V.F. committee, in D 1402/4, 'County Fermanagh committee minute book, W. B. Stack, honorary secretary'. The military training committee was set up on 25 February 1913.
49. See reports by J. Sears, the county's U.V.F. instructor, in D 1390/19/1, 'J. Sears (instructor to U.V.F.), journal detailing numbers of squads, numbers enrolled, musketry tests, 24 April–29 July 1914'. he visited Colebrooke on 24 July 1914.
50. Reports on Enniskillen Horse, in P.R.O., Co 904/27/1.
51. Police reports on arms held by the U.V.F. dated 12 March 1917, indicate that there were 510 Italian rifles at Colebrooke out of the force's estimated total of 2,318 for the county, in P.R.O. Co 904/29/2, 'Volunteers'. Almost one-third of those members of leading local families who were approached to help organise the force in December 1912 refused. See minute book of Fermanagh county U.V.F. committee, in D 1402/4, op. cit.
52. *Fermanagh Times,* 23 January, and 27 February 1913, and 26 March 1914.
53. Flackes, op. cit.
54. *Sunday News,* 14 January 1968.
55. Brooke to Sylvia, (his sister), 27 July 1913, in D 3004/C/2.
56. Brooke memoirs, op. cit.
57. Ibid.
58. Ronald Brooke to Clark, (Colebrooke land agent), 12 November 1914, in D 3004/C/2.
59. Bryant, op. cit., p. 194; also Ronald Brooke to Clark, 12 November 1914, in D 3004/C/2.
60. Brooke army records, op. cit., He had been granted commission as 2nd lieutenant, Royal Fusiliers on 24 September 1908.
61. Brooke to Sylvia, 27 October 1914, in D 3004/C/2; also Brooke to Clark, 15 September 1914, in ibid.
62. War diary of 10th Hussars, entry for 4 November 1914, records Brooke arriving with 10 other ranks, in P.R.O., W.O. 95/156, '10th Royal Hussars (Prince of Wales Own) war diary'.
63. F. H. D. C. Whitmore, *The 10th (Prince of Wales Own) Royal Hussars and the Essex Yeomanry, during the European war, 1914–1918,* (Colchester, 1920), pp 4–7.

64. 10 Hussars war diary, op. cit., entry for 11 November 1914, in P.R.O., W.O. 95/156; *Sunday News,* 14 January 1968; also Brooke to Clark, on 23 December 1914, reflecting back over his experiences since early November, in D 3004/C/2.
65. Brooke memoirs, op. cit. The 10 Hussars war diary, op. cit. mentions Brooke going on reconnaissance, on 26–7 November 1914, in P.R.O., W.O. 95/156. This appears to be the only other reference to him, in this period, apart from noting his arrival on 4 November 1914.
66. F. H. D. C. Whitmore, op. cit., pp 7, 15, also 10 Hussars war diary, op. cit., 3 February 1915, in P.R.O., W.O. 95/156.
67. Brooke memoirs, op. cit.; also Brooke to mother, 30 March 1915, in D 3004/C/2. Whilst in France the prince was mainly 'employed on paperwork and the carrying of dispatches', causing him to complain that his only real job was 'that of being prince of Wales'. See Frances Donaldson, *Edward VIII, the road to abdication,* (London, 1978), p. 39.
68. *Sunday News,* 14 January 1968, also Brooke memoirs, op. cit.
69. Brooke to mother, 16 April 1915, in D 3004/C/2; also Brooke to Sylvia, 19 May 1916, in ibid.
70. Brooke army records, op. cit. Brooke became senior A.D.C. to Byng. Also see Brooke to Sylvia, 8 May 1915, in D 3004/C/2.
71. F. H. D. C. Whitmore, op. cit., pp 44, 45, also 10 Hussar war diary, op. cit. entries for 7–13 May 1915, in P.R.O., W.O. 95/156; and Brooke to Sylvia, 31 May 1915, in D 3004/C/2.
72. See 'Byng of Vimy, an appreciation', by Sir Louis Vaughan, in the *Arm Quarterly,* xxxi, (October 1935–January 1936); and Jeffrey Williams, *Byng of Vimy, general and governor general,* (London, 1983), p. 367. It was Byng's intention that Julian should inherit Thorpe Hall with its beautiful gardens, and also his wife's considerable personal estate. He also left £5,000 to Brooke. The Byngs were childless.
73. Brooke to Sylvia, 8 May 1915, and 14 August 1915, in D 3004/C/2. On 21 April 1915, he wrote to Sylvia stating that Byng was 'one of the nicest men I have ever met, and I don't think I would have cared to go to anybody but him. It seems rather velvet', ibid.
74. Brooke to Sylvia, 29 June, and 15 August 1915, in D 3004/C/2. He wrote, 'I am just off to the Dardanelles in two hours, only four hours notice, with the general'.
75. Quoted in Flackes, op. cit.
76. Williams, op. cit., pp 99, 100.
77. Brooke to Sylvia, 31 August, and 14 September 1915, in D 3004/C/2. He observed: 'the old Turk is a great gentleman. He never shoots at the Hospital ships in the bay or at the hospitals, very different from our friend, the Bosch'.
78. Brooke to Sylvia, 21 December 1915, in D 3004/C/2; also Brooke memoirs, op. cit.
79. Brooke to Sylvia, 24 January 1916, in D 3004/C/2. In these last moments of the evacuation, 'all the men had reported in, . . . [and] . . . there was no one between [Byng and Brooke] and the Turks', see Williams, op. cit., p. 108.
80. Referred to in 'Byng of Vimy, and appreciation', by Sir Louis Vaughan, in *Army Quarterly,* xxxi, October 1935–January 1936; see Williams, op. cit., p. 109. Williams writes 'Had the operation failed, Byng knew his career would be over. Now that it had succeeded, he knew he would never be forgiven'. Kitchener had been utterly opposed to evacuation.
81. Brooke to Sylvia, 24 January 1916, also 21 December 1915, in D 3004/C/2.
82. Brooke to Sylvia, 14 September 1915, 13 February and 24 January 1916, in D 3004/C/2.
83. Brooke to Sylvia, 24 January 1916, in ibid.
84. Byng to Sylvia, 25 March 1916, and 8 April 1916, in D 3004/C/2. Brooke had written to Sylvia, on 15 September 1915, 'Sometimes we get straffed, sometimes we don't . . . but it always frightens me'. See also Brooke's army records, op. cit.; and Williams, op. cit., pp 112, 113, 125.
85. *Fermanagh Times,* 2 March 1916.
86. *Irish Times,* 30 October 1968.
87. Brooke army records, op. cit. Brooke returned to France, on 13 July 1916 having been appointed A.D.C. to G.O.C. Canadian Army Corps, on 28 May 1916. Also see *London Gazette,* 13 July 1916; and *Fermanagh Times,* 6 July 1916. Brooke was soon in the thick of battle. The *Toronto Telegram* reported that he and Byng' crawled past dead men and over shattered . . . sandbags and wire . . . [to the Canadian] . . . advance post . . . within fifteen yards of the Germans', on 12 August 1916, quoted in Williams, op. cit., pp 127, 128.
88. Alanbrooke memoirs, op. cit., i.
89. Brooke army records, op. cit. Brooke's promotion dated from 7 May 1917.

90. Alanbrooke memoirs, op. cit., i. Brooke's younger brother, Arthur, who was in the Royal Flying Corps, also served as A.D.C. to Byng for a time during this period, see Williams, op. cit., p. 180. The general sent Sir Basil out in a tank to bring him back early first-hand reports, during Cambrai. Williams describes this as 'the first use of a personal liaison officer by an army commander in an armouréd battle', p. 185; also *Sunday News,* 14 January 1968.
91. Brooke memoirs, op. cit. His Croix-de-Guerre is listed in *London Gazette* 10 October 1918. Amongst those present at the conference, on 26 March, were Poincaré, Clemenceau, Pétain, Milner, Haig and Wilson, see Williams, op. cit., p. 231.
92. From Byng's 'Special order of the day to all ranks of the Third Army', dated 11 November 1918, copy in D 3004/C/2; also Brooke to Sylvia, 1 October 1918, in ibid.
93. Brooke to Sylvia, 15 November 1918, in D 3004/C/2; Brooke memoirs, op. cit.
94. *Fermanagh Times,* 14 November, 12 December 1918, and 24 April 1919.
95. Brooke army records, op. cit.
96. F. H. D. C. Whitmore, op. cit., pp 223, 224. Byng's term as governor-general of Canada ended in a constitutional crisis and he was as a result described as 'a broken man', in September 1926, see Williams, op. cit., p. 325.
97. *Burke's peerage, baronetage and knightage,* edited by Peter Townsend, (London 1963), p. 388.
98. *News of the World,* 20 April 1919.
99. *Sussex Daily,* 5 June 1919.
100. *Fermanagh Times,* 1 September 1921.
101. *Daily Mirror,* 4 June 1919.
102. *Fermanagh Times,* 12 June 1919.
103. *Sunday News,* 14 January 1968.
104. Brooke to Sylvia, 26 October, 25 November 1915, and 24 January 1916; also Brooke to Clark, 3 August 1915, Brooke to mother, 4 June 1915, in D 3004/C/2, and Brooke to Sylvia, 26 October, and 26 November 1915, in ibid.
105. Lady Brooke diary, in D 3004/D/29, passim. The diary is very brief, kept irregularly, with entries by the month and even the year.
106. Lady Brooke diary, entry for July 1919, in D 3004/D/29.
107. *Fermanagh Times,* 13 and 27 November, 10 July 1919.
108. Brooke's oral evidence to Boundary Commission, on 29 April 1925, in P.R.O., CAB 61/66, 'Fermanagh County Council, 27 April 1925–30 April 1925.
109. *Fermanagh Times,* 17 July, and 11 September 1919.
110. *Fermanagh Times,* 5 February 1920.
111. *Sunday News,* 14 January 1968.
112. Lady Brooke diary, entry for June 1920, in D 3004/D/29.

CHAPTER III

1. W. S. Churchill, *The aftermath,* (London, 1929) p. 312.
2. See inspector general, monthly reports for June, November 1915, April 1916, and May 1918, in P.R.O., CO 904/97, 98, 99 and 106.
3. *Fermanagh Times,* 12 December 1918.
4. County inspector's report, October 1917, in P.R.O., CO 904/104.
5. Ibid., May 1916, in Co 904/100, also June 1916.
6. *Fermanagh Times,* 18 May and 1 June 1916.
7. County inspector's reports, February 1917, October 1917, December 1917, and March 1918, in P.R.O., CO 904/102, 104, 105; Livingstone op. cit. p. 282.
8. County inspector's reports, June 1916–April 1918, in P.R.O., CO 904/100–105.
9. See intelligence notes, for County Fermanagh, 1918, in P.R.O., CO 903/19, also county inspector's reports, 1918–19, passim, in P.R.O., CO 904/105–111.
10. Intelligence notes for 1919 in P.R.O., CO 903/19. Also see county inspector's reports, November 1918–October 1919, in P.R.O., CO 904/107–110.
11. Ibid., September, October and December 1919, and February 1920, in P.R.O., CO 904/109, 110, 111. District inspector J. W. Nixon was stationed at Lisnaskea. In 1924 he was dismissed from the force for inflamatory language, and later became an Independent Unionist M.P. for Woodvale. See Michael Farrell, *Northern Ireland, the Orange state,* (London, 1976), p. 346.

12. Intelligence notes, 1919, in P.R.O., CO 903/19, also county inspector's reports, September, November 1919, in P.R.O., CO 904/110.
13. Ibid., January–July 1920, in P.R.O., CO 904/111, 112.
14. Flackes, op. cit., also *Sunday News,* 21 January 1968; and Lady Brooke diary, entries for April and May 1920, in D 3004/D/29.
15. Greenwood to Bonar Law, 18 May 1920, in Lloyd George papers, F31/1/35/(C), House of Lords Record Office. Sir Hamar Greenwood was chief secretary for Ireland, 1920–22.
16. *Sunday News,* 21 January 1968.
17. *Fermanagh Times,* 6 May 1920, and *Impartial Reporter,* 22 April 1920. See also Crawford to Carson, 14 May 1920, in papers of Col. F. H. Crawford, in D 640/7, 'Correspondence concerning north-west boundary'.
18. Lady Brooke diary, June 1920, in D 3004/D/29. See also Flackes, op. cit., and *Sunday News,* 21 January 1968.
19. County inspector's report, January 1921, in P.R.O., CO 904/114.
20. Copy of Brooke to Macready, undated, but written in mid-July in reply to letter from Macready, dated 7 July 1920, in D 3004/C/2. General Sir C. F. N. Macready was general officer commanding-in-chief Ireland, 1920–22.
21. Brooke to Ernest Clark, assistant under-secretary, Belfast, undated but clearly received by Clark shortly before 28 September 1920, in papers of Sir Ernest Clark, D 1022/2/9, 'Special Constabulary, table of progress, 1920–1921.
22. Brooke to Macready, mid-July, op. cit., in D 3004/C/2.
23. County inspector's reports, June 1920, see also February, in P.R.O., CO 904/111, 112.
24. County inspector's report, August 1920, in P.R.O., CO 904/112; also intelligence notes, 1919, in P.R.O., CO 903/19.
25. Lady Brooke' diary entry for June 1920, in D 3004/D/29.
26. Brooke to Macready, mid-July 1920, op. cit., D 3004/C/2.
27. Brooke to Clark, undated but September 1920, op. cit., in D 1022/2/9. There is no reason whatever to doubt that Brooke was genuinely seeking to create a body with broad community support. There is no evidence to support Michael Farrell's view that Sir Basil was merely 'sensitive, that his force should not appear to be exclusively protestant . . .[in order to]. . . secure government recognition.' See Michael Farrell, *Arming the protestants,* (London 1983), pp 15–16.
28. Brooke to Macready, mid-July 1920, in D 3004/C/2.
29. See inspector general, monthly reports, November 1915, June 1916, May 1918, July and August 1919 in P.R.O., CO 904/98, 100, 106, and 109.
30. See note of points made by the U.U.C. standing committee to Clark, on 13 October 1920, in FIN 18/1/125, 'Ulster Unionist Council deputation to chief secretary at Belfast, on 13 October 1920', (1920).
31. Inspector general, monthly reports, June 1920, in P.R.O., CO 904/112. Also see Lady Spender diary, entry for late July 1920, in D 1633/2/23.
32. County inspector's reports, June–August 1920, passim, in P.R.O., CO 904/112.
33. See Clark's list, undated, of civilian vigilance forces in FIN 18/1/2, 'Special Constabulary, general scheme, 1920–21'. It is impossible to know how complete the list is but it is noteworthy that the only entry for Fermanagh is for a group at Lisbellaw. Brooke's 'Vigilance' is not included.
34. County inspector's report, April 1916, in P.R.O., CO 904/99. They met on 27 April 1916.
35. *Fermanagh Times,* 1 June 1916.
36. *Impartial Reporter,* 20 May 1920, also 3 June 1920.
37. *Fermanagh Times,* 27 May 1920.
38. Livingstone, op. cit., p. 142.
39. *Fermanagh Times,* 18 May 1911; also *Lisbellaw Gazette,* 15 July 1879.
40. See *Impartial Reporter,* 6 December 1920, speech by Porter-Porter, local unionist landlord.
41. Flackes, op. cit. He makes more sweeping claims in the *Sunday News,* 21 January 1968.
42. Brooke to Macready, mid-July 1920, in D 3004/C/2. He refers in this letter to visiting Dublin Castle earlier.
43. Brooke to Clark, September 1920, in D 1022/2/9.
44. Clark to Brooke, 30 April 1921, in FIN 18/1/54, 'County Fermanagh. Special Constabulary, county commandant'. Referring to the special constabulary, Clark described himself as 'not its parent but its foster parent' in letter to Wickham, 16 November 1920, in D 1022/2/9.
45. See Clark to Wickham, 16 November 1920, D 1022/2/9. The letter details his functions.

46. Clark to Sir Hamar Greenwood, 21 September 1920, in FIN 18/1/85, 'Chief Secretary. Duplicate copies of correspondence to 31 December 1920'.
47. Report by S. G. Tallents, 4 July 1922, in P.R.O., CO 906/30, 'Tallents' terms of reference, and report on the situation in Northern Ireland', from papers of S. G. Tallents P.R.O., CO 906/23–31. Tallents was private secretary to Lord Fitzalan, lord lieutenant of Ireland, 1921–22, and conducted an imperial investigation into Northern Ireland government security measures, mid-1922.
48. Clark to Sir John Anderson, 19 November 1920, in FIN 18/1/2. Anderson was joint under-secretary to the lord lieutenant of Ireland, 1920–23.
49. Lady Spender diary, entry for 29 October 1920, in D 1633/2/23.
50. Diary of Sir Wilfred B. Spender, permanent secretary, Ministry of Finance, in D 715, 7 August 1941. In later years Sir Wilfred frequently looked back on his active role in the U.V.F. and special constabulary just before and immediately after the war with deep satisfaction.
51. *Sunday News,* 21 January 1968, also Flackes, op. cit., and Lady Brooke diary, D 3004/D/29, entries for June, July 1920.
52. Clark to Anderson, 28 September 1920, in D 1022/2/9.
53. Brooke to Clark, September 1920, in 1022/2/9.
54. Clark to Anderson, 28 September 1920, in ibid., refers to this suggestion and to Brooke's overall scheme.
55. Personal note by Clark, 28 September 1920, in ibid.
56. Clark to Anderson, 28 September 1920, in D 1022/2/9.
57. See submissions from special constabulary officers in Tyrone to S. G. Tallents, 20 June 1922, in P.R.O., CO 906/27, 'Notes on police force'.
58. Copy of these instructions sent to Clark, dated 6 July 1920, in FIN 18/1/85.
59. Macready to Sir John Anderson, 25 May 1920, in P.R.O., CO 904/188 the Sir John Anderson papers.
60. Copy of instructions, 6 July 1920, in FIN 18/1/85.
61. Flackes, op. cit.; also *Sunday News,* 21 January 1968.
62. See county inspector's reports, July 1920, also June, August and September 1920, in P.R.O., CO 904/122.
63. Macready to Anderson, 18 June 1920, in P.R.O., CO 904/188, and Anderson to Bonar Law, 2 September 1920, in ibid.
64. Report of conference of ministers, 23 July 1920, attended by Lloyd George, in cabinet memoranda, in P.R.O., CO 24/109.
65. See cabinet conclusions, in P.R.O., CAB 23/22, for report of conference of ministers, on 2 September 1920, including Craig's memorandum. See also Tom Jones, *Whitehall diary,* iii, *Ireland 1918–1925,* (London, 1971), p. 28; also John McColgan, *British policy and the Irish administration, 1920–1922* (London, 1983), pp 31, 32.
66. Clark to Anderson, 28 September, also 5 October 1920, in FIN 18/1/2, and see later comments in Clark to Blackmore, 8 March 1921, in FIN 18/1/3, 'Special constabulary (general), appointments, 1920–1921'.
67. Clark to Anderson, 4 October 1920, in FIN 18/1/98, 'Press correspondence and correspondence relating to published articles etc, 1920–1921'.
68. At ministerial conference, 23 July 1920, in P.R.O., CAB 24/109 Lloyd George spoke of the merits of such a scheme in releasing troops and police. Also see cabinet conclusions, 8 September 1920, P.R.O., CAB 23/22, which approved the special constabulary scheme and the creation of an assistant under-secretary, in Belfast.
69. Bonar Law to Lloyd George, 2 September 1920, in Lloyd George papers, House of Lords Records Office, F 31/1/43. Law had initially hesitated over the scheme.
70. Clark to Anderson, 8 November 1920, in FIN 18/1/2.
71. See county inspector's reports, in P.R.O., CO 904/111, 112, passim.
72. Lady Brooke diary, December 1920, in D 3004/D/29.
73. County inspector's reports, July and October 1920, in P.R.O., CO 904/112, 113.
74. *Impartial Reporter,* 30 September 1920, and 16 December 1920.
75. *Fermanagh Herald,* 27 November 1920.
76. Spender to Clark, 15 November 1920, and Clark to Wickham, 15 November 1920, in FIN 18/1/54.
77. Clark to Collum, 11 November 1920, in FIN 18/1/56, County Fermanagh special constabulary, General scheme 1920–1921.

78. Clark to Anderson, 11 November 1920, and Clark to Wickham, 10 December 1920 in FIN 18/1/3.
79. Craig to Cole, 3 May 1921, and Cole to Craig, 5 May 1921, in CAB 9J/2/2, 'Correspondence concerning membership of the Senate, 1921'.
80. Clark to Anderson, 10 November 1920, in FIN 18/1/56.
81. Clark's private papers contain copies of the forms used in this procedure in D 1022/2/9.
82. See Clark to Anderson, 19 November 1920, where he states: 'it is not our duty to provide the men'. in FIN 18/1/2.
83. Clark to Anderson, 10 November 1920, to Wickham 29 November 1920 and to Collum, 11 November in FIN 18/1/56.
84. Clark informed Wickham, in letter dated 29 November 1920, in FIN 18/1/56.
85. See S. G. Tallents' coded descriptions of Ulster leaders, in P.R.O., CO 906/24, 'Diary and notes on Northern Ireland government personalities'.
86. *Impartial Reporter,* 16 December 1920.
87. Circular in Brooke's private papers, dated 23 November 1920, in D 3004/C/2.
88. *Impartial Reporter,* 16 December 1920.
89. Clark to Wickham, 29 November 1920, in FIN 18/1/56.
90. See statistics relating to the recruitment of specials, in FIN 18/1/170, 'Parliamentary question, Mr Raffan to ask the chief secretary in which counties recruitment for Special constabulary initiated . . . 1920'; FIN 18/1/12, 'Special constabulary, weekly returns . . . to 26 March 1921'; and FIN 18/1/13, 'Special constabulary, weekly returns . . . to 30 September 1921'.
91. Falls' speech reported in *Impartial Reporter,* 16 December 1920, also similar comments, 3 March 1921.
92. Clark to Brooke, 4 December 1920, in FIN 18/1/56; also see for example, *Impartial Reporter,* 16 December 1920.
93. Clark to Brooke, 30 April 1921, in FIN 18/1/54.
94. Ibid.
95. County inspector's reports, P.R.O., CO 904/113, 114, 115.
96. See undated submission by unionist deputation from the Fermanagh–Monaghan border area, but clearly drawn up in late March 1921, in FIN 18/1/211, 'Police protection for loyalists on borders of Fermanagh and Monaghan, 1921'.
97. Clark to Gen. Hackett-Pain, 11 May 1921, in ibid.
98. Undated border submission, late March 1921, in FIN 18/1/211, also county inspector's reports in P.R.O., CO 904/114, 115 passim.
99. Lady Brooke diary, May 1921, in D 3004/D/29.
100. Clark to Anderson, 31 April 1921, in FIN 18/1/56.
101. *Impartial Reporter,* 24 March 1921.
102. See recruitment statistics in FIN 18/1/13, passim, also Brooke's written submission to the Boundary Commission, in P.R.O., CAB 61/64, 'Fermanagh County Council, 20 December 1924–18 May 1925.
103. County inspector's report, June 1921, in P.R.O., CO 904/115, also Livingstone, op. cit. p. 293. The county inspector reported forty eight 'outrages between April–July 1921. These included ambushes of police and special constables, attacks on 'loyalist' homes, some acts of destruction on landed estates and also 'reprisal' attacks on the cottages of alleged Sinn Fein party members. See county inspector's reports, April–July 1921, in P.R.O., CO 904/115, 116.
104. Brooke to Craig, 3 June 1921, in CAB 9J/2/2; also county inspector's reports, in P.R.O., CO 904/115, passim, particularly reports for May and June.
105. Ibid., May, June and July 1921, in P.R.O., CO 904/115, 116.
106. *Fermanagh Times,* 16 June 1921.
107. *Impartial Reporter,* 14 July 1921, also FIN 18/1/13, passim; and Spender to Clark, 15 November 1920, and Wickham to Clark, 29 June 1921, in FIN 18/1/54.
108. Clark to Anderson, 28 September 1920, in D 1022/2/9.
109. Lady Spender diary, entry for 24 June 1921, in D 1633/2/24, also Frederick H. Crawford's account, in D 640/16, 'Royal visit, 1921' and *Fermanagh Times,* 16 June 1921.
110. Lady Craig diary, entry for 9 April 1921, in D 1415/B/38, 'Transcript from Lady Craig's diaries 1905–1940'.
111. Ibid., entries for 10–12 April 1921, in D 1415/D/38; also Flackes, op. cit. "Riversdale" was Archdale's home. In 1903 Craig lost North Fermanagh to E. Mitchell, an Independent, supported by unattached Liberals and Methodists, some protestant tenants and most nationalist electors.

112. Extract from stereotyped letter circulated in late April 1921, by Craig, in CAB 9J/2/2.
113. Brooke to Craig, 3 June 1921, in CAB 9J/2/2/; also *Fermanagh Times,* 16 June 1921.
114. See note of phone-call by Brooke to Clark, on 18 June 1921, in FIN 18/1/54.
115. Brooke to Wickham, 20 June 1921, in ibid.
116. Wickham to Clark, 27 June 1921, and Clark's reply, 28 June 1921, in ibid.
117. See recruitment statistics in FIN 18/1/13.
118. County inspector's reports, August and September 1921, in P.R.O., CO 904/115.
119. *Fermanagh Times,* 6 October 1921.
120. *Impartial Reporter,* 27 October 1921.
121. *Fermanagh Times,* 10 November 1921.
122. *Impartial Reporter,* 8 September 1921.
123. See FIN 18/1/13, passim.
124. County inspector's report, August 1921, in P.R.O., CO 904/115.
125. Tom Jones, op. cit., pp 137, 155; also diary of Mark Sturgis, entry for 31 October 1921, in P.R.O., 30/59/5. Sturgis, an alert Castle official noted that the Irish nationalist press was focussing increasing attention on Fermanagh and Tyrone.
126. For Churchill's remarks, see 'Notes of conference held in the prime minister's office, House of Commons, 3 December 1925', in P.R.O., CAB 61/16.
127. See Fermanagh county council minutes, 27 October and 15 December 1921, in LA 4/2GG/2. Also see E. G. Phoenix, 'Introduction and calendar of the Cahir Healy Papers', (M. A. thesis, Queen's University, Belfast, 1978), p. 3 (hereafter cited as Calendar, Healy Papers). The papers are in the Public Record Office, Northern Ireland.
128. *Fermanagh Times,* 22 December 1921, also *Impartial Reporter,* 8 December 1921.
129. *Parliamentary Debates,* (Northern Ireland, House of Commons), vol. ii, col. 9, on 14 March 1922.
130. Cabinet conclusions, on 14 March 1922, in CAB 4/36, also *Parliamentary Debates,* (Northern Ireland, House of Commons), vol. ii, cols 15–16, on 14 March 1922.
131. Lady Brooke diary, December 1921, in D 3004/D/29.
132. Tallents' report, 4 July 1922, in P.R.O., CO 906/30.
133. Ibid. See also weekly reports by Macready, general officer commanding in Ireland, 1920–1923, in cabinet memoranda, P.R.O., CAB 24/134, 135, 136, passim.
134. Mervyn Dane, *The Fermanagh 'B' Specials,* (Enniskillen, 1970), pp 9, 10, also P.R.O., CAB 21/254, 'Border incidents, February to June 1922', passim. The raid took place on the night of 7 April 1922.
135. Lady Craig diary, 9 April 1922, in D 1415/B/38, also Flackes, op. cit. Brooke met Craig on 9 April.
136. See *Parliamentary Debates.* (Northern Ireland, Senate), vol. i, col. 140, on 8 December 1921, and vol. ii, col. 11, on 14 March 1922, for Lord Londonderry congratulating Brooke; also personal interview with John Brooke, 23 February 1985.
137. Craig's telegram to Lloyd George, 8 February 1922, and a copy of Griffith to Collins, 8 February 1922, in P.R.O., CAB 21/254.
138. Cope to Tom Jones, 8 February 1922, in ibid. The political prisoners held at Londonderry were later reprieved. The Monaghan group were called locally the 'Monaghan footballers'. See also Michael Farrell, op. cit., p. 92, who claims that Collins 'approved the raid' though he 'denied knowing anything about it.'
139. *Impartial Reporter,* 9 February 1922.
140. *Sunday News,* 21 January 1968; also Flackes, op. cit.
141. See Cabinet conclusions, on 14 February 1922, in CAB 4/32, and on 1 April 1922, in CAB 4/38; also *Fermanagh Times,* 9 February 1922.
142. *Impartial Reporter,* 2 February 1922.
143. Lady Craig diary, 9 April 1921, in D 1415/B/38. The Craigs made the return journey by car.
144. Dane, op. cit. pp 12, 28, 29; also P.R.O., CAB 21/254, passim; local newspaper accounts in *Impartial Reporter* and *Fermanagh Times,* on 16 and 23 February 1922; and Brooke's submission to the Boundary Commission, in P.R.O., CAB 61/64.
145. Ibid., also Dane, op. cit., p. 12.
146. *Impartial Reporter,* 23 February 1922 and *Fermanagh Times,* 16 February 1922.
147. Lady Craig diary, 12 and 18 February 1922, in D 1415/B/38; also Lady Spender diary, 13 February 1922, in D 1633/2/26; and Lady Brooke diary, February 1922, in D 3004/D/29.
148. *Fermanagh Times,* 23 February 1922.

149. Entry for April 1922, in Lady Brooke diary, D 3004/D/29; also see special constabulary mobilisation figures in FIN 18/1/578, 'Mobilisation of special constables, 1922–1926', also *Fermanagh Times,* 16 February 1922.
150. Lady Brooke diary, March 1922, in D 3004/D/29, also *Fermanagh Times,* 9 March 1922 and *Impartial Reporter,* 23 March 1922.
151. Cope to Churchill, 7 March 1922, in P.R.O., CAB 21/254.
152. Lady Brooke diary, April 1922, in D 3004/D/29.
153. *Impartial Reporter,* 30 March 1922, also *Fermanagh Times,* 30 March 1922, and Dane, op. cit. pp 27, 28.
154. See cabinet conclusions, 14 February 1922, in CAB 4/32; also *News Letter,* 9 and 10 February 1922.
155. See cabinet conclusions, CAB 4/32, 37, on 14 February and 27 March 1922.
156. *Parliamentary debates,* (Northern Ireland, House of Commons), vol. ii., col. 344, on 4 April 1922.
157. Diary of Sir Henry Wilson, entries for 30 and 31 March 1922, microfilm copies Imperial War Museum, London, DS/MISC/80.
158. Cope to Jones, 8 February 1922 in P.R.O. CAB 21/254. See also note of conference between Craig and Sir Robert S. Horne, chancellor of the Exchequer, on 9 February 1922, in CAB 9A/4/1, '1921–23, constabulary finance, transfer of Irish services in connection with the maintenance of law and order'.
159. Cabinet conclusions, in 14 February 1922, in CAB 4/32. Craig spoke of the British government wanting 'to wash their hands of the whole affair'.
160. See Wilson diary, 8 February 1922, in Imperial War Museum, London, DS/MISC/80; also Jones op. cit., p. 194.
161. Brooke submission to Boundary Commission, in P.R.O., CAB 61/64. See also Dane, op. cit., pp 19, 27; *Fermanagh Times,* 13 April 1922; Livingstone, op. cit., p. 307.
162. *Fermanagh Times,* 13 April 1922.
163. Brooke's submission to the Boundary Commission, in P.R.O., CAB 61/64. Dane, op. cit., pp 7–10; reports in *Impartial Reporter* and *Fermanagh Times,* on 1 and 8 June 1922. The five R.I.C. barracks referred to were at Pettigo, Kesh, Belcoo, Belleek and Castlecaufield.
164. *Fermanagh Times,* 20 April and 11 May 1922. See also the report produced by G.H.Q., Ireland, dated 8 June 1922, in P.R.O., CAB 21/254.
165. Report by Lionel Curtis, adviser on Irish affairs in the Colonial Office, 1921–24, dated 6 June 1922, in ibid., also Brooke submission to Boundary Commission in P.R.O., CAB 61/64.
166. Reports by Macready, for weeks ending 3 and 10 June 1922, in P.R.O., CAB 24/136.
167. Lady Brooke diary, entry for June 1922, in D 3004/D/29. See also Flackes, op. cit. The last Sunday in May was 28 May 1922.
168. Reports by Curtis and by G.H.Q., dated 6 and 8 June 1922, in P.R.O., CAB 21/254.
169. Cabinet conclusions, on 31 May 1922, in CAB 4/46.
170. Reports by Curtis and by G.H.Q., dated 6 and 8 June 1922. in P.R.O., CAB 21/254; also Lady Brooke diary, entry for 1922, in D 3004/D/29.
171. Jones, op. cit., pp 211, 212; also Curtis report, 6 June 1922, and Collins to Churchill, 5 June 1922, in P.R.O., CAB 21/254.
172. Churchill to Lloyd George, 8 June 1922. See also his telegram to Lloyd George, 7 June 1922, and comments at the provisional government of Ireland committee on 6 June 1922, in ibid; and Jones, op. cit., pp 210, 200, and p. xx, (introduction by Middlemas).
173. Report by Curtis, 6 June 1922, in P.R.O., CAB 21/254; also Lady Brooke diary, entry for June 1922, in D 3004/29; also Jones op. cit., p. 212.
174. Cabinet conclusions, on 31 May and 19, 20 June 1920, in CAB 4/46, 48.
175. See report by Tallents, 4 July 1922, in P.R.O., CO 906/30.
176. Lady Brooke diary July 1922, in D 3004/D/29.
177. Reports by Macready, for weeks ending 10 and 17 June and 1 July 1922 in P.R.O., CAB 24/136. See also CAB 4/48, on 19, 20 June 1920, with regard to a neutral zone; and Flackes, op. cit.
178. Cabinet conclusions, 31 May 1922, in CAB 4/46, also *Fermanagh Times,* 18 May and 1 June 1922; and Lady Brooke diary, April and May 1922, in D 3004/D/29.
179. Cabinet conclusions, 19 April and 20 May 1922, in CAB 4/40, 43. See also Lady Brooke diary, entry for June 1922, in D 3004/D/29.

180. Calender, Healy papers, op. cit., pp 4, 5. See also *Impartial Reporter*, 25 May 1922. Brooke was called as a witness before the commission, on 29 April 1922, P.R.O., CAB 61/66, 'Fermanagh County Council, 27 April 1925–30 April 1925'.
181. Minutes of Fermanagh County Council, for 27 October and 15 December 1921, in LA 4/2GG/2.
182. Record of meeting held on 15 May 1922, of the north-eastern advisory committee, State Paper Office, Dublin S1011 'Minutes of the north eastern advisory committee, 1922'. Healy did say: 'we should not take life'.
183. See 'The abolition of proportional representation, 1922–38, State Paper Office, Dublin, S 2925. Consideration of this issue by the southern government related almost exclusively to County Tyrone. Also see memorandum requested by Collins, on the 'Position in the six counties in regard to the abolition of proportional representation there', dated 31 August 1922, in ibid. Milroy was a member of the north-eastern advisory committee.
184. Diary of Lady Brooke, June–August 1922, in D 3004/D/29; also FIN 18/1/578, passim.
185. Brooke's comments to boundary commissioners, on 29 April 1925, in P.R.O., CAB 61/66, also minutes of Fermanagh County Council, during September–November 1923, in LA 4/2GG/2.
186. See file on 'Belleek Fort', State Paper Office, Dublin, S 1235. The fort was handed over to the southern authorities on 25 August.
187. *Fermanagh Times,* 11 January 1923, also 6 September 1923.
188. Cabinet conclusions, on 27 July 1922 CAB 4/50; also Brooke interview with boundary commissioners, on 29 April 1922, in P.R.O., CAB 61/66.
189. See the submission, dated 19 November 1923, and Wickham's note, on 1 December 1923, in CAB 8G/28, 'Augmentation of police force in Garrison area, County Fermanagh, 1923'. See also Dane, op. cit., pp 14, 15, for account of border raids; and *Fermanagh Times*, 8 February 1923. Also see CAB 8G/3, 'Visit of the earl of Derby, secretary of state for war, to Northern Ireland, 1922–1923', passim. File contains petition to Lord Derby from Enniskillen Urban Council, dated April 1923.
190. Craig visited Fermanagh in April, August and October 1923, and spoke at Colebrooke in January 1924. See report of Craig's speech in *Impartial Reporter,* 17 January 1924.
191. See reports by Treasury and Home Office officials, dated 10 February and 11 March 1925, in P.R.O., HO 45/17418, 'Disbandment of the 'A' Special Constabulary, 1925'.
192. Wickham to Clark, 16 March 1921, in FIN 18/1/143. 'Original correspondence from the divisional commissioner, 1921'.
193. Clark to Anderson, 19 November 1920, in FIN 18/1/2.
194. See report from Tallents to Home Office, dated 18 December 1925, in P.R.O., HO 45/17418.
195. Brooke letter in *Fermanagh Times,* 2 March 1922, where Sir Basil defines his duties as commandant. Also see note dated 24 December 1925, containing Brooke's comments, in P.R.O., HO 45/17418.
196. *Sunday News,* 21 January 1968.
197. James Cooper's submission to Boundary Commission, in P.R.O., CAB 61/64.
198. *Impartial Reporter,* 23 May 1929; also typed press statement regarding the Hunt report, in D 3004/C/3.
199. *Sunday News,* 21 January 1968.
200. Typed, unsigned account entitled 'On the Ulster border with the R.I.S.C.', by a *Morning Post* reporter, in D 3004/C/2.
201. Brooke submission to the Boundary Commission, in P.R.O., CAB 61/64.
202. See Dane, op. cit., pp 21, 22, and Livingstone, op. cit. p. 305.
203. Brooke interview before boundary commissioners in P.R.O., CAB 61/66.
204. Report by Tallents, dated 4 July 1922, in P.R.O., CO 906/30. See also Tallents' Notes on police force', which contains submissions from those who had served in the special constabulary, dated 30 June 1922, in P.R.O., CO 906/27.
205. 'Notes on police force' in P.R.O., CO 906/27. General Ricardo's submission was supported by others written by Major Robert Stevenson, ex-district commandant in Dungannon, and by Colonel Perceval Maxwell, who had helped raise the U.V.F. in County Down before the war. Both Ricardo and Stevenson had resigned from the special constabulary. From county inspectors' reports it is clear that sectarian feeling was consistently greater in Tyrone than in Fermanagh throughout this period.
206. Brooke to Clark, 3 and 10 December 1920, in FIN 18/1/56.
207. Livingstone, op. cit., p. 299.

208. Report submitted by Northern Ireland Ministry of Home Affairs, dated 26 June 1922, in Tallents' papers P.R.O., CO 906/25, 'Miscellaneous correspondence with officials and prominent Roman catholics in Belfast'. This report however, conflicts with press reports, see *Impartial Reporter,* 30 March 1922.

209. See reports by assistant legal adviser to southern government, dated 19 July 1923, and by Joseph Johnston, 10 July 1923, State Paper Office, Dublin, S 3161 'Border incidents, 1923–1924'. The report also contains allegations of slight harassment.

210. See Tallents' 'Notes of police force', in P.R.O., CO 906/27. Michael Farrell describes Ricardo's comments as a 'fairly devastating indictment' of the U.S.C. but he quoted from the general's evidence selectively and omits this section of his report. See Michael Farrell, op. cit., pp 156–7.

211. See report by the secretary, provisional government of Ireland committee, dated 18 March 1922, in P.R.O., CAB 24/134, Cabinet memoranda.

212. Wilson diary, entry for 21 April 1922, Imperial War Museum, London, DS/MISC/80.

213. The strength of the force in Fermanagh, on 1 January 1920, was 115. See P.R.O., HO 184/61, records of the R.I.C. nominal returns of policemen, by county, for 1920.

214. County inspector's report, July 1920, in P.R.O., CO 904/112. There were 20 protestants out of total force of 115 on 1 January 1920, and 45 out of 132, on 1 January 1921. See P.R.O., HO 184/61, 62, records of the R.I.C. nominal returns of policemen, by county, for 1920, 1921; also report by Tallents, dated 4 July 1922, in P.R.O., CO 906/30.

215. See Tallents' 'Notes on police force', in P.R.O., CO 906/27; also *Impartial Reporter,* 30 March 1922.

216. See Clark to Wickham, 18 November 1920, also Clark to Major General Sir Hugh Tudor, chief of police, R.I.C., 1920–1922, 30 November 1920, in D 1022/2/9.

217. Tallent's interview with Cameron, on 26 June 1922, in P.R.O., CO 906/26, 'Notes of conversations with opponents and representatives of the Northern Ireland government, etc'.

218. Wilson diary, entry for 21 April 1922, in Imperial War Museum, London, DS/MISC/80.

219. Report by Tallents, 4 July 1922, in P.R.O., CO 906/30.

220. Clark to Collum, 11 November 1920, in FIN 18/1/56.

221. Minutes of meeting of north-eastern advisory committee, on 11 April 1922, State Paper Office, Dublin, S 1011.

222. Brooke interview with boundary commissioners, on 29 April 1922, in P.R.O., CAB 61/66.

223. *Fermanagh Times,* 31 May 1923.

224. Tallents interview with Ricardo, on 29 June 1922, in P.R.O., CO 906/26; also P.R.O., CO 906/27, passim, and Cooper submission to Boundary Commission, in P.R.O., CAB 61/64.

225. *Fermanagh Times,* 13 April 1922.

226. *Impartial Reporter,* 12 January 1928.

227. Brooke to Macready, mid-July 1920, in D 3004/C/2.

228. See coded descriptions of leading Ulster figures by Tallents, in P.R.O., CO 906/24, 'Diary and note on Northern Ireland government personalities'.

229. Report by Tallents, 4 July 1922, in P.R.O., CO 906/30.

230. Lady Craig diary, entry for 15 January 1924, in D 1415/B/38.

231. *Impartial Reporter,* 17 January 1924.

CHAPTER IV

1. See Brooke's letter to his sisters, 24 January 1916, D 3004/C/2.

2. *Irish Times,* 30 October 1968.

3. *Sunday News,* 21 January 1968.

4. His son remembers his father's passion for drainage, in interview with author on 23 February 1985. His main success was with Aberdeen Angus and Shorthorns. See, for example, *Fermanagh Times,* 4 September 1949. His enthusiasm for farming never subsided and was a recurring theme of his personal diary. See 'Diary of Sir Basil Brooke, 1939–1963' D 3004/D (hereafter cited as Brooke diary).

5. *Belfast Telegraph,* 6 November 1981.

6. Sir Douglas Harkness, 'But I remember', an unpublished autobiography, p. 79. (Harkness papers are not yet catalogued).

7. *Fermanagh Times,* 28 May 1921. His mother's grave inscription is terse and poignant: 'Faith, hope and charity, but the greatest of these is charity.' It is found at the church on Colebrooke estate.
8. Lady Brooke diary, 29 October 1923, D 3004/D/29. See also Harkness, op. cit. p. 79.
9. *Belfast Telegraph,* 6 November 1981; also author's interview with John Brooke, on 23 February 1985.
10. See D 3004/B/9, 'Colebrooke game and deer books,' and D 3004/B/10 'Personal game books,' passim.
11. *Daily Graphic,* 3 June 1924, in D 3004/E/9 'Press cuttings 1907–1969'. His son recalled Brooke suffering from an almost fatal attack of pneumonia in the spring of 1927 in interview with author, 23 February 1985.
12. W. D. Flackes, op. cit.; also Williams, op. cit., p. 312.
13. *Sunday News,* 21 January 1968; also Brooke to Macready, undated but mid-1920, in D 3004/C/2.
14. *Irish Times,* 30 October 1968. His son summarised his father's viewpoint by stating that 'wealth enabled the aristocracy to take a broader view', in interview with author, 23 February 1985.
15. *Belfast Telegraph,* 6 November 1968, and personal interview with John Brooke, 23 February 1985.
16. List of offices is given in Brooke's written submission to the Boundary Commission, in P.R.O., CAB 61/64, 'Fermanagh County Council, 20 December 1924–18 May 1925'. See also *Sunday News,* 28 January 1968; *Fermanagh Times,* 10 July, and 3 November 1919, and 18 April 1929; and *Impartial Reporter,* 3 April 1924.
17. Eames to Archdale, 10 April 1920, in the letter books of Fermanagh Unionist Association (Unionist headquarters, Enniskillen). (Hereafter, F.U.A. letter books).
18. F.U.A. letter books, Eames to Archdale, 2 March 1920.
19. F.U.A. letter books, passim. From March 1923 Brooke was a trustee and was throughout one of the association's main subscribers with the Ernes, Archdales and Crichtons.
20. F.U.A. letter books, passim. See Lady Brooke to Eames, 21 January 1924, 3 and 9 April 1927, 3 January and 4 May 1928. She requested that her name be added to the register, 21 May 1927.
21. *Fermanagh Times,* 29 January 1931.
22. Hungerford to Eames, 22 January 1929, in letter books.
23. Charles Falls to Eames, 18 April 1928, Eames to Brooke, 13 August 1925, and Lady Brooke to Eames, 23 January 1925, in ibid.
24. Harkness op. cit., p. 79.
25. *Belfast Telegraph,* 6 November 1981; and personal interview with John Brooke, 23 February 1985.
26. Lady Brooke to Ministry of Finance, 13 November 1932, in FIN 18/12/168 'Imperial economic conference, Ottowa, 1932'.
27. *Belfast Telegraph* obituary, 3 March 1969; also text of sermon by Bishop Peacock at memorial service, 18 March 1970, in D 3004/C/3.
28. *Irish News,* 29 March 1924.
29. Minutes of Fermanagh County Council, LA 4/2GG/2, 27 October, 21 December 1921; also Livingstone. op. cit., pp 297, 314. This happened on the same day that the local government emergency powers bill received the royal assent and three weeks after local government powers had been transferred from Westminster. See also *Fermanagh Times*, 9 December 1920.
30. See cabinet conclusions, CAB 4/41, on 12 May 1922. See also *Parliamentary Debates* (Northern Ireland, Commons), vol. ii, col. 920, 5 July 1922 (hereafter cited as *Parl. Deb.* (C)). Craig states that 'the government was pressed by . . . fifty-nine local authorities to bring forward' the local government bill.
31. Collins to Churchill, 9 August 1922, in State Paper Office, Dublin, S 2925 'Abolition of proportional representation 1922–1938.'
32. See CAB 9B/40/1 passim. 'Correspondence and memoranda concerning the local government bill, 1922–23'.
33. Eames to Archdale, 2 April 1919, in F.U.A. letter books, also Livingstone op. cit., pp 313–4.
34. Cooper to Craig, 9 August 1922, in CAB 9B/40/1.
35. Parke to Eames, 14 April 1922, in F.U.A. letter books.
36. Ibid., Eames to John Dornan, 10 March 1923.

37. Montgomery to Craig, 5 September 1922, in CAB 9B/40/1.
38. *Irish News,* 22 February 1923; also CAB 9B/40/1, passim.
39. Healy's written submission to Boundary Commission, in P.R.O., CAB 61/67, 'Fermanagh nationalist committee, 19 December 1924–2 July 1925.'
40. *Impartial Reporter,* 24 April 1924.
41. Cooper to Craig, 18 January 1924, in CAB 9B/13/1, 'Correspondence and memoranda concerning the abolition of proportional representation and redistribution of electoral areas, 1921–1927'.
42. Brooke's written submission to Boundary Commission, in P.R.O., CAB 61/64, op. cit.
43. Brooke's oral evidence to Boundary Commission, 29 April 1925, in P.R.O., CAB 61/66 'Fermanagh County Council, 27 April 1925–30 April 1925'. See also Cooper's written submission to Boundary Commission, in P.R.O., CAB 61/64. Cooper claimed that 1,000 protestant families crossed the border between 1920–25.
44. Minutes of Fermanagh County Council for 10 June, and 5 December 1924, in LA 4/2GG/2, and for 16 June 1931, in LA 4/2GG/3.
45. See his resolution on rates, 24 January 1927, and on canvassing 8 June 1925, in LA 4/2GG/2. See also *Impartial Reporter,* 7 August 1924, and *Fermanagh Times,* 2 May 1929, for full reports on Brooke's contributions on local government economy and cross-border trade; also the *'Report of the agricultural aid committee',* 1923, Cmd 17.
46. Tallents' report, P.R.O., CO 906/30, Tallents' terms of reference and report on the situation in Northern Ireland, 4 July 1922. Pre-war the *Impartial Reporter* had favoured boundary revision, see report, 1 May 1913.
47. Cooper to Spender, 19 February 1924, in CAB 9B/13/1.
48. Spender to Cooper, 21 February 1924, ibid.
49. See minutes of county council, 19 December 1924, in LA 4/2GG/2; also Livingstone op. cit., p. 312.
50. Minutes of county council, 23 January 1925, in LA 4/2GG/2.
51. Minutes of county council, 17 February 1925, in LA 4/2GG/2 also *Impartial Reporter,* 19 February 1925, and the written submissions to Boundary Commission by Cooper and by Healy, in P.R.O., CAB 61/64, 67.
52. See Brooke's written and oral submissions to the Boundary Commission, in P.R.O., CAB 61/64, 66 passim. In his written evidence, he stated: 'It would be most unjust now to hand over any portion of Fermanagh to the Free State, where it would entail . . . the handing over of one single inhabitant who has carried out his duties to his country and to the empire', in P.R.O., CAB 61/66. Essentially he argues for the retention of the existing boundary.
53. State Paper Office, Dublin, S3161, 'Boundary (border incidents) 1922–23', passim. Note report by the assistant legal adviser to the Free State government dated 19 July 1923.
54. Lady Craig diary, 3 December 1925, in D 1415/B/38; also Livingstone op. cit. p. 317.
55. See P.R.O., CAB 61/66, 'Notes of conference held in prime minister's office, House of Commons, 3 December 1925'.
56. Minutes of county council, 11 December 1925, in LA 4/2GG/2.
57. Minutes of county council, 6 June 1928, in LA 4/2GG/2.
58. Flackes op. cit.
59. *Fermanagh Times,* 20 January 1921.
60. *Fermanagh Times,* 1 September 1921; also Archdale to Eames, 9 May 1927, in F.U.A. letter books.
61. Brooke's oral evidence to Boundary Commission in P.R.O., CAB 61/66.
62. *Fermanagh Times,* 25 February 1926.
63. Wilson Hungerford, secretary to U.U.C., to Eames, 7 March 1923, in F.U.A. letter books.
64. See Miller to Spender, 20 August 1924, and Dixon to Spender, 23 August 1924, in CAB 9B/101/1 'Correspondence and memoranda concerning the abolition of proportional representation, 1922–1926'.
65. Cabinet conclusions, CAB 4/129, on 10 November 1924.
66. Hungerford to Craig, 21 December 1928, in CAB 9B/13/2, 'Correspondence and memoranda concerning the House of Commons (Method of Voting and Redistribution of Seats) Bill (Northern Ireland), 1929.
67. *Impartial Reporter,* 7 March 1929.
68. *Fermanagh Times,* 25 February 1926 and 24 January 1929, *Impartial Reporter,* 7 June 1928.
69. *Sunday News,* 21 January 1968.
70. *Fermanagh Times,* 28 April 1927, report of both speeches.

71. *Impartial Reporter,* 12 January 1928.
72. *Impartial Reporter,* 24 January and 9 May 1929. See also its favourable comments about Brooke, on 28 April 1927.
73. *Fermanagh Times,* 21 March and 16 May 1929.
74. *Impartial Reporter,* 4 April, also 24 January 1929.
75. Flackes, op. cit.
76. *Sunday News,* 21 January 1968.
77. *Impartial Reporter,* 4 April 1929.
78. *Fermanagh Times,* 25 February 1926. John Brooke believes that his father was eager to enter politics, welcomed the challenge particularly in the context of rural depression and would never have been satisfied with simply farming his estate. He is also convinced, from conversations with his father, that the latter had an implicit understanding with Craig that he would re-enter politics once the immediate security problems in Fermanagh had stabilised. Personal interview with John Brooke, 23 February 1985.
79. Personal interview with John Brooke, 23 February 1985.
80. Ibid.
81. *Fermanagh Times,* 17 July 1930.
82. See D 3004/C/2, passim, 'Bundle of draft speeches etc'. The notes are mostly undated and relate to the early 1930's. See also *Fermanagh Times,* 28 November 1929 and 30 January 1930, for reports of speeches which typify Brooke's remarks at this period.
83. *Fermanagh Times,* 3 November 1932, 16 July 1931 and 17 July 1930; also *Impartial Reporter,* 15 August 1929.
84. See Brooke correspondence with Hungerford during 1931–32, in D 3004/C/2.
85. *Fermanagh Times,* 14 August 1930, 20 August 1931 and 19 November 1931. During his speech on 14 August 1930, in justifying this policy change, he stated: 'the possibility of war cannot be dismissed'.
86. Notes for speech by Brooke, dated 30 September 1929, in D 3004/C/2.
87. *Fermanagh Times,* 16 July and 20 August 1931; and *Impartial Reporter,* 24 January 1929.
88. *Fermanagh Times,* 12 May 1932. See also 21 January, 28 April 1932 and 4 December 1930.
89. Personal interview with John Brooke, 23 February 1985.
90. *Fermanagh Times,* 27 November 1930; Gordon to Brooke, 4 November 1930, and Pollock to Brooke, 21 November 1930, in D 3004/C/2; also *Fermanagh Times,* 4 and 11 December 1930.
91. See early 1930s correspondence between Brooke and Andrews, Harkness and Jameson, president of the U.F.U. in D 3004/C/2.
92. *Parl. Deb.* (C), vol. xii, col. 2282, 30 October 1930.
93. *Sunday News,* 28 January 1968. *Parl. Deb.* (C), vol. xi, cols. 10 and 60, 29 May 1929.
94. Flackes op. cit.; also *Sunday News,* 28 January 1968.
95. *Parl. Deb.* (C), vol. xv, cols 494, 1441, 1530 and 2297, on 9 December 1932, 9 May 1933, 10 May 1933, and 12 October 1933.
96. See CAB 9F/57/1, passim, 'Imperial economic conference correspondence concerning the 1932 Ottowa conference, 1932'.
97. *Fermanagh Times,* 14 April 1932, also *News Letter,* 17 and 18 February 1932.
98. *Parl. Deb.* (C), vol. xiv, col. 253, 14 March 1932. Brooke's words were quoted in Devlin's speech.
99. Ibid., cols 253, 255, on 14 March 1932. On a number of occasions the speaker interjected to say that Devlin's speech was out of order.
100. *Parl. Deb.* (C), vol. xvi, cols 414, 416, on 21 March 1932, also draft notes for this speech in D 3004/C/2. The incident provided John Brooke, who was present in the house, with his first clear recollection of his father's political career, from personal interview, 23 February 1985.
101. Ibid., cols 416, 418, 420 and 427, 21 March 1932.
102. *Parl. Deb.* (C), vol. xvi, comments by J. F. Stewart, M.P. for East Tyrone, col. 620; and Thomas Henderson, col. 623, on 20 March 1934.
103. See Healy correspondence, D 2991/A/9C, 'Copy of newsletter issued by Healy', c. 1929, in Calendar, Healy Papers, op. cit.
104. *Fermanagh Times,* 15 June and 14 December 1933.
105. Flackes, op. cit., Henry, Duke of Gloucester was a younger son of George V.
106. Sir Wilfrid Spender, 'Financial diary', D 715 (hereafter cited as Fin. diary). See references in mid-November 1938.
107. *Fermanagh Times,* 2 March 1939.

108. See the 'Minute book of meetings of the Ulster Unionist Stormont parliamentary party', D 1327/10/1, 27 May 1929.
109. *Sunday News*, 28 January 1968, also *Fermanagh Times*, 24 January 1929.
110. *Fermanagh Times*, 30 March 1933, and also 4 April 1929.
111. *Impartial Reporter*, 24 January 1929. See also Lady Craig diary entry, 21 January 1929, in D 1415/B/38.
112. Lady Craig diary entry, 12 October 1935, in D 1415/B/38.
113. Craig to Charles Blackmore, cabinet secretary, 20 May 1930, in CAB 9B/178 'Correspondence relating to the prime minister's Fermanagh Tour, 1930'. The tablet was in memory of those specials who had 'lost their lives in the recent disturbances'. See also *Fermanagh Times*, 22 May, 1930.
114. Personal interview with John Brooke, on 23 February 1985.
115. Cabinet conclusions, CAB 4/299, on 6 April 1932. Also see correspondence between cabinet office and Ministry of Agriculture and Fisheries, on 6, 13 and 17 May 1932, in CAB 9F/57/1.
116. Memorandum by Robertson, undated, and addressed to Pollock, in Brooke's private papers, D 3004/C/2.
117. Craig to Brooke, 26 May 1932, and Brooke's reply, 30 May 1932, in CAB 9F/57/1.
118. Ibid., passim, see letter Robertson to Blackmore, 26 July 1932. Walter Runciman was at the Board of Trade, November 1931–June 1937.
119. *Sunday News*, 28 January1968. See also CAB 9F/57/1, and FIN 18/12/168, passim.
120. Robertson to Blackmore, 31 August 1932, and also see his letter to Blackmore, on 26 July 1932, in CAB 9F/57/1. In the latter, he described Thomas playing bridge with the Irish party as his 'method of getting back the annuities'.
121. William D. Scott to Blackmore, 31 August 1932. See also Robertson to Blackmore, 26 July 1932, and Pollock to Craig, 27 July and 13 August 1932, in CAB 9F/57/1.
122. Gray to Craig, 18 August 1932, also Robertson to Blackmore, 31 August 1932, in CAB 9F/57/1.
123. *Parl. Deb.* (C), vol. xv, col. 1147, on 26 April 1933, also copy of Brooke to Craig, 5 September 1932, in D 3004/C/2.
124. Pollock to Craig, 27 July and Robertson to Blackmore, 26 July 1932, in CAB 9F/57/1.
125. Robertson to Blackmore, on 31 August 1932, and also, 26 July 1932, in CAB 9F/57/1. See also undated memorandum, by Robertson to Pollock, in D 3004/C/2.
126. Robertson to Blackmore, 31 August 1932, in CAB 9F/57/1.
127. Brooke to Craig, 5 September 1932, in D 3004/C/2. The commitment is referred to in Pollock to Craig, 25 July 1932, in CAB 9F/57/1.
128. *Parl. Deb.* (C), vol. xv, col. 496, 8 December 1932. See also cols 1146–1147, 26 April 1933.
129. Brooke to Craig, 5 September 1932, in D 3004/C/2; also Flackes op. cit.
130. *Parl. Deb.* (C), vol. xv, col. 79, 23 November 1932, also *Fermanagh Times*, 3 November 1932. Such sentiments had, however, always been expressed in his speeches and had been strengthened earlier by his military experience, friendships and travel within the empire. Similarly, Pollock referred to the opening session at Ottawa as enough to 'fire the blood' in *Parl. Deb.* (C), vol. xv, col. 55, 23 November, 1932.
131. Flackes, op. cit.
132. *Fermanagh Times*, 3 and 10 November 1932.
133. Harkness, op. cit., p. 30; also *Parl. Deb.*, (C), vol. xv, cols 1475, 1532, 1533, on 10 May 1933.
134. *Fermanagh Times*, 23 March 1933, for initial rumours, and 2 November 1933, for the official statement.
135. Harkness, op. cit., pp 19, 30; also *Fermanagh Times*, 7 June 1928, on the occasion of Archdale becoming a baronet.
136. *Belfast Telegraph*, 18 December 1933.
137. *Parl. Deb.* (C), vol. xv, col. 27, on 22 November 1932. Craig was referring to the effects of Ottawa and shift to protection.
138. *Sunday News*, 28 January 1968.
139. *News Letter*, 7 December 1933.
140. Quoted in *Fermanagh Times*, 14 December 1933.
141. Livingstone, op. cit., p. 326. See also *Fermanagh Times*, 30 March 1933. With regard to the conference at Ottawa, see *Fermanagh Times*, 13 October, 3 November and 1 December 1932. One local cleric at this time described Brooke and Archdale as 'fair . . . kindly and tolerant in their personal relations . . . with all creeds and classes', in *Fermanagh Times*, 3 November 1932.

142. *Fermanagh Times,* 13 July 1933.
143. *Fermanagh Times,* 17 August 1933.
144. Ibid., 26 October 1933, and 22 March 1934.
145. *Fermanagh Times,* 13 July 1933.
146. *Impartial Reporter,* 20 July 1933.
147. Ibid., 17 August 1933.
148. *Irish News,* 17 August 1933.
149. *Parl. Deb.* (C), vol. xv, col. 2381, 17 October 1933.
150. Ibid., vol. xvi, cols 612–613, 20 March 1934.
151. Ibid., col. 616, on 20 March 1934. This speech by J. J. McCarroll, M.P. for Foyle, refers to the government of Ireland act, section V.
152. Ibid., col. 616, on 20 March 1934.
153. *Parl. Deb.* (C), vol. xvi, cols 618, 619, 20 March 1934. During 1914 local government elections a local priest arranged for a number of nationalists to rent rooms in the east ward of Enniskillen so enabling them to vote and overturn the small unionist majority there. These migrant voters were nicknamed locally 'swallows.' See Livingstone, op. cit. p. 268.
154. *Fermanagh Times,* 22 March 1934.
155. *Parl. Deb.* (C), vol. xvi, cols 1072, 1076, 1078, on 24 April 1934. For the whole speech see cols 1072–1085, passim.
156. Ibid., col. 1090, on 24 April 1934.
157. *Parl. Deb.* (C), vol. xvi, col. 1101, on 24 April 1934, remarks by J. J. McCarroll.
158. Eames to Brooke, 13 April and Ritchie to Brooke, 13 April 1934, in D 3004/C/2.
159. *Parl. Deb.* (C), vol. xvi, col. 1115, 1117, 1118 and 1120, on 24 April 1934.
160. Livingstone, op. cit., pp 327–8.
161. *Fermanagh Times,* 13 July 1933.
162. *Parl. Deb.* (C), vol. xvi, col. 620, on 20 March 1934.
163. Ibid., col. 1073, on 24 April 1934.
164. Fin. Diary, 13 July 1933.
165. *Irish News,* 17 August 1933.
166. *Parl. Deb.* (C), vol. xvi, col. 618, on 20 March 1934.
167. *Parl. Deb.* (C), vol. xvi, col. 1110 and 1111, on 24 April 1934, speech by J. J. McCarroll.
168. *Irish Times,* 30 October 1968.
169. *Irish News,* 25 and 28 April 1934.
170. Cabinet conclusions, CAB 4/303, on 22 June 1932; also Livingstone op. cit. p. 334.
171. D. F. Curran to Healy, 1 December 1934, in D 2991/A/22, Calendar, Healy papers, op. cit. The letter is bitterly critical of De Valera and his policy.
172. Cabinet conclusions, CAB 4/303, on 22 June 1932.
173. Cabinet conclusions, CAB 4/304, on 31 August 1932.
174. See cabinet conclusions, CAB 4/308, 309, on 31 January and 7 March 1933. These include the decision to make the special powers act permanent and increase the constabulary forces.
175. *Irish News,* 13 July 1933.
176. Healy to the right hon. Sir Thomas Inskip, Conservative M.P. and solicitor-general, D 2991/A/25B, in Calendar, Healy papers, op. cit.
177. Harkness, op. cit., p. 22.
178. *Parl. Deb.* (C), vol. xvi, col. 496 and 1146–1147, on 8 December 1932 and 26 April 1933.
179. *Fermanagh Times,* 26 January, 16 February and 6 April 1933.
180. Craig to Pollock, 5 August 1932, in CAB 9F/57/1.
181. *Fermanagh Times,* 9 March 1933, also 16 February, 13 April and 18 May 1933.
182. *Fermanagh Times,* 8 December 1932. Similar remarks were made during speeches in spring of 1933.
183. Quoted in ibid., 2 November 1933.
184. *Parl. Deb.* (C), vol. xv, col. 1148, on 26 April 1933; also *Fermanagh Times,* 8 June 1933, and 24 November 1938.
185. *Fermanagh Times,* 16, 23 November 1933.
186. See diary entry by Lady Craig, 20 November 1933, in D 1415/B/38.
187. These phrases recur in his controversial speeches, July 1933 to March 1934.
188. See copy of a newsletter from Healy relating to Brooke's speech at Newtownbutler, August 1948, D 2991/A/169.
189. *Parl. Deb.* (C), vol. xvi, cols 618–619, on 20 March 1934.

190. Falls to Craig, 24 February 1926, in CAB 9E/47/1, 'Correspondence concerning the granting of assistance to farmers by relief from rates, 1922–28'; also *Fermanagh Times*, 13 July 1933.
191. Ibid., 26 October 1933, and also 22 March 1934.
192. *Parl. Deb.* (C), vol. xvi, col. 1078, on 24 April 1934, during debate on the 'rights of the minority'.
193. Notes for speech, October 1933', in D 3004/C/2, reported in *Fermanagh Times*, 26 October 1933.
194. None of this correspondence was with Brooke himself, and the participants are obscure. It includes a copy of an unsigned letter to W. J. Stewart, probably the official Unionist member, for South Belfast (West), and later Progressive Unionist leader, dated 21 October 1932. The other was from J. F. Finlay to 'Dear Rev. Sir', dated 6 June 1933, in D 3004/C/2.
195. Ritchie to Brooke, 13 April 1934, in D 3004/C/2.
196. Circular, dated 10 August 1932, in D 3004/C/2.
197. *Fermanagh Times*, 26 October 1933.
198. Clark to John Anderson, dated 1 and 4 October 1920, in FIN 18/1/98 'Press correspondence and correspondence relating to published articles etc., 1920–21'.
199. See cabinet conclusions CAB 4/331, on 6 November 1934, when considering holding a further census.
200. See Fin. diary, for August and September 1934.
201. See minutes of meeting of Unionist parliamentary party, 17 May 1932, in D 1327/10/1, op. cit.; also CAB 4/320, 11 April 1934. At cabinet, the attorney-general expressed concern regarding 'how to deal with the infiltration of disloyalists from the Free State'.
202. See cabinet conclusions, CAB 4/320, 321, 324, 333, on 11 April, 25 April, 22 May 1934, and 16 January 1935.
203. *News Letter*, 18 December 1933.
204. *Ulster year book*, (Belfast, 1947), p. 40.
205. *Parl. Deb.* (C), vol. xvi, cols 1117–1118, on 24 April 1934.
206. *Belfast Telegraph*, 6 November 1981. *Parl. Deb.* (C), vol. xxvi, cols 692–693, on 25 May 1943. Campbell then asked whether Brooke meant that this threat took place in 1932, and the latter replied, 'I do not remember the exact date', col. 693.
207. *Sunday News*, 21 January 1968.
208. *Impartial Reporter*, 4 April, 1929.
209. *Irish Times*, 30 October, 1968.
210. *Fermanagh Times*, 14 July 1921.
211. Ibid. 1 September 1921.
212. See Lady Brooke diary entry, for month of December 1921, in D 3004/D/29.
213. Report by Stephen Tallents, 4 July 1922, in P.R.O., CO 906/30, op. cit.
214. *Fermanagh Times*, 13 July 1922.
215. Minutes of county council, 11 December 1925, in LA 4/2GG/2.
216. *Fermanagh Times*, 26 October 1933. It is worth noting that when Craig made his infamous speech in which he stated: 'I am an orangemen first and a politician and member of this parliament afterwards', he justified it on the grounds that 'in the south they boasted a catholic state'. See *Parl. Deb.* (C), vol. xvi, cols 1031–5, 24 April 1934.
217. *Parl. Deb.* (C), vol. xvi, cols 1117, 1118, 1120, on 24 April 1934. See also *Fermanagh Times*, 17 August and 26 October 1933, reports of Brooke's speeches.
218. Rev. J. McShane to F. J. Nugent, 10 December 1937, in D 2991/A/58B, Calendar, Healy papers, op. cit. The view that this period was one of disillusionment for Brooke was also shared by his son, in personal interview 23 February 1985.
219. *Irish News*, 29 August 1933, also Fin. diary, 17 February 1934. Unfortunately Spender does not record how Brooke reacted and gives no indication as to the final outcome of the case. Spender does, however, criticize Craig's responsiveness to 'Orange complaints.' See Patrick Buckland, *The factory of grievances, devolved government in Northern Ireland, 1921–1939* (Dublin, 1979), p. 23, (hereafter cited as Buckland op. cit.).
220. *Fermanagh Times*, 22 March 1934.
221. *Parl. Deb.* (C), vol. xxvi, col. 690, on 25 May 1943, in remarks by T. J. Campbell, Central, Belfast. Also see *Sunday News*, 28 January 1968.
222. *Belfast Telegraph*, 16 November 1981.
223. *Sunday News*, 21 January 1968.

CHAPTER V

1. *Sunday News,* 28 January 1968. It should, however, be noted that after Brooke became minister of commerce, a junior post, the title of his ministry was changed to 'Commerce and Production' and he was made deputy prime minister. Also see Brooke diary, 20 December 1940 and 31 December 1941.
2. He used this phrase in cabinet on 15 September 1938, CAB 4/401.
3. Based on K. S. Isles and Norman Cuthbert, *An economic survey of Northern Ireland* (Belfast, 1957), pp 91–114, 137–182 (hereafter cited as Isles and Cuthbert, *Economic survey); Reports of the agricultural enquiry committee,* 1947, Cmd 249, pp 11–21; *Eleventh general report of the Ministry of Agriculture,* 1931–1934, 1937, Cmd 180, pp 3–9; Greenlees, 'The structure and development of agriculture in Ulster 1900–1939' (M. Phil. thesis, New University of Ulster, 1976), chapt. 16 (hereafter cited as Greenlees); Patrick Buckland, *The factory of grievances* (Dublin, 1979), pp 52–9, 132–136; *Ulster year books,* 1932–8 (Belfast, 1932–8). A number of important P.R.O.N.I. files, open to the public some years ago, were closed to the author even after appeal. They are, however, cited in Buckland, op. cit., pp 130–49.
4. K. S. Isles and Norman Cuthbert, 'Ulster's economic structure', *Ulster under home rule; a study of the political and economic problems of Northern Ireland,* ed. Thomas Wilson (London, 1955), p. 91.
5. D. S. Johnson, 'The economic history of Ireland between the wars', *Irish Economic and Social History,* i, (1974), p. 59.
6. *Parl. Deb.* (C), vol. xxii, col. 1364, on 9 May 1939.
7. *Fermanagh Times,* 19 July 1934, also *Parl. Deb.* (C), vol. xvi, col. 223, on 6 March 1934.
8. *News Letter,* 2 January 1934.
9. *Parl. Deb.* (C), vol. xvi, col. 1130, on 25 April 1934. See also cabinet conclusions CAB 4/311, 3 May 1933, where the competence of the department was used to justify its uniquely pervasive role in devising agricultural schemes.
10. Harkness to Brooke, 4 February 1933, in D 3004/C/2.
11. *Sunday News,* 28 January 1968.
12. *News Letter,* 10 February 1931; *Parl. Deb.* (C), vol. xv, col. 72, on 23 November 1932. See Patrick Buckland, op. cit. p. 135.
13. See cabinet conclusions, CAB 4/300, 311, on 3 May 1932 and 2 May 1933.
14. Cabinet conclusions, CAB 4/311.
15. Fin. diary, 13 July 1933; also entries for 16 June, and 5 November 1934.
16. *Northern Whig,* 8 December 1933.
17. See Greenlees, op. cit., pp 367–407; Buckland, op. cit., pp 135, 145–7; Harkness, op. cit., chap. 4; Cmd 249, op. cit., pp 39–42, 105–107; Cmd 180, op. cit., pp 10–16, 94–9; *Twelfth general report of the Ministry of Agriculture, 1934–1950,* 1951, Cmd 295, pp 56–7. See also CAB 4/316, on 6 December 1933, for cabinet discussion of pig grading. For this and other marketing schemes, see Brian Barton, 'Sir Basil Brooke, the making of a prime minister', (Ph.D. thesis, Queen's University, Belfast, 1986), pp 212–51.
18. See CAB 4/319, on 27 February 1934; also *News Letter,* 15 September, 1933.
19. See CAB 4/320, on 11 April 1934. Also *News Letter,* 2 January 1935, suggests that this was the main benefit of the scheme.
20. See CAB 4/331, on 6 November 1934; CAB 4/316, on 6 December 1933; also Patrick Buckland, op. cit., p. 147.
21. See Greenlees, op. cit., pp 399–407; *Ulster year book 1938,* (Belfast, 1938), pp 53–5; Buckland, op. cit., pp 146–7; R. D. Crotty, *Irish agricultural production: its volume and structure* (Cork, 1966), pp 153–4; Cmd 180, op. cit., pp 14–16; Cmd 295, op. cit., pp 57–9.
22. Undated memorandum by Robertson, September 1932, in D 3004/C/2.
23. See cabinet conclusions, CAB 4/312, 324, 325 on 7 June 1933, 22 May 1934, and 1 June 1934. See also Greenlees, op. cit., pp 295–336; Harkness, op. cit., pp 80–82; Cmd 180, op. cit., pp 16–22; Cmd 249, op. cit., pp 101–105.
24. See cabinet conclusions, CAB 4/324, 325. On the negotiations, see also Fin. diary, 14 May 1934; also Buckland, op. cit., p. 143.
25. See Brooke speech, *Parl. Deb.* (C), vol. xvi, cols 2126–2127, on 6 June 1936.
26. *Parl. Deb.* (C), vol. xvi, col. 2126, on 6 June 1934. The act established a mixed board, meaning one not just representative of producers but also distribution and retail interests. See also cabinet conclusions CAB 4/325, 383 on 1 June 1934 and 1 October 1937.
27. Greenlees, op. cit., p. 323, also CAB 4/394, 14 March 1938.

28. *Parl. Deb.* (C), vol. xviii, col. 1384, on 7 May 1936, also col. 442, 5 March 1936, and Buckland, op. cit., pp 148–9.
29. Harkness, op. cit., pp 82–3; also *Sunday News,* 28 January 1968.
30. *Parl. Deb.* (C), vol. xviii, col. 1371, on 6 May 1936. See also Greenlees, op. cit., chap. 15; Buckland, op. cit., chap. 6, particularly pp 136–7; Cmd 295, op. cit., pp 71–75.
31. Cabinet conclusions, CAB 4/357, 358, 383, passim, 27 March and 9 April 1936, and 1 October 1937.
32. Harkness, op. cit., p. 83.
33. Cabinet conclusion, CAB 4/401, on 15 September 1938. See also Greenlees, op. cit., pp 385–6; and Cmd 249, op. cit., pp 47–8.
34. Greenlees, op. cit., pp 407–30. See also CAB 4/320, 323, 325, 350, for discussions on sugar and potato production; Cmd 249, op. cit., pp 67–73, 109–14; Cmd 295, op. cit., pp 4–11, 75–82.
35. *Parl. Deb.* (C), vol. xix, col. 1531, on 9 June 1937. See also CAB 9E/75/2, 'Correspondence with individuals and associations as regards the marketing of Fruit, 1932–44', passim, particularly correspondence between U.F.D.G.A. and the ministry, 5 December 1934 and 11 June 1937, and *Armagh Guardian,* 14 December 1934 and 18 June 1937.
36. *Parl. Deb.* (C), vol. xxii, cols 1616–17, during second reading of agricultural wages bill, on 18 May 1939.
37. Cmd 249, op. cit., p. 86.
38. *News Letter,* 2 January 1934. See also Cmd 180, op. cit., p. 96.
39. See cabinet conclusions, CAB 4/300, on 3 May 1932.
40. *Belfast Telegraph,* 20 November 1933; also Fin. diary, 6 December 1938.
41. *Belfast Telegraph,* 8 March 1939.
42. *Parl. Deb.* (C), vol. xvi, col. 2171, on 6 June 1934, and vol. xvii, col. 596, on 13 December 1934.
43. See remarks by Brown, ibid., vol. xxi, col. 759, on 27 April 1938, and by Minford vol. xviii, col. 1120 and vol. xix, col. 1554, on 28 April 1936 and 9 June 1934, and by Dehra Parker, vol. xvii, col. 275, on 28 November 1934.
44. Remarks by Midgley, ibid., vol. xvii, col. 343, on 4 December 1934, and by Grant, vol. xviii, col. 1125, on 28 April 1936.
45. Comments by Henderson, ibid., vol. xvi, cols 1137, 1378, 2151, on 25 April 1934, and 6 June 1934, and vol. xviii, col. 1124, on 28 April 1936.
46. For Brooke's speech, see *Parl. Deb.* (C), vol. xxii, cols 1616–1617, on 18 May 1939. See also *Ulster year books, 1935–38,* (Belfast, 1935–38), passim, Cmd 180, op. cit., passim; Greenlees, op. cit., pp 442–457; Isles and Cuthbert, *Economic survey,* op. cit., pp 137–183; Cmd 249, op. cit., passim; P. J. O'Hara, 'Financial returns for the seven years 1930–37 on eleven farms in Northern Ireland', *Journal of the Ministry of Agriculture, Northern Ireland,* vi, (1938), pp 13–21; J. G. Williams, 'An economic survey of small holdings in Northern Ireland', ibid., iii, (1931), pp 79–82; CAB 9E/101/1 'Correspondence and memoranda regarding inquiries from foreign countries into agricultural development in Northern Ireland, 1928–47', passim.
47. Buckland, op. cit., p. 149.
48. Cmd 249, op. cit., pp 40, 23, 75, 112.
49. Harkness, op. cit., p. 19.
50. Buckland, op. cit., p. 149.
51. Cmd 249, op. cit., p. 60.
52. Greenlees, op. cit., pp 447–58, 336–67; also Cmd 249, op. cit., pp 22–3.
53. Robertson to Blackmore, cabinet secretary, 5 December 1938, in CAB 9E/23/2, 'Development of agriculture in Northern Ireland, 1928–47'.
54. Fin. diary, 2 July 1938; and Cmd 249, op. cit., pp 62–3, 212, 261–62. See also *Report on the conditions of employment and wages of agricultural workers in Northern Ireland,* 1938, Cmd 199, passim.
55. Cabinet conclusions, CAB 4/401, on 15 September 1938. See also David Johnson, *The interwar economy in Ireland,* (Dundalk, 1985), pp 13–14.
56. *News Letter,* 22 February 1939.
57. J. G. Williams, op. cit., p. 80; also O'Hara, op. cit., p. 18; and Greenlees, op. cit., p. 351.
58. See 'Report on the mechanisation of farming, 1938', p. 31 in CAB 9E/134/1, 'Notes and correspondence in connection with the mechanisation of Farming, 1938–39'; also *News Letter,* 30 December 1937 and 20 January 1939.
59. Jameson, secretary of U.V.F., to Criag, 5 December 1938, in CAB 9E/23/2.

60. Fin. diary, 17 December 1938.
61. Cabinet conclusions, CAB 4/401, on 16 September 1938.
62. Fin. diary, 17 December, 1938, describes Craig and Brooke meeting M.P.s; also reports of these meetings in CAB 9E/23/2, passim. See *Fermanagh Times*, 22 September 1938, for account of U.F.U. delegation. On 27 October 1938, the parliamentary Unionist Party discussed labour problems, see 'Minute book of the Ulster Unionist Stormont parliamentary party', D 1327/10/1.
63. Brooke's letter to Andrews is referred to in Fin. diary, 3 January 1939. Also see ibid., 14 January 1939, *Fermanagh Times*, 18 August 1938; *News Letter*, 7 January 1939.
64. See Brooke speech in *Fermanagh Times*, 18 August 1938. Spender made strongly critical comments in Fin. diary, mid-October 1938 and early January 1939.
65. *Parl. Deb.* (C), vol. xxii, cols 318, 1189, for comments made by Nixon, on 7 March 1939 and 27 April 1939; also Fin. diary, 6 October 1938.
66. See T. W. Allen, Secretary of Ulster Fruit-Growers' Marketing Association to Craig, 11 June 1937, in CAB 9E/75/2.
67. Fin. diary, 2 July 1938. See also CAB 9E/75/2, passim. It is clear from Cmd 249, op. cit., pp 75–6 that the quality of apples produced in the area remained defective.
68. Cabinet conclusions, CAB 4/377, on 29 April 1937.
69. Cmd 295, op. cit., p. 59. See also comment by Spender who described this sector of agriculture as 'flourishing' in Fin. diary, 16 November 1938. He thus regarded the bacon industry bill as unnecessary.
70. *Belfast Telegraph*, 8 March 1939.
71. For Brooke's speech, see *Parl. Deb.* (C), vol. xxii, cols 288–300, on 7 March 1939. Also see *Report of investigators appointed by the minister of agriculture to inquire into the administrative and financial arrangements of the Pigs Marketing Board*, 1938, Cmd 205, passim, particularly pp 60–61.
72. *Fermanagh Times*, 11 May 1939. See also Cmd 205, op. cit., passim.
73. See *Report on the general administration, organisation and financial arrangments of the pig marketing scheme*, 1939, Cmd 208, passim; also letter by S. J. Crowe, board member, to *Fermanagh Times*, 2 March 1939.
74. *Belfast Telegraph*, 8 March 1939. For the debate in the commons; see also *Parl. Deb.* (C), vol. xxii, cols 287–346, 435–479, 660–672, 729–796, on 7 March, 9 March, 21 March and 23 March 1939.
75. *Parl. Deb.* (C), vol. xxii, col. 314, quoted in speech by Rowley Elliot, M.P. for South Tyrone. The other M.P.s who were ex-board members were Rev. Robert Moore and J. F. Gamble.
76. Ibid., cols 736–7, 314–5, 740; also Harkness, op. cit., pp 79–80. The latter stresses the sympathy felt in the ministry for Gordon, permanent secretary at the ministry before Scott Robertson and ex-chairman of the board.
77. *Parl. Deb.* (C), vol. xxii, cols 313, 334–5, 739, 743.
78. Ibid., col. 742.
79. Harkness, op. cit., pp 79–80. The Joint Milk Council, Eggs Marketing Association and Potato Marketing Association were also 'mixed boards'.
80. *Fermanagh Times*, 2 January 1936.
81. See Cmd 249, op. cit., p. 86.
82. Harkness, op. cit., pp 79–80.
83. Cmd 249, op. cit., p. 89.
84. Fin. diary, 14 January 1939. See also Cmd 249, op. cit., pp 87–8; and Cmd 295, op. cit., pp 57–8.
85. *Parl. Deb.* (C), vol. xxii, col. 742, comment by Moore, 23 March 1939.
86. Cabinet conclusions, CAB 4/399, on 20 April 1938; see also Cmd 249, op. cit., pp 105–7, 87–9.
87. Cmd 249, op. cit., p. 107.
88. *Parl. Deb.* (C), vol. xxii, col. 1217, 27 April 1939, remark by Lieu. Colonel Patrick, M.P. for mid-Antrim. See also *News Letter*, 28 February 1939.
89. See *Parl. Deb.* (C), vol. xvi, cols 246, 2179, on 6 March and 6 June 1934.
90. Ibid., vol. xx, col. 162; vol. xvi, cols 374, 1584; vol. xvii, cols 87, 319; vol. xxii, col. 1190.
91. Ibid., vol. xxii, col. 475, on 9 March 1939, speech by W. B. Maginess, M.P. for Iveagh, County Down.
92. *Parl. Deb.* (C), vol. xxii, col. 442, in remarks by Henderson, col. 475, by Maginess, and col. 322, by Nixon, on 7 and 9 March 1939.

93. See, for example, ibid., cols 323, 442, 452, 475, remarks by Henderson, and by Brown, M.P. for South Down, on 7 and 9 March 1939; also *News Letter,* 4 March 1939.
94. Greenlees, op. cit., p. 333.
95. *Parl. Deb.* (C), vol. xxii, cols 481, 1374, in speeches by Nixon, and by Major Panter, M.P. for Mourne, on 14 March and 9 May 1939.
96. *Belfast Telegraph,* 23 March 1939; *News Letter,* 10 March 1939.
97. Fin. diary, 11 March 1939.
98. Cabinet conclusions, CAB 4/412, on 13 March 1939.
99. Fin. diary, 11 March 1939; cabinet conclusions, CAB 4/412.
100. Fin. diary, 11 March 1939.
101. See Elliot's comments, *Parl. Deb.* (C), vol. xxii, cols 317, 344, on 7 March 1939, also Craig's support for Brooke, col. 469, 9 March 1939.
102. Fin. diary, 11 March 1939.
103. Cabinet conclusions, CAB 4/412; also for the introduction of Craig's motion, see *Parl. Deb.* (C), vol. xxii, col. 736, on 23 March 1939.
104. Cabinet conclusions, CAB 4/413, on 23 March 1939.
105. *Parl. Deb.* (C), vol. xxii, cols 731–734. For full speech, see cols 729–736, on 23 March 1939. See also *Belfast Telegraph,* 24 March 1939.
106. *Parl. Deb.* (C), vol. xxii, cols 735–736, on 23 March 1939.
107. *Parl. Deb.* (C), vol. xxii, cols 763, 764, 777–780, 755, 789–790, 660.
108. *Parl. Deb.* (C), vol. xxii, col. 1119, on 25 April 1939.
109. See Cmd 208, op. cit., passim.
110. Fin. diary, 11 March 1939.
111. Personal interview with John Brooke, 23 February 1985.

CHAPTER VI

1. Fin. diary, 11 March 1939.
2. Cabinet conclusions, CAB 4/300, 313, 316, 324, 377, passim, on 3 May 1932, 1 September 1933, 6 December 1933, 20 January 1935, 29 April 1937.
3. Ibid., CAB 4/334, 350, on 20 January and 18 December 1935.
4. Cabinet conclusions, CAB 4/334, 350, on 20 January and 18 December 1935.
5. Ibid., CAB 4/363, 369, 384, 386 on 27 August, 15 December 1936, and 18 October, 14 November 1937.
6. Ibid., CAB 4/350, on 18 December 1935; also CAB 4/403, 416, on 16 November 1938 and 4 May 1939.
7. Cabinet conclusions, CAB 4/416, on 4 May 1939; also his similar comments when introducing the bacon industry bill, *Parl. Deb.* (C), vol. xxii, col. 1364, on 9 May 1939.
8. Cabinet conclusions, CAB 4/403, on 16 November 1938.
9. Cabinet conclusions, CAB 4/403, on 16 November 1938. These views were shared by his permanent secretary.
10. Ibid., CAB 4/404, on 5 December 1938. See also Fin. diary references to negotiations in January-March 1939.
11. See Fin. diary, October-December 1938. This was a source of constant concern to Andrews and Spender throughout, so much so that the former organised a special party meeting, on 18 October 1938, to review the financial position.
12. Cabinet conclusions, CAB 4/403, on 16 November 1938; also Fin. diary, see remarks on 28 January 1939.
13. Harkness, op. cit., p. 21.
14. Fin. diary, Spender to Clark, 12 August 1935 and 10 October 1936. Clark was Governor of Tasmania from August 1933.
15. Cabinet conclusions CAB 4/403, on 16 November 1938.
16. Ibid., CAB 4/401, on 15 September 1938; see also CAB 9E/134/1, op. cit., passim. When the cabinet decided to establish a committee it failed to clarify who should be responsible for its appointment, cabinet conclusions, CAB 4/401, on 15 September 1938.
17. Gransden to Dawson Bates, 13 December 1939, in CAB 9E/134/1; also Fin. diary, 28 January 1939. Spender thought it a 'very useful precedent'.
18. See Spender's recurrent criticisms of ministry statements, including Brooke's speeches, regarding land purchase annuities, agricultural grants and the setting up of a committee of enquiry, in Fin. diary, October 1938 to January 1939.

19. Fin. diary, 21 January 1939, also, in February 1939, he insisted on a moderate estimate being inserted in the white paper relating to the bacon industry bill.
20. Ibid., 28 February 1935, 30 April and 8 May 1937, and 23 February 1938.
21. *Parl. Deb.* (C), vol. xix, col. 436, on 10 March 1937, also Fin. diary, 16 March 1937. Brooke was unable to attend nine cabinets, CAB 4/366–374 between 11 November 1936 and 16 March 1937, inclusive. Due to his absence discussion of the Clogher Valley railway was postponed, CAB 4/369, on 15 December 1936.
22. Fin. diary, 28 January 1939, and late July 1939.
23. Ibid., see comments in mid-October 1938 and mid-January 1939.
24. Fin. diary, Spender's account of meeting on 23 December 1938; also 28 January 1939.
25. Note by Gransden of Andrew's meeting with Robertson, on 2 February 1939, in CAB 9E/23/2, also see Fin. diary, 28 January 1939.
26. See personal memorandum written by Spender, Fin. diary, 2 August 1938.
27. Fin. diary, 18 October 1936, and personal memorandum, 2 August 1938.
28. Ibid., 1 October 1937 and 14 January 1939.
29. See cabinet conclusions, CAB 4/403, regarding U.F.U. opposition to wages board and P.M.P. hostility to the bacon industry bill.
30. *News Letter,* 25 January 1938; *Belfast Telegraph,* 4 February 1938.
31. *Irish Times,* 11 February 1938.
32. *Fermanagh Times,* 6 January 1938; also *Belfast Telegraph,* 4 February 1938; and J. F. Harbinson, *The Ulster Unionist party, 1882–1973* (Belfast, 1973), pp 220–21.
33. *Parl. Deb.* (C), vol. xxii, cols 316, 345–6, on 7 March 1939.
34. Hungerford to Blackmore, 26 June 1937, in CAB 9E/75/2.
35. Fin. diary, 13 July 1933. See also A. E. Muskett 'The progress of agriculture in Northern Ireland' in D 2734/4/7, op. cit.; Harkness, op. cit., p. 85; Patrick Shea, *Voices and the sound of drums,* (Belfast, 1981), p. 115. Shea describes him as 'small, bespectacled, ungracious, . . . [his] . . . rapid advancement . . . resented because he had successfully crossed the barrier between technical and administrative classes'.
36. See Buckland, op. cit., pp 141–42; see also Fin. diary, late April 1938 and 28 January 1939. Gransden told Spender that Robertson had accepted full responsibility for setting up the committee. See also CAB 9E/23/2, passim, on the setting up of the committee; also personal interview with John Brooke, 23 February 1985.
37. Harkness, op. cit., pp 83, 85.
38. Ibid., pp 78–9.
39. *Parl. Deb.* (C), vol. xxii, col. 469, on 9 March 1939, also vol. xxi, col. 762, on 27 April 1938.
40. *Parl. Deb.* (C), vol. xxii, cols 468–9, on 9 March 1939; *News Letter,* 12 January 1938.
41. See Brooke diary, 31 December 1940; D 3004/D/31–45; also *Parl. Deb.* (C), vol. xxii, col. 1214, 27 April 1939, remarks by Elliot; and personal interview with John Brooke, 23 February 1985.
42. Spender clearly indicates that Brooke was more flexible in his approach during discussions on the bacon industry bill, Fin. diary, January and February 1939.
43. *Parl. Deb.* (C), vol. xvii, col. 601, on 13 December 1934.
44. *Fermanagh Times,* 3 August 1939.
45. Spender refers to its as the 'only definite proposal' forthcoming from the management of the shipyards, Fin. diary, 16 November 1938.
46. Harkness, op. cit., pp 64–5.
47. *Parl. Deb.* (C), vol. xxii, col. 456, on 9 March 1939, comments by Gamble, also Brooke diary, 11 December 1940.
48. *Parl. Deb.* (C), vol. xxi, col. 754, on 27 April 1938, comment by Maginess. Also see Harkness, op. cit., pp 28–9, on Archdale's somewhat contrasting ministerial style.
49. Ibid., op. cit., p. 78; also *Fermanagh Times,* 23 March 1939.
50. Fin. diary, 9 May 1936, and personal memorandum dated 2 August 1938.
51. See 'Minute book of meetings of the Ulster Unionist Stormont parliamentary party', D 1327/10/1, passim, Patrick Buckland states that Brooke's 'reputation as a minister was built on the efforts of an energetic set of officials at . . . Agriculture'. However, this harsh conclusion does not accord either with the views of those leading civil servants who served under him agriculture and later commerce, or of others such as Wilfred Spender or Arther Kelly. Patrick Buckland, *A history of Northern Ireland,* (Dublin, 1981), p. 83.
52. Personal memorandum by Spender in Fin. diary, 2 August 1938, also criticism of Blackmore, early December 1938. Occassionally, Brooke spoke in cabinet on transport and linen, see CAB 4/340, 354, 396, on 12 April 1935, 25 February 1936 and 22 March 1938.

53. Personal memorandum by Spender, Fin. diary, 2 August 1938, and also October-November 1937. Spender regarded Carson as 'the greatest man of his age', Fin. diary, 27 October 1935.
54. The cabinet discussed leaks, CAB 4/333, 335, 336, 339, 344, 361, 400, passim.
55. Personal memorandum by Spender, Fin. diary, 2 August 1938, and 21 January 1939.
56. *Fermanagh Times,* 29 April 1937, also 21 November 1935 and 23 January 1936.
57. *Fermanagh Times,* 15 July 1937; *News Letter,* 25 January 1938.
58. Personal interview with John Brooke, on 23 February 1985. With regard to the opening of the bridges, see diary entry by Lady Craig, 15 April 1935, also 25 January, 22 February and 2 November 1938, and 2 March 1939 in D 1415/B/38.
59. Lady Craig diary, 20 March 1937, in D 1415/B/38; *Fermanagh Times,* 3 February 1938.
60. Craig's only recorded criticism of Brooke in cabinet was on 25 February 1936, CAB 4/354. He regarded Sir Basil's comments on transport derating as belated and expressed mild irritation.
61. Fin. diary, 16 November 1938, and 28 January 1939.
62. See personal memorandum by Spender, Fin. diary, 2 August 1938, also similar comments in October 1937, and June 1938.
63. Personal interview with John Brooke, 23 February 1985. He remembered Craig personally requesting his father to go.
64. Fin. diary, 2 November 1940, (retrospective note by Spender), and 13 January 1938; also Buckland, op. cit., pp 110–116. Andrews was given the responsibility, by cabinet, of getting reassurances from the British government regarding Northern Ireland's position, CAB 4/389. See also Robert Fisk, *In time of war,* (London, 1983) pp 46–8.
65. Undated manuscript note on the Anglo-Irish talks, in Fin. diary, (enclosed at beginning of March 1938, hereafter cited as Spender manuscript note), also early March 1938 and retrospective note, dated 2 November 1940.
66. Buckland, op. cit., pp 110–16; also Fin. diary, Spender manuscript note.
67. Fin. diary, Spender manuscript note, also mid-March 1938 and 2 November 1940.
68. Cabinet discussion with regard to letters and memoranda to be forwarded to London, CAB 4/397, on 25 March 1938.
69. Fin. diary, 10–11 April 1938.
70. Cabinet conclusions, CAB 4/397, on 25 March 1938; also Fin. diary, 23 April 1938.
71. Cabinet conclusions, CAB 4/399, on 20 April 1938. See also CAB 4/400, on 13 May 1938, cabinet discussion of leaked information relating to the Anglo-Irish talks.
72. Spender manuscript note; Fin. diary, 2 and 16 November 1940.
73. Spender manuscript note, Fin. diary, also on 27 January 1943, Sir Wilfred suggested that Andrew's reticence about coming 'out in the open' against Craig was because he was unsure of Brooke's support.
74. Ibid., 2 August 1938, memorandum by Spender.
75. *Fermanagh Times,* 12 January and 11 May 1939; interview with John Brooke, 23 February 1985; Brooke diary, 7 December 1939.
76. Fin. diary, 2 November 1940.
77. *Fermanagh Times,* 5 May 1938.
78. Buckland, op. cit., p. 143.
79. *Sunday News,* 28 January 1968.
80. *Sunday News,* 28 January 1968.
81. Fin. diary, 28 January 1939. Sir Wilfred had frequently expressed concern at southern 'propaganda', see 13 January 1938.
82. *News Letter,* 25 January 1939; also *Fermanagh Times,* 14 July 1921.
83. Fin. diary, 28 January 1939, also 22 November 1938; *Fermanagh Times,* 6 October 1938 and 17 August 1939.
84. See cabinet conclusions, CAB 4/411, 413, on 2 and 23 March 1939.
85. See letter from president, Newry Chamber of Commerce, to Blackmore, cabinet secretary, 14 May 1936, in CAB 9E/127/1, 'Correspondence and memoranda in connection with Newry Central Creamery'; also Buckland, op. cit., p. 135.
86. *Sunday News,* 21 January 1968.
87. *Parl. Deb.* (C), vol. xxii, cols 63, 65, on 21 November 1934, speech by Healy; also *Irish News,* 16 November 1934.
88. Healy to Inskip, 16 August 1935, in D 2991/A/25B; also *Parl. Deb.* (C), vol. xvii, cols 65–6, on 24 November 1934.
89. *News Letter,* 16 November 1934.

90. *Irish News,* 16 November 1934.
91. *Fermanagh Times,* 13 August 1934.
92. Fin. diary, late October 1937.
93. Brooke diary, 10 October 1940.
94. See *News Letter,* 25 January 1939; *Fermanagh Times,* 8 and 29 December 1938, 12 and 25 January 1939, reference to children and the U.V.F. in ibid. 13 August 1936.
95. *Fermanagh Times,* 11 May 1939.
96. Brooke diary, 1 September 1939.
97. Brooke diary, 4 September 1939.
98. *The Times,* 8 May 1939, letter by Lady Brooke.
99. Brooke diary, 5 September 1943.

CHAPTER VII

1. Brooke diary, 28 October 1939.
2. *Belfast Telegraph,* 18 January 1940.
3. Flackes, op. cit.
4. Brooke diary, comment about Churchill, 13 May 1940; early hopes of peace or combined action against Russia, 6 October and 30 November 1939, and prospect of German invasion of Russia, on 5, 13, 14 July, and 14 September 1940.
5. Ibid., 30 May 1940.
6. Brooke diary, 21 May, 17 and 22 June 1940.
7. *Sunday News,* 28 January 1968; Brooke diary, 31 December 1939.
8. See memorandum 'Ministry of Agriculture war services', dated 7 July 1941, in CAB 3/A/97, 'Ministry of agriculture, war service memoranda, 1936–1948', (hereafter cited as war services memorandum); J. W. Blake, *Northern Ireland in the second world war* (Belfast, 1956), pp 36–39, 403–418, Cmd 249, op. cit., passim; 'Agriculture in the war and post-war years', in *Ulster year book,* 1956 (Belfast, 1956), pp xix-x.
9. Blake, op. cit., p. 39; *Ulster year book,* op. cit., p. xix; Isles and Cuthbert, *Ecomonic survey,* op. cit., pp 290–99.
10. John Oliver, *Working at Stormont,* (Dublin, 1978), pp 35, 221, 222.
11. Blake, op. cit., pp 20, 21, 69, 105; also the volume in British war history series by K.A.H. Murray, *Agriculture,* (London, 1955), pp 47, 48.
12. Harkness, op. cit., pp 86, 87, 88, 91, 92. Sir J.D.B. Fergusson was permanent secretary at the Ministry of Agriculture and Fishines, 1936–45.
13. Harkness, op. cit., pp 88, 89, 91.
14. See comments in Fin. diary, 21 June and 18 September 1939.
15. See war services memorandum, op. cit., in CAB 3/A/97; Blake op. cit., pp 105, 106, 110, 111; and speech by Brooke during his ministry's estimates, *Parl. Deb.* (C), vol. xxiii, cols 1019, 1020, on 1 May 1940.
16. War services memorandum, op. cit., in CAB 3/A/97; also Blake, op. cit., pp 105–9; Brooke, in the Brooke diary, November 1939, frequently comments on the 'muddle' and uncertainty.
17. Fin. diary, 13 January 1940.
18. Harkness, op. cit., p. 90; also Brooke diary, 16 November 1939, and 10 January 1940.
19. *Parl. Deb.* (C), vol. xxiii, cols 462, 2002, 2221, 2222 on 6 March, 24 September, and 1 October 1940.
20. Brooke diary, 30 October 1939; also *Parl. Deb.* (C), vol. xxii, cols 2424. 2426, on 31 October 1939.
21. War services memorandum, op. cit., in CAB 3/A/97; also *Parl. Deb.* (C), vol. xxiii, col. 1024, on 1 May 1940, for Brooke's speech during estimates; also Blake, op. cit., pp 108, 109; Cmd 249, op. cit., pp 21–33, 98–101.
22. *Ulster year book,* op. cit., pp xx–xxii; war services memorandum, op. cit., in CAB 3/A/97; also Blake, op. cit., p. 109.
23. Harkness, op. cit., p. 88, also this was raised repeated in the house.
24. See Fin. diary, 27 January 1940, also 3 February 1940; and *Parl. Deb.* (C), vol. xxiii, col. 381, on 5 March 1940.
25. Brooke diary, 29 August, and 3 September 1940; and *Parl. Deb.* (C), vol. xxiii, col. 2145, on 24 September 1940.

26. Brooke diary, 14 October 1940.
27. War services memorandum, op. cit., in CAB 3/A/97; Blake, op. cit., pp 109, 413; *Ulster year book,* op. cit., pp xx–xxii.
28. Blake, op. cit., p. 417.
29. War services memorandum, op. cit., in CAB 3/A/97; Blake, op. cit., p. 416, 417, 418; Cmd 249, op. cit., pp 101–05.
30. *Parl. Deb.* (C), vol. xxiii, col. 2262, on 1 October 1940; also Blake, op. cit., pp 109, 410, 411.
31. Blake, op. cit., pp 404–10; war services memorandum, op. cit., in CAB 3/A/97.
32. *Parl. Deb.* (C), vol. xxii, cols 2027–2028, on 7 September 1939, also col. 1916, 2650, on 4 September, and 6 December 1939.
33. Brooke diary, 18 September, and 18 November 1939.
34. Harkness, op. cit., p. 88, claims to have suggested Nugent to Robertson.
35. See *Parl. Deb.* (C), vol. xxiii, cols 293, 294, on 20 February 1940 where Brown refers to Lyttle's question and the minister of food's response, and col. 859, on 18 April 1940, when Brooke concedes the unfair allocation.
36. Blake, op. cit., p. 109.
37. Harkness, op. cit., p. 88.
38. Fin. diary, 4 May 1940.
39. Harkness, op. cit., p. 92; war services memorandum, op. cit., in CAB 3/A/97; Murray, op. cit., p. 74; Blake, op. cit., pp 111, 406, 407.
40. *Ulster year book,* op. cit., p. xix; also *Parl. Deb.* (C), vol. xxii, cols 2263, 2340, on 17 and 24 October 1939.
41. Brooke diary, 3 May 1940, 31 October 1940 and 23 November 1939.
42. *Parl. Deb.* (C), vol. xxii, cols 2064–2068, on 19 September 1939.
43. *Parl. Deb.* (C), vol. xxii, cols 2466–2476, 2484, on 1 November and cols 2526–2529, on 8 November 1939; cabinet conclusions, CAB 4/426, 428, on 15 September, and 9 October 1939.
44. Brooke diary, 10 November 1939, and 18 January 1940, also 6 and 29 May 1940.
45. Brooke diary, 21 January 1940.
46. Blake, op. cit., p. 410, and war services memorandum, op. cit., in CAB 3/A/97.
47. Ibid., also Blake, op. cit., pp 110–16, 464; Cmd 249, op. cit., pp 211–15.
48. Murray, op. cit., pp 72, 73; Cmd 249, op. cit., pp 176–7; Blake, op. cit., pp 110, 111.
49. Ibid.; Cmd 249, op. cit., pp 69–73, 113–5; *Ulster year book,* op. cit., pp xxix–xxx; also CAB 4/427, 428, 432, 448, 450, 452, passim.
50. Brooke diary, 20, 30 September and 9 October 1939, and passim; also Harkness, op. cit., p. 87.
51. *Parl. Deb.* (C), vol. xxiii, col. 119, on 20 December 1939.
52. Brooke diary, 11 January 1940.
53. Blake, op. cit., pp 113, 114. See also cabinet conclusions, 6 November 1939, CAB 4/429, where due mainly to Brooke's pressure it was decided to set up 'a local publicity office'; and Brooke diary, 6 November 1939.
54. Fin. diary, 27 January 1940; also *Parl. Deb.* (C), vol. xxiii, col. 469, on 6 March 1940, remark by Elliot.
55. Brooke diary, 25 and 27 March 1940.
56. Ibid., 12 February and 2, 10 and 31 April 1940.
57. Ibid., 7 and 27 March 1940, also text of speech in D 3004/C/2.
58. Brooke diary, 12, 13, 23, 26 April, and 4, 29 May 1940. Also see *Parl. Deb.* (C), vol. xxiii, col. 460, 621, on 6 and 7 March 1940, comments by Nixon, that Brooke was 'keeping in with' the press, and 'has the press'. Kingsley Wood became chancellor of the Exchequer in May 1940.
59. Brooke diary, 6 August, describes conference at which the 13 percent was agreed. Also see Murray, op. cit., pp 108, 111, 113; and Blake, op. cit., pp 405–7.
60. Patrick Buckland, *A history of Northern Ireland,* (Dublin, 1981), p. 82; also Hugh Shearman, *Northern Ireland, 1921–1971,* (Belfast, 1971), p. 78.
61. Oliver, op. cit., pp 35, 36, 61, 62, also Blake, op. cit., p. 373.
62. *Parl. Deb.* (C), vol. xxiii, col. 1023, on 1 May 1940.
63. War services memorandum, op. cit., in CAB 3/A/97; also Blake, op. cit., p 115.
64. Blake, op. cit., pp 403–8.
65. *Parl. Deb.* (C), vol. xxiii, col. 332, on 20 February, and col. 2261, on 1 October 1940.
66. Brooke diary, 3 October 1939 and 4 January 1940; Fin. diary, 28 December 1942.
67. Flackes, op. cit.
68. Isles and Cuthbert, *Economic Survey,* op. cit., p. 297.

69. Ibid., pp 290–99, 148–153.
70. Brooke diary, 4 August 1940. On 3 November 1939. Brooke records spending his first weekend in Belfast since 1923.
71. Ibid., 17 December 1939, also 24 February 1940; see also Lady Brooke diary, brief entries for the years 1939, 1940, 1941, in D 3004/D/29.
72. Personal interview with John Brooke, on 23 February 1985; also personal interview with Sir Douglas Harkness, on 4 June 1979. The statutory salary of all Stormont ministers was £1700 per annum, 1933–7, and £2,000 from 1937–8, when the 15 percent reduction, introduced in 1931–32 was abandoned. See *Northern Ireland House of Commons papers,* (Belfast 1931–39), 'Estimates for services under the government of Northern Ireland', passim.
73. Brooke diary, 19 December, 27 June and 3 July 1940.
74. War services memorandum, op. cit., in CAB 3/A/97.
75. Personal interview with Sir Douglas Harkness, on 4 June 1979.
76. *Parl. Deb.* (C), vol. xxii, cols 2068–2069, on 19 September, 1939.
77. Brooke diary, 20 July 1940.
78. Ibid., 22 October 1940.
79. *Parl. Deb.* (C), vol. xxiii, col. 1038, on 1 May 1940, during Ministry of Agriculture estimates debate.
80. Brooke diary, 11 December 1940, he also wrote to Andrews on this subject and ultimately appointed Moore to the post after becoming prime minister.
81. Brooke diary, 31 December 1940.
82. See Fin. diary, 13 January 1940, also 12 November 1940. Sir Wilfred regarded increased government regulation in wartime as a 'necessary evil', in ibid., 12 November 1940.
83. Ibid., 13 July 1940; Brooke diary, 18 July 1940.
84. Brooke diary, 7 September 1940.
85. Fin. diary, 14 and 21 September 1940; also *Parl. Deb.* (C), vol. xxiii, cols 2000, 2001, on 17 September 1940.
86. Fin. diary, 20, 21 September 1939, and 24 February and 27 October 1940.
87. Fin. diary, 9, 10 February 1940.
88. Brooke diary, 6 October 1939; Fin. diary, 27 January 1940.
89. Fin. diary, 21 February 1940.
90. *Parl. Deb.* (C), vol. xv, col. 496, on 8 December 1932; also Brooke diary, 28 February 1940, 20 and 28 January 1941; and Oliver, op. cit., p. 222.
91. Brooke diary, 6 November 1939.
92. Fin. diary, 23 March 1940.
93. See comments by Minford, *Parl. Deb.* (C), vol. xxiii, col. 2145, on 24 September 1940, and by Brown, col. 2245, on 1 October 1940. Also see Oliver, op. cit., p. 44, where he remarks regarding Brooke's department, that the ministry was 'the legal entity and corporate body', unlike Britain where it is usually the minister. This may have contributed to its austere public image.
94. See *Parl. Deb.* (C), vol. xxiii, col. 198, on 13 February 1940, remarks by Nixon; also Brooke diary, 14 November 1939, and 2 November 1940. Brooke believed that the question of farmers working on Sunday should be left to the individual farmer, ibid., 14 November 1939.
95. *Parl. Deb.* (C), vol. xxiii, cols 2593, 2594, 2597, 2598, on 12 November 1940.
96. Ibid., (C), vol. xxiii, cols 2621, 2632, on 19 November 1940.
97. Fin. diary, 21 November 1940; Brooke diary, 19, 20, 26 November and 4 December 1940.
98. Brooke diary, 5, 6 March 1940.
99. *Parl. Deb.* (C), vol. xxiii, col. 2243, on 1 October 1940, remarks by Brown.
100. Brooke diary, 3 November, 6 and 15 December 1940.
101. *Sunday News,* 28 January 1968.
102. Brooke diary, 11 September, 5, 24 October and 8 November 1939.
103. Ibid., 14 March and 1 May 1940; also *Parl. Deb.* (C), vol. xxiii, col. 1031, on 1 May 1940.
104. *Parl. Deb.* (C), vol. xxiii, col. 465, on 6 March, comment by Minford.
105. See remarks by Nixon and Brown, in ibid., cols 541, 2243, on 7 March and 1 October 1940. Also see ibid., cols. 470, 2104, on 6 March and 24 September 1940, comments by Elliot.
106. Ibid., cols 1435, 1439, on 11 and 18 June 1940.
107. *Parl. Deb.* (C), vol. xxiii, col. 1891, on 6 August 1940.
108. Brooke diary, 25 April 1940.
109. Ibid., 25 April, 28 May, 11 and 18 June 1940.

CHAPTER VIII

1. *Manchester Guardian,* 4 December 1916.
2. Buckland, op. cit., p. 1. The comment was made by Sir Wilfrid after he had been considering the hostile attitudes which local authorities in Northern Ireland held towards Stormont, in Fin. diary, late September 1939.
3. Blake, op. cit., p. 116.
4. Fin. diary, 9, 23 December 1939, 4 May, 3 August 1940 and 20 February 1942.
5. *Parl. Deb.* (C), vol. xxiii, col. 975, on 25 April 1940. Craig's annual salary, 1937–40 was £4950 (including allowances). See *Northern Ireland House of Commons papers* (Belfast 1937–40), 'Estimate for services under the government of Northern Ireland,' passim.
6. Fin. diary, 25 May 1940, also 11 May 1940. Spender observed, on 25 May, that Andrews 'should be apprised' of important decisions.
7. Ibid., 8 June 1940, also 28 September and 19 October 1940. This was an increasingly insistent cause of concern to Spender.
8. Ibid., 25 May 1940, also 29 January and 9 March 1940.
9. Fin. diary, 25 May 1940. Also see entry for 28 September 1940, where Spender notes that Milne Barbour's spinning firm was prosperous due to government contracts, whilst others had closed down, and implies that this made him politically more vulnerable.
10. *Parl. Deb.* (C), vol. xxiii, col. 1505, 1506, on 19 June 1940.
11. Fin. diary, 15 June 1940.
12. Brooke diary, 20 June 1940, also see minutes of party meeting, on 20 June 1940, in 'Minute book of meetings of the Ulster Unionist Stormont parliamentary party' D 1327/10/1.
13. *Parl. Deb.* (C), vol. xxiii, col. 1923, on 15 August and col. 1964 on 10 September 1940; Fin. diary, 14 September 1940.
14. *Parl. Deb.* (C), vol. xxiii, cols 2155, 2161, 2162, 2171, on 25 September 1940.
15. Ibid., col. 2190, remark by Campbell, on 25 September 1940.
16. Fin. diary, 24 September and 16, 21 November 1940.
17. Fin. diary, 14 May 1940, also see comment on 25 May 1940, that 'Andrews feels . . . the position of the government is so shaky . . . it is necessary to make concessions of a political nature which he himself deprecates'.
18. Ibid., 12 October 1940.
19. *Northern Whig,* 29 May, 20 June, and 27 September 1940.
20. See cabinet conclusions, in CAB 4/441, on 1 June 1940; also Fin. diary, 24 July 1940; Blake, op. cit., p. 77 comments on unemployment levels; Fisk, *In time of war,* (London, 1983), pp 227, 228, 240, on the province's inadequate defences.
21. See Fin. diary, 15, 26 October 1940, and 23 November 1940, comments on electricity, and early January 1940, regarding local authority nepotism; also Blake, op. cit., pp 97–117, passim.
22. See cabinet conclusions, CAB 4/429, 451, on 6 November 1939, and 1 October 1940.
23. Fin. diary, 8 June, 6 July, 14 October, and 21 December 1940.
24. Personal interview with Sir Douglas Harkness, on 4 June 1979.
25. Brooke diary, 10, 11 February, 15 May, 14, 15, 22 June 1940; also *Sunday News,* 28 January 1968.
26. Brooke diary, 26 May, 15 June 1940; also cabinet conclusions, on 15 June 1940, in CAB 4/443.
27. Ibid., on 22 June and 1 July 1940, in CAB 4/445, 446.
28. Brooke diary, 15 June and 16 July 1940; Michael Farrell, *Northern Ireland, the Orange state,* (London, 1976), pp 151, 152.
29. Fin. diary, 15 May 1940; Lady Craig diary, entry for 15 May 1940, in D 1415/B/38.
30. Cabinet conclusions, on 20 May, in CAB 4/438, and on 25 May, in CAB 4/439; also St John Ervine, *Craigavon; Ulsterman,* (London, 1949), p. 553.
31. *Parl. Deb.* (C), vol. xxiii, cols 1422, 1426, on 11 June.
32. The Tom Harrisson Mass Observation Archive, Brighton (henceforth cited as M-OA) mass observation diary, (diarist 5462), entry dated 24 May 1941, Fisk, op. cit., p. 389.
33. Brooke diary, 25 May 1940; also *Parl. Deb.* (C), vol. xxiii, cols 1283–1286, on 28 May 1940.
34. Brooke diary, 3, 4, 5, 16 July and 28 August 1940.
35. Cabinet conclusions, on 29 October 1940, in CAB 4/453.
36. Blake, op. cit., pp 182, 183.
37. Brooke diary, 5 December 1940.

38. Cabinet conclusion, on 20 May 1940, in CAB 4/438; also Fisk, op. cit., p. 388; and Blake, op. cit., p. 199.
39. Brooke diary, 3 June 1940; also *Parl. Deb.* (C), vol. xxii, col. 1430, on 11 June 1940, for Craig's statement to House regarding Brooke's new responsibility.
40. Brooke diary, 1 August 1940.
41. Ibid., 25 May, 4, 18 June 1940. The War Office indicated to Craig that equipment was scarce during his talks in London, on 22–4 May.
42. Fin. diary, 15 June 1940.
43. Brooke diary, 12, 22, 23, 24 July 1940.
44. *Parl. Deb.* (C), vol. xxiii, col. 1860, on 6 August 1940, remark by Nixon.
45. Brooke diary, , 1 and 2 July 1940, and entries from 15 July to late August, passim. Also see Fisk, op. cit., p. 397 with regard to Lord Londonderry, and Spender's remarks in Fin. diary, mid-September 1939, on public criticism of Londonderry.
46. Brooke diary, 5 August and 1, 17, and 21 September 1940.
47. Blake, op. cit., p. 199; also Fisk, op. cit., p. 388; and *Parl. Deb.* (C), vol. xxiii, col. 1894, on 6 August 1940, for remarks by Warnock. Nixon made similar comments.
48. Flackes, op. cit.
49. Brooke diary, 12 August 1940.
50. Brooke diary, 10 October, 21 November 1940.
51. See letter from Healy to director of bank in Belturbet, Co. Cavan, 22 May 1940, in D 2991/A/148.
52. Fin. diary, 30 March 1943.
53. Ibid., 23 January 1941. Spender himself considered the number of Roman catholics in Brooke's ministry to be 'not unduly large', and consistently urged the necessity for even-handed treatment of the minority.
54. Fin. diary, 12 November 1940.
55. *Sunday News,* 28 January 1968.
56. Cabinet conclusions, 30 April 1940, in CAB 4/437.
57. Brooke diary, 2, 3, 7, and 8 May 1940.
58. Ibid., 22 May 1940; and Fin. diary, 25 May 1940.
59. See Fisk, op. cit., pp 161–72; John Bowman, *De Valera and the Ulster question, 1917–1973,* (Oxford, 1982), pp 220–38; Joseph T. Carroll, *Ireland in the war years, 1939–1945,* (Newton Abbot, 1975), pp 49–59.
60. Brooke diary, 22 May 1940.
61. Bowman, op. cit., p. 222, based on letter from Gray to Roosevelt, on 6 June 1940.
62. Brooke diary, 19 June 1940. With Mackenzie King was the prime minister of Canada.
63. Ibid., 5 June 1940.
64. Ibid., 7 June 1940, and cabinet conclusions, 7 June 1940, in CAB 4/442.
65. Fisk, op. cit., pp 185, 186; also personal interview with John Brooke, on 23 February 1985.
66. Brooke diary, 25 June 1940; Bowman, op. cit., p. 232.
67. Fisk, op. cit., p. 186, and personal interview with J. C. MacDermott, (minister of public security, 25 June 1940–9 November 1941); on 11 May 1979. MacDermott recalled also suggesting to Andrews that he would support a council for Ireland in exchange for Britain introducing conscription into Northern Ireland. After making the remark he could see 'doubt in Andrews' eyes', the latter was horrified at the idea.
68. Bowman, op. cit., p. 237.
69. Brooke diary, 25 June 1940.
70. Brooke diary, 23 June 1940. This reference disproves Fisk's account, given in Fisk, op. cit., p. 209, which suggests that it was the Unionist senator himself who made contact with southern leaders. Fisk's account is based on an inaccurate reference in the Mulcahy papers, (University College Dublin, Archives Department), P7/C/111.
71. Brooke diary, 23 June 1940.
72. Bowman, op. cit., p. 237. The meeting took place on 25 June.
73. Brooke diary, 26 June 1940.
74. Craig to Chamberlain, 26 June 1940, in 'Mr Chamberlain's negotiations with Mr De Valera and Lord Craigavon, 1940', prime minister's office, operational papers, P.R.O. PREM 3/131/2. The letter was not discussed by the Northern Ireland cabinet. The reference in Brooke diary removes any doubt that Craig's 'friend' was Pat Herdman, hitherto the identity was uncertain.
75. Brooke diary, 1 July 1940; Fin. diary, 6 July 1940.

76. Brooke diary, 10 and 11 July 1940; also cabinet conclusions, CAB 4/447, dated 10 July 1940.
77. Fin. diary, 15 August 1943.
78. Brooke diary, 4 September 1940, also 29 October 1940, for similar comments.
79. Memorandum written by Morrison, dated 16 October 1946, in British cabinet papers, P.R.O., CAB 129/13.
80. Brooke diary, 19 September 1946.
81. Brooke diary, 29 October 1940; also *Parl. Deb.* (C), vol. xxiii, cols 2486–2493, on 29 October 1940.
82. Brooke diary, 24 November 1940.
83. Lady Craig dairy, 24 November 1940, in D 1415/B/38.
84. *Parl. Deb.* (C), vol. xxiii, col. 2669, on 26 November 1940; see also Brooke's public statement quoted in Lady Craig diary, 26 November 1940, in D 1415/B/38; also Brooke diary, 24 November 1940. Lady Brooke recorded similar comments, D 3004/D/29, entry for 1940. Lady Brooke recorded similar comments, D 3004/D/29, entry for 1940, though noting the 'terrible moral loss to Ulster', she added that he had been 'very ill . . . off and on for years'.
85. Quoted in Lady Craig diary, late November 1940, in D 1415/B/38.
86. Fin. diary, 26, 27 November 1940.
87. Cabinet conclusions on 25 November 1940, in CAB 4/454; also Brooke diary, , 25 November 1940.
88. *Northern Whig,* 26 November 1940.
89. Brooke diary, 25 November 1940.
90. Fin. diary, entries on 7, 11, and 28 December 1940.
91. Based on Brooke diary, passim; and personal interviews with Sir Arthur Kelly, (a member of the cabinet secretariat in 1940), on 11 May 1979. Also see memorandum by Lord Wakehurst, 'Change of prime minister', dated 29 March 1963, in Wakehurst papers, House of Lords, Record Office, 'Note on Northern Ireland affairs.'
92. *Northern Whig,* 26 November 1940.
93. See *Parl. Deb.* (C), vol. xxiii, col. 2156, on 25 September 1940, Warnock also suggested Brooke be promoted, and MacDermott be brought in. Craig agreed to the latter after a party meeting two days later.
94. Fin. diary, 4 December, 30 November 1940.
95. St John Ervine, op. cit., p. 562; also personal interview with John Brooke, on 23 February 1985.
96. Fisk, op. cit. pp 244, 392.
97. *Belfast Telegraph,* 18 January 1940.
98. *Northern Whig,* 18 December 1940, 10 January 1941, also 6 November 1940.
99. Andrews to Morrison, 2 January 1941, in CAB 9CD/208, 1940–45, 'correspondence and memoranda concerning Northern Ireland's industrial production'.
100. Fin. diary, 4 December 1940.
101. Personal interview with Sir Arthur Kelly, 28 April 1979. MacDermott soon came to believe that Brooke ought to have succeeded Craig, in interview, 11 May 1979.
102. Fin. diary, personal memorandum, written by Spender, dated 2 August 1938.
103. Cabinet conclusions, 1 October 1940, in CAB 4/451.
104. Brooke diary, 9 December 1940.
105. The correspondence between Craig and Barbour was published in the *News Letter,* 21 April, 1937.
106. Brooke diary, 12 and 19 July 1940.
107. Brooke diary, 15 September, 5 and 9 November 1939, and 13 February 1940.
108. *Parl. Deb.* (C), vol. xxiii, col 165, on 6 February 1940, and col. 530, on 6 March 1940. Brooke records that Craig had agreed to answer a motion tabled by Brown, critical of the Ministry of Agriculture, in Brooke diary, 5 February 1940. The motion was actually withdrawn.
109. Interview by author with Arthur Kelly, on 28 April 1979.
110. Brooke diary, 27 November 1940.
111. Brooke diary, 18 June 1940. Writing earlier about the overall effects of the war, he observed that, if it continued, there would be 'no class distinction', and added that this would be 'no bad thing'.
112. Ibid., 20 June 1940, also, on 21 August 1940, he noted that the government would not be able to get its transport proposals through the house 'in its present mood'.
113. Ibid., 26 and 27 November, 1 and 18 December 1940.
114. Fin. diary, 30 November 1940.

115. *Northern Whig,* 18 December 1940. (The editorial referred to the commons report on unemployment as 'a serious indictment of the government and the minister of commerce'. Milne Barbour); see also ibid., 19 December 1940, and 10 January 1941.
116. In Brooke diary, 31 December 1941, Brooke states that Andrews was 'first of all anxious' that he become minister of finance and move from agriculture. Also see Fin. diary, 28 December 1940, Sir Wilfred does not disclose the name of the person under consideration.
117. Fin. diary, 13 January 1941; also *Parl. Deb.* (C), vol. xxiii, cols 1523, 1524, for Warnock's speech on 18 June 1940, in which he refers to the appointment of Bevin. In 1938 Spender commented that Captain Herbert Dexon was staying in politics to achieve some unfulfilled ambitions. If this is so he was successful, as he now become minister of agriculture having earlier, on 8 July 1939, been raised to the peearge as first Baron Glentoran of Ballyalloly. See personal memorandum by Spender, 2 August 1938, in Fin. diary, op. cit.
118. See Lady Spender diary, op. cit., for 18 January 1941 in D 1633/2/40, also Fin. diary, 18 January 1941.
119. Brooke diary, 3 and 18 December 1940, 9 January and 31 December 1941.
120. Fin. diary, 13 January 1941.
121. Brooke diary, 11 December 1940 and 9 January 1941.
122. Fin. diary, 11 May 1940.
123. *Northern Whig,* 15 January 1941.

CHAPTER IX

1. W. D. Flackes op. cit.
2. Speeches by Beattie, *Parl. Deb.* (C), vol. xxv, col. 986, 21 April 1942, and Henderson, ibid., col. 1397, 2 June 1942.
3. *Northern Whig,* 17 January 1941.
4. *Sunday News,* 28 January 1968.
5. Interview with Sir Arthur Kelly, on 28 April 1979. Kelly served on the cabinet secretariat and was liaison officer with the imperial government 1943–56.
6. Brooke diary, 28 and 31 January 1941.
7. *Sunday News,* 28 January 1968.
8. Harkness, op. cit., p. 104; also Fin. diary, 26 December 1941.
9. Brooke diary, 24 January 1941.
10. Fin. diary, 5 May 1943.
11. Harkness, op. cit., p. 103.
12. Fin. diary, 12 November 1940.
13. Flackes, op. cit.
14. Harold Wilson's Report, 2 January 1941, in COM 61/440, '1940–1944 Northern Ireland's manpower resources. Report by Harold Wilson'. See also Brooke to Keir, 5 March 1941 and Keir to Brooke 27 February 1941, in ibid. (Lindsay Keir was vice-chancellor of Queen's University, Belfast).
15. Note by Ince on the use of resources in Northern Ireland, 24 March 1941, in ibid. (Ince became permanent secretary, Ministry of Labour and National Service, 1944–56).
16. Blake, op. cit., pp 39–42; See also Ministry of Commerce memorandum, 19 April 1943, in COM 61/694, '1941–44 diversion of work to Northern Ireland'.
17. COM 61/440, passim.
18. Wilson report, 2 January 1941; also Fisk, op. cit., p. 391. Fisk's very severe criticisms of the Northern Ireland government fail to take into account the many other factors which contributed to the province's unemployment.
19. Brooke to Keir, 5 March 1941, COM 61/440.
20. In introduction to booklet on the function of his ministry, October 1941, in COM 61/667, '1941–2, preparation of a guide for the service departments'; also Brooke diary, 10 January 1941.
21. Fin. diary, 16 December 1940.
22. Andrews to Morrison, 1 and 20 January 1941, and Morrison to Andrews, 3 January 1941, in CAB 9CD/208, '1940–45, correspondence and memoranda concerning Northern Ireland's industrial production'. (Morrison was at the Home Office, 1940–45).

23. Blake, op. cit., p. 372.
24. Scott to Gransden, cabinet secretary, 18 March 1941, in COM 61/440.
25. Churchill to Ernest Bevin, 23 January 1941, in ibid. (Bevin was minister of labour and national service, 1940–45).
26. Memorandum by Scott, 1 March 1941, in ibid.
27. See memorandum by Brooke, 3 February 1942, in COM 61/694. Also see the minutes of the production executive of the war cabinet, 8 April 1941, in P.R.O., HO 45/20268, 'Manpower resources and organisation of war production in Northern Ireland, 1941'.
28. Memorandum by Bevin, 3 April 1941, in ibid.
29. Minutes of production executive of war cabinet, 8 April 1941, in ibid. (Duncan was minister of supply, October 1940–June 1941).
30. Churchill to Morrison, 4 May 1941, and Morrison to Andrews, 13 May 1941, in CAB 9CD/208.
31. See Brooke diary 29 January 1942, and Brooke to Lyttelton, 25 March 1942, in COM 61/694; also, Fin. diary, 5 and 7 April 1941, and Ministry of Commerce memorandum, 12 January 1942, in COM 61/694; and CAB 9CD/208 passim.
32. Brown to Scott, 2 February 1942 in COM 61/694. Fisk, op. cit., p. 391, gives a very different interpretation, which would appear to be at variance with the evidence.
33. Brooke diary, 15 and 18 May 1941.
34. Andrews to Chruchill, 21 May 1941, in CAB 9CD/208; also Brooke to Andrews, 12 June 1941, in COM 61/585 "committee on utilisation of manpower".
35. Churchill to Morrison, 4 May 1941 in CAB 9CD/208.
36. Minutes of production executive of war cabinet, 8 April 1941, in P.R.O., HO 45/20268; also Brooke diary, 8 April 1941. (Beaverbrook was minister of aircraft production, May 1940–May 1941).
37. Ibid., 3 February and 27 January 1941.
38. See cabinet discussion, CAB 4/419, 22 June 1939, and CAB 4/451, 1 October 1940.
39. Fin. diary, 28 December 1940, 28 April and 16 December 1941.
40. See cabinet conclusion, CAB 4/470, 29 April 1941; also Fin. diary, 3 May 1941.
41. CAB 4/472, 5 May 1941. Also see Brooke diary, 16 April, 3 May and 10 June 1941.
42. Brooke diary, 3 and 25 November 1941; also CAB 4/480, 488, 489 on 19 August, 1 and 25 November 1941; Fin. diary, 26 November 1941; and Beaverbrook to Brooke, 20 November 1941, in House of Lords, Record Office, Beaverbrook papers, BBK/D/111.
43. Fin. diary, 26 April, 3 May, 19 November and 17 December 1941.
44. See cabinet conclusions CAB 4/489; also CAB 4/480, 488.
45. Fin. diary, 18 October 1841.
46. CAB 4/489; also Fin. diary, 11 and 19 November 1941; and Brooke diary, 11 June and 24 November 1941.
47. CAB 4/489; also Brooke diary 25 and 26 August 1941, and 13 October 1941.
48. Ibid., 7 October, 15, 19 and 22 November 1941.
49. See cabinet conclusions, CAB 4/489.
50. Brooke diary, 15 and 20 June, 25 November 1941; Fin. diary, 11 December 1941.
51. Brooke diary, 27 November, 2 and 11 December 1941; also cabinet conclusions, CAB 4/490, 28 November and CAB 4/491, 2 December 1941.
52. Brooke diary, 28 June 1942.
53. Fin. diary, 10 December 1941 and 17 February 1942; also cabinet conclusions, CAB 4/500, 510, 512, on 16 February, 2 June, and 8 June 1942.
54. Brooke diary, 23 June 1942; Fin. diary, 13 May and 17 July 1942; and *Parl. Deb.* (C), vol. xxv, cols 1605–1642, 23 June 1942, and 2133–2185, 16 July 1942.
55. Fin. diary, 10 and 17 December 1941.
56. Memorandum by Brooke, 18 April 1943, in COM 61/694.
57. *Sunday News,* 28 January 1968; also Blake, op. cit., pp 370–72.
58. Andrews to Morrison, 8 January 1941 in CAB 9CD/208.
59. Brooke diary, 31 December 1941.
60. Brooke to Duncan, minister of supply, 7 February 1941, in COM 61/459, '1941–2, Ministry of Supply services contracts in Northern Ireland'; also Brooke diary, 7 February 1941.
61. Minutes of the production executive of the war cabinet, 8 April 1941, in P.R.O., HO 45/20268.
62. Brooke diary, 19 March 1941; Fin. diary, 5 April 1941.
63. Brooke diary, 13 May 1941; also Brooke to Bevin, 3 June 1941, in CAB 9CD/208.

64. Bevin to Gransden, 22 January 1941, in ibid. See also Bevin memorandum, 3 April 1941, in P.R.O., HO 45/20268.
65. Minutes of production executive of the war cabinet, 17 June 1941, in P.R.O., HO 45/20268.
66. Brooke diary, 17 and 18 June 1941.
67. War cabinet conclusions, P.R.O. CAB 65/66; also Morrison to Andrews, 23 June 1941, in CAB 9CD/208.
68. Blake, op. cit., pp 369–80; also COM 61/590, '1941–44, production advisory committee', passim.
69. Blake, op. cit., p. 379.
70. Brooke diary, 11 and 13 September 1941. See also 27 September 1941; and Fin. diary, 28 February 1941.
71. Blake, op. cit., p. 379; and Brooke diary, 3 October 1941 and 17 March 1942.
72. Brooke to Lyttelton, 29 May 1942, in CAB 9CD/208 (Lyttelton was minister of production, 1942–5). See also Brooke diary, 17 June 1942.
73. Lyttelton to Brooke, 3 July 1942; also Scott to Gransden, 23 June 1941 and 9 July 1941, in CAB 9CD/208.
74. Memorandum by Brooke, 19 April 1943, in COM 61/694.
75. Brooke to Lyttelton, 28 May 1942, in CAB 9CD/208.
76. Brooke diary, 18 January 1942. This is deduced from diary references. See also Brooke's memorandum, 3 February 1942, in COM 61/694. See also *Sunday News,* 28 January 1968.
77. See Blake, op. cit., pp 367–9. Also Scott to Maxwell, 17 February 1942, Scott to Gransden, 13 February 1942, and Brooke to Beaverbrook, 12 February 1942, in COM 61/694.
78. See cabinet conclusions, 2 February 1942, CAB 4/499.
79. Lyttelton to Brooke, 22 April 1942, in COM 61/694; also cabinet conclusions, 30 September 1941, in CAB 4/483.
80. Andrews to Beaverbrook, 10 February 1942, in COM 61/694.
81. Fin. diary, 7 April 1941; and Brooke diary, 8 April 1941.
82. See COM 61/694, passim.
83. Brooke diary, 25 April 1941; also cabinet conclusions, 15 May 1941, CAB 4/473; and Harkness, op. cit., p. 108.
84. Fin. diary, 26 December 1940 and 4 January 1941.
85. *Sunday News,* 28 January 1968.
86. Minutes of production executive of war cabinet, 8 April 1941, in P.R.O., HO 45/20268. Also Brooke to Duncan, 7 February 1941, in COM 61/459, and Brooke diary, 6 February and 31 March 1941.
87. Brooke diary, 21 April, 27 August 1941, and 4 February 1943.
88. Ibid., 7 and 20 August 1941, 2, 3 and 8 September 1941 and 23 January 1942; also with regard to military visits, see COM 61/598, '1941–43, production drive visits to factories by military'.
89. Kelly to Scott, 20 September 1941, in COM 61/589, '1941–44, Production Council'.
90. See COM 61/589; and COM 61/773, passim, '1942–44 production executive committee'.
91. Brooke diary, 27 June, and 15 and 22 July 1942.
92. Ibid., 25 October 1941, 12 June and 2 July 1942.
93. W. P. Kemp to Cooper, 8 July 1941, in COM 61/589.
94. Scott to Gransden, 25 February 1941, in COM 61/440.
95. Brooke diary, 10 June 1941. See also cabinet conclusions, 17 June 1941, CAB 4/476; and COM 61/586 passim, '1941–2, conclusions of the manpower committee'.
96. Brooke diary, 26 June 1941.
97. Minutes of production executive of war cabinet, 17 June 1941, in P.R.O., HO 45/20268. Scott to Wickham, 13 April 1942, in COM 61/939 '1942–44, Short & Harland Ltd, correspondence between Brooke and Llewellin'; also See cabinet discussion, CAB 4/501.
98. Brooke diary, 23 February 1942.
99. Denholm report, 23 January 1942, in CAB 9CD/208.
100. Barnes to Sir John Anderson, lord president, 15 April 1943, in P.R.O., CAB 123/92, war cabinet committee records relating to 'Shipbuilding in Northern Ireland'.
101. Scott to Brown, 15 November 1941, in COM 61/589. Also regarding the firm's strike record see CAB 9C/22/1, passim, '1926–42, arbitration in strikes and industrial disputes'.
102. Brooke diary, 7 July 1941.
103. See COM 61/589 passim, particularly notes by Scott dated 8 and 17 July 1941; also Brooke diary, 28 July 1941; and COM 61/861 '1941–45, censorship intercepts'.
104. Brooke to Lyttelton, 7 September 1942, in COM 61/939; Brooke diary, 10 September 1941.

105. He refers to acting as an 'umpire' in *Sunday News,* 28 January 1968. See Brooke diary, 17 March and 27 October 1942.
106. P.R.O., CAB 123/92, war cabinet sub-committee records relating to 'Shipbuilding in Northern Ireland'.
107. Bevin to Churchill, 13 April 1943, and minutes of cabinet sub-committee, 20 April 1943, in ibid.
108. Memorandum by A. V. Alexander, first lord of Admiralty, dated 20 April 1943, also minutes of cabinet sub-committee, 22 April 1943, in P.R.O., CAB 123/92.
109. Fin. diary, 10 December 1941. (Linlithgow was civil lord of the Admiralty, 1922–4, and later viceroy of India).
110. Ibid., 23 January 1942.
111. P.R.O., CAB 123/92, passim. Also P. W. Buhrman, American consul general, Belfast, report to Department of State, 16 February 1943, The National Archives, Washington, 841E.642/3.
112. See report produced by Smiles for the Ministry of Aircraft Production, dated 20 November 1942, in COM 61/939.
113. Report by Smiles, op. cit., in COM 61/939. See also Scott to Kemp, 1 April 1943, and memorandum by Gordon, minister of labour, 20 November 1942, in ibid.
114. M-OA, FR 1309, 'Ulster shipping situation', dated 12 June 1942.
115. Smiles to Schuster, 14 December 1942, in COM 61/939.
116. *Northern Whig,* 14 April 1943, report of speech by Lord Geddes, in House of Lords, on 13 April. Geddes claimed that each aircraft had taken 120,000 man hours for completion at Shorts compared with 40,000 hours at mainland firms. He laid the blame, without equivocation, on the directors.
117. Scott to Wickham, 13 April 1942, in COM 61/939.
118. Llewellin to Brooke, 1 and 11 September 1942, in ibid. (J. J. Llewellin was minister of aircraft production from February to November 1942). Also Brooke diary, 10 August 1942.
119. Brooke memorandum, 24 September 1942, in CAB 9CD/208; and Brooke to Andrews, 1 December 1942 in COM 61/939.
120. Notes by Scott, 22 February 1944, and 31 March 1944, in ibid. (Stafford Cripps was minister of aircraft production, November 1942–May 1945).
121. Brooke to Morrison, 20 August 1943, in COM 61/694.
122. Brooke memorandum, 12 January 1942, in ibid; also Gordon to Andrews, 14 May 1941, in CAB 9CD/208; Harkness, op. cit., p. 104; Blake, op. cit., pp 386–7.
123. In note initialled I.A.N. to Osbert Peake, 6 May 1941, in P.R.O., HO 45/20268; also Brooke memorandum, 3 February 1942, in COM 61/694.
124. Bowman to Andrews, 20 August 1941, in COM 61/589.
125. Brooke diary, 17 October, 31 December 1941, 9 January 1942; also CAB 4/496, 21 January 1942.
126. Gordon to Andrews, 26 November 1942, in COM 61/894, '1942–3, correspondence concerning worker transfer'.
127. Brooke to Morrison in letters dated 22 May and 14 October 1942, in COM 61/694, and passim.
128. Blake, op. cit., pp 395, 401–02.
129. Brooke to Morrison, 14 October 1942 in COM 61/694.
130. Brooke memorandum, 19 April 1943, in ibid.
131. These were made particularly by Bevin. For Brooke's response see Brooke diary, 1 March 1943, and for Spender's reaction Fin. diary, 24 February 1943.
132. Brooke diary, 31 December 1942, 8 April 1943.
133. Brooke to Morrison, 20 August 1943, in COM 61/694.
134. Scott to Kipping, 27 July 1943, in COM 61/911, '1943, Effect on Northern Ireland of changes in production programmes'.
135. Flackes, op. cit.
136. Initialled note by I.A.N. to Peake, 6 May 1941, in P.R.O., HO 45/20268.
137. Flackes, op. cit.
138. Brooke diary, 29 March 1941, and 10 April 1941.
139. *Sunday News,* 4 February 1968; and Brooke diary, 10 September 1942.
140. Brooke diary, 21 February, 17 September, 10 and 14 October, 10 November 1941, 26 and 27 January, and 2 and 16 February 1943.
141. Fin. diary, 9–10 February 1942. See also Brooke diary, 19 February 1942.

142. Fin. diary, 1 March, 3 June 1941, 10 April, 6, 22 July, 15 August 1942.
143. Flackes, op. cit.
144. Fin. diary, 16 December 1940, 22 February 1941.
145. See ibid., 14 June 1941. Also F. D. Anderson, colonel, Northern Ireland district, report to undersecretary of state, War Office, 29 May 1941, in CAB 9CD/217, '1941–42, correspondence and memoranda concerning the air-raids on Belfast'.
146. Brooke diary, 19 February 1942; Fin. diary, 28 February 1942; Blake, op. cit. p. 379.
147. Fin. diary, 15 February 9, 14 June 1941, 21 February 1942.
148. Brooke diary, 9 June 1941.
149. Notes on Northern Ireland's war effort, 6 November 1942, in COM 61/637, '1941–45, contribution of Ministry of Commerce to war effort'.
150. Brooke diary, 7 January 1942; Flackes, op. cit.
151. War cabinet conclusions, in P.R.O., CAB 65/8.
152. Brooke diary, 26 January, 1 and 2 September 1942.
153. M-OA, FR 1306, 'Americans in Ireland,' dated 8 June 1942.
154. Brooke diary, 26 April 1943.
155. Brooke diary, 21 June, 21 November 1941.
156. Brooke diary, 3 February, 17 June, 13 December 1942.
157. Shaw was a southern Irish unionist, assistant secretary of the Irish convention and secretary to Lord French when lord lieutenant of Ireland. He visited the province in December 1940 and submitted a report to the Foreign Office, dated 1 January 1941, P.R.O., FO 371/29108.
158. *Parl. Deb.* (C), vol. xxv, col. 2503 and col. 327, 30 July and 24 February 1942; also col. 927, 30 March 1942, col. 986 and col. 1560, 21 April 1942 and 17 June 1942.
159. Fin. diary, 23 January 1942.
160. *Parl. Deb.* (C), vol. xxv, col. 63, 4 February 1942, col. 649, 12 March 1942; col. 107, 4 February 1942.

CHAPTER X

1. *Sunday News,* 28 January 1968.
2. John F. Harbinson, '*The Ulster Unionist party, 1882–1973*' (Belfast 1973), pp 142–3; also Fisk, op. cit., p. 394.
3. Fin. diary, 20 February 1942.
4. Churchill to Andrews, 6 May 1943, in P.R.O., PREM 4/53/1, 'Northern Ireland, 1942–1945'.
5. *Parl. Deb.* (C), vol. xxiii, col. 2708, 14 January 1941.
6. *News Letter,* 5 May 1943.
7. Fin. diary, 18 April, 13 May 1942. See Spender's earlier comments in his memorandum, in ibid., dated 2 August 1938.
8. *News Letter,* 24, 26 and 29 March 1941.
9. Comments by Shaw, dated 1 January 1941, in P.R.O., FO 371/29108, op. cit. He added: 'No one can say who would lead [a revolt] but Mr. Warnock, K.C. has been suggested to me as a possible prime minister.'
10. Fin. diary, 1 March and 8 March 1941.
11. Fin. diary, 1 March 1941, 30 April 1942.
12. Home Office report on Andrews' resignation, dated 30 April 1943, in P.R.O., PREM 4/53/1.
13. *Parl. Deb.* (C), vol. xxiii, col. 2710, 14 January 1941.
14. Fin. diary, 16 December 1940, 4 January 1941; also see cabinet conclusions, CAB 4/459, 9 January 1941.
15. CAB 4/457, 458, 459, 463, 467, 468, passim; also Fin. diary, 14 March 1942.
16. See cabinet conclusions, CAB 4/461, 464, on 4 and 24 February 1941.
17. See CAB 4/456, on 23 December 1940. Also interview with J. C. MacDermott, minister of public security from 25 June 1940 to 9 November 1941. The interview was on 11 May 1979 (hereafter MacDermott interview).
18. See cabinet conclusions, CAB 4/469, 16 April 1941.
19. Scott to McCorquodale, 19 April 1941, in COM 61/459.
20. Fin. diary, 3, 10 May, 5 and 19 July 1941; also Brooke diary, 4 May 1941; and CAB 4/470, 472, 473, on 29 April, 5 and 15 May 1941.

21. CAB 4/471, 473, 474, on 30 April, 15 May and 20 May 1941. See also the 'Minute book of meetings of the Ulster Unionist Stormont parliamentary party; in D 1327/10/1, for 5 and 20 May 1941 (hereafter, Minutes of Unionist parliamentary party).
22. See CAB 3A/71, '1935–44, miscellaneous notes on civil defence in Northern Ireland,' entry for 25 July 1941.
23. Fin. diary, 15, 31 May 1941.
24. Brooke diary, 15 May 1941. Also cabinet discussions, CAB 4/473, on 15 May 1941.
25. Brooke diary, 4 April 1941, and 8 April 1941; Blake, op. cit., p. 195.
26. Andrews to Morrison, 4 April 1941, in CAB 9CD/208.
27. War cabinet conclusions, P.R.O., CAB 55/49, 51, on 12 and 19 May 1941.
28. See CAB 4/475, on 21 May 1941; Brooke diary, 21 and 23 May 1941.
29. Oscar Henderson, the governor's secretary summarised the conversation in a letter to Gransden dated 13 May 1941, in CAB 9CD/217.
30. War cabinet conclusions, P.R.O., CAB 65/52, 53, 54, on 22, 26 and 27 May 1941.
31. War cabinet conclusions, P.R.O., CAB 65/53, 54, on 26 and 27 May 1941.
32. Fin. diary, 29 May 1941; also see cabinet conclusions, CAB 4/540, on 28 April 1943 and earlier discussion, in CAB 4/492, on 4 December 1941.
33. Fin. diary, 11 April 1942, and 7 June 1941.
34. Brooke diary, 20 March 1942. See also Fisk, op. cit., p. 449, on MacDermott's response. Fisk, however, ignores the evidence for the belated change in Andrew's attitude towards conscription.
35. Brooke diary, 24 March 1942.
36. Ibid., 8 March 1944. See also 9 February 1943.
37. Fin. diary, 29 May 1941.
38. Brooke diary, 8 March 1944.
39. Fin. diary, 18 October, 9 December 1941, 27 February, 28 March and 13 May 1942.
40. Ibid., 17 May 1941; also 5 February, 8 April and 25 June 1942.
41. See cabinet conclusions CAB 4/500, 506 on 16 February and 22 April 1942, also war cabinet conclusions, P.R.O., CAB 65/91, on 13 July 1942.
42. Fin. diary, 8, 14 July 1942, and 24 February 1943; also *Parl. Deb.* (C), vol. xxv, col. 2549–2551.
43. Fin. diary, 11 December 1941. Andrews assumed a commons vote of censure after the Willowfield defeat, see Brooke diary, 5 December 1941.
44. Fin. diary, 30 April 1942, and 30 March 1943. Compare this with Brooke's attitude in CAB 4/537, on 25 March 1943. See also Fin. diary, 3 September 1941, for Spender's own view.
45. CAB 4/503, 505, 507, on 24 March, 20 and 28 April 1942; also Fisk, op. cit., pp 398–9.
46. Fin. diary, 29 May 1942.
47. See memoranda by the Department of Industry and Commerce, dated 12 November 1942, and by the Department of Finance, 4 November 1942, in State Paper Office, Dublin, S 1582, '1940–48, Irish labour emigration to Great Britain and Northern Ireland'.
48. CAB 4/505, on 20 April 1942; *News Letter,* 14 June 1941.
49. See CAB 4/508, on 11 May 1942. It was so described by Lowry, parliamentary secretary, Ministry of Home Affairs; also Fin. diary, 7 March 1942.
50. Fin. diary, 23 November 1942.
51. Cabinet conclusions, CAB 4/505, on 20 April 1942.
52. Fin. diary, 18 October 1941.
53. CAB 4/512 on 8 June 1942.
54. CAB 4/512, 513, 516, 517, 518, passim; Brooke diary, 30 June 1942, Fin. diary, 23 and 25 July 1942.
55. Ibid., 29 July 1942; see also *Parl. Deb.* (C), vol. xxv, col. 2344–2348, 28 July 1942.
56. Fin. diary, 29 July and 8 September 1942.
57. See CAB 9C/22/1, passim.
58. R. R. Bowman to Gransden, 11 September 1942. in ibid.
59. MacDermott to Andrews, 2 November 1942 and Andrews to MacDermott, 3 November 1942, in ibid.
60. Fin. diary, 24 January 1942.
61. Stevenson & Son Ltd to Andrews, 9 October 1941, also Bates to Andrews, 15 April 1942, in CAB 9C/22/1; Fisk, op. cit., p. 402.
62. W. P. Kemp to Andrews, 23 September 1941, in CAB 9C/22/1.
63. Brooke diary, 2 March 1942.

64. Report of court of enquiry, 28 October 1942, in CAB 9C/22/1.
65. Churchill to Andrews, 15 October 1942, in ibid.
66. Memorandum by Morrison, 16 October 1942, in P.R.O., PREM 4/53/1.
67. Andrews to Churchill, 16 and 29 October 1942, in CAB 9C/22/1.
68. Ormeau Unionist association to Andrews, 26 October 1942, in ibid; also Fin. diary, 19 January 1943.
69. Fin. diary, 27 October 1942.
70. MacDermott to Andrews, 2 November 1942, in CAB 9C/22/1.
71. Churchill to Roosevelt, 11 April 1943, in war cabinet conclusions. P.R.O., CAB 66/36.
72. Andrews to Gordon, 4 November 1942, in CAB 9C/22/1.
73. Brooke diary, 21 December 1942.
74. Andrews to Gordon, 4 and 9 November 1942, and Gordon to Andrews, 5 November 1942, in CAB 9C/22/1.
75. See Brooke diary, 21 March 1943; Fin. diary, 2 April 1943.
76. Fin. diary, 10, 16 December 1941, and 18 April, 8 May 1942.
77. Ibid., 31 December 1941, 13 May 1942.
78. Fin. diary, 31 December 1941 and 13 May 1942; also CAB 4/517, 21 July 1942.
79. Fin. diary, 18 April 1942, also 23 January, 9 May, and 29 June 1942. See also R. J. Lawrence, *The government of Northern Ireland* (Oxford, 1965), p. 63, on causes of large contribution.
80. Cabinet conclusions CAB 4/510, 513, on 2 June and 19 June 1942; also Fin. diary, 6 June 1942.
81. Andrews to Wood, enclosed in Fin. diary, 19 August 1942. Also see *Parl. Deb.* (C), vol. xxv, cols 2450–2454, 30 July 1942.
82. Fin. diary, 31 July 1942; also *Parl. Deb.* (C), vol. xxv, col. 2456, 30 July 1942.
83. See Fin. diary, 5 and 7 August 1942, and Wood to Andrews enclosed, 15 August 1942. The correspondence is also contained in P.R.O., T 160/1327/32563, 'Northern Ireland post-war reconstruction, 1941–45.' At departmental local negotiations had taken place over the previous nine months, aimed at devising structures which would ensure that the Northern Ireland government was adequately informed by imperial thinking on post-war reconstruction. Hence the complaint by one Treasury official, Brittain, of Andrews' 'disregard . . . for even the elements of inter-governmental courtesy', in letter to Horace Wilson, 5 August 1942, T160/1327/32563.
84. Initialed note by H. S. to Sir Horace Wilson on 4 August 1942, in P.R.O., T160/1327/32563, op. cit.
85. Sinclair to Andrews in Fin. diary, 18 August 1942; also notes by Brooks dated 31 July, by Gilbert dated 11 August, and by Brittain dated 5 August 1942, in P.R.O., T160/1327/32563, op. cit.
86. Andrews to Wood, enclosed in Fin. diary, 19 August 1942, also Wood to Andrews, enclosed in ibid. 14 September 1942.
87. Ibid., 24 September 1942. See also enclosed correspondence, Andrews to Wood and Andrews to Barbour, both 22 September 1942.
88. Lawrence, op. cit., p.69.
89. Fin. diary, 19 and 24 September 1942.
90. P.R.O., PIN 18/26, '1946–48, interim agreement on 8 September 1946 between Treasury and Ministry of Finance, Northern Ireland,' passim. Had a major point of principle been conceded by Wood, as Lawrence claims, one might have expected it to have been referred to during these negotiations.
91. *Parl. Deb.* (C), vol. xxv, col. 2453, 30 July 1942; also cabinet conclusions, CAB 4/510, 513, on 2 June and 19 June 1942.
92. See cabinet conclusions, CAB 4/524, on 7 September 1942, for the case put forward by Bates; also CAB 4/504, 30 March 1942.
93. Brooke diary, 22 and 23 July 1942, and 7 September 1942.
94. CAB 4/524, on 7 September 1942.
95. Brooke diary, 10 September and 27 November 1942; Fin. diary, 7 December 1942.
96. *Parl. Deb.* (C), vol. xxv, cols 2786–2820, 20 October 1942, and cols 3143–3144, 15 December 1942; Fin. diary, 22 October 1942.
97. Brooke diary, 10 September 1942.
98. Fin. diary, 15 August 1942; also CAB 4/513, on 19 June 1942.
99. Brooke diary, 24 November 1942. For post-war planning see CAB 4A, '1941–50, cabinet committees: post-wartime reconstruction programme,' passim; also Lawrence, op. cit., pp 71–73.

100. Brooke diary, 14 November 1941, and 8, 30 June, 24 September, and 18 October 1942.
101. Brooke diary, 4 and 8 April, 24 and 27 May 1941.
102. Ibid., 24 July 1941; 20 April 1942; also Fin. diary, 24 July 1941 and Harkness, op. cit., p. 107.
103. Brooke diary, 21 April 1943, 23 October 1941, see also 6 October 1941.
104. Brooke diary, 19 February 1942. The comment was in response to Andrews' suggestion of a parliamentary enquiry into production, days after Brooke had been made minister of commerce and production.
105. Ibid., 26 November, 10 December 1941, 27 January, 9 March 1942, 23 January 1943.
106. *Sunday Dispatch,* 28 February 1943. See also Home Office report, 30 April 1943 in P.R.O., PREM 4/53/1.
107. Fin. diary, 26 July 1941, 4 May 1943. Lady Spender described him as a 'nice kind man', 18 January 1941, in D 1633/2/40.
108. Fin. diary, 19 November 1941, 22, 27 October 1942, 9, 13 January 1943.
109. Fin. diary, 13 January 1943, also 19 March 1942, 14 January 1941; also see Patrick Shea, *'Voices and the sound of drums'* (Belfast 1981), p. 138.
110. Fin. diary, 11 January, 21, 28 June, 1 August 1941, 8 and 13 May 1942. Treasury officials regarded the constabulary pay increase as 'indefensible', see Brittain to Wilson, 5 August 1942, in P.R.O., T160/1327/32563.
111. Fin. diary, 13 January 1943; Brooke diary, 14 July 1942.
112. Fin. diary, 10 December 1942.
113. *News Letter,* 19 February 1943; also see Fin. diary, 27 March, 5 April, 19 and 26 November 1941, and 25 June 1942. Spender felt that poor party organisation contributed to by-election defeats.
114. CAB 4/473, on 15 May 1941.
115. M-OA, FR 1309 'Ulster shipping situation', dated 12 June 1942.
116. *Parl. Deb.* (C), vol. xxv, col. 2454, 30 July 1942.
117. M-OA, FR 1309, 'Ulster shipping situation', dated 12 June 1942.
118. Fin. diary, 18 January 1943, 19 November 1942, 8 December 1941.
119. Brooke diary, 21 January 1942, 4 December 1941.
120. *Parl. Deb.* (C), vol. xxv, col. 2569.
121. Fin. diary, 30 April 1941. MacDermott and Spender shared this view of Beattie. See also Shaw's comments on the lack of clear leadership amongst the back-benchers, in his report, 1 January 1941, in P.R.O., FO 371/29108.
122. Fin. diary, 20 December 1941, and 25 November 1942. Also *Parl. Deb.* (C), vol. xxiv, cols 2511–2519, 16 December 1941, and vol. xxv, cols 3051–3068, 25 November 1942.
123. Report by P. W. Buhrman, American consulate general to Department of State, dated 25 February 1943, National Archive, Washington, 841E.00/100.
124. See Fin. diary, for 10 and 16 December 1941; also D 1327/10/1, minutes for 15 December 1942; also *Parl. Deb.* (C), vol. xxv, col. 165, 10 February 1942, Carnwath's report raised in housing debate.
125. Brooke diary, 19 and 29 June 1942, 4 December 1941.
126. See D 1327/10/1, for 9 December 1941, 27 January and 17 March 1942; also Brooke diary, 2 April 1943.
127. D 1327/10/1, 17 March 1942.
128. Ibid., at party meeting on 21 April 1942. Glentoran had recently resigned as chief whip.
129. Fin. diary, 8, 14 July 1942; Brooke diary, 1 July 1942; also *Parl. Deb.* (C), vol. xxv, col. 1964, 7 July 1942.
130. MacDermott interview.
131. *Parl. Deb.* (C), vol. xxv, cols 2902–2906, 28 October 1942 and cols 3120–3132, 15 December 1942.
132. Fin. diary, 16 December 1942; Brooke diary, 17 December 1942.
133. Fin. diary, 30 December 1942 and 11 January 1943.
134. Ibid., 15, 19 January, 2, 15 and 27 February 1943. The precise wording of the reference caused friction between Andrews and the ministry of Finance.
135. Fin. diary, 13 January 1943; Brooke diary, 11 January 1943.
136. Quoted in Fin. diary, 4 January 1943.
137. *News Letter,* 12 January 1943.
138. Fin. diary, 10 December 1942.
139. *The Times,* 14 January 1943.

140. Fin. diary, 25 April, 14 June, 18 October 1941, 30 March 1943. See *Parl. Deb.* (C), vol. xxv, col. 702, 29 April 1941, remarks by Beattie.
141. MacDermott to Andrews, 2 November 1942, in CAB 9C/22/1; also his talk with Brooke, in Brooke diary, 4 January 1943; and MacDermott interview.
142. Fin. diary, 6 June 1942. See also CAB 4/510, 2 June 1942.
143. *News Letter,* 18 January 1943.
144. Fin. diary, 3 and 21 June 1941, also Kelly interview.
145. CAB 4/510, on 2 June 1942.
146. Sinclair to Andrews, enclosed in Fin. diary, 13 August 1942.
147. Ibid., 25 and 26 June, 18 July, 7 August, 10 December 1942.
148. Fin. diary, 6 June 1942.
149. CAB 4/508, on 11 May 1942.
150. Fin. diary, 21, 29 July, 7 August 1942, 26 January, 24 February, and 4 July 1943.
151. See for example his comments at party meeting on 19 January 1943, in D 1327/10/1.
152. Brooke diary, 4 January 1943; Kelly interview.
153. Fin. diary, 14 January 1943.
154. Brooke diary, 13 January 1943.
155. *Sunday News,* 4 February 1968.
156. Brooke diary, 10, 11 and 12 January 1943; Fin. diary, 13 January 1943.
157. Brooke diary, 4 and 14 January 1943.
158. Fin. diary, 23 January 1943, also 19 January 1943.
159. Fin. diary, 14 January 1943, also 4 and 9 January 1943.
160. *News Letter,* 12 January 1943.
161. Fin. diary, 14 January 1943; Brooke diary, 12 January 1943.
162. *News Letter,* 16 January 1943.
163. Fin. diary, 16 January 1943.
164. Brooke diary, 13 and 27 January 1943. The letter irritated Andrews.
165. See minutes in D 1327/10/1, for 19 January 1943; *News Letter,* 20 January 1943; Fin. diary, 24 February 1943.
166. Brooke diary, 26 January 1943.
167. *The Times,* 14 January 1943; *Sunday Dispatch,* for 28 February 1943. See Spender on local press attitudes, the governor and the mood in the country in Fin. diary, 16, 20, and 31 January, 27 February and 16 April 1943; also Brooke diary, 19, 20 and 27 January 1943, and 16, 18 and 22 February 1943.
168. Brooke diary, 19 January, 20 and 25 February 1943.
169. Ibid., 19, 26, 27 and 29 January, 2 and 16 February 1943. He offered to resign on 2 February 1943.
170. *News Letter,* 20 January 1943.
171. Fin. diary, 20 January, 24 February 1943. He was considering attitude of *News Letter.*
172. Ibid., 12 February 1943. See also *Parl. Deb.* (C), vol. xxvi, cols 4–8, king's speech, 23 February 1943.
173. Brooke diary, 23 February 1943; Fin. diary, 24 February, 10 March 1943.
174. Fin. diary, 22 March 1943.
175. *News Letter,* 23 February, also 11 February, 31 March 1943. May became minister of education, April 1957 to March 1962.
176. *Sunday Dispatch,* 28 February 1943. Bates was Donegall's solicitor, and this may have been the source of his information. Certainly the article was very complimentary to Bates. See also CAB 4/533, on 2 March 1943.
177. Brooke diary, 22 and 25 February 1943.
178. Brooke diary, 16 March 1943.
179. Ibid., 25 February 1943.
180. *News Letter,* 16 March 1943, refers to reports to this effect having circulated over the previous two weeks; also MacDermott interview.
181. Minutes of meeting, 19 March 1943, in D 1327/10/1; also *News Letter*, 20 March 1943.
182. Brooke diary, 19 March 1943.
183. Fin. diary, 20 March 1943.
184. Ibid., 30 March 1943.
185. Fin. diary, 16 April 1943. See also Home Office report on Andrew's resignation, 30 April 1943, P.R.O., PREM 4/53/1.
186. Brooke diary, 25 March, 6 April 1943; *Sunday News,* 4 February 1968.

187. Brooke diary, 25 and 28 March 1943.
188. Brooke diary, 1 and 2 April 1943.
189. Ibid., 16 April 1943; also *News Letter,* 17, 26 April, and 5, 6 May 1943.
190. Andrews to Churchill, 30 April 1943, in P.R.O., PREM 4/53/1.
191. Quoted in W. D. Flackes, op. cit.; also Kelly interview.
192. Fin. diary, 17 April 1943.
193. Ulster Unionist Council, annual report, (Belfast, 1943), p. 3.
194. Brooke diary, 19, 20, 21 April 1943.
195. *News Letter,* 26 April 1943.
196. Fin. diary, 28 April 1943. Barbour complained bitterly to Spender.
197. *News Letter,* 26 and 28 April 1943; also Fin. diary, 23 April 1943.
198. Brooke diary, 28 April 1943.
199. Account based on minutes of meeting, 28 April 1943, in D 1327/10/1. See also Fin. diary, 29 April 1943; Brooke diary, 28 April 1943; Kelly and MacDermott interviews; W. D. Flackes, op. cit.; and *News Letter,* 29 April 1943.
200. Brooke diary, 28 April 1943. Robb was at the time minister of education and leader of the Senate.
201. Minutes in D 1327/10/1, on 28 April 1943.
202. Brooke diary, 28 April 1943.
203. Minutes in D 1327/10/1, on 28 April 1943.
204. Fin. diary, 29 April 1943; Flackes op. cit.; minutes in D 1327/10/1, 28 April 1943.
205. Memorandum by Lord Wakehurst 'Change of prime minister', dated 29 March 1963, in House of Lords record office, the Wakehurst papers, 'Notes on Northern Ireland affairs'.
206. Fin. diary, 30 April 1943.
207. Ulster Unionist Council, *Annual report* (Belfast, 1943) p. 3.
208. Fin. diary, 1 May 1943. See also Brooke diary, 10 May 1943.
209. *News Letter,* 29 and 30 April 1943.
210. Fin. diary, 30 April 1943.
211. Brooke diary, 30 April, 1 May 1943.
212. Fin. diary, 1 and 4 May 1943.
213. Andrews to Churchill, 30 April 1943, and Home Office report, dated 30 April 1943, in P.R.O., PREM 4/53/1.
214. Fin. diary, 5 May 1943; Brooke diary, 4 May 1943.
215. Fin. diary, 23 March 1943.
216. Brooke diary, 30 April, 1 May 1943.
217. Fin. diary, 5 May 1943.
218. MacDermott interview.
219. Fin. diary, 5 May 1943.
220. John Brooke to author, 9 October 1985.
221. W. D. Flackes, op. cit.
222. Andrews to Churchill, 10 May 1943 in P.R.O., PREM 4/53/1.
223. Second memorandum by Lord Wakehurst, 'Change of prime minister,' 11 April 1963, in House of Lords record office, Wakehurst papers.
224. Kelly interview.
225. Andrews to Churchill, 10 May 1943, P.R.O., PREM 4/53/1. He continued to serve Mid-Down in parliament until 1953, three years before his death on 5 August 1956. See *The Times,* 6 August 1956.
226. Fin. diary, D 715/21, draft letter, Spender to Andrews; also John Andrews to Brooke, 6 February 1968, D 3004/C/3; and Churchill to Andrews, 6 May 1943, P.R.O., PREM 4/53/1.
227. Kelly interview.
228. Brooke diary, 6 May 1943. Of the new cabinet, Grant had been a minister, and Sinclair and Lowry junior ministers. Midgley, Corkey and Moore had no ministerial experience.
229. Andrews to Midgley, 8 December 1941, in CAB 9C/22/1.
230. *News Letter,* 29 April 1943.
231. Andrews to Churchill, 30 April 1943, in P.R.O., PREM 4/53/1.
232. *Parl. Deb.* (C), vol. xxv, col. 2098, 15 July 1942.
233. Fin. diary, 28 April, 9 January 1943.
234. Fin. diary, 28 June 1941, also 13 January 1943.
235. Andrews to Churchill, 30 April 1943, in P.R.O., PREM 4/53/1.
236. Fin. diary, 18 January 1941, also 26 July 1941, and 22 March 1943.

237. Comment by Herbert Shaw, dated 1 January 1941, P.R.O., FO 341/29108.
238. Fin. diary, 28 April 1943.
239. Ibid., 4 May 1943.
240. Ibid., 23 January, 3 March 1943.
241. Fin. diary, 1 November 1941.
242. *Parl. Deb.* (C), vol. xxv, col. 2498, comment by Brown on 30 July 1942; also Fin. diary, 8 May 1942.
243. *Sunday News,* 4 February 1968.
244. Andrews to Churchill, 10 May 1943, in P.R.O., PREM 4/53/1.
245. MacDermott interview. Certainly Glentoran entirely misjudged the gravity of the crisis. Lady Spender gave the definitive popular view of him, writing; 'every man you meet will tell you what a good fellow Lord Glentoran is.' see diary entry, 18 January 1941, in D 1633/2/40.
246. Fin. diary, 1 and 3 May 1943.
247. Andrews to Churchill, 30 April 1943, in P.R.O., PREM 4/53/1.
248. John Andrews to Brooke, 6 February 1968, D 3004/C/3.
249. Quoted in *News Letter,* 1 May 1943.
250. *Sunday News,* 4 February 1968.
251. Fin. diary, 20 January 1943.
252. *Sunday News,* 4 February 1968.
253. Brooke diary, 26 and 27 November 1940 and 1 December 1940.
254. *Sunday News,* 4 February 1968.
255. Brooke diary, 17 December 1941.
256. Ibid., 26 March 1943.
257. W. D. Flackes, op. cit.
258. Brooke diary, 25 April 1943.
259. Brooke diary, 14 January and 2 September 1942.
260. Brooke to Macready, undated–mid 1920, D 3004/C/2.
261. *Sunday News,* 4 February 1968.
262. Brooke diary, 31 December 1942.
263. *The Times,* 14 January 1943; Brooke diary, 16 and 20 January 1943.
264. *Sunday News,* 4 February 1968.
265. Interviews with MacDermott and Kelly.
266. *Belfast Telegraph,* 1 May 1943.
267. Brooke diary, 2 May May 1943, also 31 December 1943, when reviewing the year.
268. Report by P. W. Buhrman, American consul general, Belfast, to Department of State, 1 March 1943, (National Archives, Washington, op. cit., 841E.00/101).
269. Brooke diary, 24 September 1942.
270. Fin. diary, 12 May 1943. Spender was clearly relieved at this. Shaw had predicted that in the event of a 'revolt . . . the task of the northern civil service would become arduous indeed'. See his report, 1 January 1941, P.R.O., FO 371/29108.
271. Ibid., 12 May 1943. This view was shared by Brooke. See Brooke diary, 11 May 1943. Midgley's appointment was the most controversial in the new cabinet. He later described himself as 'a great admirer and devoted colleague' of Brooke's, though 'poles apart' on social and economic questions. See Graham Walker, '*The politics of frustration*' (Manchester, 1985) p. 179.
272. Interviews with Kelly and MacDermott.
273. M-OA FR 2101, 'Ulster outlook, by Tom Harrisson, dated 20 May 1944.'

CONCLUSION

1. In personal interview with John Brooke, on 23 February 1985, the latter was strongly of the opinion that the war did have this effect on his father.
2. In Paul Bew, Peter Gibbon, and Henry Patterson, *The state in Northern Ireland, 1921–72,* (Manchester, 1979), Brooke is not clearly identified with either the 'populist' or the 'anti-populist' group in cabinet; see p. 106. It is, in any case, far from certain that these terms have great value in interpreting the period up to 1943. Craig (a 'populist') does not seem to have favoured 'populists' in the pattern of his ministerial promotions, most notably in preferring Barbour, an 'anti-populist', for finance in May 1937. The 'populists' (Craig, Bates and Andrews) did not form a cohesive grouping let alone an inner cabinet. Also this

classification takes insufficient account of Andrews' dramatic change of course after becoming premier. Prior to this, whilst minister of finance, Spender (an 'anti-populist') had complete confidence in his judgement and even, on occasion, criticised his frugality. Andrews' career would suggest that ministerial perceptions were determined to a very large extent by the specific departmental responsibility the individual concerned held within the government. See also Buckland, op. cit., p. 13, when he states: 'ministers took up postures appropriate to their departments', and his comments on Brooke and Archdale, p. 135.

3. Interview with Miss Emara MacNeill, Brooke's private secretary, on 12 May 1979; Brian Faulkner, *Memoirs of a statesman,* (London, 1978), p. 23.

4. *Belfast Telegraph,* 18 August 1973.

5. Remarks by Thomas Passmore, grandmaster of the Orange Order, in *Belfast Telegraph,* 31 August 1973.

6. Brooke diary, 28 April 1949, also 3 May 1949. Brooke had been heartened by support in the British press for his position, particularly a headline in *The Times,* stating: 'Ulster is not for sale'. See Brooke diary, 31 July 1948.

7. C. R. Atlee, *As it happened,* (Surrey, 1984), pp 191, 192. See also Brooke diary, 28 July 1945, where he expresses his worries with regard to the election of a Labour government in Britain and analyses the causes of Churchill's defeat.

8. Comment by James A. Kilfedder, in *Belfast Telegraph,* 18 August 1973. Kilfedder was Unionist M.P. for West Belfast 1964–6, and for North Down from 1970, before breaking with the party in 1979.

9. Comment by William Craig, ex-Stormont minister and Unionist party chief whip, in *Belfast Telegraph,* 18 August 1973.

10. See Brooke diary, 19 and 26 November 1959. These comments were made in the context of 'much rage' over speeches by Brian Maginess and Sir Clarence Graham (chairman of the standing committee of the Unionist Council) 'on the line of allowing Roman catholics to enter the Unionist party'. See Brooke diary, 4 November 1959.

11. See *Belfast Telegraph,* 28 August 1973. The remarks were made during Brooke's memorial service at St Anne's Cathedral.

12. Brooke diary, 21 February 1963. Allegations had been made that Glentoran had used his influence as a government minister to further the interest of the insurance company of which he was a director.

13. Comment by Mr. Eddie McAteer, leader of the Nationalist party at Stormont, 1964–1969, in *Belfast Telegraph,* 18 August 1973.

14. See *The Times,* obituary, 20 August 1973.

15. *Belfast Telegraph,* 28 August 1973. Butler was born in Dublin in 1911 and educated at Trinity College, Dublin. He had served as an army chaplain in world war two, and subsequently had worked mainly in southern dioceses. He was made bishop of Connor in September 1969, and was a leading figure in the ecumenical movement. The memorial service was attended by William Whitelaw and Edward Heath. Butler's remarks were strongly criticised by amongst others, Brian Faulkner, James Kilfedder and Ian Paisley. Roy Bradford commented that the bishop was 'honestly dealing with a widespread view'. See *Belfast Telegraph,* 29 August 1973.

16. *Parl. Deb.* (C), vol. lxxiv, cols 1585–1586, 28 March 1972.

17. Faulkner, op. cit., p. 79.

18. Terence O'Neill, *The autobiography of Terence O'Neill* (London, 1972), p. 40.

19. Patrick Buckland, A history of Northern Ireland, op. cit., p. 83.

20. John Cole, *The Thatcher years, a decade of revolution in British politics* (London, 1987), p. 183.

21. *Sunday News,* 21 January 1968.

22. John Bowman, *De Valera and the Ulster question, 1917–1973,* (Oxford, 1982), p. 339.

23. See T. Ryle Dwyer, 'The partition question, in *De Valera and his times,* edited by J. P. O'Carroll and J. A. Murphy, (Cork, 1983), pp 80, 82.

24. Ibid., p. 84. Dwyer writes of 'institutionalised discrimination in favour of those able to use the Gaelic language' in the civil service and education. See also Bowman, op. cit., pp 311, 316–317, 281, 127–128. A. C. Hepburn, *The conflict of nationality in Modern Ireland,* (London 1980), pp 136–137, provides an extract from De Valera's Dail speech, on 17 June 1931, in which he stated: 'I say that if I had a vote on a local body, and if there were two qualified people who had to deal with a catholic community, and if one was a catholic and the other a protestant, I would unhesitatingly vote for the catholic'.

25. J. P. O'Carroll and J. A. Murphy, op. cit., p. 83.

26. Leader article in *Irish Times,* 20 August 1973, written at the time of Brookeborough's death.

Index